D0123835

Published by The Philanthropy Roundtable, 1120 20th Street N.W., Suite 550 South,Washington, D.C., 20036

Free copies of this book are available to qualified donors. To learn more, or to order more copies, call (202) 822-8333, e-mail Main@PhilanthropyRoundtable.org, or visit PhilanthropyRoundtable.org

Books are available for purchase at Amazon.com. Online versions of all book sections are available at PhilanthropyRoundtable.org/Almanac

Cover: © Megin/shutterstock, jgroup/istockphoto, Kativ/istockphoto, James Hayes/istockphoto, jorgeantonio/istockphoto

ISBN 978-0-9978526-0-8
LCCN 2017952957

First printing, October 2017

TABLE
of
CONTENTS

PREFACE

The Almanac of American Philanthropy was first published in 2016 after a major, multi-year commitment from The Philanthropy Roundtable and some long-sighted donors. We wanted the great American undertakings of private giving and voluntarism to have a worthy standard reference—one that captured the power of these institutions, and profiled the fascinating citizens and philanthropic accomplishments that have transformed our country in thousands of ways.

This was an entirely new work, of a sort that had never previously existed. And it quickly became the authoritative reference on one of the most distinctive aspects of American culture, one of our largest economic sectors, and the most inventive way that we solve national problems. Many users have come to describe *The Almanac of American Philanthropy* as the "bible" of giving and civil society in the U.S.

The full-size *Almanac* also weighs in at 1,342 pages! That's what it requires to chronicle this epic part of our civilization. But we recognized that many readers would like to have a slimmed-down version of the book they could more easily carry around, give to interested colleagues, and quickly dip into for information and inspiration. So we have created this *Compact Edition* of *The Almanac of American Philanthropy*—and updated it with the very latest achievements, statistics, and donor profiles, right up through 2017.

We remain very open to future improvements, corrections, and expansions of this rich resource. If you have suggestions, please contact us at the address below. We will continue to update and extend this *Almanac* so it remains a living document, and continues to serve as the central, trusted window into one of the most potent and defining of our national activities.

The Philanthropy Roundtable exists to serve donors of all sorts, equipping them with information that will make them as discerning and efficacious as possible in all of their charitable actions. If you know of givers who could benefit from the information contained in this book, let us know and we will share a copy with them. Copies of this *Compact Edition* and of the full-length *Almanac* can also be purchased at very reasonable prices at Amazon. And all of the information contained in both of these books is available for free online at PhilanthropyRoundtable.org/Almanac.

Please enjoy this lively and important new resource!

Adam Meyerson
President, The Philanthropy Roundtable

Feedback welcome:
AlmanacEditor@PhilanthropyRoundtable.org

HOW PHILANTHROPY
Fuels
AMERICAN SUCCESS

By Karl Zinsmeister

This rollicking essay introducing *The Almanac of American Philanthropy* races through America's fascinating tradition of private giving and describes why it is so effective and important to our nation. You can read this argument as one flowing narrative, or in six distinct sections, one following another:

HOW PHILANTHROPY FUELS AMERICAN SUCCESS

By Karl Zinsmeister

P hilanthropy is a huge part of what makes America America.
Start with the brute numbers: Our nonprofit sector now employs 11 percent of the U.S. workforce. It will contribute around 6 percent of GDP in 2017 (up from 3 percent in 1960). And this doesn't take into account volunteering—the equivalent of an additional 5 to 10 million full-time employees (depending on how you count), offering labor worth hundreds of billions of dollars per year.

America's fabled "military-industrial complex" is often used as a classic example of a formidable industry. Well guess what? The nonprofit sector passed the national defense sector in size way back in 1993.

And philanthropy's importance stretches far beyond economics. Each year, seven out of ten Americans donate to at least one charitable cause. Contributions are from two to ten times higher in the U.S. than in other countries of comparable wealth and modernity. Private giving is a deeply ingrained part of our culture—a font of social creativity and crucial source of new solutions to national problems. Voluntary efforts to repair social weaknesses, enrich our culture, and strengthen American community life are and always have been a hallmark of our country.

Yet, somehow, there exists no definitive resource that chronicles American philanthropy broadly and explains it in a context where it can be fully understood and appreciated. Until now.

This *Compact Edition* of *The Almanac of American Philanthropy* offers everyday citizens, givers, charity workers, journalists, local and national leaders, and others the information needed to put in perspective the vital role that philanthropy plays in all of our daily lives. The facts, stories, and history contained in these pages can fill gaping practical and intellectual holes in our self-awareness.

You will find here an accessible collection of the major achievements of U.S. philanthropy, lively profiles of the greatest givers (large and small), and rich compilations of the most important ideas, statistics, polls, literature, quotations, and thinking on this quintessentially American topic.

There are also *Iliad*s and *Odyssey*s of human interest in this volume. Some tremendously intriguing Americans of all stripes have poured time and treasure into helping their fellow man. You'll meet lots of them here.

Absent the passion and resources that our fellow countrymen devote to philanthropy, it's not only our nation that would be less thriving. Our individual days would be flatter, darker, uglier, more dangerous, and less happy. You'll find vivid evidence of that in machine-gun presentations throughout this book. Let's get a taste by meeting a few of the many philanthropists who populate this almanac.

LARGER-THAN-LIFE CHARACTERS

Ned McIlhenny, born and raised on a Louisiana bayou, was an expert on camellias, on alligators, on the hundreds of varieties of bamboo that grow around the world, and on wild turkeys. He was an Arctic explorer. His skills as a hunter once helped save the lives of 200 ice-bound sailors. He was an ornithologist who personally banded more than a quarter of a million birds. He also had a day job selling the hot-pepper condiment invented by his family: McIlhenny Tabasco sauce.

It turns out there is real money in burning mouths, and McIlhenny used his for an amazing array of good works. For one thing, he got very attached to a fellow native of Louisiana's bayous: the snowy egret. When McIlhenny was young, hats bearing egret plumes were for ladies what Coach handbags are today. This fashion mania had the effect of nearly driving the snowy egret to extinction, and no one was doing anything about it. So the philanthropist swung into action.

McIlhenny beat the bushes in wild parts of the island his family owned, and managed to find eight baby egrets in two nests. He raised

these hatchlings in a protected area, paid for their care over a period of years, and by 1911 had built up a population of 100,000 egrets on his private refuge. He simultaneously recruited John Rockefeller, Olivia Sage, and other philanthropists to buy up and preserve swampy land in Louisiana that is important as winter habitat of migratory waterfowl, including egrets. And in this way he rescued a magnificent creature that was on the verge of disappearing from the Earth.

Later in his life, McIlhenny took action to stave off a very different kind of extinction. He had been raised with Negro spirituals in his ears, and loved them dearly. Around his 60th birthday, McIlhenny realized that these songs —which then existed only in an oral tradition—were dying out and at risk of being forgotten forever. So he again sprang into action with both his checkbook and his personal involvement.

He used his contacts to find two elderly singers who still remembered many of the songs. He hired a musicologist to sit with him, and as these ladies sang their hearts out, the two men wrote down the lyrics and melodies and harmonies as fast as they could scribble. In this way they preserved the music in scrupulous detail, exactly as it had been handed down among generations of slaves.

McIlhenny then published these songs as a book, which became a classic of the genre. All but a handful of the 125 spirituals he captured were unrecorded in any other place—he single-handedly saved these soulful artifacts of American history for future generations. McIlhenny's songs included one that provided Martin Luther King Jr. with his most famous line:

> When we allow freedom to ring...from every village and hamlet... we will...speed up that day when all of God's children, black men and white men, Jews and Gentiles, Protestants and Catholics, will be able to join hands and sing in the words of the old Negro spiritual:
> > *Free at last! Free at last!*
> > *Thank God Almighty, we are free at last!*

Another red-blooded American philanthropist who helped freedom last was Alfred Loomis. His philanthropic field was national defense. Many of us think of defense as the ultimate government responsibility, and a place without room or need for philanthropy, so it may come as a surprise to learn that throughout our history private donors have played important roles in securing our nation. Private donors financed our Revolution. They created the modern field of code-making and -breaking. Donors single-handedly developed the field of rocketry, and fanned private space launch into fiery

success. (See "Donors Who Come to the Aid of their Country" in the Summer 2015 issue of *Philanthropy* magazine for details on how philanthropy has repeatedly bolstered our national defense.)

No donor was more crucial in building America's military strength than Alfred Loomis. After financing much of the electrification of rural America as a Wall Street dealmaker, he became convinced that the stock market was overvalued and converted everything he owned to cash and T-bills in 1929. When the October 1929 Crash came he was not only protected but in a perfect position to go shopping at bargain prices. By the early 1930s Loomis was one of the richest men in America, and at age 45 he retired from finance to put all of his time and energy, and much of his money, into his true love: science. He set up one of the world's great science labs in a mansion near his home, invited top researchers from around the world to experiment there, and conducted his own state-of-the-art investigations.

While visiting Berlin in 1938, Loomis was disturbed to find how popular Hitler was, and how good German scientists were. He returned home convinced that war was brewing, and that science would have a lot to do with who won. So he poured himself and his money into one new field where he thought science might be able to contribute to the war effort: using radio waves to detect moving objects. His lab

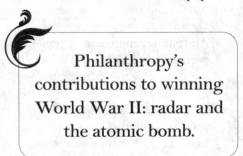

Philanthropy's contributions to winning World War II: radar and the atomic bomb.

quickly became the national leader in what we now call radar. Thanks to Loomis's funding and leadership, practical radar sets were created under his supervision and delivered to the Army and Navy by the thousands, turning the tide of World War II.

If radar won the war, the atomic bomb ended it. And as it happens Alfred Loomis had a lot to do with that as well. The method he used for his radar triumphs was to relentlessly gather the best scientific minds, without regard to their prior specialties, give them rich resources, and protect them from bureaucratic interference. When it became apparent how powerful Loomis's modus operandi was, it was directly copied for the Manhattan Project; indeed most of his scientists were transferred over to work on the bomb. Franklin Roosevelt later said that aside from Winston Churchill, no civilian did more to win World War II than Alfred Loomis.

By the way, it isn't only Alfred Loomis's brilliant model for conducting crash research that lives on today. He also left behind a flesh-and-blood

embodiment of his whirlwind entrepreneurial philanthropy. His great-grandson is Reed Hastings—who as CEO of Netflix, and one of the nation's most influential progenitors of charter schools as a donor, has been a huge game-changer in both business and philanthropy.

DONORS + PASSION = POTENT ACCOMPLISHMENT

Another entrepreneurial philanthropist who put deep imprints on America was George Eastman. He popularized photography in the early 1900s as founder of Kodak in upstate New York. When he began, the photographic process was all art and guesswork, and no science. During the frantic start-up phase of his company, for example, a calamitous failure of the gelatins used in his photo-developing process threatened to kill his firm. It eventually turned out that the cows whose carcasses were being boiled down to create the industrial gelatin had been shifted to new pastures where their forage lacked sulfur, and that tiny missing ingredient was enough to wreck the delicate chemical process.

Determined to figure out the basic chemistry of photography so he wouldn't be prisoner to these inconsistencies, Eastman started hiring chemists from an obscure little school in New England known as Boston Tech. Grateful for the well-trained minds he came to rely on, Eastman later funded much of the transformation of Boston Tech into today's MIT, including building the entirely new campus where that university now resides. At the moment Eastman presented his offer, the college was on the verge of failing and shutting down. Eastman likewise nurtured the University of Rochester into a great research and educational facility, including creating its medical school from scratch.

Eastman adored music, and had a huge pipe organ installed in his home and played every morning to wake him as his alarm clock. One friend who accompanied him on a New York City trip where they took in 12 operas in

six days described Eastman as "absolutely alcoholic about music." This passion led to one of the great cultural gifts in American history, as Eastman methodically created and built to world prominence the Eastman School of Music at Rochester, which currently enrolls 500 undergraduates, 400 graduate students, and 1,000 local child and adult students. The Eastman School was important in Americanizing and popularizing classical music, which had previously existed as a European transplant, and remains one of our country's top cultural institutions.

Another great American donor was Milton Hershey. Many readers will insist that his crowning gifts to humanity came in brown bars and silver kisses. By transforming chocolate from expensive rarity to treat affordable by all, he did create an explosion in new ways of making Americans feel happy.

Hershey's deepest passion, though, was his remarkable school for orphans, which he and his wife created and ultimately gave their entire company to. Hershey's father was a neglectful drinker, and the separation of his parents turned his boyhood into a shoeless and hungry trial. To relieve other children of similar ordeals he built

> One friend described George Eastman as "absolutely alcoholic about music."

up his orphanage in a gradually surging ring of family-like houses encircling his own home, where each small group of youngsters was overseen by a married couple who lived with them. The school also provided a thorough basic education and excellent training in industrial crafts.

Hershey was a constant physical presence among his youngsters until his death in 1945. At one point he announced, "I have decided to make the orphan boys of the United States my heirs." And he did—endowing the Milton Hershey School with a nest egg currently worth $12 billion. That allows the school to serve 2,000 endangered children from around the U.S. every year, putting many of them on a dramatically elevated life path.

Philanthropists come in all stripes. That's one of the field's strengths: Different givers pursue different visions, so you get many solutions to problems rather than just one. If Milton Hershey's cure for child neglect was large-scale fostering, Katharine McCormick's attempt was to make orphans rarer by manipulating biology. It's pretty widely known that medical breakthroughs like the polio vaccine and hookworm eradication were products of philanthropy. But how many people know that the birth-control pill was the creation of a sole private funder?

A reaper of the International Harvester fortune, McCormick was an early women's rights activist. She initiated a connection with Gregory Pincus, a brilliant biologist who had been fired by Harvard for ethical lapses, to discuss whether it might be possible to prevent pregnancy by means as easy as taking an aspirin. Before leaving the room after their first meeting, McCormick wrote Pincus a check for $40,000.

She funded his private laboratory steadily thereafter, eventually investing the current equivalent of about $20 million in their quest to develop a daily birth-control pill. McCormick was the sole and entire funder of this work, and hovered constantly over the lab, influencing many of its research choices. By 1957 this duo had an FDA-approved pill, and the Earth wobbled a little on its axis. McCormick reveled in her accomplishment, even taking her own prescription to be filled at a local pharmacy—despite being a matron in her 80s at that point—just for the sheer frisson.

LOTS OF LITTLE GUYS

Dwight Macdonald once described the Ford Foundation as "a large body of money completely surrounded by people who want some." (Back when the foundation's headquarters was on a southern California desert estate, the staff sometimes called the place "Itching Palms.") It's easy to look at a big pile of silver like Ford and think that's what American philanthropy is all about. But philanthropy in the U.S. is not just a story of moguls. In fact, it is not even primarily about wealthy people or (even less) big foundations.

Do you realize that only 15 percent of charitable giving in the U.S. comes from foundations? And only 5 percent from corporations? The rest comes from individuals—and the bulk of that from everyday givers, at an annual rate of about $2,600 per household. Even among foundations there is a strong tilt toward the small. Less than 2,000 foundations (2 percent of all) have assets of $50 million or more today. Most foundations are modest in size. And most giving is even smaller—but it is practiced very widely.

It is inexorable giving by humble Americans that constitutes the main branch of U.S. philanthropy. Take Gus and Marie Salenske, a plumber and nurse who lived quietly into the first decade of this millennium in a small house in Syracuse, New York. Their one indulgence was weekly square dancing; other than that they were savers. After they died, this simple couple left more than $3 million to good causes, mostly their beloved Catholic Church.

Anne Scheiber was a shy auditor who retired in 1944 with just $5,000 in the bank. Through frugal living and inspired stock picking she turned this into $22 million by the time she passed away in 1995 at the age of 101. She

left it all to Yeshiva University so that bright but needy girls could attend college and medical school.

Minnesota farmer Harvey Ordung consumed modestly and invested prudently. When he passed on, he left $4.5 million to 12 charities in his home region. The largest portion went to a program that gives college scholarships to local kids.

Elinor Sauerwein painted her own home, kept a vegetable garden, and mowed the lawn herself until she was in her 90s. She eschewed restaurants, cable TV, and other expenses as unnecessary luxuries. But when she died in 2011, she left $1.7 million to the local Modesto, California, branch of the Salvation Army. "Her goal for years and years was to amass as much as she could so it would go to the Salvation Army," reported her financial adviser.

Millicent Atkins earned a teaching degree in 1940, but eventually left that profession to help manage the family farm in South Dakota. She developed a keen eye for productive land and an appetite for buying, eventually owning 4,127 acres. When she died in 2012 she left $38 million to two nearby universities and her church.

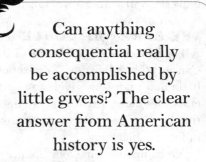

> Can anything consequential really be accomplished by little givers? The clear answer from American history is yes.

Albert Lexie shined shoes in Pittsburgh for more than 50 years, and made a decision decades ago to donate every penny of his tips to the Free Care Fund of the Children's Hospital of Pittsburgh, which benefits families who can't afford treatment. From 1981 to 2013, Lexie handed over more than $200,000 to Children's Hospital—a third of his total earnings.

One of these humble givers you may have heard of is Oseola McCarty. I tell her story in detail in our Philanthropy Hall of Fame section. Her life could not have started much harder—she was conceived when her mother was raped on a wooded path in rural Mississippi. And it didn't get easier with age. She started to work ironing clothes in elementary school, and dropped out at sixth grade to support her ailing aunt by taking in washing.

Hers wasn't a standard-issue home laundry. McCarty scrubbed her clients' clothes by hand on a rubboard. She did try an automatic washer and dryer in the 1960s, but concluded that "the washing machine didn't rinse enough, and the dryer turned the whites yellow." After years of boiling shirts and linens and then doing four fresh-water rinses, that wasn't good enough

to meet her high standards. So she went back to her bubbling pots, Maid Rite scrubboard, and 100 feet of open-air clothesline.

Early in her life, McCarty reported, "I commenced to save money. I never would take any of it out. I just put it in…. It's not the ones that make the big money, but the ones who know how to save who get ahead. You got to leave it alone long enough for it to increase." This was a life secret she mastered, and when she retired in 1995, her hands painfully swollen with arthritis, this washerwoman who had been paid in little piles of coins and dollar bills her entire life revealed another secret: She had $280,000 in the bank. Even more startling: She decided to give most of it away—not as a bequest, but immediately.

Setting aside just enough to live on, McCarty donated $150,000 to the University of Southern Mississippi to fund scholarships for worthy but needy students seeking the education she never had. When the community found out what she had done, more than 600 men and women in Hattiesburg and beyond made donations that more than tripled her original endowment. Today, the university presents several full-tuition McCarty scholarships every year.

THE POWER OF LITTLE GUYS AND BIG GUYS JOINED TOGETHER

Can anything large and consequential really be accomplished by these little and middling givers, or by the very limited population of big givers? The clear answer from American history is yes. Many remarkable things have been achieved by dispersed giving, which often aggregates in formidable ways.

Once upon a time, our country even built its naval ships via dispersed giving. When newborn America was having terrible troubles with pirates in the Mediterranean and revolutionary French raiders off our coasts, many communities took up subscriptions and gathered voluntary funds to build warships and hire captains. The good people of Salem, Massachusetts, for instance, contributed $74,700, in amounts ranging from $10 given by Edmund Gale to a pair of $10,000 donations from Elias Derby and William Gray, and built the frigate *USS Essex*, which became one of the most storied vessels in our new Navy.

When the War of 1812 arrived it was dispersed giving that saved us from calamity. As the conflict broke out, the U.S. Navy possessed a total of seven frigates and less than a dozen other seagoing ships. The British Navy at that same moment numbered a thousand warships, including 175 double-gundeck "ships of the line," of which the United States had none. The comparison by firepower was even starker: a total of 450 cannons carried by the U.S. Navy versus 27,800 afloat in the Royal Navy.

So how did America avoid obliteration by the English juggernaut? Individually funded, decentralized warfighting—in the form of privateers. Not long after hostilities were declared there were 517 privately equipped and manned corsairs defending the U.S. "Let every individual contribute his mite, in the best way he can to distress and harass the enemy, and compel him to peace," urged Thomas Jefferson in 1812. During the course of the War of 1812, the U.S. Navy captured or sunk about 300 enemy ships, while U.S. privateers captured or sunk around 2,000, blasting British trade.

The American merchants and ordinary sailors who voluntarily organized themselves into fighting units got everything they hoped for. No more impressment of U.S. seamen. A restoration of free trading. And deep respect for the ability of America's small colonies—weak of government but strong of civil society—to defend their interests.

That same pattern has been followed in many other sectors of American society. In chronicling the astonishing bloom of colleges in the U.S., author Daniel Boorstin noted that the state of Ohio, with just 3 million inhabitants, had 37 colleges in 1880. At that same time, England, a nation of 23 million people, had four. Why the difference? Education philanthropy.

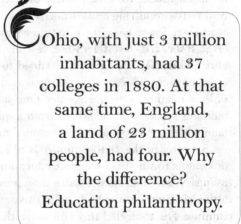

Ohio, with just 3 million inhabitants, had 37 colleges in 1880. At that same time, England, a land of 23 million people, had four. Why the difference? Education philanthropy.

Education philanthropy in the U.S. stretches back to our earliest days, a century and a half before we even had a country. The New College was established in the Massachusetts Bay Colony in 1636. Three years later it was renamed, after young minister John Harvard donated his library and half of his estate to the institution.

America's first recorded fund drive was launched in 1643 to raise money for the college; after 500 British pounds were collected it was deemed a "great success." The next year, colonial families were asked to donate a shilling in cash or a peck of wheat to support the citadel of higher learning in their midst. These voluntary donations, known as the "college corne," sustained Harvard for more than a decade.

Fast forward to 2015. Nearly 50 American colleges were in the midst of fundraising campaigns aimed at raising at least a billion dollars in donations. Private gifts power even our public universities—institutions like the

University of Virginia and the University of California, Berkeley now receive more revenue from voluntary giving (gifts and interest off previous gifts) than they do from state appropriations.

Relying on private individuals to train up the next generation of leaders, rather than leaving that responsibility to the crown or church, was an entirely new development in higher education. It burst forth across our new land, producing the College of William & Mary in 1693, the precursor to St. John's College in 1696, Yale in 1701, and many others. Sub-innovations followed, like the spread of the endowed professorship from a first example in 1721. The pervasiveness of the endowed chair in the U.S. today tempts one to assume that this practice must be common everywhere, but actually it remains rare outside America, where it has helped drive our universities to international pre-eminence.

Our nation's great bloom of universities illustrates perfectly the fruitful mixing of little and big givers. Institutions like the Rensselaer Polytechnic Institute in upstate New York—a pioneer of science-based education that granted the first civil engineering and advanced agriculture degrees in the English-speaking world—relied on big gifts from major patrons like Stephen Van Rensselaer. Other places such as Western Reserve University in Ohio, founded just two years after Rensselaer and likewise destined to become a science powerhouse, relied on an entirely different philanthropic model—the sacrificial giving of thousands of local neighbors on the frontier. One supporter spent a whole winter hauling building supplies to the school from a quarry ten miles away. Another typical family pledged a portion of their annual milk and egg sales.

Starting in the 1840s, hundreds of Eastern churches began to pool small donations to support collegiate education across the western frontier. Within 30 years they had raised more than a million dollars to sustain 18 colleges. Hillsdale College was built up at this same time after professor and preacher Ransom Dunn circled through more than 6,000 miles of wild lands collecting nickels and dimes and dollars from settlers.

THE POWER OF PERSONALISM

Pledging your family egg sales to a local institution. Hauling stone all winter for a good cause. Donating your shoeshine tips. In our country, giving is often very *personal*.

Michael Brown was a Broadway lyricist with a hit musical under his belt, so his family was enjoying a burst of unanticipated prosperity. For their 1956 Christmas celebration he and his wife and two sons hosted a close friend, a young writer who was far from her home in the South. At the end of their gift exchange, the Browns handed their guest an envelope. Inside was a note that read: "You have one year off from your job to write whatever you please. Merry Christmas."

The writer's name was Harper Lee. When she had decided to try to make it as a novelist, she relocated (like many before her and since) to New York City. After getting there she found (like many before her and since) that she was so preoccupied with paying her rent—by working at an airline office and bookstore—that she had little time left over to focus on her literary craft. The Browns noticed this, and through some very personal philanthropy changed the course of U.S. literature.

With their donation in hand, Harper Lee quit her retail jobs. And during that gift year she wrote *To Kill a Mockingbird*. It won the Pulitzer Prize in 1961 and became one of the most influential American books of all time.

While this was an especially intimate contribution, this kind of personalism is not at all unusual in American philanthropy. In fact, gifts where the givers and recipients are involved with each other, familiar with one another's characters, and committed to each others' flourishing, are some of the most successful forms of philanthropy. You can see this yourself any day. Volunteer at a Habitat for Humanity building project and you will often work next to the person who is going to occupy the house as soon as you get the roof on and the oven in. Sponsor a child in an inner-city Catholic school (or an overseas village) and you will have opportunities to follow the life progress of the beneficiary, share in his or her dreams, and perhaps attend a graduation.

Knowing the character of the person you are trying to help—strengths and weaknesses, needs and temptations—allows the giver to focus his help much more effectively and to avoid wasteful or mistaken or perverse forms of "help." As William Blake put it, "If you would help another man, you must do so in minute particulars." One man's medicine can be another man's poison; donors must prescribe for particular people, not treat "mankind" as some cold abstraction. Much of the best anti-poverty work carried out during America's immigrant waves and transitions to industrialism during the 1800s and early 1900s took highly personal forms, where givers rolled up their sleeves and offered not only money but mentoring and guidance and support to specific men and women in need.

Stephen Girard was one of the five richest men in American history, when his wealth is measured as a percentage of GDP. But when the yellow-fever epidemics swept his hometown of Philadelphia—as they did many summers in the years before anyone realized that the deadly malady was carried up from the tropics on sailing ships, and spread by mosquitoes—Girard was a tireless personal leader in the efforts to tamp down the disease. This required courage, as the terrifying affliction would kill hundreds of people per day in a horror of delirium and bloody vomiting.

Residents who could afford it generally fled the city when epidemics

roared through. Not Girard. He stayed in Philadelphia in 1793, 1797-1798, 1802, and 1820 to guide relief efforts, fund hospital operations, and provide direct care for individuals—often bathing and feeding the dying himself. Benjamin Rush (whose profile you can find in our Philanthropy Hall of Fame) did likewise. He worked himself to exhaustion assisting thousands of Yellow Fever victims, even after he contracted the disease himself. Both givers put their personal and business affairs entirely on hold during outbreaks. "As soon as things have quieted down a little you may be sure I shall take up my work with all the activity in my power," Girard wrote to a friend in 1793. "But, for the moment, I have devoted all my time and my person, as well as my little fortune, to the relief of my fellow citizens."

Nicholas Longworth grew up poor, apprenticed to a shoemaker for a period, before eventually earning great wealth. He gave much of it away to what he called "the devil's poor," whom he identified and helped in extremely personal ways. "Decent paupers will always find a plenty to help them, but no one cares for these poor wretches. Everybody damns them, and as no one else will help them, I must," he concluded.

Longworth distributed food directly to these most abject cases, built apartments to salve their homelessness, and held personal sessions where he would listen patiently to sad stories and offer solace and assistance. When he died in 1863 in Cincinnati, Longworth's funeral procession numbered in the thousands, a great many of them outcasts. Drunkards, prostitutes, beggars, and criminals sobbed at the loss of their one true friend.

The Tappan brothers, Arthur and Lewis, were successful New York merchants and among this country's most accomplished philanthropists at changing society and politics. They worked on a much more national scale than Longworth or Girard. Yet their machinations were often just as personal.

Fired by their evangelical Christian convictions, the Tappans were leading donors to the cause of abolishing slavery. After their funding turned the American Anti-Slavery Society into a mass movement with 250,000 members, mobs attacked their homes and businesses. Arthur escaped with his life only by barricading himself in one of the family stores well supplied with guns. Lewis's home was sacked that same evening, with all of his family possessions pulled into the street and burned by slavery apologists.

The brothers did not buckle. Lewis left his house unrepaired—to serve, he said, as a "silent anti-slavery preacher to the crowds who will flock to see it." More substantively, the two men decided to flood the U.S. with anti-slavery mailings over the following year. This brought them more death threats and harassment, none of which slowed them down.

When a group of Africans who had been captured by Spanish slavers rose

against the crew of the ship transporting them and eventually came ashore on Long Island, Lewis immediately organized their defense against murder charges for having killed a crewmember. He decamped to Connecticut, where he clothed and fed the defendants, located and hired an interpreter of their African dialect, and brought in Yale students to tutor them in English, American manners, and Christianity. Then he retained top lawyers to represent their interests. He attended the court proceedings himself every day, organized a public-relations campaign, and eventually got the Africans freed after pushing their case all the way to the U.S. Supreme Court. His personal devotion and single-handed financing turned abolitionism into a cause célèbre. (For more details on the remarkable culture-changing philanthropy of the Tappan brothers, see their joint entry in our Philanthropy Hall of Fame later in this book.)

If the campaigning of the Tappans on behalf of slaves was impressively personal, the devotion of Joseph de Veuster to miserable lepers was out-and-out heroic. Better known as Father Damien after he became a Catholic priest, de Veuster thought it inhumane that when leprosy reached the Hawaiian Islands victims were forced to live in isolation on a wild peninsula without any buildings or goods or services. The newly diagnosed would be dropped off with nothing but a few tools and some seeds, and proceed to live miserably in shelters made of sticks.

Father Damien moved into the leper colony himself in 1873, brought anti-social residents into line, rescued orphans, provided medical care, and organized building and gardening efforts. He organized large fundraising campaigns by mail that brought in donations sufficient to pay for his many improvements, and to decently bury the 1,600 people whose funerals he presided over in a period of six years. He died himself at age 49 from complications of leprosy. The sacrifices made by Father Damien are especially piercing, but there are many examples of philanthropists who risked happiness, health, and even life itself to carry out their good works.

Philanthropy regularly grows out of pain. The death of John Rockefeller's grandson from scarlet fever in 1901 cemented his desire to build a medical research facility that could banish such afflictions. The result was the great Rockefeller University, whose researchers over the years have been awarded dozens of Nobel prizes. The organizer and funder of today's wildly successful National Kidney Registry, which matches donors to patients with organ failure, acted after his ten-year-old daughter was nearly lost to kidney disease.

America's most fecund artist colony, known as Yaddo, was created by Thomas Edison's financial partner Spencer Trask and his wife, Katrina, as a cathartic effort after the couple endured the profound pain of losing all four of their young children, in separate incidents, to disease and early death. The

Trasks envisioned a place where "generations of talented men and women yet unborn" would be "creating, creating, creating." Since its opening in 1926, Yaddo has nurtured a Nobel literature laureate, dozens of Pulitzer Prize and National Book Award winners, and countless other productive musicians, playwrights, and novelists. The Trasks sweetened and softened a world that may have felt hard and bitter when they started giving.

Though it sometimes grows out of pain, philanthropy is more frequently sparked by opposite emotions like gratitude and joy. The first charity hospital in America was created in, of all places, 1735 New Orleans—at that point a ragingly ragged and largely ungoverned city first populated just 18 years earlier by people drawn from jails, poorhouses, and urban gutters. The hospital benefactor was a dying sailor named Jean Louis, who had made some money for the first time in his life by going into the boatbuilding business in the brand-new French colony. He wanted to pass on his good fortune. And his Charity Hospital offering free care to the indigent became one of the most useful of its type, finding a vast market in a town known even then for creativity in vice.

Sticking to that same unlikely place and time, we can easily pluck up another example of great philanthropy growing out of gratitude. Judah Touro arrived in New Orleans in 1801, where he set up as a merchant and rode to great fortune the city's rise and incorporation into the United States of America. Touro became a noted patriot and philanthropist, gratefully donating all across the country to a society that offered freedom and fair play to Jews like him. In his appreciation for the value of sincere faith, Touro financed synagogues and churches alike. He built hospitals, orphanages, almshouses, asylums, schools, and libraries. He bequeathed even more when he died in 1854, a human advertisement for what a determined donor can accomplish.

GOOD CHARITY, BAD CHARITY?

Some activists today are eager to define what is good or bad, acceptable or unacceptable, in other people's giving. Princeton professor Peter Singer has lately made it almost a career to pronounce that only certain kinds of philanthropic contributions ought to be considered truly in the public interest. Only money given directly to "the poor" should be counted as charitable, he and some others argue.

Former NPR executive Ken Stern constructed a recent book on this same idea that charity must be "dedicated to serving the poor and needy." Noting that many philanthropists go far beyond that limited population, he complains that it is "astonishingly easy to start a charity; the IRS approves over 99.5 percent of all charitable applications." He disapprovingly lists nonprofits that have "little connection to common notions of doing good: the Sugar Bowl, the U.S. Golf Association, the Renegade Roller Derby team in Bend, Oregon, and the All Colorado Beer Festival, just to name a few."

> Who is to say that Ned McIlhenny's leaps to preserve the Negro spiritual, or rescue the snowy egret, were less worthy than income-boosting?

Is that a humane argument? Without question, the philanthropy for the downtrodden launched by people like Stephen Girard, Nicholas Longworth, Jean Louis, the Tappans, Milton Hershey, Albert Lexie, and Father Damien is deeply impressive. But the idea that only generosity aimed directly at the poor (or those who agitate in their name) should count as philanthropic is astoundingly narrow and shortsighted. Meddling premised on this view would horribly constrict the natural outpouring of human creativity.

Who is to say that Ned McIlhenny's leaps to preserve the Negro spiritual, or rescue the snowy egret, were less worthy than income-boosting? Was the check that catalyzed Harper Lee's classic novel bad philanthropy? Were there better uses for Alfred Loomis's funds and volunteer management genius than beating the Nazis and Imperial Japanese military?

Even if you insist on the crude utilitarian view that only direct aid to the poor should count as charity, the reality is that many of the most important interventions that reduce poverty over time have nothing to do with alms. By building up MIT, George Eastman struck a mighty blow to increase prosperity and improve the health and safety of everyday life—benefiting individuals at all points on the economic spectrum. Givers who establish good charter schools today are doing more to break cycles of human failure than any welfare transfer has ever achieved. Donors who fund science, abstract knowledge, and new learning pour the deep concrete footings of economic success that have made us history's most aberrant nation—where the poor improve their lot as much as other citizens, and often far more.

> The Brown family changed the course of U.S. literature with some very personal philanthropy.

And what of the private donors who stoke the fires of imagination, moral understanding, personal character, and inspiration? Is artistic and religious philanthropy just the dabbling of bored and vain wealthholders? Aren't people of all income levels lifted up when the human spirit is cultivated and celebrated in a wondrous story, or haunting piece of music, or awe-engendering cathedral?

When a donation is offered to unlock some secret of science, or feed an inspiring art, or attack some cruel disease, one can never count on any precise result. But it's clear that any definition which denies humanitarian value to such giving, because it doesn't go directly to income support, is crabbed and foolish. Much of the power and beauty of American philanthropy derives from its vast range, and the riot of causes we underwrite in our millions of donations.

To illustrate this rather than just claim it, let's take a somewhat random whirl through some of the evidence packed into the back of this book. We'll scroll through a few dozen of the thousands of philanthropic accomplishments accumulated in the full-length version of *The Almanac of American Philanthropy*. We will begin with very tangible products like historic

buildings and parks, consider services like medicine and education, and touch on more ethereal accomplishments in fields like the arts.

THE WILD RICHNESS OF AMERICAN PHILANTHROPY

How many readers know that some of America's top cultural treasures—the homes of our founders—are preserved and kept open to the public not by the National Park Service or other agency of government but rather by privately funded nonprofits? George Washington's Mount Vernon was saved from ruin by thousands of small donors and today thrives under the ownership of the Mount Vernon Ladies' Association. The separate home where Washington was born was also retrieved from oblivion by a mix of small donors plus John Rockefeller Jr. Likewise, Monticello—Thomas Jefferson's residence sometimes described as his "greatest creation"—has been protected and interpreted to visitors for about a century by a private foundation that receives no government funding. Ditto for Montpelier, the nearby home of the father of our Constitution, James Madison.

The summer cottage where Abraham Lincoln spent a quarter of his Presidency and made some of his most momentous decisions, including for-mulating the Emancipation Proclamation, was a neglected part of American history until private donors came along to restore it and open it to the pub-lic in 2008. Williamsburg, Virginia; Touro Synagogue; Greenfield Village; Mystic Seaport; Sturbridge Village; Plimoth Plantation; Old Salem—these beloved historic sites and scads of others have been saved for future genera-tions by philanthropy, not taxpayers.

Our great cathedrals are products of private giving. St. John the Divine, one of the most monumental Christian edifices in the world, was begun in New York City with gifts from J. P. Morgan, and then raised up over decades via thousands of small donations. Riverside Church, a grand gothic pile just another ten blocks up Broadway, was a gift of John Rockefeller Jr. On the other hand, the National Cathedral in Washington, the second-largest such church in the country after St. John (and probably the last pure Gothic cathe-dral that will ever be built), was a flowering of mass philanthropy, and built over a period of 97 years as small funds donated by the public pooled up.

Our cathedrals of human learning—libraries—are also an invention of philanthropy. Ben Franklin promulgated the idea that in a democratic nation like America, everyday people should have easy access to books, and that making them available is a worthy calling for the generous. Even the rough-and-ready city of New Orleans in 1824 got a Free Library courtesy of Judah Touro, who also helped endow the Redwood Library in Newport. John Jacob Astor, James Lenox, and Samuel Tilden gave millions between 1849 and

1886 to create what became the New York Public Library. Financier Joshua Bates launched the Boston Public Library, and Enoch Pratt provided brilliant planning as well as money for a magnificent multibranch library in Baltimore that inspired Andrew Carnegie to create more than 2,800 other libraries in the decades following. Today there are 16,000 public libraries in the U.S. and they are visited a billion and a half times every year.

Many magnificent parks are also fruits of philanthropy. In the mid-1850s, donors started giving lovely botanical gardens to the public in various cities. The list of national parks sparked by donors is long and stretches from Maine's Acadia to the Virgin Islands, from Great Smoky to Grand Teton.

> Many of the most important interventions to reduce poverty have nothing to do with alms. They are gifts that increase the prosperity of everyday life—benefiting individuals at all points on the economic spectrum.

A recent research report declared that thanks to philanthropy we are currently living in the golden age of urban parks. Inspired by the success of the Central Park Conservancy, which donors created to bring New York's green haven back from the brink of disastrous decay and disorder, conservancies have spread all across the country, creating parks that delight citizens by the millions. Manhattan's High Line, Discovery Green in Houston, Chicago's 606 trail, the new $350 million oasis springing up in Tulsa, Dallas's Klyde Warren Park carved out of thin air over a busy freeway—these are all new gifts. And tired or underdeveloped older recreation areas like Shelby Farms in Memphis, Piedmont Park in Atlanta, Buffalo Bayou in Houston, the Olmsted parks in Louisville, and our National Mall are also being renovated and expanded in much-loved ways thanks to generous givers.

Clever private ideas as well as private money have been at the center of miraculous recoveries of several endangered species. The peregrine falcon is the fastest creature on earth when flying, but as a reproducer it had become such a snail that it was flirting with extinction. Government biologists tried to speed its breeding but failed. Then a grant from the IBM Corporation mixed with small donations from falconry hobbyists allowed birders to experiment with some unconventional ideas (including that city skyscrapers might be among the best places for the height-loving, pigeon-dining creatures to make their comeback). Today, the peregrine is out of danger. Fresh ideas and

donor funds were similarly crucial in the comebacks of the wolf, the bluebird, whooping cranes, wild turkeys, the swift fox, and many threatened waterfowl.

Philanthropy isn't going to bring dinosaurs back to life. It has, however, fueled much of the paleontology that has dramatically transformed the field in recent decades. Jack Horner has leveraged $12 million of donations into radical new understandings that some dinosaurs exhibited mothering behaviors, that millions-of-years-old bones can contain soft tissue residues that explain biological secrets, and that the T. Rex may have been as much scavenger as predator. And voluntary donations have been vital in making dinosaurs real for their fans, via imaginative new museum exhibits in places like Montana, the Smithsonian, and New York City's Museum of Natural History.

THE PHILANTHROPY OF SCIENCE

Science in general is deeply entwined with philanthropy in America. Take the high-end telescopes with which astronomers and astrophysicists have made many of the most important discoveries about our universe. They have all been filled with light by philanthropy. Donors created the Lick and Yerkes Observatories before the twentieth century. It was Carnegie money that placed 60-inch and later 100-inch reflecting telescopes on Mount Wilson, and Rockefeller funding that built the 200-inch Hale telescope on Mount Palomar. The Keck Foundation made possible the pair of 33-foot reflectors that opened in Hawaii in 1993. And the two massive instruments under construction today—the Giant Magellan and the 30-Meter Telescope—are both being built with donations. *Big* donations, like the $250 million that Intel founder Gordon Moore slapped down to design and kick off the 30-Meter instrument (which will produce images *12 times* sharper than NASA's Hubble telescope).

Certain large areas of science have been spurred especially hard by donors. Aeronautics, for instance. The Guggenheim family took a very early interest in the field, and in the first half of the 1900s created most of America's infrastructure for supporting flight, including nearly all of our original university aeronautical engineering departments. The Guggenheims were also virtually the sole funders, starting with a 1930 grant of $100,000, of Robert Goddard—the world's greatest genius in rocketry, and the man most responsible for putting the U.S. on the path to world leadership in space flight.

Oceanography is another field mostly created by donors. Ellen Scripps made possible the Scripps Institution of Oceanography in San Diego, and the Rockefellers spawned a similar research operation on the Atlantic at Woods Hole in Massachusetts. There are likewise great research aquariums on both the West Coast (thanks to David Packard) and the East Coast (paid for by Bernie Marcus).

It would be hard to exaggerate the importance of some of these science gifts. In 2013, *Philanthropy* magazine undertook some deep historical investigation on John Rockefeller's pioneering funding for medical research, which commenced in 1901. We found that an astonishing 47 Nobel science-prize winners had received significant financial support from Rockefeller before they earned their awards. Another 14 Nobel laureates were supported by Rockefeller money sometime after their award, allowing them to expand their research or to mentor a new generation of scientists. The discoveries made by these men and women included blood typing, penicillin, the yellow-fever vaccine, electrical signaling in the nervous system, the operation of optical nerves, fundamental understandings of DNA and genetics, and much more.

These kinds of breakthroughs fueled by intensive philanthropy are by no means just something from history. A number of philanthropists have of late made brain research a high priority of their giving. Four donors alone have put a billion and a half dollars into this area in recent years, and their efforts are beginning to cumulate in important findings. When President Obama announced a human-brain initiative as a $100 million federal project in 2013, his roadmap was drawn by researchers involved in the much larger philanthropic brain-science blitz already underway.

SAVING LIVES

Medical philanthropy has had many splendid triumphs. After World War II, the entire budget of the National Institutes of Health was less than $10 million, and the major forces in biomedical research were smart donors. The John Hartford Foundation was smart indeed, catalyzing many advances in health care during the 1950s, '60s, and '70s with its grants in areas like immunology, organ rejection, development of the artificial heart, microneurosurgery, and cancer research.

Hartford was a special savior for the many people suffering from kidney failure. They funded some of the world's first successful kidney transplants at Boston's Brigham Hospital, and underwrote creation of the important professional societies where kidney specialists exchange information. Hartford made kidney dialysis practical, funding the machines created for the world's first out-of-hospital dialysis center. For the one out of every 100,000 Americans who experience kidney failure, these gifts lifted a death sentence.

In similar fashion, Uncas Whitaker more or less willed the new field of biomedical engineering into legitimacy by leaving $700 million for that sole purpose when he died in 1975. The trustees of his bequest pushed the money out the door quickly and wisely, at a time when most universities and the government medical-funding agencies opposed a blending of engineering

and medical disciplines. The Whitaker efforts created curricula for the new field and funded inaugural research projects. They paid for classrooms, labs, and 13 entire buildings. They gave dozens of colleges the money to hire dual-purpose faculty, fellows, and interns, and otherwise encouraged talented people to take up work at the intersection of technology and medicine. They spawned professional societies and launched the careers of 1,500 biomedical engineers who founded more than 100 companies and accumulated over 400 patents or property licenses.

The results are dramatic. Biomedical engineering has become the fastest growing specialty in all of engineering. And revolutionary products like lab-grown skin and organs, laser surgery, advanced prosthetics, large-scale joint replacement, cochlear implants, and hundreds of other miracles are now commonplace.

Like overlooked medical disciplines, philanthropy has been helpful in bringing new attention to overlooked diseases. Autism was barely understood when philanthropists offered the funds for deeper research and wider public education. Schizophrenia, certain kinds of blindness, and prostate and breast cancer have all receded in the face of donor pressure.

Huntington's disease afflicts one out of every 10,000 Americans, and there is no cure for the slow, suffocating killer. It gets modest attention from the NIH. Throughout the past decade and a half, though, philanthropist Andrew Shechtel has stimulated expansive new research on the affliction via $732 million in donations.

> Uncas Whitaker willed the new field of biomedical engineering into legitimacy with $700 million and a determination to buck the university, government, engineering, and medical establishments.

Philanthropists have also done marvelous things on the social side of medical care. They have, for instance, funded giant advances in palliative care and patient comfort—creating the Fisher Houses, which now unite wounded servicemembers with their families during treatment, and the Ronald McDonald houses, which do the same for sick children. Humane hospice care was brought to America by philanthropists starting in 1974.

It isn't just in the field of medicine that donors have been able to save and improve lives. Literally hundreds of millions of people have avoid-

ed starvation thanks to the crucial foundation investments that created the Green Revolution. Today, the Gates Foundation is putting money into extending the agricultural progress of the Green Revolution across Africa.

It is estimated that tobacco could kill a billion people globally during the present century. Philanthropists are investing hundreds of millions of dollars in educational efforts to head off many of those deaths. Dangerous roads that kill thousands of people in developing countries every year are another area where donors have recently started working creatively to save lives.

Disaster zones are one of the most visible realms where the philanthropic impulse does battle against danger and chaos. From the Red Cross and Samaritan's Purse to World Vision and Doctors Without Borders, there are many vehicles through which the generous now act to rescue the perishing. Entries in the full-length *Almanac* chronicle multiple philanthropic outpourings in response to earthquakes, for instance: San Francisco in 1906, Italy in 1909, Armenia in 1989, Haiti in 2010, and so on. The largest recent charitable gushes in response to cruel twists of fate were the $2.8 billion donated by Americans after the 9/11 attacks and the $5.3 billion offered up after Hurricane Katrina.

ELEVATING MINDS

Philanthropy doesn't just fill bellies and fill pockets. It also fills heads with productive knowledge, and souls with inspiration and ideas. Education, religion, culture, and the arts are primeval philanthropic imperatives.

Philanthropy is, for instance, the central factor behind the greatness of American universities. Donors like Mary Garrett didn't just give the money to create learning citadels (in her case, the Johns Hopkins medical school), they also demanded business-like procedures and reforms that separated U.S. colleges from their European predecessors. Garrett insisted, in return for her support, that Hopkins raise academic standards, and accept women into its medical school on equal footing with men, making it the first place those two things were accomplished.

As I am writing, more than a half-billion dollars of private giving is creating a remarkable new campus on New York City's Roosevelt Island where cutting-edge engineering and entrepreneurship training will be combined under the aegis of Cornell University. Donors also brought in as a partner Technion, the Israeli university that has proven one of the most effective in the world at spinning off lab discoveries as useful products. Cornell Tech, as the new institution will be called, has great promise of becoming a hub that not only provides superb student training but also generates a flood of economic productivity in the surrounding region, à la MIT or Stanford (two other products of entrepreneurial philanthropy).

In addition to dominant universities, philanthropy has yielded many remarkable academies for younger students. From the Catholic schools that serve as lifelines for families stranded in neglected urban neighborhoods, to superb vocational instruction at institutions like the Williamson School, to alternative programs like Waldorf schools, to many privately supported schools that provide top-flight academics, generous scholarship and endowment gifts have done wonders for generations of American children. Donors have created and sustained distinctive American institutions like the Hershey School and the Kamehameha Schools in Hawaii. The Hawaiian institution was bequeathed 365,000 acres of land by Bernice Bishop, allowing it to educate more than 7,000 youngsters every year at almost no charge to their parents.

Within just the last 20 years, donors have powered what I suspect historians will someday categorize as the most important social invention of our time—the charter school. As this book is published, 3 million children are attending 7,000 charter schools, and both of those numbers are rising rapidly (from zero just a couple decades earlier). Even more remarkably, the top charters have invented starkly original techniques and procedures that allow them to take children with harsh life disadvantages and dreadful conventional schools in their neighborhoods and lift them into well-above-average academic results.

> Philanthropy is the rain that keeps the tree of artistic life in bud.

The 9,000 students at the Uncommon Schools charter network are 98 percent minority and 78 percent low-income, yet all seniors take the SAT and their average score is 20 points above the college-readiness benchmark. At KIPP schools, 95 percent of their 70,000 students are minority and 86 percent are low-income, yet 83 percent go to college. In New York City, the average charter-school student now absorbs five months of extra learning per year in math and one extra month in reading compared with counterparts in conventional public schools.

CREATIVE JUICES

In the U.S., philanthropy is the rain that keeps the tree of artistic life in bud. Consider symphony orchestras. Fully *half* of their income today comes from donations (33 percent from annual gifts, 16 percent from revenue off of endowments given previously). Only 6 percent of symphony funds come from local, state, or federal government support. (The rest comes from concert income.)

The story is about the same for other arts. Nonprofit arts institutions as a whole currently get 45 percent of their budgets from donors.

Subtract the philanthropy and our lives immediately become duller, flatter, darker, more silent.

Voluntary support for artistic activity in our country sprawls across a delightful range of fields. The little gems are often just as sparkly as the big diamonds. Take the Van Cliburn piano competition. Established in Fort Worth, Texas, in 1962 by local donors anxious to encourage gifted players like their native son Mr. Cliburn, it is a kind of Olympiad for piano players. Every four years, the greatest rising stars in the world descend on Bass Hall and play until their fingers can flutter no more. Spectacular performances are available not only to the live listeners but also to broadcast, Internet, and film audiences.

George Eastman's pet project, his School of Music and the 3,100-seat hall he built for it, remains one of the treasures of American culture. He created the venue to be much more open and welcoming to audiences than European concert halls, and programmed it from the very beginning not only with classical music but also with other arts like film (which was then considered a vulgar and unserious trifle). Eastman made Martha Graham's career by bringing her in to choreograph avant-garde dances that could be presented between film reels to mass audiences who would never darken the door of a ballet performance.

> Fully 47 Nobel science-prize winners received significant financial support from Rockefeller before they earned their awards.

Now that it is recognized as both a potential art form and a potent shaper of popular culture and opinion, film has become a field of interest to other savvy philanthropists. The individual most committed at present is the former co-founder of eBay, Jeff Skoll, who has poured hundreds of millions of his dollars into an operation that makes popular movies with a message. He also funds a "social-action campaign" for each release, which encourages people to alter their thinking and behavior based on what they have seen. Skoll has convinced big names like Matt Damon, Julia Roberts, and George Clooney to take roles in his filmanthropy, which has hit some popular and creative nerves. A charmed Hollywood establishment has given more than 30 Oscar nominations to his pictures—which include works like *The Help*, *Syriana*, *Lincoln*, *Charlie Wilson's War*, *Waiting for Superman*, and *An Inconvenient Truth* (which brought Al Gore his Nobel Peace Prize).

Creative work undertaken under the banner of art and culture can also yield practical progress in unexpected ways. In the days before mass

media, two donors—library and art patron Ada Moore, and the Carnegie Corporation—gave money to the American Foundation for the Blind to fund a crash program to bring books to the sightless in some practical audio form. The foundation decided to see if a brand-new patent for what was being called the "long-playing record," or L.P., might work.

L.P.s were much larger and slower-spinning than the 78-rpm records that were then popular, and thus allowed four times as much material on each side, making them practical for extended readings from books. The AFB experimented with making discs out of various materials, seeking one durable enough to stand up to shipping from house to house among blind subscribers. They eventually settled on vinyl. The foundation also had to build the first players for the records.

This philanthropic product-development effort succeeded, and "talking books" began to be shipped around the country, leaving blind Americans wide-eyed with wonder at the joys of literature. For the first 14 years of its existence, the L.P. record funded by Moore and Carnegie was enjoyed exclusively by the blind. Only later did CBS turn it into a medium for the general public to play music. A charitable creation thus became a big part of American pop culture.

FIXING PROBLEMS
VIA PHILANTHROPY
VS. GOVERNMENT

Philanthropy is not interchangeable with government spending. It typically takes quite different approaches to solving problems.

John Updike once wrote an essay about how government administrators view change—noting that their every incentive is for continuation of the status quo. Change disrupts bureaucracies and creates work for those who man them. People working in government thus tend to shun departures from prevailing procedure, and to seek more of the same, *not* innovation. Updike

writes poetically that "the state, like a young child, wishes that each day be just like the last." Whereas an inventive private actor "like a youth, hopes that each day will bring something new."

This pierces to the heart of why government problem-solving is generally so sluggish and uninspired. Of course, philanthropy can also become bureaucratic and timid—as can any human activity under certain conditions. But there are fundamental structures and incentives to private giving that, in the main, make it much more imaginative, flexible, and interested in transformation, as well as more individualized, more pluralistic, more efficient. One at a time, let's look at some of the distinctive qualities of private giving that set it apart from public spending.

PHILANTHROPY IS INVENTIVE

Both in its approach to problems and in the forms through which it operates, American philanthropy has shown itself to be highly experimental and creative.

For instance, the institution of the charitable foundation itself—which allowed donors to codify their giving and extend it to future generations—is an invention of American philanthropy. The first foundations emerged in the U.S. around the turn of the twentieth century. By 1915 there were 27 in operation; in 1930 the total was over 200. The British began to copy the foundation structure in 1936; it was 1969 before the French and Japanese got some of their first examples. Today the foundation (and U.S.-style philanthropy in general) is just beginning to be understood and copied in places like China, the Middle East, Russia, and India.

Heaps of examples illustrate the inventiveness of private philanthropy in substance as well as form. Take just the past decade of grantmaking in a single field—education. Five donors recently set up a fascinating effort to trim the soaring costs of college by producing top-quality, low-cost textbooks for the country's 25 most-attended college courses. They will use the open-source method commonly applied to producing great software, along with an expert-review process. And the resulting books will be free to students. Given that college students spent an average of $1,200 on texts in the 2013 school year, this effort is expected to save collegians $750 million in its first years. The donors are now expanding it to the high-school level.

In the same year that this clever venture was launched, other donors paid to bring a new testing yardstick to schools so they can measure their performance against peers in other countries. Yet others provided the means to set up MOOCs—massive open online courses from top colleges that can be taken for free by anyone—thanks to philanthropic sponsorship. Simultaneously, philanthropists concerned about the low quality of many of the colleges that

train schoolteachers created a new guide, in collaboration with rating expert *U.S. News and World Report*, that scores every one of the nation's 1,668 teacher colleges for effectiveness.

There were creative educational thrusts by other givers at about the same time. One donor paid for a major experiment in Chicago that is testing whether at-risk preschoolers get a bigger academic boost from long-term training for parents, or from special financial incentives for teachers who produce results in a year, or from small weekly payments that reward specific achievements by parents, teachers, or children. Other givers paid for Khan Academy to offer "a free, world-class education for anyone, anywhere" via thousands of free online seminars. A contemporaneous donor-driven innovation was a practical new system that allows school districts to measure how far students progress from their starting point during a school year, and then to reward the teacher accordingly.

Meanwhile, several radically different and effective new ways of drawing fresh talent into teaching were created with charitable funds. Philanthropy invented a superb math and science initiative that spread rapidly to 560 schools in its first seven years. (It causes the number of students earning passing scores on math and science Advanced Placement exams to jump 85 percent in the first year, on average, and to nearly triple within three years.) And it was thanks to generous givers that

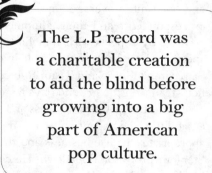

The L.P. record was a charitable creation to aid the blind before growing into a big part of American pop culture.

less than a decade after Hurricane Katrina wiped out every one of its miserable public schools, New Orleans had an entirely new 100-percent-charters school system in place that allowed the city's students to mostly catch up with the performance of students in the rest of the state, for the first time in state history.

And so on. We could walk through similar bursts of philanthropic invention in medicine, economic development, overseas aid, and other areas. You'll find examples in the sample Philanthropic Achievement lists at the heart of this book.

PHILANTHROPY IS NIMBLE

Private giving is light years quicker than government action, and it tends to adapt effectively to changing conditions on the ground. A simple example

is donor John Montgomery's provision of lifesaving radio gear in central Africa. Residents of that region had been terrorized for years by warlord Joseph Kony and his mercenary army that routinely popped out of the jungle to kill, steal, and kidnap children from remote villages. Montgomery suggested that if a radio network were created so information on Kony's movements could be quickly shared, imperiled villagers could be warned in time to flee. In very short order he had tribal chiefs equipped with the necessary transmitters and receivers, and many families were spared.

Another illustration of the responsiveness of philanthropy came during the 2014 Ebola scare. As the disease swept into new nations, neither the international nor American health bureaucracies showed much capacity to adjust or speed up their distribution of resources. Enter philanthropist Paul Allen with an almost instant $100 million pledge, rapidly matched by $50 million from the Gates Foundation, $25 million from Mark Zuckerberg, and other gifts. By, for instance, immediately establishing protocols for aid workers who get infected, providing financial support for their evacuations and insurance-coverage gaps, and paying for the dispatch of 500 emergency respondents and their equipment to west Africa, Allen's quick gift was credited by experts with stanching the bleeding (literally). The comparative speed of charities is often visible in disaster relief—where organizations like Samaritan's Purse and Team Rubicon are routinely able to put supplies and help-teams on the ground days faster than public authorities.

Interestingly, the nimbleness and speed of philanthropy coexist with a proven ability to be patient and take an extraordinarily long-term approach when appropriate. "Unlike business and the state, foundations can 'go long,' " writes Stanford professor Rob Reich. He cites the multi-generation creation of public libraries, the decades-long Green Revolution, the painstaking creation of our national 911 emergency call system by philanthropists, and other examples.

PHILANTHROPY IS INDIVIDUALIZED

Howard Husock once wrote in *Forbes* that "the more individualized attention a problem calls for, the less well-suited government is to dealing with it—and the more likely that independent, charitably supported groups can help." This is indubitably true.

Many of the most successful mechanisms in the charitable world—like microlending circles, Alcoholics Anonymous, the successful mentoring programs for prisoners, college-dropout preventers like the Posse Foundation, and good job-training programs for welfare moms and the homeless—rely heavily on one-to-one human linkages and accountability. They take advantage of all the useful information that becomes available when you actually

know someone, instead of dealing with a stranger. And they use the power of relationships to help people change behavior.

I once did a study of the informal lending circles that many immigrants use to build economic success after they come to the U.S. Typically, a group of six to ten individuals who are related or know each other will band together, and each month every participant will put a few hundred dollars into the circle. When your turn comes up you get to collect that month's kitty—which recipients typically use for things like starting a business, or making a downpayment on a car or house, or buying some equipment or education that can be used to make a living. These circles almost never have contracts or receipts or any legally binding structure. So what prevents someone from walking off with the pot then refusing to kick in their share of contributions in the future? Relationships!

There is the pressure of not letting down your relatives or friends or neighbors whom you will see in the future. There is also the confidence that comes from entering the circle with valuable knowledge of the character of the other people in it, making it less likely you will be taken advantage of yourself. These are not anonymous strangers in a transfer program, they are people whose strengths and weaknesses are known to each other. These are personal, not impersonal, transactions.

> Gifts where the giver and recipient are involved with each other, familiar with one another's character, and committed to each other's flourishing are some of the most successful forms of philanthropy.

"I never think about crowds. I think about individuals," Mother Teresa used to say. The administrator of a government helping program, on the other hand, has to focus wholly on the crowd. Government programs can't have different approaches and different rules for different kinds of people; they are all about equal opportunity, about being strictly the same for all participants in all places at all times. Cramped minds sometimes romanticize this "consistency" of government programs, and contrast it favorably to the "patchwork" variations of charitable aid. But consistency is not really how humans work.

If you have one child who needs a very structured environment, and another who blooms when left to navigate on her own, and a third who

doesn't do any kind of book learning well but has vibrant creative skills, you don't want "consistent" schools; you don't want one size fits all. You want individualized services that recognize and work with intimate differences of personality. You'll have a hard time finding that in government-run programs, but it's a hallmark of philanthropic efforts.

Great philanthropists know all of this. That's why many donors prefer to work in their own backyards, where they know the characters of many recipients. When allying themselves with social entrepreneurs, donors tend to seek out neighborhood operators who have intimate acquaintance with the problem at hand, and the persons suffering through it. Donors sift through competing petitions for help and choose those where they have some direct knowledge, and confidence the transactions will be personal enough to keep people accountable and tuned in to real needs.

Successful benevolence uses the power of intimate knowledge. That greatly improves the chances of social success. An individually tailored approach is often the central difference between philanthropy done right and ineffective government check writing.

> "I never think about crowds. I think about individuals," Mother Teresa used to say.

The great giver Julius Rosenwald once described the aim of philanthropy as "healing the sore spots of civilization." This is easier to achieve by working in personal rather than impersonal ways. Consider the story of a young woman named Liz Murray who grew up as the neglected daughter of two drug addicts.

In her teenage years Murray began reaching out to potential allies for help in saving herself. On one particular day she had two back-to-back human interactions that were climactic in her life. The first was in a New York City welfare office where she attempted to qualify for aid for the first time so she could have an apartment instead of living on the street as she had been for two years. The transaction was all about forms and rules. It was impersonal. And it ended in yelling, her being mocked by the government caseworker, and a refusal of aid—which was disastrous given her precarious circumstance at that moment.

Murray's next interview that day was at the *New York Times* headquarters, where she sat down with the committee in charge of awarding the charitable college scholarships handed out every year by the New York Times Company Foundation. This transaction was highly personal. She told them how her

mother sold their donated Thanksgiving turkey for drugs; how she had slept in stairwells since her mother died of AIDS; about not eating and living off a food pantry; and about what kept her spirits intact throughout these trials. She was soon awarded one of the foundation's six scholarships (with which she eventually graduated from Harvard). And when a very personal story about her life was published by the *Times*, donations poured in which not only allowed Murray to occupy an apartment and start eating regularly, but also provided the means for the foundation to award 15 more college scholarships than expected.

Murray herself makes clear how important personal factors are in any helping interaction. "During my more vulnerable moments, I was always seeing myself through the eyes of others." If they looked at her as a failure, "then I was one." And if they looked at her as "someone capable, then I was capable. When teachers like Ms. Nedgrin saw me as a victim—despite her good intentions—that's what I believed about myself too. Now I had teachers who held me to a higher standard, and that helped me rise to the occasion. The deeply personal relationships in this intimate school setting made me believe." With the help of just a few well-placed helping hands—philanthropists as it happens, though that is too cool and Greek a word to capture the intimacy of what they did for her—Murray eventually wrenched herself out of a death-spiral. It could not have been done without human closeness.

PHILANTHROPY FREQUENTLY SEEKS TO TRANSFORM, NOT JUST TREAT

Philanthropists are often driven by a deeper, wider, more comprehensive ambition than just giving aid. Instead of merely compensating for ills, philanthropy often tries to correct them. It works preemptively to stop the flow of hot lava, rather than simply putting out the fires it creates.

An early advocate for this aspect of American philanthropy was Ben Franklin. His own extensive giving aimed not so much to relieve men in their misfortune as to reform them into a healthier state. "The best way of doing good to the poor is not making them easy in poverty, but leading or driving them out of it," he wrote. Improving the world that strugglers live in was Franklin's notion of the best way to do good for fellow men. Libraries, schools, occupational training, and all forms of education, self-improvement, and character-building were his favorite causes.

This connects to the previous point about philanthropy being individualized and intimate. If improving private behavior and building self-governance is what you are trying to do, a personal approach is essential. And in our country, the goal of charity has always been individual competence and independence, not just social quiet.

As a Polish journalist who traveled across the U.S. in 1876 observed to newspaper readers back in Europe, the charitable impulses of Americans are very specific. "A man who is old and infirm, a woman, or a child receive more assistance in the United States than anywhere else," he noted. But "a healthy young man will almost invariably hear one piece of advice: 'Help yourself!' And if he does not know how to follow this advice, he may even die of starvation."

Strong citizens and strong communities make most palliative aid unnecessary. In law enforcement it is a truism that heading off bad behavior is much preferable to cleaning up after a crime. American philanthropists often take a similar approach to social reform—better to help people build sturdy habits than to rescue them after they fall.

In a free society, one doesn't really want government, with its coercive powers, to get into the business of personal transformation. There's too much risk of Big Brother authoritarianism in that. But donors can do this work well on a voluntary basis. They offer carrots that encourage individual reform, while at the same time assisting recovery from prior mistakes. This has great value to society.

> Better to help people build sturdy habits than to rescue them after they fall.

In 2015 The Philanthropy Roundtable published a book called *Clearing Obstacles to Work* which catalogues the secrets of hundreds of successful charities that help homeless people, released prisoners, welfare moms, and other at-risk populations succeed economically and stand on their own two feet. These effective charities don't just give out jobs and apartments and checks. Without exception, they require their clients to rise to the occasion—they expect them to learn and cooperate and expend effort. In short they treat them as equal partners and ask them to contribute, rather than patronizing them with undemanding alms.

PHILANTHROPY IS PLURALISTIC

Polyarchy. That's a great $50 word for any American to know. It refers to a society in which there are many independent sources of power. Contrast it to monarchy. The United States has a notably polyarchic culture, and independent grassroots philanthropic giving is one big aspect of this.

The polyarchy fed by philanthropy increases variety in our lives and protects non-mainstream points of view. There is only one federal government, and it necessarily applies a uniform approach to all who approach the throne. At the state level we have 50 power centers but only one applies to our own

life. If you count every single school board and village administration and water district in the U.S. there are about 100,000 government entities all told, but again only one holds sway where we live, and we usually have no alternative to what it presents us.

Meanwhile, there are about *two million* independent organizations in our civil society, and *hundreds of millions* of separate adult donors. These overlap and compete; none have an exclusive franchise; we can pick and choose, mix and match. And as alternate sources of resources and organizing power these voluntary elements are antidotes to any uniform authority that could become oppressive, or just ineffective. ("The legislator is obliged to give a character of uniformity...which does not always suit the diversity of customs and district," observed Tocqueville.)

Yale law professor Stephen Carter points out that "the individual who gives to charity might measure the needs of the community by different calipers than centralized policy makers, and will therefore contribute to a different set of causes. These millions of individual decisions lead to a diversity in spending that would be impossible if we adopted the theory that the only money spent for the public good is the money spent by the state." Philanthropy "also helps resolve an information problem: Government officials, no matter how well-intentioned, cannot know all the places where donations are needed, or the form that will be most useful." Philanthropy is thus "democracy in action."

Give away houses built by bleeding-heart church volunteers! Ask small business owners to have coffee with a prisoner every month, and college kids to spend a day with his children! Adapt Mormon welfare programs to other hungry and homeless people! Recruit school teachers from the Ivy League! It is much easier for private givers to invent and experiment in these sorts of ways. They can try liberationist models, authority-based models, religious approaches, mentoring influences, and other strategies that would be off-limits to public agencies.

The sprawling, multi-dimensioned society that America has grown into is often too complex for government-provided single-solution answers. In areas like family life, schooling options, health, and so forth, many citizens would prefer to choose from independent and voluntary social solutions rather than have a government-provided version forced on them. Do we really want public authorities deciding what's in our art galleries, who trains our children in moral virtues, and the size of soda we should drink? It will often be more realistic and desirable to address these sorts of issues through multifarious private voluntary efforts. Let a thousand flowers bloom.

Philanthropic solutions, right-leaning professor Les Lenkowsky has pointed out, are "especially important for people with ideas that may be unpopular, innovative, or directed at a minority of the population.... Philanthropy, in

short, is an expression of pluralism." Left-leaning professor Rob Reich makes the very same point. Because they "decentralize production of public goods and curtail government orthodoxy," he writes, philanthropists provide "pluralism of public goods."

In addition to reinforcing freedom and innovation, this aspect of private giving has many practical advantages. What works to reverse homelessness or alcoholism or loneliness in old age may be quite different in Nebraska than in Newark (or Namibia). Yet in public programs it's hard to allow different rules and pursue varying strategies. In philanthropy that's easy. Indeed that's one of the field's inherent strengths.

One of the distinctive (and for many of us encouraging) aspects of contemporary life is the rapid "nicheification" of choices. Not long ago we had three national news networks, and three national car makers, and three national entertainment channels. Many neighborhoods had one hospital choice, one public school, one department store, and one dominant employer. Today we have many more options, allowing us to select from quite different priorities, and values, and tastes. Philanthropy has always enjoyed this rich variety.

Another subtle way that philanthropy protects diversity and options is by giving the social visions of different time periods their chance to chip away at problems, allowing points of view that are out of fashion, or just forgotten, to retain a foothold. "The great thing about the legal protection of charitable trusts over time is that we don't all have a bunch of institutions in 2013 that are wholly determined by what trustees happen to think in 2013. That would lead to an appalling homogenization of our cultural, social, and educational landscape. Instead, people set up different projects in 1880, or 1938, or 1972, and those visions, sometimes gloriously out of step with how we currently think…continue to thrive."

So wrote a trustee of a college in the rural West whose founder stipulated a hundred years ago that it had to be one of the most academically selective in the country, yet require its students to put half of their time into ranch work, that it had to be all male, and never bigger than a few dozen students per class. We wouldn't want every American college to have that signature, but how wonderful that there is one that does. Thanks to its donor's rules, Deep Springs College offers a rare and perfect education for a special type of student, while producing results and insights that the rest of the educational establishment can learn from.

PHILANTHROPY IS FLEXIBLE

If you talk to problem-solvers who rely on both private donors and government grants to support their operations, they will tell you that one of the

most invaluable things about philanthropy is its flexibility, its trust in social entrepreneurs, its comparative lack of red tape, its willingness to adapt.

This can be seen with crystalline clarity in science philanthropy. It was donors like John Rockefeller, John Hartford, and Lucille Markey who created modern biomedical research and set the template for the way government funders like the National Science Foundation and the National Institutes of Health operate today. Even after the federal science agencies began gushing billions of dollars in all directions, philanthropy remains crucial to the field because it is more flexible.

MIT professor Fiona Murray recently studied the 50 universities that top the list for science-research spending in the U.S. She found that private donors now provide about 30 percent of the total research funding at these places. So the sheer volume of dollars is consequential.

But what's even more important about science philanthropy is the way it is structured. Private funders often take up work that is neglected by federal funders because it is too experimental, too obscure, pursued by scientists too young to have a record, and so forth. "Government research is powerfully conservative. I've been an NIH researcher for decades, and to get an NIH grant today you essentially have to already have solved the problem in question," says Charles Marmar, a top medical scientist at New York University. Private funding is not only more willing to take risks, it is also much faster and less bureaucratic, according to Marmar. "On the philanthropic side donors tend to have business acumen and know how to get things done," he notes.

Philanthropic money often functions as venture capital, supporting high-risk, high-payoff science that is at an early stage or taking an unconventional approach. "What I've always loved about philanthropy is it's money that has a potential to be flexible. It's money that can catalyze new ideas. It's money that lets you push the frontiers, follow the leading edge," states Leroy Hood, one of today's leading biologists. "At the National Institutes of Health, if you haven't completed two thirds of your research, you're probably not going to get a grant, because everything is so competitive and so conservative. So a philanthropist who is willing to say 'Yes, I'll step in and help you find something new' is a jewel."

Hood has relied on donors over and over in his illustrious career. When he was creating a machine to automate the labor-intensive process of sequencing DNA, he applied for NIH grants and "got some of the worst scores the NIH had ever given. People said it was impossible, or they said, 'Why do this? Grad students can do it more easily.'" So Hood turned to Sol Price, the entrepreneurial whiz who originated the warehouse superstore concept that

produced Costco and Sam's Club, and then later Bill Gates. With support from these two donors, Hood produced the technology that made much of today's genomic revolution possible.

There are many simple things that make science philanthropy so valuable. For example, the federal bureaucracies are hugely biased toward scientists who have already made their mark—the average age at which researchers receive their first federal grant is 43, and only 1 percent of NIH grants go to researchers 35 or younger. Yet most science breakthroughs originate from precisely those young inquirers who haven't yet fallen into conventional ways of approaching topics. Private funders are vastly more likely to support young investigators.

Private donors are also vastly more willing to buy machines, and erect buildings, and hire technology aides—creating the infrastructure within which discoveries can take place. Government grants are notoriously unwilling to pay for this sort of foundation-laying. Federal grants must be tailored for one discrete experiment and its immediate costs only. That makes it hard for directors to keep their labs operating and continuously improving.

> Science lab directors describe private giving as "gold" and "magic"— for one thing because it usually arrives without onerous strings attached.

Philanthropy has special importance in bringing resources to new fields, new places, new approaches. Ignoring conventional advice that they give only to established health centers, donors have built top-flight new medical facilities from scratch in places like Kansas City, San Diego, and Houston. Eminent neuroscientist Steven Hyman, who is investigating the genetic bases of mental illness, wanted to do work in Africa because of its unusually diverse genetic pool, "but it would take a huge administrative or bureaucratic effort to run federal grants there. We couldn't think of doing that without private money."

As easily as it fills geographical gaps, philanthropy fill gaps in popularity, conventional wisdom, and intellectual fashion. The list of "orphan" maladies that neither government nor corporate funders were much interested in before donors became involved is long. Trachoma, schistosomiasis, Guinea worm, onchocerciasis, and many other tropical diseases. Geriatric medicine. Retinitis pigmentosa blindness. Huntington's disease. Malaria. "Diseases like schizophrenia, bipolar disorder, and autism have moved out of this black box," reports Hyman. "Without private philanthropy, we wouldn't be able to take risks or get our research up to scale."

The medical establishment was dismissive of his idea when George Papanicolau used a "highly speculative" grant from the Commonwealth Foundation to invent the Pap smear. The AIDS epidemic was still a blurry terror when the Aaron Diamond Foundation ripped into it with a nimbleness, speed, and tolerance for risk that allowed it to pioneer many of the key research and treatment findings needed to battle the disease.

Lab directors prize the fact that private giving usually comes without onerous strings attached. "Unrestricted funds are gold; they're magic," says Eric Lander, director of the Broad Institute and another of the nation's top scientists. "We're able to say when we have a good idea, 'Let's start investing in it now rather than write a grant and start working on it two years from now after it wends its way through the NIH system.'"

In combination, these practical advantages can have remarkable effects. The trust set up by Lucille Markey to support biomedical careers is an excellent illustration. It operated only from the mid-1980s to 1997, when it shut its doors for good after distributing more than $500 million in 200 grants.

The Markey funding was everything that government granting isn't. It was tremendously flexible. Preliminary investigations and risky science of the sort that give NIH or NSF funders lockjaw? No problem. Spend money recruiting great new scientists or graduate students whose exact roles will be determined in the future? Can do. Build or equip a lab before the exact experiments that will unfold there have been plotted? Sure. Shift money from one year to another, or one project to another, to fuel the most promising avenues as they open up? Yup. Dramatically change research directions in response to unexpected experimental results? You'd be stupid not to! Yet almost none of those things can be done with government funding.

The rules which allowed the Markey grants to fuel so much innovation by recipients were explicit: favor young investigators with promise and nurture them through the "valley of death" that extends from the end of their training until their reputations are established. Trust outstanding researchers with wide discretionary powers in using their funds. Support fields with the biggest upside. Fund areas that are important but not popular. Allow not just basic science but also "translational" research that turns new discoveries into useable treatments and technologies. Pay for the infrastructure necessary for great research, not just the research itself. Be patient.

The Markey Scholar Awards offered funding for five to seven years to each recipient, plus money to establish his or her own lab. The 113 Markey awardees turned out to be extraordinarily successful and productive. Eric Lander is an example—during his fellowship he refined new concepts of

gene mapping in the lab Markey supported, and today he heads the largest genome center in the world.

A current example of how different philanthropy-funded science can be from state-funded science is the Howard Hughes Medical Institute. The eccentric billionaire who founded it created the institute primarily to conduct its own research instead of handing money to facilities with their own agendas. A 1985 sale of gifted stock made it the wealthiest medical philanthropy in the country.

About 350 Hughes Investigators operate at more than 70 universities, hospitals, or labs across the country in an unusual organizational structure. Their dispersal allows them to benefit from cross-fertilization of ideas, yet they are employed by the institute rather than their host, and benefit from its independence and patience. As a companion to these investigators working far afield, Hughes recently created a major research campus of its own outside Washington, D.C., where it has concentrated more than 400 biologists to do high-risk, long-term research in large interdisciplinary teams. Their more corporate style of investigation is quite different from the traditional individual-researcher model favored by government funders (and by Hughes in its other support), and brings special advantages to certain kinds of discovery work.

> The goal of charity in our country has always been individual competence and independence, not just social quiet.

A 2009 study by the National Bureau of Economic Research found that these philanthropic models are unusually effective. "Investigators of the Howard Hughes Medical Institute, which tolerates early failure, rewards long-term success and gives its appointees great freedom to experiment…produce high-impact papers at a much higher rate than a control group of similarly accomplished NIH-funded scientists," the study concluded. This meshes with many other observations. "Philanthropy fuels new opportunities in exciting ways," concludes Leroy Hood. "At really excellent places like MIT or Caltech or Harvard, new innovation almost always comes from philanthropy."

PHILANTHROPY IS EFFICIENT

A few years ago, academics collected 71 different studies comparing the efficiency of offerings when the same basic service was available from both public agencies and private organizations. They found that in 56 out of the 71 cases, the philanthropic provider was more cost-effective. In ten cases there was no clear difference, and in only five cases was the public provider more efficient.

The public senses and understands this reality, which is one root of its deep affection for charitable operations. Americans know most philanthropic efforts get a lot of bang for the buck. That's why they voluntarily handed $390 billion to charities in 2016.

Asked in 2011 "Which do you think is more cost-effective in promoting social good—private charities or the government?," 73 percent of adults nationwide said charities were the most cost-effective, while 17 percent selected government agencies. (Perhaps you've heard the old definition of social science: "Elaborate demonstrations of the obvious, by methods that are obscure.") Asked in 2010 whether they most trust government, business, or nonprofits to solve "the most pressing issues of our time," 71 percent of Americans picked nonprofits.

To gather more evidence on public attitudes toward philanthropy, The Philanthropy Roundtable commissioned its own national poll in 2015. The results revealed deep public confidence in both the effectiveness and the efficiency of private giving. The results are laid out in the full-length version of *The Almanac of American Philanthropy*.

COMMON CRITICISMS OF PHILANTHROPY

It's very easy to underestimate philanthropy. After all, it is carried out in radically decentralized ways, and most of us rarely see anything other than small fragments in operation. Most philanthropy takes place on a local level. It is often private, anonymous, or simply happening out of the public eye.

Even most donors and nonprofits grossly underestimate the problem-solving power of charitable action and how crucial it is to our national flourishing. So not surprisingly there are plenty of out-and-out critics who discount or even mock the idea that major concerns can be addressed via private responses. Philanthropy can be cute, but if you're *serious*, they suggest, get big and governmental or go home.

You've all heard the complaints: Philanthropy is a drop in the bucket! Philanthropy is amateurish! Philanthropy is chaotic and uncoordinated! Its

51

programs are a crazy patchwork! Some donors are mean, or vain, or in it for all the wrong reasons!

Let's look at a few of those claims.

IT'S A DROP IN THE BUCKET!

The next time you hear the gibe above, recall the numbers at the very beginning of this Introduction: The U.S. nonprofit sector now totals to 11 percent of our workforce and 6 percent of GDP, making it much bigger than the "military-industrial complex" and many other important sectors of our society. Let me add one more number: Nonprofits currently control total assets of about $3.5 trillion. That's trillion with a "t."

And here's a little perspective: The Gates Foundation alone (which is just a tiny sliver of our entire philanthropic apparatus) distributes more overseas assistance than the entire Italian government. It is estimated that in just its first two decades, the Gates Foundation's overseas vaccine and medical program (only one element of its total giving) will directly and immediately save the lives of 8 million preschool children. Is that a drop in the bucket?

Then absorb this: Members of U.S. churches and synagogues (who are, in turn, just one part of America's philanthropic army) send *four and a half times* as much money overseas to needy people every year as the Gates Foundation does! Indeed, private U.S. philanthropic aid of all sorts sent overseas now substantially exceeds the official foreign aid of the U.S. government. As of 2014, the annual totals were $44 billion of philanthropy versus $33 billion from government. (And on top of that, individual Americans, mostly immigrants, sent an additional $109 billion abroad to support relatives and friends in foreign lands.)

When Tocqueville made his classic visits across America he wrote, "In the United States I am even more struck by the innumerable multitude of little undertakings than by the extraordinary size of some of their enterprises.... One is therefore in daily astonishment at the immense works carried through without difficulty by a nation which, one may say, has no rich men." The power of innumerable little undertakings is even clearer today—when wealth and power are spread all across our sprawling continental nation.

Getting seduced by giantism is easy, but it's an egregious mistake. Just because something is big and shiny and official doesn't mean it is effective. And just because certain actions are small doesn't mean they can't accumulate into mighty rivers of joined effort. When private citizens in every community take care of little things, nearby things, civic needs in their own towns, the net result will often be mightier than any bureaucratic mobilization.

The best metaphors for the achievements of philanthropy are not marching armies or triumphant grand-slam home runs. Think instead

of the gradual changes wrought by nature. "For many years a tree might wage a slow and silent warfare against an encumbering wall, without making any visible progress," writes Lloyd Douglas in his novel *The Robe*. Then one day the wall topples over. "The patient work of self-defense… had reached fulfillment."

In one of his poems, Arthur Clough offers a similar image of the power of subtle, gradual action:

> …while the tired waves, vainly breaking,
>   seem here no painful inch to gain,
>   far back, through creeks and inlets making,
>   comes silent, flooding in, the main.

These descriptions capture well the way that philanthropy works. Drop by drop, yes. But inexorable, omnipresent, and adding up forcefully.

IT'S AMATEURISH!

It's easy to caricature grassroots solutions. You've probably seen the wise-guy bumper stickers saying things like "It'll be a great day when social issues get strong public funding and the Pentagon has to hold bake sales to buy bombers." Well, I'm here to tell you that bake sales, and other small-scale acts like them, can do great things.

> The Gates Foundation alone (which is just a tiny sliver of our entire philanthropic apparatus) distributes more overseas assistance than the entire Italian government.

Lizzie Kander was working as a truant officer in Milwaukee in the 1890s when she discovered that the home conditions of Russian immigrant families were "deplorable…threatening the moral and physical health of the people." Believing that women were the keys to household success and acculturation, she devoted herself to charitable initiatives teaching cleanliness, child education, good nutrition, household skills, and economically useful trades to Russian women. By 1900 she was deeply involved in running a settlement house that assimilated Jewish immigrants using funds donated by Milwaukee businessmen.

When additional money was needed, Kander compiled a 174-page cookbook-cum-housekeeping-guide to sell as a fundraiser. The board of directors would not pay the $18 needed to print the book, so she paid for production by

selling ads. It became known as the *Settlement Cook Book*, with the very polit- ically incorrect subtitle, "The Way to a Man's Heart." Goofy little bake-sale project, right? Well, the book eventually sold two million copies. And the revenue stream from this idiosyncratic effort paid for the mainstreaming of Jewish immigrants in the upper Midwest for 75 years, along with many other charitable projects.

Let me extend the point with another example from the same era and a similar cause. Amid the turmoil of World War I and pogroms breaking out in Eastern Europe and the Near East, many American Jews became concerned for the safety of co-religionists abroad. So, in classic American fashion, a charitable fundraising committee was formed to help resettle refugees, and a goal of $5 million was announced. To kick things off, four anonymous donors pledged $100,000 each if another $600,000 could be raised in New York at a single event. A gala was scheduled at Carnegie Hall for December of 1915. Very soon, requests for tickets were triple the hall's capacity. On the day of the fundraiser more than 3,000 people congregated outside the building in the hope of being admitted at the last minute.

The event featured a string of speakers describing the dangers Jews faced abroad. Then people began walking to the stage one by one to drop off donations. In addition to cash, slips of paper pledging monthly gifts piled up. The *New York Times* reported that some in attendance left rings, necklaces, and earrings. When the event ended, the gifts exceeded $1 million. This inspired major donors like Julius Rosenwald, Jacob Schiff, Nathan Straus, and Felix Warburg to make big pledges. Throughout the next few years an estimated 3 million Americans donated, raising many millions for this urgent cause.

Even when they don't make a big wave like the Carnegie Hall fundraiser, or Lizzie Kander's cookbook-fed-charity, quirky human-scale projects can do lovely things. There is a little $5 million foundation in Baltimore called the Anna Emory Warfield Fund that has one simple mission: help elderly women who want to stay in their homes do so "in the style to which they are accustomed." Grants can be as little as a few hundred dollars to pay for a handyman to repair overflowing gutters, or a few thousand dollars to catch up on mortgage payments or weather a temporary health crisis. No one has any illusions that these grants are changing the world. But for a widow at risk of outliving her savings, or a retired teacher who doesn't have the means or inclination to enter a nursing home, this quiet support can be a godsend that prevents life from spiraling out of control.

Programs that grow naturally from the bottom up rather than the top down not only collect together into larger actions, but have overlapping

qualities that can magnify their effect. Piece together a handyman grant here, a meal-delivery service there, and a volunteer program for driving people to doctor's appointments, and independent life remains possible. Add a video-medicine program that lets you consult with out-of-town specialists, and a hospice when the end draws near. A family-building effort down the street, an alternative school across town, and a county-wide college scholarship program might make all the difference to a young person. Take an inspiring donor-funded museum nearby, and a devoted effort to get local kids out of foster care, and your community feels different. Cumulate these kinds of philanthropic projects and soon you have a gorgeous, continually regenerating, transcontinental quilt that covers millions of local needs and longings.

Amateur webs of giving and volunteering make every one of our home towns more livable, richer, safer, more charming, more interesting. The varied and sometimes underappreciated gifts that donors offer their fellow citizens fill human hungers that would otherwise be ignored or foisted on impersonal and less effective state agencies. This work is a great strength of our country.

IT'S UNCOORDINATED!

Even loyal donors will sometimes complain that the factor limiting philanthropy is that it's not coordinated. Rules vary all over the place. It lacks uniformity. There are holes. Everybody gets to make their own decisions. People go off in many different directions. No one's in control. Chaos! The Wild West! Some observers are really bothered by a lack of standardizing forces that get everyone marching in the same direction (as government programs do).

There's one problem with that rather authoritarian critique: Non-coordination can just as easily be considered an advantage as a problem. Recent decades have taught us that in economics, technology, social practice, and community life, decentralized multiplicity can be a saving grace. That is even truer in philanthropy than in many other areas.

I worked for three years in the West Wing, overseeing domestic policy for the President, and one of the deepest impressions that work made on me was how heavy the tread of the federal government is. We'd take up a problem and I'd realize, "whatever we do, however well-considered our reforms, we are going to discombobulate millions of people." Since the entire federal apparatus swings in one direction with any rule change, it is very hard to test competing policies, to turn faucets on slowly, or to allow differing solutions in different places. Almost every new federal policy turns over the apple carts of many completely innocent parties and disrupts the settled expectations of large numbers of families and

communities. I left the White House hungry for less monolithic, less uniform, more decentralized ways of attacking problems.

Humans are not predictable robots, so the healthiest forms of society-building often proceed in an empirical way: test, experiment, undertake lots of trials, recognizing that many—perhaps most—will fail. But so long as our whole society isn't swerving in unison in one direction, the errors will generally cancel each other out, the failures will be exposed, and the successful ventures will become visible and then be copied.

This is an argument for dispersal of resources. For divided attacks. For independent assessment. Exactly the things that private philanthropy provides.

Yes, you will be told that breaking the responsibility for social problem-solving into hundreds of pieces and then handing these off to thousands of charities and foundations and private doers of good is medieval, and will never be effective in our modern world. Critics will portray it as mere dabbling in the face of giant pressures. Such criticism, however, seriously misunderstands the power of the human anthill, at least under American organization.

> Humans are not predictable robots, so the healthiest forms of society-building often grow out of small tests, divided attacks, independent assessments—exactly the things that private philanthropy excels at.

A wonderful new word was coined in 2003 to describe a reliance on dispersed authority to fix things: crowdsourcing. The effectiveness of chewing through big issues via lots of small bites by dispersed participants is a fundamental reality understood by wise humans for millennia. But it has been brought into high relief by aspects of the computer revolution.

In the early years of computing (not very long ago), the largest supercomputers were extraordinarily complex centralized devices, where all the wires led to one extremely expensive custom-made processing chip. Today, there is no king processor in a supercomputer. The latest versions are made with around 40,000 plebeian, everyday chips just like the one in your Dell, all working in democratic parallel. And this so-called "distributed intelligence" has turned out to be vastly more potent than the elegant genius of the old centralized Cray supercomputers that worked from the top down.

Forms of distributed computing are being applied to many of today's most difficult problems. For instance, the vast amounts of astronomical data that

need to be sifted through in order to discover a possible planet transiting a distant sun, or a possible radio signal from another civilization, are being processed by hundreds of thousands of volunteers on their home computers.

Or take the Linux computer operating system—the computer code which has become the backbone of the digital business world. There is no master control over what goes into Linux. Software drafts are passed around over the Internet, where thousands of informal contributors just add and subtract and tinker with the code and then put the result out there in the marketplace. If that sounds like chaos, you haven't been paying attention. This so-called open-source method of creating software solutions has turned out to be remarkably orderly and powerful, and the result is that Linux quickly turned into the most flexible and effective computer operating system available.

The pattern of complex problems being solved by small actors working locally and independently without heavy central direction is not just the story of the Internet, it is a phenomenon common to much of technology, and biology, and human history.

Some years ago, I read a book called *Ants at Work*, written by a Stanford entomologist who spent 17 years studying a large colony of harvester ants. The author's goal was to learn how these tens of thousands of tiny creatures coordinate the specialized tasks essential to colony health—food harvest and storage, care of offspring, tunnel digging, garbage toting, war fighting, etc. Who's directing the show to make sure the right work gets done at the right time?

The answer, she discovered, is that *nobody* is in charge. No insect issues commands to another. The colony operates without any central or hierarchical control. These complex societies are instead built, she reports, on thousands of simple decisions made by individual creatures based on what they see around them, with those many microdecisions melding together to yield an efficient macro-result. I suggest the right term for this is *self-organization*, and it's something of an iron rule throughout the natural world, not only among bugs, but also at the very top of nature's pyramid—in human society.

As a simple example of the general superiority of decentralized problem-solving, consider what happens every fall weekend in football stadiums. Even a boozy crowd can drain itself from a packed oval in a matter of minutes. Yet emptying that stadium by commanding each person from some master perch, as readers with some background in mathematics or statistics will know, is an almost insoluble problem. You could cover the field from goal post to goal post with computers and programmers, and you'd end up frustrated. There are just too many variables—80,000 people, 25 exits, scores of

stairways, thousands of stairs, pillars that block certain routes, backups in specific aisles; it's just too much to orchestrate.

Yet leave each Joe to himself and he'll be opening the door to his Chevy before the scoreboard lights are cool. He may not realize that he's exhibiting what scientists call "large-scale adaptive intelligence in the absence of central direction." But he is. Less trivial examples abound: vast and absolutely crucial human tasks like food distribution, for instance, are managed in the U.S. without any central organization. This is not just acceptable, it is an *advantage,* increasing variety and innovation and customization to meet specific circumstances.

Thanks to technology making the mechanics easier, crowd-based problem-solving is on a sharp upswing today, including in philanthropy. Did you know that way back in 2012, Kickstarter roared past the National Endowment for the Arts in providing money for arts and culture projects? Charities like DonorsChoose.org offer remarkable opportunities for Americans to fund grassroots educational help. The fascinating philanthropy SpiritofAmerica.net collects ideas from U.S. Special Forces operators in poor, dangerous countries on ways to enhance stability and reduce the temptation to violence and radicalism by making small improvements in community life. Donors view choices online and sign up to send sewing machines to Iraqi women, or educational supplies to a school destroyed by terrorists in the Philippines, or handheld spotlights for police working the Pakistan-Afghanistan border. Even the Smithsonian launched a crowdfunding campaign in 2015, seeking $500,000 to restore the space suit worn by Neil Armstrong on the moon. The effort quickly exceeded $720,000, given by 9,500 people.

> The decentralized multiplicity of philanthropy increases variety in our lives, and protects non-mainstream points of view.

Dispersed authority and funding may be new to military work, or to the Smithsonian. But it is the longstanding backbone of philanthropy. I'll plant my little seeds over here, and you till your garden over there, and soon the world turns green and lovely.

This is not a matter of ideology, or of sweet-breathed philanthropists trumping wicked government officials. It is a simple matter of practicality and surrender to the facts about how humans accomplish things most effectively. Local citizens tend to have better information than remote authorities on the optimal ways to solve their problems. Trying to separate good schools or good doctors

from poor ones is a very hard task from Washington, but people in the neighborhood can usually steer you right away to either. Nearby helpers are also likelier to tailor solutions to specific circumstances and to create varied answers instead of just one template for everybody. Decentralized solutions tend also to be more respectful of individual sovereignty and personal preferences.

So lack of coordination and uniformity needn't be considered a problem. Indeed, it is often helpful. To take just one example, philanthropists can take much bigger risks than a government program creator would dare because the philanthropist knows he's not betting the entire national farm. He can try something new, retune as it unfolds, and expand or walk away depending on how it succeeds.

What do you suppose ran through the minds of the foundation officials who were first pitched on the idea of a bank built on $27 loans to rag pickers and fruit-cart pushers in Bangladesh? Probably that it sounded wildly improbable. Thank goodness they gave it a shot anyway. And thus was microfinance born, which grew quickly into a strapping poverty-squashing grownup.

IT'S A PATCHWORK!

Our society has rapidly moved beyond the old industrial-revolution paradigm of the one big factory. We now rely much more on networks and ecosystems of smaller providers working in loose synchronization. A perfect example of this is one of the great philanthropic creations of the last generation—charter schooling.

The very largest charter-school chain in the nation, KIPP, operates a total of 183 schools. Meanwhile, there are now more than 7,000 charter schools in total. So this is a radically decentralized sector. Most schools are solo operations or part of a very small group running just a handful of campuses.

And this allows a riot of choices. There are math and science schools. Schools built around the Great Books. Hippie schools without walls, doors, or other controlling features! Work oriented schools! Quasi-military schools where the all-male student body wears uniforms and has ranks! Academies that only assign books by gentle left-handed poets! The charter movement is built on the idea that there is no single definition of what constitutes a good school, that education is an exercise in matching each child's temperament and gifts with an institution that can bring out his or her best self.

Part of this bubbling variety is churn. Every year now, about 650 new charter schools open their doors and offer their new neighborhood some fresh approach. And in that same year, more than 200 schools will close down, because their offerings were not well embraced.

Here's a Rorschach test: Are those wildly different schools, and that annual churn, signs of inconsistency, patchwork, and trouble? Or are they healthy signs of adaptation to what people want? If you prize stability and predictability, the conventional public school (which is basically impossible to close down even when it's abysmal!) may be your preference (at least for other people's children). But if it seems humane to offer citizens more of what they prize, and less of what they are choosing to walk away from, then the constant gurgling and gap-filling may be a reflection of the very kindest and gentlest sort of philanthropy.

Within the charitable sector itself there are even further levels of customization and "inconsistency." The KIPP schools are an example. While they have a few bedrock principles and uniform high standards, schools in various regions are given a wide degree of independence and autonomy for coping with their own particular needs.

Goodwill Industries, another extraordinarily successful charity, is likewise more interested in results than in uniform rules and operations. Goodwill's operation is vast: workforce training provided to 26 million persons annually in a great variety of fields; over $5 billion in revenues; more than 3,000 stores in the U.S., Canada, and 13 other countries. Yet each of the 165 Goodwill regional branches is autonomous in policy and funding, and has its own board of directors. Local branches can assist each other, and can request advice or aid from the world headquarters. But the central office's budget is dwarfed by those of affiliates in cities like Milwaukee and Houston.

This same lack of monolithic uniformity can be seen across the philanthropic sector—in everything from the 1,400 independent local chapters of Habitat for Humanity, to the very different regional branches of the Appalachian Mountain Club that maintain thousands of miles of hiking trails in their own distinctive ways. This locally varying "nicheification" of service provision is also a strong trend in private business today. The Netflix company actually has a catchphrase for the way it puts this principle to work inside the firm. It wants its various corporate teams to be "highly aligned, yet loosely coupled." The vision, in other words, needs to be shared, but the execution should be decentralized.

That's how the Marriott company now does hotels, for instance. Instead of one big company offering one standardized service, they offer customers more than 30 different kinds of lodging choices, depending on where you are and what you need. Someone staying put for a while can pick a Residence Inn or Fairfield Suites. If you want a luxury experience, Marriott has its Ritz-Carlton and St. Regis subsidiaries. Aloft or W are for people wanting a boutique experience.

These aren't just fake nameplates on the same company. Each of these spinoffs of Marriott has its own rules, its own managers, a separate budget,

and special ways of serving different needs. Even further out on the spectrum of decentralized, personalized solutions in business today you have Airbnb. It is a loose network of tens of thousands of independent local service providers, and is incredibly varied, efficient, and helpful to people in need.

This is the direction in which American businesses are racing at high speed. The charitable world has operated that way for generations.

SOME DONORS AREN'T NICE!

Another reality which sometimes gets critics fulminating and makes philanthropists defensive is the fact that certain donors are mean, or selfish, or seem more interested in getting their name on a building, or a tax break, than in altruism. In my experience, human kindness and empathy are commoner among loyal donors than among an average cross-section of the population. And while journalists love to mock "philanthro-me" and "egonomics," the truth is that vain, peacock donors are not the norm. "Humility is far more common in the top tiers of philanthropy than egotism," agrees philanthropy writer David Callahan. "Our writers at Inside Philanthropy have come across innumerable donors who are engaged in high-level giving, with barely a peep. They issue no press release about their gifts, maintain no website, turn down all media inquiries, and otherwise stay mum about great acts of generosity."

> Trying to separate good schools or good doctors from poor ones is a very hard task from Washington, but people in the neighborhood can usually steer you right away to either.

That said, it is unquestionably true that there are some philanthropists who do their good for not-so-good reasons. Indeed, certain of these men and women are laughably far from angelic in their motivations.

J. Paul Getty was a cheapskate who made visitors to his estate use a pay phone at a time when he was one of the richest men in the world. He was a serial womanizer whose own father didn't trust him. When his grandson was kidnapped for a $17 million ransom he kept dickering for a lower payment until the criminals cut off the boy's ear and mailed it to grandpa. Even then, Getty only put up as much of the ransom as was tax-deductible ($2.2 million), and gave his son the rest as a loan—at 4 percent interest. Yet Getty gave the world one of its most sublime collections of Greek and Roman art, a gift that will elevate souls for centuries to come.

Russell Sage was a notorious miser and convicted usurer. He cheated his wife's father in business. When a mad extortionist dynamited his office, he used a clerk as a human shield, then refused to pay compensation for the man's injuries. Yet Sage's fortune created one of the most influential early charitable foundations in the country.

There is no denying that corruption made Leland Stanford rich. To build his railroad fortune he employed kickbacks, bribes, stock watering, collusion, monopolization, and political manipulation. Yet genuine grief over the death of his son motivated Stanford to use his ill-gotten lucre to benefit the children of California (and ultimately all of humanity) by creating Stanford University.

George Eastman could be as cold-blooded as he was brilliant and generous. He asked his doctor to outline the exact location of his heart on his chest. Later he reclined on his bed, centered a pistol where the doctor had drawn, and committed suicide rather than face old age.

> The genius of the philanthropic mechanism is that it takes people just as they are and helps them do wondrous things, even when they're not saints.

So philanthropists are not always pretty. And even when they do bring the best of motives to the task, their efforts can disappoint. As Andrew Carnegie established the Carnegie Endowment for International Peace with a $10 million grant, he optimistically included a stipulation on what the group should do after it ended all armed conflict: "When the establishment of universal peace is attained, the donor provides that the revenue shall be devoted to the banishment of the *next* most degrading evil." He wrote that in 1910. Oops.

Are there stupid or cruel givers? Are there dumb projects launched by donors? Of course. But charitable programs that don't produce results soon die or transform into something more useful. When was the last time you saw a dumb government program die?

And here's the fascinating secret of philanthropy: Charity doesn't have to come from people who are charitable. You don't need to be an angel to participate. In fact, motivations of any sort aren't that important. The genius of the philanthropic mechanism is that it takes people just as they are—kind impulses, selfish impulses, confusions and wishes and vanities of all sorts swirling together in the usual human jumble—and it helps them do wondrous things, even when they're not saints.

Philanthropy is a machine that is able to convert the instincts and actions of even the meanest of men into truth, uplift, and beauty. Adam Smith taught us that freely conducted commerce can take normal human behaviors, including ugly and mercenary ones, and turn them to broadly productive uses. This is as true in the world of philanthropy as in business. Base impulses like greed, insecurity, image-laundering, and egotism can become gold, or at least good useful brass.

Happily, most philanthropy is the work of decent and earnest men and women. Even the worst misanthropes, however, are regularly redirected into doing useful, and even great, things for all of society. That is part of the power of America's charitable structure.

* * *

BIG-PICTURE BENEFITS OF PHILANTHROPY

Let's close this introduction by looking at some of the broadest and deepest ways that philanthropy makes our lives and our nation better. I don't mean the good done to recipients of aid, or the pragmatic value of donated money and time, or other obvious advantages. In this final section we'll look at some of the philosophical, moral, and political gains to America that grow out of our giving tradition.

PRIVATE GIVING SATISFIES DEEP HUMAN NEEDS

It's easy to overlook the fact that philanthropy doesn't just help the recipients—it offers profound life satisfaction to givers as well. It opens avenues to meaning and happiness and ways of thriving that aren't easily found otherwise. When I was in college I had a philosophy professor named Louis Dupre who told me a story I've never forgotten. He had a wonderfully generous friend from whom he eventually fell away for the most paradoxical reason: this friend was unable to let Dupre be generous and giving in return.

Receiving gifts and favors can be lovely, but there is also a potent and irreplaceable joy of giving that most people need to express.

The joy of giving is captured frequently in literature:

> It is one of the most beautiful compensations of life that no man can sincerely try to help another without helping himself.
> — *Ralph Waldo Emerson*

> As the purse is emptied the heart is filled.
> — *Victor Hugo*

> If you want happiness for a year, inherit a fortune. If you want happiness for a lifetime, help someone else.
> — *Confucius*

> The best recreation is to do good.
> — *William Penn*

> If you want to lift yourself up, lift up someone else.
> — *Booker T. Washington*

> A man there was, though some did count him mad, the more he cast away, the more he had.
> — *John Bunyan*

Giving is an ancient impulse. Way back in 347 B.C., Plato donated his farm to support students at the school he founded. It is also a widespread impulse. Even people who have very little money are eager to give, and feel good when they do, as documented in several places later in this *Almanac*.

The book *Breaking Night* tells the true story of a neglected girl and the kind people who intervened to help her succeed in spite of her horrendous upbringing. "What was most moving about all of this unexpected generosity," writes the now-grown child, "was the spirit in which people helped. It was something in their moods and in their general being…how they were smiling, looking me right in the eyes."

She describes a woman named Teressa who came up to her and said, "Since I didn't have any money to help you out, I thought I couldn't do anything for you at all. And then last night, I was doing my daughter's laundry, and I thought, how silly of me, maybe you had laundry I could do for you." Every week for the remainder of the author's time in school, Teressa picked

up dirty clothes and returned them clean and folded, taking great pleasure in this little thing she could do to help.

Lots of research shows that this is a common phenomenon. A 2014 book by two Notre Dame social scientists called *The Paradox of Generosity* combined national surveys with in-depth interviews and group observations. It concluded that "the more generous Americans are, the more happiness, health, and purpose in life they enjoy. This association…is strong and highly consistent…. Generous practices actually create enhanced personal well-being. The association…is not accidental, spurious, or an artifact of reverse causal influence." They conclude with the observation that "People often say that we increase the love we have by giving it away…. Generosity is like love in this way."

In a 2008 paper published in *Science*, three researchers gave study participants money, asking half of the group to spend it on themselves, and the other half to give it to some person or charity. Those who donated the money showed a significant uptick in happiness; those who spent it on themselves did not. In his book *Who Really Cares*, economist Arthur Brooks cites a host of similar studies showing that Americans who make gifts of money and time are much more likely to be satisfied with life than non-givers who are demographically identical.

> Philanthropy doesn't just help the recipients— it offers profound life satisfaction to givers as well.

PRIVATE GIVING IMPROVES CAPITALISM

Capitalism and philanthropy have always been closely tied. In the 1600s when the Netherlands was gestating free trade and many modern business patterns, there were alms boxes in most taverns (where business negotiations generally took place), and a successful deal was expected to conclude with a charitable gift.

Philanthropy and business are entwined especially tightly in America. One of the most distinctive aspects of American capitalism is the deep-seated tradition of philanthropy that has evolved among American business barons. Our capitalism also differs from the capitalism practiced in other countries in two other important ways—in its linkage to religiosity, and its preference for entrepreneurial forms. Both of these are also connected to philanthropy.

Let's unpack this a bit, starting with religion. In 2014, the Pew Research Center released data comparing the per capita wealth of nations with the religious beliefs of their people. The U.S. stands out like a sore thumb:

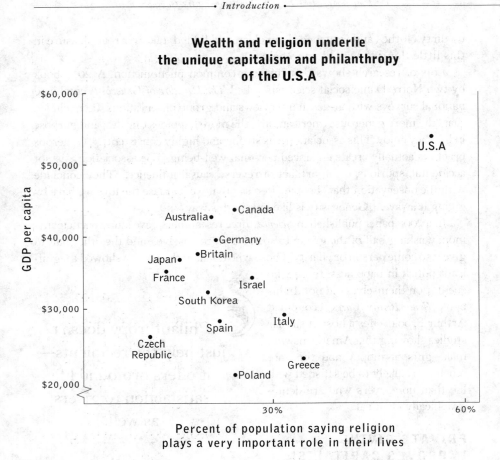

Wealth and religion underlie
the unique capitalism and philanthropy
of the U.S.A

GDP per capita

$60,000

$50,000

U.S.A

$40,000

•Canada

Australia•

•Germany

Japan•   •Britain

France•

•Israel

South Korea•

$30,000

•Spain   Italy•

Czech
Republic•

Greece•

$20,000

•Poland

30%   60%

**Percent of population saying religion
plays a very important role in their lives**

Source: Pew Research Center, 2013 data

The Calvinism that came to the U.S. with the Pilgrims (and continued to dominate our religious views for generations right up to the present) treats wealth as something that passes through the hands of a successful person— with the steward expected to apply it to uplift his fellow man. Thus John Rockefeller gave away 95 percent of his fortune by the time he died. Bill Gates is in the process of giving away tens of billions of dollars, leaving his three children only $10 million each.

That is different from the pattern in Europe, where many of the same dynasties have dominated the rolls of the wealthy for generations. The Howard family, for instance, has been one of Britain's richest for more than 500 years. In the U.S., wealth tends to be extremely transient. Only 15 to 20 percent of the individuals on today's *Forbes* list of richest Americans inherit- ed wealth. About half the the *Forbes* 400 had parents who didn't go to college

at all. Even the foundations left behind by the previously wealthy rapidly get eclipsed in America: the Rockefeller Foundation, once our richest, now ranks a mere number 15, while the Carnegie Corporation has fallen to number 24.

A second distinctive aspect of American capitalism is its entrepreneurial bent. As economists Zoltan Acs and Ronnie Phillips write, "American capitalism differs from all other forms of industrial capitalism" in two ways. One is its emphasis on the creation of new wealth via entrepreneurship. New firms, new ideas, and nouveau riche wealthmakers are at the core of our economic success.

This can be demonstrated in many ways. If you look at the 500 largest companies in the world today, you find that 29 percent of the U.S. firms were founded after 1950, compared to just 8 percent of the European firms. On a per capita basis, the U.S. has four times as many self-made billionaire entrepreneurs as Europe.

Entrepreneurialism and philanthropy are often tightly connected, and linked directly with economic success. In their book *Super-Entrepreneurs*, Swedish researchers Tino and Nima Sanandaji investigated about 1,000 self-made billionaires from around the world. They found "a very strong correlation" between entrepreneurship, wealth, and philanthropy.

> Dispersed authority is the backbone of philanthropy. I'll plant my little seeds over here, and you till your garden over there, and soon the whole world turns green and lovely.

Acs and Phillips argue that in addition to its distinctive means of creating wealth through new enterprises, the U.S. has a distinctive means of "reconstituting" wealth via philanthropy. "Philanthropy is part of the implicit social contract that continuously nurtures and revitalizes economic prosperity," they write. Philanthropy is a very important mechanism for recycling wealth in America, agree the Sanandajis. "The notion exists that wealth beyond a certain point should be invested back in society to expand opportunity for future generations," they write. " 'The legitimacy of American capitalism has in part been upheld through voluntary donations from the rich'.... Much of the new wealth created historically has thus been given back to society. This has had several feedback effects on capitalism. For one, the practice has limited the rise of new dynasties. Another positive

feedback mechanism is that the donations to research and higher education have allowed new generations to become wealthy."

PRIVATE GIVING STRENGTHENS DEMOCRACY

Civil society and charitable action sprang up in the U.S. even before government did. In most of our new communities, mutual aid among neighbors was solving problems long before there were duly constituted agencies of the state.

> Americans of all ages, all conditions, and all dispositions constantly form associations...religious, moral, serious, futile, general or restricted, enormous or diminutive. The Americans make associations to give entertainments, to found seminaries, to build inns, to construct churches, to diffuse books, to send missionaries to the antipodes; in this manner they found hospitals, prisons, and schools. If it is proposed to inculcate some truth or to foster some feeling by the encouragement of a great example, they form a society. Wherever at the head of some new undertaking you see the government in France, or an aristocrat in England, in the United States you will be sure to find an association.

That was Tocqueville's observation in *Democracy in America* close to 200 years ago.

As the title of the French visitor's book suggests, what impressed him about voluntary action in the U.S. was not just its practical ability to solve problems, but the way it exercised and built up the social muscles needed if people were to govern themselves in a healthy democracy. Tocqueville considered American voluntary associations not just signs, but the *source*, of effective self-rule. He wished aloud that this American tradition could be transferred to Europeans, who had lost "the habit of acting in common" on their own, due to generations of smothering by the state.

Some people, Tocqueville wrote,

> claim that as the citizens become weaker and more helpless, the government must become proportionately more skilled and active, so that society should do what is no longer possible for individuals.... I think they are mistaken.... The more government takes the place of associations, the more will individuals lose the idea of forming associations and need the government to come to their help. That is a vicious circle of cause and effect.... The morals and intelligence

of a democratic people would be in [danger]. Feelings and ideas are renewed, the heart enlarged, and the understanding developed only by the reciprocal action of men upon another.

Edmund Burke also viewed local association as the nursery for broader loyalty to one's fellow man. "The little platoon we belong to in society is the first principle (the germ as it were) of public affections. It is the first link in the series by which we proceed towards a love to our country, and to mankind," he wrote.

The great advantages that accrue to America from possessing a bubbling voluntary sector that acts independently have been under threat since the Great Depression, cautions author Richard Cornuelle. The economic crash gave American confidence a knock and planted the idea that "only government seems big enough" to solve serious social issues. "Our habit of sending difficult problems to Washington quickly became almost a reflex" and parts of the public and some of our leaders have turned their back on our deep tradition of indigenous alternatives to government action.

Cornuelle complains that we often now

> speak of American life in terms of only two "sectors": the public sector (government), and the private sector (commerce). We leave out the third sector in our national life, the one which is neither governmental nor commercial. We ignore the institutions which once played such a decisive part in the society's vibrant growth... [which] made it possible for us to build a humane society and a free society together.

This third sector, operating in the space between the individual and the state, between the coercion of law and the profit-seeking of commerce, goes by various names: civil society, the voluntary sector, charitable action. Back in 1970, the Peterson Commission pointed out the crucial need for "institutions standing outside the frame of government but in support of the public interest." Cornuelle called these philanthropic institutions the "independent sector," and warned that they have

> a natural competitor: government. Both sectors operate in the same industry: public service and welfare..... The quality of life in the U.S. now depends largely on the revival of a lively competition between these two natural contenders for public responsibility. The struggle would enhance the effectiveness of both.

In some quarters, Cornuelle observes,

> the very idea of competition with government is, by a weird public myth, thought to be illegitimate, disruptive, divisive, unproductive, and perhaps immoral.... Far from being illegitimate, lively competition with government is essential if our democratic institutions are to work sensibly....
>
> The government doesn't ignore public opinion because the people who run it are naturally perverse. It isn't wasteful because it is manned by wasteful people.... Without competition, the bureaucracy can't make government efficient.... Innovation painfully disrupts its way of life. Reform comes only through competitive outsiders who force steady, efficient adjustment to changing situations.
>
> The independent sector will grow strong again when its leaders realize that its unique indispensable natural role in America is to compete with government. It must be as eager as government to take on new public problems.

There are times and places where governmental rulers feel threatened by the philanthropic process. Philanthropy practiced on a mass level, as in America, becomes a kind of matrix of tens of thousands of private legislatures that set goals and priorities, define social ills, and methodically marshal money and labor to attack them—without asking the state's permission. Some rulers prefer dependent citizens who are *consumers* rather than *producers* of governance.

Certainly tyrants hate philanthropy. They want government to be the only forum for human influence and control. "Everything within the state, nothing outside the state, nothing against the state," was Mussolini's encapsulation. Independent associations and private wielders of resources must be co-opted or suppressed. The charitable sector is not only denied a seat at the table, it is put on the menu to be eaten. One of the first things every totalitarian government has done upon assuming power—from Nazis, to communists, to radical imams—is to destroy charities, private giving, and voluntary groups.

We're seeing the same phenomenon today in authoritarian countries like Russia, China, and Iran, where charities are being shut down out of fear that they will provide alternate sources of ideas, cultural solutions, and social legitimacy. Only the freest societies have had flourishing philanthropic sectors. In America, our freedom to expend charitable resources without supervision or control is ultimately sheltered by the First Amendment of our Bill of

Rights, which protects our right to assemble and act outside of government, to dissent, to take heterogeneous, unpopular, or minority-supported action to redress grievances.

Enlightened, practical, democratic leaders shouldn't just tolerate the independent actions of donors and volunteers, they should embrace and encourage them. Social entrepreneur Neerav Kingsland, who gained prominence by helping build the nation's most extensive web of independent charter schools in New Orleans after the Katrina disaster, has argued that the most effective and humane thing that many public servants can do today to help needy populations is to let go of their monopolies on power. He uses the term "Relinquishers" to describe progress-minded officials who are willing to transfer authority away from centralized bureaucracies in order to allow experimentation and improvement driven by philanthropy, commerce, grassroots activism, and other independent forces.

To illustrate how quickly societal conditions can improve when intelligent Relinquishers cede power to civil actors, Kingsland cites examples from the U.S. and abroad. He charts the explosion of per capita income in India since 1991, where economist and then Prime Minister Manmohan Singh promulgated new policies that made him "one of the greatest Relinquishers of the modern world. Over the past 20 years, his work in transferring power to India's citizens…improved the well-being of hundreds of millions."

> Tyrants hate philanthropy. They want government to be the only forum for human influence and control. "Everything within the state" was Mussolini's encapsulation.

Another Relinquisher triumph unfolded in New Orleans after philanthropists were allowed to pour resources and expertise into restructuring that city's schools. Government continued to provide funds, fair rules, and accountability, but it allowed independent operators to take over the running of classrooms and academies. The result was that the number of classroom seats rated "high-quality" quadrupled in four years. The fraction of students testing at the proficient level leapt from 35 percent to 56 percent. The ACT scores of graduating seniors hit an historic high.

Sharing responsibility for societal improvement with funders and volunteers in civil society will often be a government policymaker's speediest path to excellence and success—as well as a more democratic course.

IT'S NOT WISE TO RELY SOLELY ON GOVERNMENT

"Every single great idea that has marked the twenty-first century, the twentieth century, and the nineteenth century has required government vision and government incentive." That was Vice President Joe Biden. "The ballot box is the place where all change begins in America." That was Senator Ted Kennedy.

These speakers overlooked the vast improving powers of free enterprise. (Government didn't produce the air conditioning that transformed the South, or the mobile phone that is now revolutionizing everything from news to conversation to human attention spans.) They also ignored the profound role of independent philanthropy in altering American history.

Let's take the civil-rights movement—a favorite example of advocates who would have you believe that nothing good happens unless government does it. Back in 1704—when 1,500 African Americans in New York City were held as slaves with full government sanction, and educating them was forbidden, private donors set up schools to instruct hundreds of slaves on the quiet. In the early 1830s, when state and federal governments still made it a crime to teach a slave to read, private donors like Arthur Tappan were paying for African Americans to go to college. Less than two years after the bullets of the Civil War stopped flying,

> Philanthropy is crucial to keeping America operating as that exceedingly rare society where most individuals can steer their own lives.

philanthropist George Peabody was distributing millions of his own dollars across the South to train teachers and set up schools without racial considerations so that freed slaves and other illiterate people could get education—despite the ferocious antipathy of state and local governments for that cause. In 1891, philanthropist Katharine Drexel gave her entire fortune (half a billion dollars in contemporary terms) to create a new religious order devoted to assisting blacks and Indians. She established 50 schools for African Americans, 145 missions and 12 schools for Native Americans, and the black college Xavier University in New Orleans. In these same years, governments at all levels were doing little more than breaking promises to Native Americans and neglecting African Americans.

As the twentieth century opened, hundreds of governments were fiercely enforcing Jim Crow laws that stunted the education of blacks. But John Rockefeller was pouring money into his new General Education Board

for providing primary education to African Americans. Then he boosted up 1,600 new high schools for poor whites and blacks. He eventually put almost $325 million of his personal fortune into the venture. Simultaneously he was spending millions to improve the health of poor blacks and whites by nearly eliminating hookworm.

Numerous private givers followed the leads of George Peabody and John Rockefeller and donated millions of dollars to improve the education and social status of African Americans at a time when they had no friends in government. The philanthropic help came from Anna Jeanes's Negro Rural Schools Fund, the Phelps Stokes Fund, the Virginia Randolph Fund, the John Slater Fund, and others. These all continued their work until government finally caught up and started desegregating schools in the 1960s.

African-American children whose education and social conditions were being wholly neglected by the state got their biggest lift of all from philanthropist Julius Rosenwald. Starting in 1912, he donated the current equivalent of billions of dollars to build schoolhouses in hundreds of counties where black education was ignored. In less than 20 years, the Rosenwald program erected 4,977 rural schools and 380 companion community buildings in most of America's locales with a substantial black population. At the time of Rosenwald's death in 1932, the schools he built were educating fully 27 percent of all the African-American children in our country.

Many economic producers and sensible leaders were produced by these philanthropic projects. Absent these private efforts by donors, racial improvement and reconciliation in our country would have been delayed by generations. Government not only had little to do with this philanthropic uplift—many arms of government did their very best to resist or obstruct it.

A curmudgeon might say, "Well that's nice, but it's ancient history. Today, the government leads all necessary change." That is gravely mistaken.

Guess where America's most segregated and often most inadequate government-run schools are located at present? All in Northern cities with activist governments: Detroit, Milwaukee, New York, Newark, Chicago, and Philadelphia, research shows. According to the UCLA Civil Rights Project, New York is the state with the country's most segregated schools—thanks to New York City, where the proportion of schools in which at least 90 percent of the students are black or Hispanic rose sharply from 1989 to 2010.

The government-operated schools in New York City drip with rhetoric about "social justice." But it is private philanthropy that is shaking up the city's complacently bad educational establishment today—by launching charter schools. As of 2016, there were 106,600 New York City children in charters, nearly all of them minorities and low-income, and 44,000 more

remain on waiting lists. Stanford investigators and others find that these children are receiving significantly better educations than counterparts in conventional government-run schools, in some cases outscoring comfortable suburban schools in annual testing. Yet donors and charter-school operators continue to have to fight through the resistance of reactionary progressives in city hall and the New York City Council.

Or let's look at another area where conventional wisdom says nothing important will happen except under governmental banners: Who saved the refugees disrupted by the two World Wars and the ethnic genocides of those decades? When the U.S. Ambassador to Turkey discovered that Ottomans were starving and killing Jews in Palestine, he sent an urgent telegram to philanthropist Jacob Schiff in New York. A fundraising committee was set up, and over the years to come it distributed hundreds of millions of dollars, donated by more than 3 million private givers, saving many thousands of Jews.

> Philanthropy has a long history of taking up crucial burdens in the face of government failure.

It wasn't only Jews who needed saving. At that same time, Muslims were carrying out a jihad against Armenian Christians that ultimately took 1.5 million lives. The U.S. government did little, but everyday Americans, missionaries, church members, and philanthropists sprang into action to both save lives immediately and then sustain the Armenians dislocated by the genocide. Nearly 1,000 Americans volunteered to go to the region to build orphanages and help refugees. They assumed responsibility for 130,000 mother- and fatherless children, and rescued more than a million adults.

It was a similar story when fascism swept Europe. The U.S. government dragged its feet and failed to organize any speedy effective effort to save the Jews, gypsies, Christians, and others targeted by the Nazis. Private donors jumped into the breach. The Rockefeller Foundation, for instance, established two special funds that worked, under the most difficult wartime conditions, to relocate mortally endangered individuals to Allied countries.

As with our civil-rights example, philanthropy taking up crucial burdens in the face of government failure is not just a story in the past tense. In 1993, all Western governments were pathetically slow and inadequate in their response to the ethnic cleansing in Bosnia that killed tens of thousands. The most effective actor by far was philanthropist George Soros—who used $50 million of his own money to insert a highly effective relief team into the city of Sarajevo while it

was under siege, re-establishing gas and electric service during the bitter winter, setting up an alternate water source, and bringing in desperately needed supplies. It has been estimated that Soros's gift saved more lives than the efforts of all national governments plus the United Nations *combined.*

The list of great ideas and dramatic improvements instigated by philanthropy while government was AWOL could be expanded endlessly, from the Green Revolution and invention of microlending abroad, to domestic achievements like the recovery of desolated urban parks, control of drunk driving, and creation of the country's best job-training programs for economic strugglers. And philanthropic change tends to come with much less friction. As one social entrepreneur has put it, philanthropy generally practices "the politics of addition and multiplication," while government action often comes via "the politics of subtraction and division."

WHY PHILANTHROPY IS INDISPENSABLE TO AMERICAN FREEDOM

Let's open this final section with a bit of extended historical analysis by Richard Cornuelle, from his book *Reclaiming the American Dream*:

> We wanted, from the beginning, a free society, free in the sense that every man was his own supervisor and the architect of his own ambitions. So our founders took pains to design a government with limited power, and then carefully scattered the forces that could control it.
>
> We wanted as well, with equal fervor, a good society—a humane, responsible society in which helping hands reached out to people in honest distress, in which common needs were met freely and fully. In pursuit of this ambition, Americans used remarkable imagination. We created a much wider variety of new institutions for this purpose than we built to insure political freedom. As a frontier people, accustomed to interdependence, we developed a genius for solving common problems. People joined together in bewildering combinations to found schools, churches, opera houses, co-ops, hospitals, to build bridges and canals, to help the poor. To see a need was, more often than not, to promote a scheme to meet it better than had ever been done before.
>
> The American dream was coming true. Each part of it supported another part. We were free because we limited the power of government. We prospered because we were free. We built a good society because our prosperity yielded surplus energy that we put directly to work to meet human needs. Thus, we didn't need much government,

and because we didn't, we stayed uniquely free. A sort of supportive circle, or spiral, was working for us.

The part of the system least understood, then as now, was the network of non-governmental institutions that served public needs. They did not leave an easy trace for historians to follow. They did not depend on noisy political debate for approval, nor did civil servants have to keep very detailed records of what they did. [Yet] they played a significant role.... They took on almost any public job and so became the principal way Americans got things done.

For years the leading colleges and universities were created by the churches. Hospitals began in a variety of ways, and in the era before the Civil War, under Clara Barton's leadership, they blossomed into today's major system of independent institutions. Many of our giant commercial firms, notably in insurance and mutual savings, grew out of early self-help organizations.

Urgent problems filled the agenda of public business in early America. Citizens, acting on their own, took the heavy load. Localities and states took most of what was done by government. We rarely needed the federal government, a distant thing to the frontiersman. We limited government, not only because people knew its limitations and wanted it limited, but because we left little for it to do.

As the great social thinker Michael Novak once put it: "The secret to the psychology of Americans is that they are neither individualists nor collectivists; their strong suit is *association*, and they freely organize themselves, cooperate, and work together in superb teamwork." Novak points out that "the social system of the United States is constituted of three independent, yet interdependent, systems of institutions, organized along different axes and even different values: A political system. An economic system. And a moral-cultural system." Our politics and economy are freedom-focused. Our moral-cultural system is focused on goodness, decency, and fairness.

These descriptions of America's social order, and its dual devotion to freedom and goodness, are helpful in understanding why philanthropy is indispensable to American society. I view it as indispensable in two senses: 1) Philanthropy is not able to be replaced by something else. And 2) bad things will happen to the nation if it is not adequately continued.

The aspect of America that many of us cherish most is the latitude allowed individuals to chart their own course, to be responsible for themselves, sometimes to reinvent themselves if they choose and are able. Historically, this

degree of individual independence and freedom is highly unusual. Every preceding society was in one fashion or another paternal. On the wide spectrum stretching from starchy monarchy to socialist beehive, all pre-American governments basically took responsibility for every individual, and in return reserved the right to tell him or her how to live. More specifically, a small caste of strongmen at the top of the heap (king, tribal chief, warlord, bishop, emperor) told everyone else how to live.

One can't really claim that's unfair—it's how all but a thin sliver of humanity has always existed. The individual liberty and self-reliance carved out in America was the anomaly. And one of great preciousness, because it has allowed a quality of life and existential autonomy never approached by people in other times and places.

Our non-paternalized freedom is also a somewhat frail arrangement, however. For the reality is that all of us will occasionally misuse our independence in various ways, and a substantial minority of us will make a complete hash of our lives under a system of profound freedom. And when elderly profligates start dying in the street, or neglected children peer up at us with starving eyes, all the old solutions to governance will immediately be proposed.

Monarchy or socialism or blanketing welfare-state all boil down in one way or another to setting up a paternal fief under which individual freedoms will be traded away in exchange for more secure and predictable lives. Then the shirkers and the drunks and the abandoned are no longer at risk of perishing on the street. But personal liberties also evaporate, and the ceiling under which we must all fly falls down to match the lowest common denominator. Life becomes less risky, but all citizens are debased—not only the failures who are henceforth ordered how and where to live, but also everyone who had succeeded independently, and even members of the master class who must cage and feed the failures. All experience a decline in dignity, self-determination, and life satisfaction.

Lovers of freedom object: "That's too high a price, we must therefore let the failures fail, else our whole system will tumble into busybodying

> The miserable must be lifted up from the sidewalks where they sprawl. Empathy will not tolerate the alternative. Yet when the lifting is done in conventional collective ways, it leads to enslavement on both sides of the transaction.

oppressiveness." But stepping over wasted children or dead bodies will soften many citizens to the idea of trading independence for security. Which is why nearly all human societies have ended up in one of the many paternal structures.

It's just a fact of human empathy: one way or another, the miserable *must* be lifted up from the sidewalks where they sprawl. Common decency will not tolerate the alternative. Yet when the lifting is done in conventional collective ways, it leads to enslavement on both sides of the transaction.

It was voluntary action and private giving that allowed America to escape this terrible dilemma. We made the magical discovery that voluntary action can be a non-enslaving kind of paternalism, enabling us to meet Judeo-Christian and humanitarian responsibilities to fellow men without setting in motion the statist spiral which kills individual sovereignty. In solving basic security hungers and primal fears of a "jungle" freedom, philanthropy thus enabled enormous liberty. Philanthropy turned out to be indispensable to personal independence and national success. It kept America functioning as that exceedingly rare society where average people can steer their own lives.

This is why philanthropists are different from doctors, or teachers, or businessmen, who also do social good, and different from soldiers or ministers or others who sometimes sacrifice their own interests to aid fellow citizens. Doctors, businessmen, and soldiers are valuable contributors, but they are not essential to maintaining America's basic social contract. They are not indispensable.

Effective philanthropists are indispensable. They allow us to have a good society without a paternalist state. They are the prophylactic against public lurches for freedom-killing security blankets.

Philanthropy is the guardian of our self-rule. It is one of just a few *sine qua nons* essential to our national health. Without it there is no America as we know it.

As you amble through the multifarious and sometimes quirky human actions described on these pages, and absorb the colorful stories of charity as it has been practiced in our land over four centuries, I hope you will also keep sight of this profound reality that underlies voluntary giving in America.

GREAT MEN & WOMEN

=== *of* ===

AMERICAN PHILANTHROPY

1706-present

On the pages following you will find a series of profiles bringing to life
the greatest donors from American history. These include individuals like
Franklin, Rockefeller, Carnegie, Rosenwald, Packard, and many others you have
never heard of. They all made large imprints on the course of our country
and the texture of our lives.

THE PHILANTHROPY
HALL OF FAME

59 GREAT DONORS WHO CHANGED OUR NATION AND WORLD

he great deceased donors described in this section transformed
society through their charitable giving. In the entries that follow
we offer brisk biographical narratives that capture the essence of
each man and woman, the sources of their fortunes, and the motivations,
tactics, and results of their philanthropy.

BERNICE BISHOP

Bernice Pauahi Bishop was a Hawaiian princess, the last direct descendant of the Royal House of Kamehameha. With her husband, Charles, she is remembered as one of the most remarkable philanthropists in the history of the Islands. Her bequest endowed the Kamehameha Schools, which to this day specialize in educating the children of native Hawaiians. After her death, Charles Bishop spent many years bringing her vision to fruition.

She was born in December 1831, the great-granddaughter of King Kamehameha the Great, conqueror and unifier of the Hawaiian Islands. In her earliest years, she was raised as an *ali'i* (noble), steeped in native traditions. At the age of seven, however, she was sent to the Royal School. Run by a pair of married Protestant missionaries, the school was committed to providing the children with the finest possible course of Western education. "Miss Bernice" quickly became a star pupil, excelling in both academics and etiquette, and a devout Christian. She was often compared favorably to her spoiled, misbehaving *ali'i* classmates—including Prince Lot Kapuaiwa, the future King Kamehameha V.

In 1846, Charles Bishop arrived in Hawaii. The 24-year-old clerk had sailed from New York aiming for Oregon, but after a rough passage through Cape Horn the ship put in at Honolulu for provisions. Bishop decided to wait out the winter in the Islands. He found work with local Yankee merchants, then became a clerk at the U.S. consulate. He met Pauahi and soon began regularly calling on her at the Royal School. Though her family firmly reminded her of her obligation to marry Hawaiian royalty, Pauahi resisted. In June 1850, in a small ceremony which her parents refused to attend, Pauahi became Bernice Bishop.

Bishop reconciled with her family within a year, and by 1857 had inherited from them an estate totaling 16,011 acres. With it came a wide range of responsibilities. Throughout her mid-20s, Bishop served as a traditional Hawaiian philanthropist, offering guidance, support, and assistance to those who approached her. She spent many working hours in her garden, seated under a tamarind tree, taking visits from fellow islanders and working through their problems in her native Hawaiian tongue.

At the same time, Bernice grew ever more involved in American forms of civic engagement. She was a leader in several charitable organizations, including the Stranger's Friend Society, which aided sick travelers, and the Women's Sewing Society, which provided clothing for the poor. An accomplished contralto singer and pianist, she conducted performances of the works of Haydn and Verdi with the Amateur Musical Society, and gave

music lessons at the Royal School. A devout Protestant, Bishop regularly taught Sunday school at Kawaiaha'o Church.

Charles Bishop, meanwhile, found mounting success as a businessman, opening a bank that profited from the booming sugar trade. (It would eventually become First Hawaiian Bank, which remains the oldest and largest bank in the state, with assets totaling $16 billion and branches in Guam and Saipan.) Before the islands were annexed, he held a series of public offices, even serving as minister of foreign affairs from 1873 to 1874. With her royal lineage and his growing fortune, the Bishops were the social leaders of Honolulu.

In 1872, Bernice was summoned to the deathbed of King Kamehameha V, where he named her successor to the throne. Bishop refused, simply saying, "Do not think of me." Rather than assume the crown, she spent the next decade traveling the world. In 1883, the royal governess of the Islands passed away, leaving nearly 353,000 acres to her cousin Bernice. Bernice was instantly the largest landowner in Hawaii, possessing about 9 percent of its landmass.

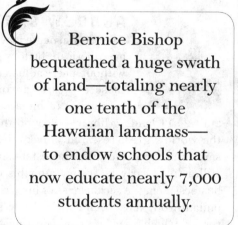

Bernice Bishop bequeathed a huge swath of land—totaling nearly one tenth of the Hawaiian landmass— to endow schools that now educate nearly 7,000 students annually.

With this newfound wealth, the Bishops decided to write their wills. Bernice made individual provisions for a number of charities, friends, and servants. The great bulk of her estate—some 378,569 acres of land—was to be held in trust, for the purpose of opening "two schools, each for boarding and day scholars, one for boys and one for girls, to be known as, and called the Kamehameha Schools." Her will further stipulated that the schools give preference to "Hawaiians of pure or part aboriginal blood," providing them with an English-language education and inculcating strict Protestant morality. It was an ambitious project, unprecedented in Hawaiian history.

The future of the schools was left to five trustees, including her husband. An accomplished philanthropist in his own right, Charles Bishop had already helped found the Hawaiian Historical Society, the Honolulu Public Library, and dozens of kindergartens throughout the Islands. In 1889, he founded the Bishop Museum, home to the world's largest collection of Polynesian cultural artifacts. To launch the Kamehameha schools, Bishop drew on his

previous service on the board of the Punahou School, where he funded the construction of several buildings and labs.

In November 1887, 39 students formed the first class at the boys' school; in 1894, 35 students filled out the first class at the girls' school. Today the schools have campuses on Oahu, Hawaii, and Maui, educating nearly 7,000 children annually. Thus do Charles and Bernice Pauahi Bishop, childless themselves, rank among the greatest patrons of Hawaii's children.

Mithun Selvaratnam

Further information

○ George Kanahele, *Pauahi: The Kamehameha Legacy* (Kamehameha Schools Press, 1986)
○ Harold Kent, *Charles Reed Bishop: Man of Hawaii* (Pacific Books, 1965)

ANDREW CARNEGIE

Andrew Carnegie may be the most influential philanthropist in American history. The scale of his giving is almost without peer: adjusted for inflation, his donations exceed those of nearly anyone else in the nation's history. The magnitude of his accomplishments is likewise historic: he built 2,811 lending libraries around the globe, founded what became one of the world's great research universities, endowed one of the nation's most significant grantmakers, and established charitable organizations that are still active nearly a century after his death. And, perhaps uniquely among businessmen, the seriousness of his writing has ensured that his thoughts on philanthropy have been continuously in print for more than a century, and remain widely read and studied to this day.

Carnegie was born in 1835 in Scotland, one of two sons of a linen weaver and his wife. Advances in looming technology rendered his father's occupation obsolete, threatening the family with dire poverty. Seeking a better future, in 1848 the Carnegies borrowed money to go to the United States. They settled near Pittsburgh, where young Andrew began an extraordinary rags-to-riches business career.

Starting as a "bobbin boy" in a cotton mill for a weekly salary of $1.20, he advanced rapidly, eventually becoming a manager with the Pennsylvania Railroad Company. There Carnegie came to appreciate the importance of iron and steel for the future of the American economy and shifted his efforts toward producing them.

Carnegie had consummate—some might say ruthless—financial and organizational skills, as well as an unremitting appetite for cost-efficiencies

and a keen eye for innovations (most notably the Bessemer process, the first industrial method for converting pig iron to steel). He consolidated several smaller manufacturers and mines to create the largest maker of steel and iron products in the world. In 1901, Carnegie sold his business to financier J. Pierpont Morgan for nearly $500 million. His stake was almost half the total. Thus did the poor son of a laboring immigrant become one of the wealthiest individuals in American history.

As his fortune increased, Carnegie came to associate with the most eminent political, financial, and intellectual figures of the time, both in the United States and abroad. Especially after moving to New York City in 1870, he became a patron of numerous schools, museums, libraries, and churches on both sides of the Atlantic. (Though not particularly religious himself, Carnegie adored the hymnody of his youth, and provided some 7,500 organs to congregations around the world.)

Carnegie is best known for the nearly 3,000 public libraries he helped build. As a young man in Allegheny City, Carnegie spent most of his evenings in the book collection of Colonel James Anderson, a prosperous local businessman who gave working boys free access to his 1,500 volumes. It was clearly a formative experience, and one which Carnegie later attempted to re-create for similar benefit to others. Starting in 1885, Carnegie began funding the construction of thousands of libraries. At the time of his death in 1919, the tally stood at 2,811. To ensure that communities were invested in the success of these institutions, he would only pay for buildings—and only after local authorities showed him credible plans for acquiring books and hiring staff.

During his lifetime, Carnegie created a number of charitable institutions that bore his name. In 1900, he founded the Carnegie Technical Schools, later the Carnegie Institute, and known today as Carnegie Mellon University, one of the world's great research universities. In 1904, he created what he called his "pet child," the Carnegie Hero Fund Commission, which recognizes and rewards individuals who spontaneously risk life and limb to aid others. A year later, he launched the Carnegie Foundation for the Advancement of Teaching, whose many accomplishments include the Flexner Report, which revolutionized American medical education, and the provision of pensions to college faculty members (which increased the attractiveness of an academic career).

Other organizations would bear his name, including the Carnegie Relief Fund (for the benefit of injured steelworkers), the Carnegie Dunfermline Trust (to support his hometown), and the Carnegie Trust for the Universities of Scotland (to bolster higher education in his native land). The Manhattan

concert venue was not supposed to bear its patron's name, but when European notables declined to perform in a simple "music hall," its benefactor relented. In 1893 the facility was renamed Carnegie Hall.

Not all of Carnegie's efforts were successful. For much of the final third of his life, he devoted his fortune and personal influence to encouraging the peaceful resolution of international conflicts. He created and closely attended to the Carnegie Endowment for International Peace and the Carnegie Council for Ethics in International Affairs. The outbreak of World War I dashed his hopes of world amity and precipitated his retreat from the public stage.

A somewhat ambiguous achievement was the creation of the Carnegie Corporation. This foundation was among the first (and remains among the largest) grantmaking foundations in the United States, with consequential achievements including early support for the National Bureau of Economic Research, the research of Gunnar Myrdal, and the development of "Sesame Street." And yet, creation of a perpetual foundation represented a failure of sorts for Carnegie, whose stated goal was to give away his entire fortune while living, and die penniless.

The fact that Carnegie's philanthropic goals are well known is a testament to the third source of his enduring influence: his extensive public writings. In several widely read books, articles in serious British and American magazines, and frequent newspaper interviews and speeches, the colorful Scot's opinions on a range of economic, political, and philosophical issues attracted public attention.

None of his writings had more influence than those about philanthropy, which were published as two articles in the *North American Review* in 1889 and collected in a 1901 book called *The Gospel of Wealth and Other Timely Essays*. His views grew out of an economic and political philosophy that owed a lot to English classical liberalism and social theorists such as Herbert Spencer.

Carnegie attributed his business success not only to his own talents, but also to an economic system that valued enterprise, protected property, and encouraged competition. This system brought dramatic improvements in living standards to the public at large, while enabling successful competitors like himself to become extremely wealthy. Yet Carnegie acknowledged that there were costs as well as triumphs, which included a wide gap between rich and poor and social frictions between employers and workers.

Carnegie saw philanthropy as essential for addressing these shortcomings. He called on those enjoying the largest fruits of the economic system to use their wealth "to produce the most beneficial results for the community." This would ensure that all of society benefited,

reducing resentments that could ultimately lead to replacement of a bountiful system of free enterprise with a less productive one built on envy and redistribution.

Carnegie believed, however, that just giving away money was not enough—in fact, it could make things worse. "Of every thousand dollars spent in so-called charity today," he opined, "it is probable that nine hundred and fifty dollars is unwisely spent—so spent, indeed, as to produce the very evils which it hopes to mitigate or cure." The problem, as he saw it, was "indiscriminate charity"—providing help to people who were unwilling to help themselves. That sort of philanthropy only rewarded bad habits rather than encouraging good ones. He argued that philanthropy should instead support universities, libraries, hospitals, meeting halls, recreational facilities, and similar projects that strengthened and refreshed individuals so they could become more independent and productive themselves.

Carnegie urged his wealthy peers to provide for themselves and their dependents and then make it their "duty" to use the rest of their funds for their communities. They should apply their "wisdom, experience, and ability to administer" to lift up "poorer brethren" who "would or could not do for themselves." He warned successful men who failed to help others that "the man who dies thus rich dies disgraced."

> Successful men should help lift the unsuccessful into more productive lives, thought Andrew Carnegie, and a man who neglects this duty and dies rich "dies disgraced."

Carnegie's "gospel" has attracted generations of successful businessmen, including the one whose current wealth rivals that of the steel magnate— Bill Gates. By linking giving not just to religious and moral imperatives to care for the needy, but also to preservation of the American economic and political system, Carnegie extended the rationale for philanthropy. In the process, he imbued charitable giving with an extra appeal for the generations of entrepreneurs and self-made men and women who came after him.

— Leslie Lenkowsky

Further information

o *Philanthropy* magazine article, philanthropyroundtable.org/topic/donor_intent/the_carnegie_corporation_turns_100

○ Andrew Carnegie, *The Autobiography of Andrew Carnegie* (Northeastern University Press, 1986)

○ David Nasaw, *Andrew Carnegie* (Penguin Books, 2006)

PETER COOPER

Peter Cooper was a first-rate inventor who also— uncharacteristically of inventors—was a first-rate businessman. He became an industrialist, a civic leader, and a philanthropist. Cooper knew what he wanted to make of his life. In his old age, he said he spent the first 30 years of his life getting a start, the next 30 making a fortune, and the last 30 doing good with that fortune.

Cooper was born in 1791, the fifth of nine siblings. His father worked at various occupations—as a hatter, storekeeper, brickmaker, and brewer. He was not particularly good at any of them, however, and the family eventually left New York City for Peekskill upstate. As a result, young Peter became widely acquainted with business practices as he tried to help the family breadwinner in creative ways. While still a child, he constructed a device for pounding laundry, perhaps the world's first washing machine. He also designed a machine for mowing lawns, in an age when lawnmowers were called "sheep."

Because his family was always short of money, Cooper received only one year of formal education, a lack he felt keenly. But he studied on his own and, when he could afford it, hired tutors to teach him subjects. Apprenticed to a carriage maker, Cooper proved so valuable an employee that the carriagemaker voluntarily doubled—and then *tripled*—his salary. Shortly after completing his apprenticeship, Cooper married Sarah Bedell. It would be a long and happy marriage, producing six children, although only two lived to maturity.

When he was 30 years old, Cooper acquired a glue factory, just north of the settled part of Manhattan. He paid $2,000 in cash, a considerable sum at that time. Adept at chemistry, Cooper greatly improved the product line. That proved immensely rewarding, yielding him $10,000 in profit the first year. Among the new products he developed was instant gelatin. (His wife developed recipes for mixing it with fruit, so in a sense it can be said they invented Jell-O.) Soon he was earning $100,000 annually, a vast income for the 1820s.

Cooper lived simply and poured his profits into his business and investments. With two partners, he bought extensive waterfront property

in Baltimore, hoping to benefit from the increased commerce between the harbor and then-under-construction Baltimore & Ohio Railroad. When the steam locomotives arrived from Britain, however, it was discovered that they could not climb the steep grade and make the narrow turns west of the city. Cooper was undeterred. He built from scratch a steam engine—later nicknamed the "Tom Thumb"—that was capable of handling American conditions. It was the first steam engine built in the United States.

By the 1850s, he was among the richest men in the country. He remained open as ever to new ideas and new technology, including the transatlantic telegraph cable project of his neighbor Cyrus Field. Cooper invested in the cable—which was successful only after four failures and 11 years.

Contemporaries of Cooper sometimes observed that he had no sense of humor whatsoever. He never joined any of the men's clubs that were springing up in mid-nineteenth-century New York. His idea of leisure was to spend an afternoon discussing the finer points of Protestant theology with clergymen. The great joy of his life, it appears, was philanthropy.

As Cooper approached middle age, charitable work became increasingly important to him. He sat on numerous boards of eleemosynary institutions and was a generous contributor to his church and to worthy causes throughout the city and state. In 1853, he laid the cornerstone of his signature project, Cooper Union.

Cooper intended for his school to provide a practical education, free of charge, to working people who wanted to improve themselves. Modeled after the École Polytechnique in Paris, the Cooper Union offered many of its classes at night so that those who had to earn a living could fully avail themselves of the school. And thanks to Cooper's extraordinary generosity, the college was completely tuition-free.

When Cooper Union first opened its doors in 1859, more than 2,000 people applied to take classes. The Union's reading room was also open to the public and, unlike New York City's other libraries at that time, was open until 10:00 p.m., again so that working people could use it. As many as 3,000 people took advantage of the reading room every week.

Cooper required that there be no discrimination on the basis of race, religion, or sex—almost unprecedented in the mid-1800s—and that the institution provide an education "equal to the best" available. Among its early alumni was Thomas Edison. The impoverished Edison could never have afforded tuition at a regular engineering school.

The building, located at Astor Place in Manhattan's East Village, is itself interesting. It was the first fireproof building in New York, constructed with

iron I-beams invented and manufactured by Cooper himself. It contained an elevator shaft, though commercial elevators were not yet in existence, because Cooper was confident that a safe elevator mechanism would soon be developed. Soon enough, the circular shaft was fitted with a mechanism created by Elisha Otis, which is still in use.

Cooper Union's Great Hall occupied the basement level and immediately became one of the most important venues in New York for major political addresses. Abraham Lincoln gave his "House Divided" speech there early in 1860, propelling him into serious contention for the Republican nomination that year. Many Presidents have spoken there since.

Cooper devoted over half of his fortune to the Union's endowment, including much Manhattan real estate, which has allowed the endowment to grow along with the city. (Cooper Union, for instance, owns the land under the Chrysler Building, from which it derives a considerable rent.) Prominent among the school's later benefactors was Andrew Carnegie, who praised Cooper in *The Gospel of Wealth* and donated $600,000 to the institution in 1902. Cooper Union became one of the premier engineering, architecture, and art schools in the country.

> Peter Cooper's great goal in setting up a free college in New York City was to boost up poor people ambitious to improve themselves. Thomas Edison was an early alum.

"I have always recognized that the object of business is to make money in an honorable manner," wrote Cooper not long before his death in 1883. "I have endeavored to remember that the object of life is to do good." He remembered that well, and tens of thousands of young men and women over the last 150 years have benefited as a result.

John Steele Gordon

Further information

- Edward Clarence Mack, *Peter Cooper: Citizen of New York* (Duell, Sloan, and Pearce, 1949)
- Rossiter Raymond, *Peter Cooper* (Houghton Mifflin, 1901)
- J. C. Zachos, *A Sketch of the Life and Opinions of Mr. Peter Cooper* (Murray Hill, 1876)

BILL DANIELS

Bill Daniels was a pioneer of the cable TV industry and a major philanthropist in Denver and the Rocky Mountain region. Throughout his life, his charitable giving ranged widely. He reached out to those down on their luck, those who abused alcohol and drugs, and those who suffered from mental and physical disabilities. He provided scholarships, with a focus less on academic achievement and more on demonstrated character and leadership potential. He funded efforts to integrate ethics into business schools and created a bank meant to teach young people the principles of finance and personal responsibility. Through it all, his giving was largely personal; Daniels routinely enclosed a note with each check, explaining to the recipient what he hoped his money would do.

Born in 1920, Daniels grew up in Hobbs, New Mexico. He became a rowdy, rough-and-tumble teen who needed discipline, and he found it at the New Mexico Military Institute. Daniels entered the Navy after graduating and became a highly decorated aviator, serving in combat at Guadalcanal, Midway, and the Coral Sea.

In 1952, after serving in the Korean War, Daniels moved to Casper, Wyoming, where he made the discovery that would yield his fortune. The two-time Golden Gloves state champion stopped at Murphy's Bar in Denver one night. To his surprise, a fight at Madison Square Garden was visible on a television behind the bar. It was the first time he had seen a television. He was instantly transfixed.

But, as was the case with many small rural communities, there was no television available in Casper—a mountain range prevented the signal from reaching his town. Daniels did some research and found that several towns in the eastern United States had resolved the same issue by transmitting TV signals through coaxial cable. A single large antenna might be set up on a mountaintop or hill to pick up the nearest signal, which would then be run through cables strung on telephone poles to the homes of subscribers.

In 1953, Daniels started a cable system in Casper, at great initial expense. But his bet paid off. For a single black-and-white channel that broadcast for only eight hours daily, he won 4,000 subscribing households—about a third of the total homes in the area. Before long, he found himself traveling all across the West, securing investors, finding customers, and recruiting talent. In 1958, as small cable systems began to proliferate, Daniels sensed the need for a coordinating firm for the nascent industry. In Denver, he founded Daniels and Associates, which became a center of the burgeoning industry.

"Bill may have been the prime architect of cable's capital structure—the whole way in which the cable industry decided to make money," explained

cable entrepreneur John Malone. "In the very early days, the theory was that you charged people a lot to hook them up and then you'd charge them hardly anything after that. Bill took it the other way, arguing we'll have much more success if we treat it as an ongoing revenue stream."

With the cable boom in the 1980s and '90s, Daniels's fortune exploded. He had always been generous to his employees and to people in need. He would anonymously make cash gifts to families whose homes burned down, or who were suffering medical emergencies. He also gave generously to homeless shelters, food pantries, and organizations that served the disabled. But his wealth made philanthropy on a large scale possible.

Daniels had a soft spot for kids—like him—who needed a hand up to succeed, and he often gave scholarships to put these young people through school. They need not have been straight-A students. Daniels was looking for hard-working kids with strong values and leadership potential. He did expect satisfactory grades to keep the scholarship funds coming, and he also expected the student to live by high moral standards and hold down a part-time job.

> Daniels had a soft spot for kids who needed a second or third chance to succeed (as he had), and often gave scholarships to put these "diamonds in the rough" through college.

In 1986, the work-hard, party-hard playboy faced a reality check when his closest friends and business associates confronted him about his drinking. He committed himself to the Betty Ford Center, where he kicked alcohol for good. He never forgot hitting rock bottom, and for the rest of his life he attended Alcoholics Anonymous meetings, sponsored drug and alcohol addicts, referred friends to the Ford Center, and even paid for their treatment. In 1988, he became the first Ford Center alumnus to join its board. At the time of his death in 2000, he was one of the center's largest funders.

Daniels sensed after his recovery that he had much more philanthropic work ahead of him. In the 1980s, he became concerned that the nation's leading business schools did not teach business ethics. In the 1980s and 1990s, he gave over $22 million to what became the Daniels College of Business at the University of Denver, where he insisted that ethics and etiquette become a mandatory part of the MBA curriculum—one of the first business schools in the nation to do so.

Daniels created Young Americans Bank with the hope of preparing young people to participate in the free-enterprise system. Daniels personally backed the bank, which he insisted would be fully functioning, state-chartered, and FDIC-insured. After two years of wooing skeptical regulators, Daniels opened YAB in 1987. The bank serves people under 21, who can open checking and savings accounts, apply for credit cards designed to teach them how to spend wisely, and obtain small-business loans. By 2011, YAB had served nearly 70,000 young customers.

As the bank grew, so did its mission—YAB spun off its financial literacy teaching into an elementary-school classroom curriculum and created Young AmeriTowne, where students run model businesses and learn how to be financially responsible citizens. When asked in 1996 what his proudest accomplishment was, Daniels didn't miss a beat. "Young Americans Bank," he said.

"I think God told me as a young man to share my good fortune with others," Daniels said near the end of his life. "I have tried to do it. And my foundation will see to it when I die. Believe me, it is a real joy to me to be able to help people."

— Evan Sparks

Further information

○ *Philanthropy* magazine article, philanthropyroundtable.org/topic/donor_intent/back_to_bill

○ Daniels Fund, *The Life and Legacy of Bill Daniels*, danielsfund.org/Legacy.asp

○ Stephen Singular, *Relentless: Bill Daniels and the Triumph of Cable TV* (Daniels Estate, 2003)

KATHARINE DREXEL

Katharine Drexel of Philadelphia is known for many things: She was heiress to a banking fortune, a fierce advocate for the poor, a foundress of the American religious order Sisters of the Blessed Sacrament, and a canonized saint in the Catholic Church. Her greatest accomplishment may have been her role in helping blacks and Native Americans improve their lot.

Drexel's birth in 1858 was traumatic; her mother died a month later and doctors expected to lose the baby as well. But the weak newborn battled back and eventually was sent, with an older sister, to live with relatives. After her father's remarriage she and her sister came home, and it would be years before the girls realized that their father's new wife, Emma Bouvier, was not their biological mother. They were soon joined by a third sister.

Drexel's family was one of the wealthiest in America, and Katharine was related to many prominent figures in American financial and political history. Her great-grandfather founded the firm that eventually became Drexel Burnham Lambert. Her grandfather partnered with J. P. Morgan to found the banking giant Drexel, Morgan & Co., later renamed J. P. Morgan. Her uncle founded Drexel University. Drexel is also related to Nicholas Biddle—the great Philadelphia banker, president of the Second Bank of the United States, and scourge of Andrew Jackson.

The Drexels were a French-Catholic family, deeply religious and intensely philanthropic. Her father had an active prayer life; her mother opened up the family house three times every week to feed and care for the poor. They gave roughly the equivalent of $11 million to charitable causes annually. The family lived on a 90-acre estate not far from Philadelphia, in a house dominated by a large stained-glass window depicting the archangel Michael.

> After growing up in one of the wealthiest families in America, Katharine Drexel became a nun and devoted her inheritance and talents to charitable work among Native Americans and African Americans.

At the death of Katharine's parents, the three Drexel sisters inherited the bulk of their massive estate. Picking up the thread of an earlier trip to the West, Katharine began to devote a significant amount of her personal fortune to missionary and charity work among American Indians, starting with the establishment of the St. Catherine Indian School in Santa Fe in 1887. Later, she visited Pope Leo XIII to ask him to send missionaries to staff the Indian missions she had financed. He turned the request back on her: the missionary she needed, the Pope suggested, was herself. To the disbelief of Philadelphia society, she decided to become a Catholic nun and devote her inheritance and talents to missionary and charitable work among Native Americans and African Americans.

Drexel entered religious life in 1889 with the Sisters of Mercy in Pittsburgh. The death of her sister in 1890 momentarily shook her resolve, but in 1891 she and 15 companions took their vows and founded a new order: the Sisters of the Blessed Sacrament for Negroes and Indians. Added to the normal vows of poverty, chastity, and obedience was a special vow, not to "undertake any work which would lead to the neglect or abandonment of the Indian or Colored races."

Drexel postponed sending sisters to missions in the American West until she felt they were well prepared. The first step for the order was to open a home for parentless African-American children at her family's estate. The home provided both a refuge for these orphans and a place to train her young novices before they were sent off into the still-wild West. Ahead of her time when it came to the education of women, Drexel arranged for the sisters to take classes at Drexel University so they could be prepared to teach their young charges when the time came.

To Katharine, education was the key to opportunity. The bulk of her order's efforts went into developing a network of 145 missions, 12 schools for Native Americans, and 50 schools for African Americans throughout the South and West. These Catholic schools were staffed by laypersons, often attached to a local church, and offered religious instruction and vocational training. Unlike many religious mission schools, students did not have to be or become Catholic to enroll.

In 1915, with a $750,000 grant from Katharine, the sisters founded Xavier University in New Orleans. The only historically black Catholic college in the United States, Xavier was designed to train teachers who could staff the order's burgeoning network of schools. Much of the cost of opening these schools, as well as Xavier, was covered by Drexel's personal fortune, and it is estimated (there is no official figure) that she gave nearly $20 million during her lifetime to support the work of her order, or more than $500 million today.

Drexel was also an outspoken advocate for the rights of poor blacks and Native Americans. She supported petitions to Congress to increase aid to reservation schools, wrote letters to newspaper editors whose reporting on Indian affairs she found to be biased, and started a letter-writing campaign in support of a federal anti-lynching law.

The wealthy heiress displayed a hard-headed pragmatism when dealing with local authorities in the segregated South. Adopting the maxim "render to Caesar what is Caesar's," Drexel decreed that the order's churches in the South, instead of the customary roped-off section in the rear for blacks, would have two long pews running front to back for the races. This tactic kept the sisters within the letter of local segregation laws—and protected the schools from closure—while flouting racist intentions. She also used dummy corporations and other legal shell games to hide her land purchases until the schools were too entrenched for local authorities to close. Nonetheless, there were regular conflicts with local bigotries: the order's mother house in Bensalem, Pennsylvania, received a bomb threat when it was under construction; an order school in Rock Castle, Virginia, was destroyed by arson in 1899; and the Ku Klux Klan threatened the same for another in Texas in 1922.

Katharine's travels and work continued until 1938, when a stroke left her almost completely immobile and forced her to give up leadership of the sisters. Because she died without issue, the corpus of her father's estate passed not to the order she founded, but to various charitable and religious institutions designated in his will.

In 2000, Pope John Paul II canonized Drexel, the second native-born American to be named a saint. The ceremony in St. Peter's Square likely would have pained Katharine Drexel, servant of the poor, whose only request when Xavier University was founded was that the school make no mention of her bequest, and who, at the college's dedication, sat in the back of the room, quiet and unnoticed.

～ Justin Torres

Further information

- Katherine Burton, *The Golden Door: The Life of Katharine Drexel* (P. J. Kennedy, 1958)
- Daniel McSheffery, *Saint Katharine Drexel* (Catholic Book Publishing, 2002)
- Ellen Tarry, *Saint Katharine Drexel: Friend of the Oppressed* (Farrar Strauss, 1958)

JAMES DUKE

James Buchanan Duke built two massive fortunes, the first in tobacco and the second in hydroelectric power generation. He became one of the greatest philanthropists in the history of the Carolinas, perhaps best known today as the patron of Duke University.

Born in December 1856 near Durham, North Carolina, Duke grew up on a small farm with a widowed father. After the Civil War devastated the Carolina countryside, the Duke family began growing, curing, and selling tobacco. In 1874, the Dukes opened a tobacco factory in Durham, where they were among the first cigarette manufacturers in the South. The family was—at young J. B.'s recommendation—among the very first to adopt machine production on a large scale. The Dukes were able to produce much faster than manufacturers using older methods, and to build consumer demand for the Duke brands they pioneered national cigarette advertising, including tradable "cigarette pictures" and billboards. J. B.'s devout Methodist father was concerned about the suggestive pictures, and his competitors sniffed at "this damned picture business" that "degraded" the cigarette industry, but smokers across the country increasingly asked their local tobacconists for Duke brands by name.

Like many of his era's industry titans, Duke sought to limit competition. His firm joined four others in 1890 to form the American Tobacco Company,

which accounted for upwards of 90 percent of the domestic cigarette business. Duke, who had orchestrated the merger, was at the helm of the new monopoly. In 1901, he bought a major British tobacco company. He again joined forces with competitors and formed the British-American Tobacco Company. "Duke's keenest satisfaction from this international triumph," said business partner William Whitney, "came to him in the knowledge that he had gotten an almost unlimited and more lasting market for the tobacco made by his own people on their small farms." But in 1911 the federal government dissolved his conglomerate under the Sherman Antitrust Act.

Duke was already planning his next enterprise: hydroelectric development of the western Carolinas. Lasting growth and prosperity in the South would require cheap, abundant electricity, he believed, especially in the textile-producing regions. Duke's foresight put him a generation ahead of government efforts to electrify the Tennessee River Valley during the Great Depression. He bought land and built dams, then persuaded mill owners to use the new source of energy. By the 1920s, Duke's Southern Power Company was the leading electric utility in the western Carolinas. Today the firm is known as Duke Energy.

> James Duke channeled his large donations tightly into the Carolinas—where he had made his fortune, and where the limited scale gave him chances to exert a clear positive influence.

Duke's brother, Ben, handled most of the family's giving. ("I am going to give a good part of what I make to the Lord," J. B. Duke was fond of saying, "but I can make better interest for Him by keeping it while I live.") But in 1924, Duke gave $40 million to create the Duke Endowment. Unlike many of his peers who created foundations with vague mandates, Duke's indenture gave his trustees very specific instructions: they were to support hospitals, orphan care, rural Methodist churches, and four Carolina colleges. The men and women who have run the Duke Endowment since have hewed loyally to Duke's designs.

These philanthropic interests grew out of Duke's life. He always attributed his family's success to its Methodist faith. ("If I amount to anything in this world," he would say, "I owe it to my daddy and the Methodist church.") His interest in orphans came from his own experience without a mother. And the Duke family had for many decades generously supported Trinity College, which Duke had

designated to receive the gifts that would transform it into Duke University as a memorial to his father and brother. "I have selected Duke University as one of the principal objects of this trust because I recognize that education, when conducted along sane and practical, as opposed to dogmatic and theoretical, lines, is, next to religion, the greatest civilizing influence," he wrote. He intended that Duke University attain "a place of real leadership in the educational world."

Duke even allocated specific percentages of his endowment's payout to each charitable category: 46 percent devoted to higher education, 32 percent for hospitals, 10 percent for orphan care, and 12 percent to Methodist causes. He also limited his endowment's giving to the Carolinas—to give elsewhere, he thought, "would be productive of less good by reason of attempting too much." Duke also produced a statement of principles to guide his trustees, with many details—urging, for instance, that "adequate and convenient hospitals are assured in their respective communities, with especial reference to those who are unable to defray such expenses of their own." As for orphans, he wrote, while "nothing can take the place of a home and its influences, every effort should be made to safeguard and develop these wards of society."

Per Duke's instructions, the Duke Endowment's trustees are paid for their service. Every year, they read aloud the full text of Duke's indenture. "After the reading, there is always a time of reflection and comment about Mr. Duke, his ideas, and our mission," said the late Mary D. B. T. Semans, a longtime board member and grand-niece of Duke. "This closeness to the founder renews us and gives us a sense of new energy." Duke's successors have continued the program he laid out, with some adjustments for changes in how health care and orphan care are delivered.

In its early years, the endowment helped North Carolina's hospitals to grow at twice the rate of other Southern states. It also helped make Duke University one of the world's highest-ranked institutions. "Trinity was a small Methodist college," notes endowment president Eugene Cochrane. "Mr. Duke said, 'I want it to become a great university'—and it has."

James Duke is memorialized in a statue in front of Duke University's monumental chapel. In the years before his death in 1925, he took a special pleasure in the design of Duke's Gothic campus. "Don't disturb me now; I am laying out the university grounds," he said to his nurse days before he died. "I am looking to the future, how they will stand and appear a hundred years from now."

↦ *Evan Sparks*

Further information

○ *Philanthropy* magazine article, philanthropyroundtable.org/topic/donor_intent/duke_of_carolina

○ Robert Durden, *Bold Entrepreneur: A Life of James B. Duke* (Carolina Academic, 2003)

○ *Lasting Legacy to the Carolinas: The Duke Endowment, 1924–1994* (Duke University Press, 1998)

○ John Wilber Jenkins, *James B. Duke: Master Builder* (George Doran Co., 1927)

HARRY EARHART

Harry Earhart made his fortune as a manufacturer of lubricating oils, and used that fortune to support some of the most influential thinkers of the twentieth century through his philanthropy. He established two foundations, Earhart and Relm, to support free-market and American ideals. He also exercised bold leadership in structuring his board, thereby ensuring that his work would continue after his death, and providing a model for organizing philanthropic entities to safeguard donor intent.

Earhart was born in 1870, one of 11 children, the son of a respected local businessman (and the first cousin once removed of pilot Amelia Earhart). Earhart started several businesses, including stints brokering cargo and designing logging machinery. But his greatest success came from the lubricant industry. He took a job with the White Star Refining Company, a struggling oil company based in Buffalo, New York. In 1909, he was sent to Detroit as the company's sales agent.

Earhart saw the opportunity. With the automobile industry about to take off, he bought White Star and moved the company to Detroit. Thirsty for lubricants, auto manufacturers soon made White Star a thriving business. Under Earhart's leadership, the company operated its own refineries and sold petroleum products throughout the Midwest and into Canada, becoming one of the largest oil refining companies in the region. In 1930, Earhart sold White Star to the Vacuum Oil Company (a company later acquired by Mobil); he retired shortly thereafter. The White Star logo earned a good reputation, and would remain on Mobil gas station signs and maps until well after World War II.

Earhart and his wife, Carrie, settled into retirement in Ann Arbor and began to devote their full attention to philanthropy. They founded the Earhart Foundation in 1929 and gave it a broad charitable and religious mandate. It was a conventional family foundation, with their children included on the board.

As time passed, however, Earhart became concerned about the structure and future of his foundation. He saw increasing threats to free enterprise and traditional American values. Though he tried to get his children to see the urgency of promoting free-market ideals, he met with little success.

In 1949, Earhart moved boldly to refocus the work of his foundation—and ensure that it would continue long after him. He asked all of his children to step down and appointed a new and independent board to oversee the Earhart Foundation. He then established a second board made up of family members who shared his vision. The purpose of the second board was to elect trustees to the operating board, and to see to it that the trustees of the operating board remained true to the founder's vision. It is one of the first known instances in which a donor reconfigured his board to ensure future compliance with his intent.

At the same time, the Earhart Foundation instituted a new strategy of influencing ideas and scholarship. It would restrict its activities to funding fellowships for individual scholars whose work advanced the principles of a free society. The foundation's "talent scouts" were to identify promising students, writers, or researchers engaged in uncovering the role of economic freedom in creating a free society. Earhart fellowships eventually funded the work of more than 2,500 graduate students.

> Nine winners of the Nobel Prize in economics were supported by Earhart fellowships in early phases of their careers.

A year later, Earhart also established the Relm Foundation, which funded institutions devoted to furthering economic freedom, like the London-based Institute for Economic Affairs and the Mont Pelerin Society. It also supported individual scholars like Leo Strauss, Eric Voegelin, and Peter Bauer. Relm was given a limited life of 20 years, and in 1977 the foundation was closed and all of its remaining assets went to the Earhart Foundation.

The Earhart Foundation had a peerless record for identifying talented, influential scholars. Nine winners of the Nobel Prize in economics were supported by Earhart fellowships early in their careers: Friedrich Hayek, Milton Friedman, Gary Becker, James Buchanan, Ronald Coase, Robert Lucas, Daniel McFadden, Vernon Smith, and George Stigler.

Though Harry Earhart died in 1954, his foundation remained true to his vision by supporting hundreds of individuals and playing a key role advancing freedom. The foundation's board decided to spend down its assets and close at the end of 2015. That decision would likely have pleased Harry Earhart, who insisted that "giving should serve to strengthen recipients rather than to make them increasingly and perhaps permanently dependent upon help from others."

↪ *Kari Barbic*

Further information

○ *Philanthropy* magazine article, philanthropyroundtable.org/topic/excellence_in_ philanthropy/measuring_success_in_generations

○ Lee Edwards on the Earhart Foundation, FirstPrinciplesJournal.com/articles. aspx?article=561

○ Elizabeth Earhart Kennedy, *Once Upon a Family* (Fithian, 1990)

GEORGE EASTMAN

His talented but erratic father died when he was seven years old, leaving debts. His devoted mother coped as widows had for millennia: she took in boarders. The young boy had two older sisters, one of them afflicted with polio. Thus, when George Eastman dropped out of school in 1868 and took a job at age 14 as an office boy, he did so as the man of the family, with weight on his shoulders.

George was serious, extremely orderly, and thrifty, and he made himself useful at a pair of insurance companies and then a bank, where he rose from clerk to bookkeeper. His private passion was the brand new hobby of photography. He experimented with the variety of crude techniques available in the 1870s, haunted photo shops, and swapped tips with professional portraitists.

Eastman was a methodical self-educator, and began to experiment with the tricky chemistry and mechanics of creating photographic emulsions, which were then coated by hand on glass plates. He tinkered, invented, and even took a trip to England (then the technology center for photography) in an attempt to procure partners and patents for his innovations. He was racing scores of other nascent entrepreneurs situated around the world, trying to figure out the science and business model of a brand-new and rapidly emerging field.

Fortunately Eastman was a worker with enormous stamina. He would toil at the bank all day, six days a week, then spend his evenings in a rented room where he was experimenting tirelessly with various photo emulsions— devilishly sensitive concoctions subject to mysterious failure given the slightest variation in the chemical recipe or production process. He would work into the night, grabbing catnaps in a hammock he strung in one corner of the room and waking himself to stir the emulsions at exact intervals.

Soon he was building his own business producing photographic supplies and cameras, in an industry where the engineering was in constant flux, and the commercial competition was cutthroat. He moved aggressively and became the leading force in the sector during the 1890s. From the beginning,

he worked to establish a presence not just in the U.S. but in countries around the world. By early in the twentieth century, when hobby photography was exploding in popularity, and filmed movies were emerging as mass entertainment, the Eastman Kodak Company had become one of the first firms to dominate a market across the globe.

Throughout it all, Eastman remained humble, shy, and unassuming. His reticence and boyish face gave him a low profile for many years, even in his hometown of Rochester, New York. When he identified himself, at the peak of his success, to a newly hired gate guard outside his own factory, the watchman scoffed, "Glad to meet you; I'm John D. Rockefeller." One of his friends observed that he "could keep silent in several languages." It took 25 years of close collaboration before Eastman and University of Rochester president Rush Rhees began to address each other by their first names. Eastman could be brisk and unemotional, and he never married, though he enjoyed his extended family and a number of close friendships.

He was a stern and no-nonsense businessman, but generous in sharing successes with employees and shareholders. He was a pioneer in creating sick pay, disability compensation, pensions, and hospital benefits. After one highly successful stock offering he set aside a large sum from his personal proceeds and had it distributed to 3,000 startled Eastman Kodak employees with a note reading: "This is a personal matter with Mr. Eastman and he requests that you will not consider it as a gift but as extra pay for good work." It was one of the first corporate bonuses.

Eastman was a high mix of homebody and adventurer. He would work ceaselessly in Rochester, relaxing only in mundane house and garden duties, then explode into some exotic and extended foreign jaunt. He bicycled across Europe several times (and also enthusiastically bicycled to work much of his life, even in Rochester winters). He would go on music and theater jags where he'd attend several performances or plays each day. On African safari once he stood filming a rhino on an early hand-cranked movie camera, and calmly continued as the snorting animal charged directly at him, simply sidestepping and actually brushing the animal as it passed. As the very large rhino began its second charge, with Eastman still methodically filming, the terrified hunter-guide accompanying him shot the creature dead just a few paces from his intrepid client.

By the time Eastman Kodak became a secure juggernaut in the early 1900s, its founder had lost interest in accumulating wealth. He was one of the richest men in the world, but much of his fortune sat in low-interest bank accounts. Instead of wanting more money he was now gripped by a powerful desire to put his funds to work in the rest of society. Over the next couple

decades he would give away more than anyone except John Rockefeller and Andrew Carnegie. In current dollars, his gifts totaled in the range of $2 billion.

Eastman built brand-new campuses for two universities that became among the best of their kind. He established a medical school, and did pioneering work in improving the dental health of children in the U.S. and Europe. He built one of the greatest music schools in the world. And he was the largest contributor to the education of African Americans during the 1920s.

He also strayed into a few of the dead ends and dangers of those who become hypnotized by "science" and "progress" and "reason." He insisted that Kodak abandon tradition and lead the rest of mankind into use of a new rational calendar of 13 equal months of 28 days each. Kodak found it a lonely parade, but continued through the 1980s to use the so-called Cotsworthian calendar for accounting, sales, planning, and other purposes. More seriously, like others in the progressive era, he became a major funder of eugenics. And when his health began to fail, his utilitarian approach to life led Eastman to commit suicide, at age 77, via a pistol shot to the heart.

In general, though, Eastman was an exceptionally thoughtful and effective philanthropist. As much as or more than any other large American donor he worked hard at being a wise giver. "A rich man should be given credit for the judgment he uses in distributing his wealth, rather than in the amount he gives away," he stated in a rare public speech. To discipline his giving he followed several crucial principles.

> Donors should give while they are living and able to intelligently guide the use of their money, Eastman insisted. And he worked hard at being a wise patron, researching groups personally and making his own decisions with great care.

Along with Julius Rosenwald, his contemporary and confrère on this topic, Eastman believed strongly that donors should give while they are living and able to intelligently guide the application of their money. "Men who leave their money to be distributed by others are pie-faced mutts," he once said famously (just before signing away $39 million in one sitting). Eastman would never have locked up his money in a foundation, like Rockefeller and Carnegie, with money to be dribbled out after his death, in perpetuity, by succeeding waves of professional

staff and trustees favoring who knows what causes. Eastman distributed the vast bulk of his fortune before he died in 1932, and bequeathed the remaining $25 million or so by last will and testament.

Rather than hiring a professional manager or teams of functionaries to distribute his largesse, Eastman did it himself, with very personal attention. He researched carefully, often acted without being asked, and made all of his own decisions. In addition to giving them money, he actively advised, guided, and assisted groups and causes. One of the reasons he concentrated his giving in the Rochester area was so he could personally supervise the execution, completion, and operation of his good works. He also took pains to avoid "scattering" his resources, and tried instead to "bunch" them for greatest effect.

Eastman ultimately had as much effect as any giver in America. He was a catalytic funder of universities. His $51 million in gifts made the University of Rochester into a top-tier school. The $22 million he gave to MIT in 1912 (the equivalent of $550 million in 2017 dollars) reoriented it from local commuter facility to international leader. At the moment Eastman presented himself as a giant voluntary backer of the school, MIT was in such desperate financial straits it had decided to sell its campus and fold itself into Harvard as simply the engineering department of that university. After a court blocked that as a violation of the college's charter, MIT's president resigned and the institution tottered. When Eastman stepped up, unbidden and unknown, and built the university a new campus, he turned it into one of the great technology fountains of the world. And this (like much of the rest of Eastman's philanthropy) was carried out completely anonymously, leaving many Americans then and now unaware of his huge philanthropic footprints.

In addition, Eastman gave hefty sums, without solicitation, and loyally over decades, to black colleges like Tuskegee, Hampton, Howard, and Meharry. He also acted close to home, for instance, creating a model school for the black children living around his hunting camp in North Carolina. Between his college and lower-school gifts, George Eastman became the largest donor to African-American schooling of his era.

He was also a pioneer in medical philanthropy, with an ahead-of-his-time emphasis on prevention. Having watched in horror as a boy while his mother had eight teeth pulled at their kitchen table without anesthesia, Eastman established the country's first free dental clinic for children in Rochester in 1901. He later built it a large central facility that was beautifully decorated for young patients, including with live birds in cages to entertain them. The success of this dispensary led him to build others, including in European cities where Kodak did business. Eastman's dental clinics in London, Rome, Stockhom, and Paris still exist today.

Eastman single-handedly created the University of Rochester School of Medicine and Dentistry. He built extensive hospital complexes throughout Rochester (which he identified as "the town I am interested in above all others," and where two thirds of his public gifts were centered).

George Eastman's most personal gift blessed Rochester and the world alike. "GE is absolutely alcoholic about music," wrote one friend, after accompanying him on a 1925 culture trip to New York City. They attended 12 operas and plays in six days, as well as visiting the Morgan Library, the Metropolitan Museum, the Frick Museum, and taking in two movies. ("The rest of the time we loafed," Eastman summarized in his own account.)

Eastman described listening to music as "a necessary part of life," and installed one of the country's largest organs in his house (6,175 pipes), then paid an organist to play it every morning as a kind of alarm clock and breakfast accompaniment. "There are no drawbacks to music: you can't have too much of it," he opined. "There is no residual bad effect like overindulgence in other things."

The charmed donor loved to share beautiful music with others, and made many innovative efforts to expose everyday citizens to great performances. He created elaborate music-instruction programs for the community at large, purchased hundreds of instruments for children, and subsidized the best ensembles to play in Rochester. He insisted tickets at all performances he had anything to do with should be sold first-come/first-served to avoid any "class distinctions." He required that operas be sung in English so people could understand them. He sent the conductor of the local orchestra to Europe for a year of full-time study and practice, then brought him back to lead a large professional orchestra in popular concerts.

With intense attention to detail, Eastman painstakingly created the Eastman Theater, still one of the largest and most wondrous concert halls in the country, into which he introduced imaginative programming. He popularized a new art form—and scandalized many in an era when movies were considered disreputable and trivial—by marrying his two loves of music and film. Every week in his 3,500-seat auditorium a fine orchestra was assembled to accompany the screening of silent films.

In philanthropy and in business, George Eastman was unusually open to novel creative combinations, while always insisting on excellence and the highest of standards. With the Eastman School of Music he was as demanding as he was generous; 12 years after his death this entity, which he had created from scratch by sheer willpower and financial devotion, had been called the best graduate conservatory in the nation (and one of the best in the

world). Eastman likewise aimed to make MIT a world paragon in technology education. He also got that wish.

Observers sometimes characterized George Eastman as having a "success complex." Hard achievement was everything for him. Failure was not to be tolerated. Remarkably, he often met his own lofty standard.

☞ *Karl Zinsmeister*

Further information

○ Elizabeth Brayer, *George Eastman: A Biography* (Johns Hopkins University Press, 1996)

○ Kodak corporate biography for founder, kodak.com/ek/US/en/George_Eastman.htm

○ PBS profile, "The Wizard of Photography," pbs.org/wgbh/amex/eastman/index.html

○ George Eastman Papers, University of Rochester, lib.rochester.edu/index.cfm?page=864

THOMAS EDDY

Thomas Eddy, one of New York City's top financiers, led some of the most innovative philanthropic efforts of the early nineteenth century. He founded the first mutual insurance company in New York, and was among the first commissioners of the Erie Canal. But Eddy was best known for his charitable work. He guided the efforts to reform penal laws. He helped construct the New York Hospital. And he founded the New York Savings Bank, a spectacularly successful charitable bank designed specifically to serve the working poor.

Born in 1758 to Quaker immigrants from Ireland, Eddy grew up in Philadelphia. During the Revolutionary War he sided with the Loyalists, and remained engaged in commerce as hostilities flared around him. When he turned 21, he moved to New York City, where he and his brothers set up a merchant house. The business prospered for a while, and Thomas opened a satellite office in Philadelphia. He won a lucrative contract for transporting remittance money from the British headquarters in New York to the troops who were taken prisoner after the fall of Yorktown.

In 1791 Thomas returned to New York, where he set himself up as the city's first insurance underwriter. He made a fortune speculating in the first issue of federal debt, and was asked to become a director of the Mutual Insurance Company. As his reputation grew, he was invited to join other boards, including that of the Western Inland Navigation Company, which had been established in 1792 for the purpose of developing a navigable route along the Mohawk River to Lake Ontario. When it proved impractical, he proposed building a canal rather than relying on river navigation. His idea became the basis for the Erie Canal.

When the project was presented to the legislature in 1810, Eddy was appointed one of the project's first commissioners.

"There is no benevolent or charitable institution founded of which he was not the serious promoter," proclaimed New York grandee Cadwallader Colden in 1833. Eddy was chosen to meet with the Indians of the Six Nations, negotiating treaties and working to alleviate distress. He was a charter member of the New York Manumission Society. He was a founding trustee of the New York Bible Society. He established and served as the primary benefactor of the House of Refuge, one of the first charities dedicated to turning around the lives of juvenile delinquents.

One of Eddy's most notable philanthropic achievements was the reform of New York's penal laws. In the early 1790s he began a campaign to end branding, whipping, and solitary confinement in state prisons. In 1796, he shepherded a bill through the state legislature that established new standards for the penitentiary system. He was appointed to oversee the construction of the first state prison and served from 1797 to 1801 as its first director. On the basis of those experiences, in 1801 he published *An Account of the State Prison or Penitentiary House in the City of New York*, a landmark book in the history of prison reform.

> Eddy was one of New York City's earliest philanthropists, and a leader in nearly all of the good causes of his day.

Equally significant were his efforts to open the New York Hospital. Efforts to build a free hospital for the poor of New York City were begun in 1771. A fire destroyed the first building; the Revolutionary War interrupted the construction of its replacement. Progress stalled. Eddy took it upon himself to drive a new charitable subscription, to which he contributed liberally, to get the project finished. For his efforts, he was made governor of the hospital in 1793. In 1815, he launched another such project, establishing a humane mental asylum in Bloomingdale, New York.

But Eddy's greatest philanthropic accomplishment was almost certainly the Savings Bank of New York. Largely forgotten today, the mutual savings banks of the nineteenth century were invaluable to the working poor. "The utility of these institutions to industrious persons of small means," wrote Samuel Knapp, "fired his soul" and opened Mr. Eddy's checkbook.

Unlike commercial banks of the era, mutual savings banks sought out small depositors of modest means, investing their funds at minimal risk while

providing at least a 5 percent return. The banks did not pay dividends, and most were run by trustees who volunteered their time. At a time when banks were unsecure, deposits were not guaranteed, and the only other method of saving was to hoard cash, the mutual savings bank offered a safe way for persons of modest income to accumulate capital.

Eddy did not invent the idea of a mutual savings bank. By the time he floated his first proposal in 1803, Boston and Philadelphia had already pioneered the model. Eddy's great accomplishment was making the Savings Bank of New York an unparalleled success. Optimistic predictions suggested that the bank would accumulate $50,000 worth of deposits in its first year. Instead, writes historian Kathleen McCarthy, "it drew $155,000 in the first six months. And its resources grew exponentially thereafter. In 1825, 9,000 investors had $1.4 million on deposit; ten years later, the number of investors had risen to 23,000, with $3 million in funds; by 1860 over 50,000 passbook holders had nearly $10 million on deposit."

Thomas Eddy died at age 69 in 1827. "His death was as sudden as his life was serene," wrote his biographer Samuel Knapp. "He who had done so much to alleviate the sufferings of others was not doomed to suffer much himself."

↦ *Christopher Levenick*

Further information

○ Freeman Hunt, *Lives of the American Merchants* (Derby & Jackson, 1856)
○ Samuel Knapp, *The Life of Thomas Eddy* (Conner and Cooke, 1834)
○ Alan Olmstead, *New York City Mutual Savings Banks: 1819–1861* (University of North Carolina, 1976)

DON FISHER

Don Fisher founded the Gap, one of the most successful retail chains of the twentieth century, and became the savviest education-reform philanthropist of his era. Born in 1928 to a middle-class family in San Francisco, Fisher always credited his parents with encouraging him to take risks while making practical, smart decisions. "Change or fail" was the lesson he often said he learned from his father, a cabinetmaker and businessman.

Fisher had the opportunity to go into the family business when he graduated from the University of California, Berkeley, but instead chose to branch off on his own. He tried real-estate development for a while, then noticed an unfilled niche in retail fashion. While leasing space to a Levi's store in one of the properties he owned, Fisher found that he could not find

a pair of jeans that fit him right. He had a 31-inch inseam, but the pants in the store only came in even numbers. He went to other stores and found a similar lack of selection.

"What if," he wondered, "someone put together in one store all the styles, colors, and sizes Levi Strauss had to offer?" In 1969, he secured space on Ocean Avenue in San Francisco and opened up a clothing store that was comprehensive and geared specifically toward young people. His wife Doris suggested that they capitalize on the perceived generation gap, and perhaps the gap in retail choices. "The Gap" was emblazoned on their tags and signs.

The Fishers learned the retail business as they went along. Within a few years, they had launched their own line of clothing. By the time Don Fisher passed away at age 81, he had expanded that single store into a worldwide chain with more than 3,100 outlets, nearly $15 billion of annual sales, and more than 134,000 employees.

In 1995, when he stepped down as CEO, Fisher began to think strategically about ways to improve K-12 education in America. A graduate of San Francisco public schools, Fisher considered excellent education a moral imperative. But public-school results were crying out for application of his father's "change or fail" mandate.

Fisher approached Scott Hamilton, who was then working in Massachusetts as associate

> The pioneer in finding, founding, and funding effective school reforms over the last generation, Don Fisher was a lead supporter of nearly all of the major educational innovations of the last 20 years.

commissioner of education for charter schools, asking about schools that had real quality and the potential for replication. "I want to do something where we can touch a lot of kids," Fisher told Hamilton. "I don't want to support just one school; I want to support something that has a broad opportunity around the country."

Hamilton found the "Knowledge Is Power Program," or KIPP, which at that point consisted of two fledgling charter schools. It was clear they were getting powerful results. According to Hamilton, KIPP's track record of success, its central belief that skin color or family income should not limit a child's ability to learn, its focus on college as a goal for all students, and its ferocious commitment to excellence made it different from anything else offered in urban public education.

Over the next decade, the Fishers donated more than $70 million to KIPP—which allowed the chain to grow to 183 top-flight schools by 2015. While 87 percent of its students are eligible for subsidized school meals, and 95 percent are African-American or Latino, more than 90 percent of KIPP middle-school students graduate from high school and more than 80 percent of KIPP alumni go on to college—vastly higher numbers than in other urban schools.

Recognizing that new networks like KIPP could succeed only if they were able to recruit talented educators, Fisher turned his attention to Teach For America, eventually donating more than $100 million to that organization, which recruits top students to take up the teaching of disadvantaged students as a calling. Thanks in no small part to Don Fisher's generosity, the TFA corps grew to around 10,000 active instructors in classrooms during peak years, most of them hailing from the nation's most selective colleges and universities.

Just as in his business, Fisher was always concerned with both quality and scale in his philanthropy. To make sure that excellent charter schools grew beyond the occasional curiosity, he co-founded the Charter School Growth Fund with the late John Walton. This venture has made early-stage investments of over $100 million to high-promise charter-school networks that have shown the ability to grow. Today, CSGF is invested in 32 networks serving over 100,000 students. These networks operate the highest-performing schools in their cities, and many have completely closed the achievement gap between low-income and affluent students.

Fisher also helped found the California Charter School Association, whose membership is open only to those schools that meet exacting educational standards. The movement "mustn't accept mediocre or poor charter schools," Fisher explained, "because they'll bring down the rest of the schools."

Don and Doris Fisher were active donors outside of education too. They assembled a large collection of contemporary art—some 1,100 works by the likes of Alexander Calder, Roy Lichtenstein, Gerhard Richter, and Andy Warhol—which they donated to the San Francisco Museum of Modern Art. Fisher was a major booster of the Boys & Girls Clubs of America, where he served as governor. He endowed the Fisher Center of Real Estate and Urban Economics, as well as the Fisher Center for the Strategic Use of Information Technology, both at Berkeley's Haas School of Business.

Don Fisher was one of the most consequential education reformers of the last century. He was first to find and fund almost *all* of the pioneering ideas and top programs of the last 20 years. His uncanny knack for discovering

effective people was coupled to a fierce independent streak that encouraged him to back brave mavericks long before anyone else would.

⤙ Naomi Schaefer Riley

Further information

○ *Philanthropy* magazine article, philanthropyroundtable.org/topic/excellence_in_ philanthropy/closing_the_gap

○ Jay Mathews, *Work Hard. Be Nice: How Two Inspired Teachers Created the Most Promising Schools in America* (Workman, 2009)

○ Gap website founder bio, "Don Fisher, 1928–2010," gapinc.com/content/dam/gapincsite/ documents/DonFisher_Bio.pdf

ZACHARY FISHER

Zachary Fisher, with his brothers Martin and Larry, built a fortune as a real-estate developer in New York City. That fortune has since been devoted to a wide variety of philanthropic initiatives, from supporting the New York Police Department to funding charitable projects in Israel. But the Fisher family, and Zachary himself, are best known for their extensive work on behalf of America's military servicemembers and veterans.

Zachary Fisher was born in 1910, the son of Jewish immigrants from Lithuania. His father was a general contractor, and at 16 years of age Zachary dropped out of high school and went to work as a bricklayer. Soon he joined his brothers in forming Fisher Brothers, a company that initially focused on building residential properties around the boroughs of New York. The firm flourished. By the early 1950s, it had expanded to commercial real estate, and within two decades was involved in financing, erecting, and leasing properties throughout the city. Fisher Brothers came to construct, own, or manage upwards of 10 million square feet of New York real estate. The Fishers, proclaimed the *New York Times* in its obituary for Zachary, rank among "the royal families that over two or three generations have molded the Manhattan real-estate market."

Throughout their lives, Zachary and his wife, Elizabeth, had an unusually deep respect for the men and women of the United States military. "It's a privilege to live in this great country of ours," Fisher said in an interview late in life. "I owe them."

Zachary Fisher never served in the military. After the bombing of Pearl Harbor he attempted to enlist in the Marine Corps. He was denied, however, because of a knee injury he sustained while working as a teenager on a construction site. Undeterred, Fisher volunteered his

The Intrepid Sea, Air & Space Museum

115

building expertise for civil defense, helping build coastal fortifications along the Atlantic seaboard.

In the late 1970s, Fisher learned that the USS *Intrepid*—a storied aircraft carrier which had survived several kamikaze attacks, played a critical role in the Pacific during World War II, served in Korea and Vietnam, and even recovered two NASA space capsules—was scheduled to be retired and sold for scrap metal. Fisher hated the idea that the nation would "cut up our own history for razor blades."

He decided to acquire and rebuild the *Intrepid*, converting it into a floating museum moored off the banks of Manhattan. It was a monumental undertaking. He put up the first $25 million. Then he shepherded along an act of Congress. (Since this would be the first time an aircraft carrier had ever been sold to a private party, it required a federal statute to complete the transaction.) Next he battled the New York City building commission. (Lacking any precedent for an aircraft-carrier museum, the city inspectors originally treated the *Intrepid* as a multi-story skyscraper lying on its side.) Five years later, the Intrepid Sea-Air-Space Museum opened—the world's largest naval museum. "I watched kids in sneakers wandering all over this piece of history," remarked Fisher on the museum's opening day. "I wondered if any of them would be inspired to do something for their country."

> Zachary Fisher launched some of the most inventive efforts ever seen to honor and aid men and women of the United States military.

Soon after the 1983 bombing of a U.S. Marine barracks in Beirut, the Fishers offered an additional $10,000 beyond the standard government death benefit to each of the families of fallen service members. Having come to the conclusion that these death benefits given to families of fallen military personnel were too low in all cases, the Fishers created the Intrepid Fallen Heroes Fund. Its mission was to supplement the government's benefits, in all future cases, with as much as $25,000 in cash. The Fishers continued these efforts for more than two decades, closing the direct-payment program only after the federal government significantly increased the monetary benefits offered to the families of servicemembers killed on active duty.

Zachary and Elizabeth Fisher are perhaps best known for launching the Fisher House Foundation. In 1990, Fisher learned about a servicewoman who had recently received medical treatment at a military hospital. Her

husband, unable to afford a hotel, spent the duration of her hospitalization sleeping in his car. Fisher was shocked to learn that the military made no provision for the families of hospitalized veterans and servicemembers—and he decided to do something about it.

With an initial donation of $20 million, Zachary and Elizabeth began building "comfort homes" within walking distance of V.A. and military medical centers. These multi-unit complexes were designed to provide free housing for families of military personnel and veterans who were hospitalized at nearby medical facilities. Fisher limited his mission to building the houses, a task for which he had proven expertise. By the time of Zachary's death in 2000, the Fisher House Foundation had built 26 houses. The program continues to expand; as of 2017 there were 72 houses in operation and five more in the process of being built.

Fisher was deeply involved in creating new philanthropic ventures of all sorts throughout his life. After his wife developed Alzheimer's, he joined forces with David Rockefeller, donating $5 million to establish the Fisher Center for Alzheimer's Research. Based at Rockefeller University, it focuses on supporting research that addresses the cause, care, and cure of Alzheimer's, as well as providing public-education programs on the disease.

After Zachary's death, the Fisher family continued and expanded his philanthropic mission of supporting the military and veterans. Between 2000 and 2012, the Intrepid Fallen Heroes Fund provided $120 million in support to wounded servicemembers and their families, first through direct payments to the families of soldiers lost in war, and later through the construction of new medical research and rehabilitation facilities for wounded military personnel. The Center for the Intrepid in San Antonio is focused on treatment of soldiers with amputations, burns, or loss of limb use. The National Intrepid Center of Excellence in Bethesda, Maryland, is focused on the care of brain injuries and psychological health. In 2012, it was announced that several satellite centers will be constructed to bring advanced brain-injury care to other parts of the country.

Also in 2012, the Fisher House program was expanded to Great Britain, where local partners helped build a facility to serve the families of British military patients. There was already a facility at a U.S. Army post in Germany. There is also a house for grieving families receiving the remains of loved ones at Dover Air Force Base.

As of 2015, the Fisher House Foundation has provided the families of hospitalized servicemembers and veterans with 9 million days of free lodging. In addition to saving those families a great expense, the opportunity to commune with other families in similar situations has proven invaluable for many beneficiaries. The foundation also administers complementary programs sponsored by others—such as Hero Miles,

which uses donated frequent-flyer credits to pay for loved ones to travel to wounded servicemembers, the Newman's Own Award, which provides grants for projects to support troops at local military bases, and Scholarships for Military Children.

Zachary Fisher never sought any special recognition for his work on behalf of American servicemen and women. The work was its own reward. Six months after his death, though, Fisher was honored with a new law that conferred upon him the honorary status of veteran of the Armed Forces of the United States.

↳ Thomas Meyer

Further information

○ John Culhane, "The Man Who Bought an Aircraft Carrier" (*Reader's Digest*, 1990)

○ *New York Times* obituary, nytimes.com/1999/06/05/nyregion/zachary-fisher-88-dies-helped-alter-new-york-skyline.html

HENRY FORD

Henry Ford ranks among the most important figures of the industrial era. He founded the Ford Motor Company, which pioneered assembly-line production, driving down costs and making automobile ownership a staple of middle-class American life. Through it all, he maintained a highly idiosyncratic style of charitable giving. He saw work as the purpose of human existence, and he deeply disliked anything—especially something well-intentioned, like philanthropy—that seemed to undermine its discipline. He distrusted organized charities, although he created a few himself. Despite his misgivings, Ford seems to have dedicated about one third of his income to philanthropy.

Henry Ford was born on a Michigan farm in July 1863. He absorbed the farmer's tireless work ethic but hated agriculture. His inclination was mechanical, and as a boy he would strip down and reassemble any machine he could find. ("Every clock in the Ford house shudders when it sees Henry coming," a friend once quipped.) At the age of 16, he left the farm and headed to Detroit, where he found work first as a machinist, and later as an engineer.

Ford settled into a comfortable middle-class life in Detroit, marrying Clara Bryant in 1888 and getting a job at the Edison Illuminating Company in 1891. Every night, he tinkered in the garage behind his house. The neighbors called him "Crazy Henry" for his obsession, but in 1896 he rolled out his first self-propelled vehicle: the Ford Quadricycle. With encouragement from Thomas Edison, Ford kept experimenting—and began to believe he could create his own automobile company.

By the time Ford turned 39 he had founded two car companies. Both had failed—one with a bang, the other with a whimper—yet he was undeterred. In 1903, he borrowed $28,000 to establish the Ford Motor Company. The early cars produced by this firm generated enough profit to make Ford wealthy, and to give him time to take on a more long-range project: the Model T.

When it rolled off the assembly line in October 1908, the Model T revolutionized the automobile industry. In relentless pursuit of efficiency gains, Ford had developed unprecedented production methods. He used machine-made, standardized parts, which were put together along a continuously moving assembly line. The results were staggering. At a time when cars regularly sold for $1,000, he was soon selling the Model T for $345. Orders poured in. By 1915, about half of all cars on earth were Fords. Eventually, some 15 million Model Ts were sold.

Henry Ford owned the Ford Motor Company until his death. By the mid-1920s, his net worth was estimated around $1.2 billion, and though Ford's market share gradually diminished, the company's stunning success made its namesake one of the wealthiest men in American history.

Yet Ford seemed almost indifferent to money and all it could buy. A dry cleaner once returned a $125,000 check Ford had accidentally left in his suit pocket. Ford once declined a dinner invitation at the White House to honor the King and Queen of England. His wife, he explained, had a previously scheduled meeting of her garden club.

> In average years, Henry Ford gave away about a third of his income, and he preferred to give money to individual people, face to face and with a firm handshake.

Being unimpressed by money may help explain Ford's extensive charitable giving during his lifetime. In average years, Ford gave away about 33 percent of his income. By way of comparison, most people in his tax bracket gave away 5 percent. What Ford himself considered to be the most genuine philanthropy were small gifts to individuals, of which he gave many. Biographer William Greenleaf records "impulsive and warm-hearted acts of individual generosity that saw him give away money, food, automobiles, or other articles." While driving through the Massachusetts countryside, for example, Ford came across an elderly couple whose farmhouse had just been

destroyed in a storm. He asked a few questions, then reached into his pocket and gave the farmers all the cash he had on him, some $200.

To Ford's mind, writes Greenleaf, charitable giving should be "a private and individual act," one that is "spontaneous on the part of the giver, unanticipated and unsought by the beneficiary, and a gratuitous gesture without any element of calculation." By contrast, Ford despised virtually all institutional charity. To his mind, it "degrades recipients and drugs their self-respect," while creating a "feeling of resentment which nearly always overtakes the objects of charity." He preferred to give money to individual people, face to face and with a firm handshake.

Ford did launch a few projects of his own. In 1911, he and his wife created Valley Farm, an 80-acre home for orphan boys. During the First World War, he housed Belgian war refugees at Oughtrington Hall, and in 1915, he headed a "peace ship" that sailed for Europe with 120 American representatives, hoping to persuade the European powers to quit the conflict. He built a trade school in Detroit and a school for African Americans in Georgia. During the Great Depression, he paid for two work camps for boys.

Two of his philanthropic projects, however, were particularly conspicuous, because of both their size and their strategy. The first was the Henry Ford Hospital in Detroit. In 1914, the residents of Detroit started a subscription campaign to build a modern medical facility. Construction began, but was halted when the half-completed facility foundered in debt. Ford took over, completed the project with his own funds, served as its first president, and over the course of his lifetime gave it about $14 million. To this day, it remains one of Detroit's largest hospitals.

Ford wanted the Henry Ford Hospital to reflect his philosophy of work and self-reliance. The hospital's patients were workingmen and their families—solid citizens who wanted excellent health care but did not want to beg for charity to settle the bills. He thus subsidized some of the cost of the medical care, but took pains to ensure that patients would still have to bear some of the costs they incurred. "There are plenty of hospitals for the rich," Ford explained. "There are plenty of hospitals for the poor. There are no hospitals for those who can afford to pay only a moderate amount and yet desire to pay without a feeling that they are recipients of charity."

Ford's other major philanthropic passion was historical preservation. Many biographers have noted the irony of the industrialist who brought about the future spending money to preserve the past. His interest was whetted in 1919 when he restored his family's homestead in Dearborn. His first major preservation endeavor was the Wayside Inn, near South Sudbury,

Massachusetts, a tavern celebrated in verse by Henry Wadsworth Longfellow. To enhance the property, Ford bought up surrounding buildings and restored them, too, at a total cost of $15 million.

Ford was a lifelong collector of Americana, and in 1926 he decided to house his collection in Dearborn. For over 20 years, Ford had collected everything from locomotives to fabric samples to historic buildings—including the courthouse where Abraham Lincoln practiced law and the Wright Brothers' bicycle shop. His collection opened to the public in 1929, with President Hoover officiating. It remains one of the country's great living-history museums, known as Greenfield Village.

Ford was born in 1863, a few weeks after the Battle of Gettysburg; he died in 1947, a few months before Chuck Yeager broke the sound barrier. His life spanned from the steam engine to the jet engine—and Ford himself was responsible for much of that technological revolution. Yet his vision for philanthropy tended toward the nineteenth century. "I have no patience with professional charity or with any sort of commercialized humanitarianism," Ford wrote in 1923. "The moment human helpfulness is systematized, organized, commercialized, and professionalized, the heart of it is extinguished, and it becomes a cold and clammy thing."

➳ Martin Morse Wooster

Further information

○ Peter Collier and David Horowitz, *The Fords: An American Epic* (Simon and Schuster, 1987)

○ Garet Garrett, *The Wild Wheel: The World of Henry Ford* (Cresset Press, 1952)

○ William Greenleaf, *From These Beginnings: The Early Philanthropy of Henry and Edsel Ford, 1911-1936* (Wayne State University Press, 1964)

BENJAMIN FRANKLIN

Benjamin Franklin is perhaps the greatest polymath of American history. He was known by turns as a scientist and satirist, an inventor and entrepreneur, a printer and politician. Within his lifetime, Franklin won international admiration for his discoveries relating to electricity, optics, thermodynamics, and other elements of science. He was a skilled diplomat and distinguished public servant, an intimate of many of the eighteenth century's most significant political and intellectual leaders. He was a profligate inventor, who devised the Franklin stove, the lightning rod, bifocals, and the glass armonica—an instrument for which Mozart, Handel, and Beethoven all composed works. And not least

among his many accomplishments, Franklin is often considered the father of American civil society.

Franklin was born in Boston in 1706, the youngest of ten children. His father, a soap- and candlemaker, wanted Franklin to attend college but was only able to afford two years of formal education. At the age of 15, Benjamin was apprenticed to his brother James, a newspaperman. The brothers often clashed, and after two years Benjamin broke his apprenticeship and left New England, moving first to Philadelphia and then to London. In 1726, he returned to the City of Brotherly Love and soon began publishing the city's leading newspaper and the popular annual *Poor Richard's Almanac.*

Franklin also started methodically acquiring property. His investments in real estate in Philadelphia, plus holdings as far afield as Boston, Ohio, Georgia, and Nova Scotia, made him one of the colonies' wealthiest men. By some estimates, indeed, Franklin became one of the wealthiest men in American history.

> "It is prodigious the quantity of good that may be done by one man, if he will make a business of it," Franklin observed.

Franklin retired from active business at the age of 42, and devoted himself to public service. He rose rapidly through a series of appointments: councilman, justice of the peace, assemblyman, and deputy postmaster general for North America. During this same period, Franklin was studying and writing about the properties of electricity, for which he was awarded honorary doctorates from St. Andrews and Oxford. He eventually returned to London, where he worked at the highest levels of government, eager to advance the interests of the British Empire.

As relations with the North American colonies deteriorated, Franklin tried to ameliorate tensions, becoming an ardent patriot only after being attacked before the king's Privy Council in 1774. He returned to Philadelphia, where he helped draft and then signed the Declaration of Independence. The Continental Congress appointed him Ambassador to the Royal Court at Versailles, where he achieved what may be the most remarkable success in the history of American diplomacy: winning French support for the independence of the United States. At the conclusion of hostilities, he helped negotiate the peace treaty with Britain, returned to the United States, and represented Pennsylvania at the Constitutional Convention. He died in 1790, one of the most accomplished men of our Founding era.

Throughout his life, but most notably while living in Philadelphia, Franklin led a number of private, voluntary initiatives to enhance civil

society. "It is prodigious the quantity of good that may be done by one man, if he will make a business of it," he once observed. Historian Edmund Morgan suggested he "was behind virtually every scheme that made Philadelphia an attractive place to live."

The city was in many respects an ideal laboratory for Franklin's experiments in civil society. For most of his life, Pennsylvania lacked capable governing institutions. The province was essentially a feudal possession of the long-absent Penn family. Philadelphia nevertheless flourished—by 1750, it was a major center of transatlantic commerce and ranked among the largest cities in the British Empire—and its surplus wealth made large philanthropic initiatives possible. Civic life was further bolstered by the Quakers' strong communitarian ethic.

Back in 1727 when he was a young man, Franklin organized a group of 12 artisans—including a glazier, a shoemaker, a printer, a cabinetmaker, two surveyors, and several clerks—who began to meet for the purpose of mutual betterment. Calling themselves the Junto Club, the men met on Friday evenings to share dinner and engage in edifying conversation. "The rules that I drew up," Franklin noted in his *Autobiography*, "required that every member, in his turn, should produce one or more queries on any point of Morals, Politics, or Natural Philosophy, to be discuss'd by the company; and once in three months produce and read an essay of his own writing, on any subject he pleased." A recurring topic of conversation involved opportunities for civic improvement.

One of the Junto's first such projects was the creation of a public subscription library. Members of the group shared books among themselves and soon decided to coordinate their efforts and share it with the public. In 1731, they incorporated the Library Company of Philadelphia, the first such library in British North America. Franklin initially found it difficult to arouse public interest in the project. The problem, he realized, was "the impropriety of presenting one's self as the proposer of any useful project." He resolved to "put myself as much as I could out of sight" and thereafter adopted the lifelong habit of presenting his ideas as a "scheme of a number of friends."

In December 1736, Franklin conceived and founded the Union Fire Company, the first volunteer fire brigade in Pennsylvania. All of the company's 30 charter members pledged to protect one another's homes against fire. Each member agreed to keep at the ready two leather buckets (to carry water) and four heavy cloth bags (to rescue endangered property). Failure to maintain the required equipment resulted in a fine—five shillings per infraction—and the fire company met eight times annually to review its procedures. In 1751, Franklin convened representatives from the other

volunteer fire companies that had sprung up across the city and organized the Philadelphia Contributorship Fire Insurance Company.

Franklin also played a crucial role in the movement to bring higher education to Philadelphia. Around 1743, he began circulating his proposal for the Academy of Philadelphia. Unlike other colonial colleges, which preferred the sons of leading families, Franklin's college would be open to all deserving young men. It also differed from other schools in that it lacked a denominational affiliation. Franklin was elected president of the nascent institution, and saw it through to its opening day. The Academy of Philadelphia, later the University of Pennsylvania, opened its doors in 1750 and had 300 students within two years.

Once the academy was underway, Franklin turned his attention to founding a charitable hospital. "In 1751," he recalled in the *Autobiography*, "Dr. Thomas Bond, a particular friend of mine, conceived the idea of establishing a hospital in Philadelphia, for the reception and care of poor, sick persons, whether the inhabitants of the province or strangers—a very beneficient design, which has been ascribed to me but was originally his." When it began admitting patients in 1756, this organization became the nation's first hospital, a philanthropic enterprise that served all comers, regardless of their ability to pay.

In addition to the many institutions he founded, Franklin supported scores of others. Franklin's name, notes one of the editors of his collected writings, appears "at the head of many a subscription list, whether for the College of Philadelphia, to support the botanizing of John Bartram, or to construct a synagogue for Mikveh Israel Congregation. (He was often the most generous contributor as well.)" Although not himself a churchgoer, he funded any denomination that sought his aid. And even late in life, he was an inveterate joiner. Only a few years before his death, Franklin became the president of the Society for Promoting the Abolition of Slavery and the Relief of Negroes Unlawfully Held in Bondage.

"Liberality is not giving much," Poor Richard wrote in 1748, "but in giving wisely." Franklin was a tireless improver, and his inventiveness made lasting contributions to American philanthropy. For example, Franklin led the first effort in British North America to offer tax relief to charitable activity. Encouraged by the success of the Union Fire Company, and eager to see the model replicated throughout Philadelphia, Franklin persuaded municipal authorities to offer a property tax abatement in exchange for participation in a volunteer fire company.

Franklin likewise pioneered the concept of the matching grant. While raising funds for the Pennsylvania Hospital, he approached the colonial legislature to propose that once the hospital had raised £2,000 in private

contributions, the colonial government should contribute another £2,000 to the effort. "Every man's donation would be doubled," Franklin later wrote. "The subscriptions accordingly soon exceeded the requisite sum."

Perhaps Franklin's best-remembered charitable donation was his final bequest. Franklin left £1,000 to his native Boston and another £1,000 to his adopted Philadelphia. Both bequests were held in trust, to gather interest for 200 years. At the end of the first century, each city had the right to withdraw capital from the trust; by the close of the second, each was directed to spend it down. In 1990, the trusts were required to sunset. Philadelphia elected to spend its remaining $2 million on scholarships for local high-school students. The $5 million in Franklin's Boston trust was used to establish a trade school: the Franklin Institute of Boston.

In the first pages of *The Protestant Ethic and the Spirit of Capitalism*, Max Weber describes Franklin's essay "Advice to a Young Tradesman" as an expression of the capitalist ethos in "almost classical purity." Weber, however, recognized that Franklin did not always adhere to the unrelenting profit-maximizing ethic he seemed to champion. The example of Benjamin Franklin offers a deeply American symbiosis between energetic profit-seeking and creative not-for-profit activity, and between enlightened self-interest and charitable concern for others.

↳ *Christopher Levenick*

Further information

○ Whitfield Bell, "B. Franklin on Philanthropy" (American Philosophical Society, 2006)

○ Edmund Morgan, *Benjamin Franklin* (Yale University Press, 2002)

○ Gordon Wood, *The Americanization of Benjamin Franklin* (Penguin Books, 2005)

○ The Papers of Benjamin Franklin, franklinpapers.org/franklin

John Singer Sargent portrait (Alan Mason Chesney Medical Archives of the Johns Hopkins Medical Institutions)

MARY GARRETT

Mary Elizabeth Garrett ranks among the nation's most significant benefactors of higher education for women. Born in 1853 to wealth and privilege, Garrett was the third child of railroad tycoon John Work Garrett, the president of the Baltimore & Ohio Railroad. Mary Garrett's inheritance would make her one of the wealthiest women in the United States, but it was her business savvy and shrewd philanthropy that helped her to achieve some of the greatest social improvements of her generation.

As John Garrett's daughter, Mary could not enter the family business or exert influence on their financial empire. She nevertheless gained invaluable

business training as her father's personal secretary. She would accompany him on many of his business trips, recording his correspondence and meeting some of the most influential businessmen of the time, including titans like Andrew Carnegie, J. Pierpont Morgan, and Cornelius Vanderbilt.

John Garrett also taught his daughter by example in his philanthropy. Garrett's giving was influenced by his friend George Peabody, and he maintained close ties with Johns Hopkins, serving as a trustee of both Hopkins's university and hospital. Mary Garrett would employ the lessons she gleaned from the example of her father and his friends when she inherited nearly $2 million upon her father's death and became a philanthropist in her own right.

She relied heavily on her intimate circle of friends, known as the "Friday Evening." The intellectually curious group included Carey Thomas, Mamie Gwinn, Elizabeth "Bessie" King, and Julia Rogers—all but one of them daughters of trustees of Johns Hopkins University, the hospital, or both. It was with this group that Garrett collaborated on her two key philanthropic achievements: the Bryn Mawr School and Johns Hopkins Medical School.

> Garrett cleverly mastered the art of "coercive philanthropy" to promote high standards and fairness at the same time.

The Bryn Mawr School was Garrett's first philanthropic undertaking. The Friday Evening group was appalled by the lack of a serious college preparatory school for girls in Baltimore. Garrett's inheritance provided the means to remedy the situation. They decided to act.

They named the new preparatory school for Bryn Mawr College in Philadelphia, and acquired the school's permission to do so. (They also maintained close ties to the college, and Bryn Mawr school students were required to pass the college entrance examination in order to graduate.) Garrett not only provided the necessary funds to establish and build the school, she also closely oversaw the project. Her hands-on involvement extended to the selection of gym equipment and artwork for the school, which was located but a few blocks from Garrett's home in Baltimore. The Friday Evening served as the governing body of the school. Garrett was its president.

Garrett and the Friday Evening then set their sights higher—the education of women at Johns Hopkins University. Garrett first attempted to open the doors of Johns Hopkins to women in 1887 by offering the university $35,000 to establish a coeducational school of science. The university

president and trustees rejected her offer. Just a few years later, however, Johns Hopkins found itself on unsure financial footing. The opening of its medical school had been delayed due to insufficient funds. The Friday Evening saw an opportunity.

Garrett enlisted her friends and sought support from other influential women around the country (including Frances Morgan, Jane Stanford, and Caroline Harrison) to raise funds to approach the university with a new offer. Garrett offered the trustees $100,000 (half of which she contributed personally) to pay for the opening of the medical school on one condition: that men and women would be admitted on equal standing. The board accepted the offer, but told the group that the school could not open with less than $500,000.

When the university and the newly formed Women's Medical Fund Committee struggled to approach this number, Garrett stepped in and covered the difference with a donation of $307,000. But her additional funding came with additional conditions. These new conditions required that the medical school be a full graduate program leading to a medical degree and that all applicants be required to have a bachelor's degree in the field of science. (Neither of these stipulations were normal for medical schools at the time.)

Garrett's funding and her clearly outlined conditions not only opened medical education to America's women, it also turned Johns Hopkins into the first modern medical school in the United States. In his history of the school, Alan Chesney concludes: "To this lady, more than any other single person, save only Johns Hopkins himself, does the School of Medicine owe its being."

Throughout the rest of her life, Garrett would continue to use her wealth and influence to promote women's education and opportunity. She gave generously to Bryn Mawr College and later became a major funder of the cause of women's suffrage. Her final years were spent at Bryn Mawr with her close friend Carey Thomas, who was president of the college, to whom Garrett left her fortune upon her death in 1915.

For her bargain with the Johns Hopkins medical school, Garrett is sometimes criticized as America's greatest "coercive philanthropist." William Osler, one of the school's four founding physicians, famously replied: "It was a pleasure to be bought."

ᴗ Kari Barbic

Further information

- Alan Chesney, *The Johns Hopkins Hospital and the Johns Hopkins School of Medicine, A Chronicle* (Johns Hopkins Press, 1943)
- Helen Horowitz, *The Power and Passion of M. Carey Thomas* (Alfred Knopf, 1991)
- Kathleen Sander, *Mary Elizabeth Garrett: Society and Philanthropy in the Gilded Age* (Johns Hopkins Press, 2008)

J. PAUL GETTY

J. Paul Getty was one of America's most successful oilmen who was, if anything, an even more successful art collector. Getty acquired a number of oil companies before discovering and mining major oil deposits in Saudi Arabia, a feat which made him for some years the richest living American. Getty then used his fortune to assemble one of the world's greatest collections of art and antiquities, a collection that today forms the core of the Getty Villa and the Getty Museum in Los Angeles.

Jean Paul Getty was born in Minneapolis in 1892. His father, George Getty, was an insurance-agent-turned-wildcatter, and J. Paul grew up wealthy. Sent to Oxford by his father, J. Paul became a committed Anglophile—indeed, he spent the last 25 years of his life in a sixteenth-century Tudor estate near Guildford. After college, the younger Getty returned to the States, where he worked in his father's oil fields before striking out on his own. He made his first $1 million at age 24.

> Getty was haughty, cheap, and cruel. But his great philanthropic achievements in presenting classical art to the public were something nobler.

Despite his son's manifest talents, George never quite trusted him. J. Paul was a serial womanizer—"A lasting relationship with a woman is only possible if you are a business failure," he proclaimed—and George worried his son's string of hasty marriages and casual divorces (three by the time George died in 1930) would destroy the family business. J. Paul received just $500,000 of his father's $10 million estate.

Luckily for J. Paul, the Great Depression was a buyer's market, and even a diminished inheritance could go a long way toward acquiring cash-poor businesses. Getty began systematically acquiring assets. He started with oil companies: Pacific Western, Tidewater, Skelly. Then he bought Manhattan's Hotel Pierre; later he set up a realty company. During the Second World War, the Navy asked him to take over and turn around Spartan Aircraft, an aircraft-parts supplier; he did, and after the war made it a mobile-home manufacturer.

The majority of Getty's fortune came from an investment he made in 1949. Getty obtained a lease from King Ibn Saud to drill on a sandswept tract of barren land adjoining Kuwait. In exchange for $9 million up front and $1 million annually, Getty purchased exclusive mineral rights for 60

years. Four years and $18 million of sunk costs later, Getty struck oil. The wells produced such quantities that by 1957, *Fortune* placed Getty's net worth somewhere between $700 million and $1 billion. "A billion dollars isn't what it used to be," Getty quipped, but it did not change the fact that he was now the wealthiest citizen in the land.

After his success in Saudi Arabia, thousands of unsolicited requests for money poured in every week. They grated on him, not least because he had little use for what he considered soft-headed humanitarianism. "If I were convinced that by giving away my fortune I could make a real contribution toward solving the problems of world poverty, I'd give away 99.5 percent of all I have immediately," he wrote in one of his many articles on wealth and business. "But a hard-eyed appraisal of the situation convinces me this is not the case.... However admirable the work of the best charitable foundation, it would accustom people to the passive acceptance of money."

He was similarly suspicious of higher education. He was once approached by several members of the Rockefeller family, who urged him to make a large contribution and suggested that he consider giving to an institute of higher education. Getty sat silently for a moment. Then he burst into a tirade, demanding to know why the Rockefellers had not expelled the socialists from the University of Chicago.

If charitable giving could do little to remedy poverty and was a dubious way to promote learning, to Getty's mind it still had one distinct advantage: it could help preserve the artistic achievements of Western civilization. Philanthropy provided the means by which his private collection could become a public resource, which was precisely what Getty hoped to do with it. "As I learned in my youth," he wrote, "a gift—whether to the public or an individual—is something given of one's own volition and without strings attached. Otherwise, it is no longer a gift but a business transaction. And if I had wanted to do business with my collection, I would have gone all-out and sold it off."

A serious art collector since the 1930s, Getty had a good command of art history and criticism. He wrote a history of nineteenth-century Europe and was fluent in German, French, and Italian. He could speak passable Arabic, Greek, Russian, and Spanish, and he was able to spot-read Latin and ancient Greek. He was disciplined in his collecting, restricting himself largely to a few categories: Greek and Roman marbles and bronzes, Renaissance paintings, sixteenth-century Persian carpets, and eighteenth-century French furniture and tapestries. He owned three of the "Elgin Marbles" and acquired the "Lansdowne Herakles," a first-century A.D. Roman sculpture that was a personal favorite of the Emperor Hadrian.

Getty had exhibited some of his art in his California mansion, but in 1968 he decided to house it in a permanent museum. He told his trustees: "I refuse to pay for one of those concrete-bunker type structures that are the fad among museum architects—nor for some tinted-glass-and-stainless-steel monstrosity." Getty also insisted that his museum have free admission and free parking. (The museum continues to offer free admission but has reversed Getty's latter commitment.) He followed its construction closely, even once berating his architect for the unauthorized purchase of a $17 electric pencil sharpener.

The original Getty Museum, now the Getty Villa in Malibu, was completed in 1974. A reproduction of a Roman villa, it is considered a masterful reproduction of classical architecture. Getty, aged 82 and in poor health when the building opened, never saw it complete. On his death in 1976, he left most of his estate to the museum, and after a nine-year probate fight (which included the 1984 sale of Getty Oil to Texaco for $10 billion), it became the best-endowed museum in the world. In 1997, the J. Paul Getty Trust opened a second facility, the Getty Center, at a cost of $1.3 billion. With stunning views of Los Angeles, this Brentwood museum houses the collection's non-antiquarian holdings, as well as a research library, conservation laboratories, sculpture gardens, and educational facilities.

J. Paul Getty was haughty ("One is very nearly always let down by underlings," he often said), cheap (visitors to his estate had to use a pay phone), and cruel (when a grandson was kidnapped, he paid only as much ransom as was tax-deductible: $2.2 of the $17 million). But his great philanthropic achievement aspired to something nobler. "In learning about ancient Greek and Roman art," Getty wrote, "one cannot help but also learn about the civilizations and the people who produced the art. This will unquestionably serve to broaden the individual's horizons and, by increasing his knowledge of past civilizations, greatly aid him in knowing and understanding his own."

☛ *Martin Morse Wooster*

Further information

○ J. Paul Getty, *As I See It: The Autobiography of J. Paul Getty* (Prentice-Hall, 1976)
○ J. Paul Getty, *The Joys of Collecting* (Hawthorn Books, 1965)
○ Robert Lenzner, *The Great Getty: The Life and Loves of J. Paul Getty* (Crown, 1986)
○ Russell Miller, *The House of Getty* (J. Curley, 1987)

STEPHEN GIRARD

Stephen Girard amassed enormous wealth as a merchant and banker; if his wealth is viewed as a percentage of GDP, he was one of the five richest men in American history. That fortune was dedicated to an extensive program of philanthropy. Girard was the patron of a variety of charitable causes in his adopted home of Philadelphia, most notably offering comfort to the sick, at real personal risk, during the city's yellow-fever outbreaks. During the War of 1812, Girard staked virtually everything he owned on bond purchases for the federal government; in doing so, he saved the nation's credit, less in pursuit of profit than as an act of patriotism. And his final bequest funded the creation of a college for orphaned boys, which was at the time the best endowed charity in the country.

Born in Bordeaux in 1750, Girard was the son of a sea captain and merchant. At 14 years of age, he followed in his father's footsteps, serving as an apprentice pilot on a voyage to the West Indies. For over a decade, he plied the seas, traveling between France, the West Indies, and North America. In 1776, Girard moved to Philadelphia, where he started his own shipping business. He instituted a number of revolutionary business practices, including warehousing goods until he was satisfied with prices and offering ship captains a straight wage rather than a percentage, thereby encouraging speed rather than market timing. His business expanded worldwide, and his ships traded in China and South America as well as Europe and the Caribbean.

When the charter of the First Bank of the United States expired in 1811, Girard purchased a majority of its shares (as well as its headquarters on Philadelphia's South Third Street). The timing was fortuitous. Over the next few years, the newly established financier effectively saved the U.S. Treasury.

As the War of 1812 ground on, confidence in American credit collapsed. In late 1813, Albert Gallatin, Secretary of the Treasury, was only able to sell $6 million worth of a $16 million bond issue. Gallatin approached Girard in Philadelphia and John Jacob Astor in New York, pleading with them to purchase the remainder. Girard and Astor consented, on the condition that the Madison administration agree to re-charter the Bank of the United States. It was not philanthropy in the strict sense—Girard ultimately turned a tidy profit—but it was nevertheless a saving grace to the American people, undertaken largely from patriotic motives, with a high likelihood of costing Girard his fortune.

During his lifetime, Girard supported a wide variety of civic associations in his adopted hometown of Philadelphia. He contributed

to (among many other groups) the Pennsylvania Hospital, the Society for Relief of Distressed Masters of Ships and Their Widows, the Société de Bienfaisançe Francaise, the Public School Fund of Philadelphia, the Pennsylvania Institution for the Deaf and Dumb, the Fuel Saving Society, and the Orphan Society. He joined the Masons, and donated his time and money to its various charitable activities.

Such close, personal involvement was evident in the charitable efforts for which Girard was best known during his lifetime. Girard was a tireless leader in the efforts to contain and combat the yellow fever epidemics that hit Philadelphia in 1793, 1797-98, 1802, and 1820. Nineteenth-century medicine was all but helpless against the terrifying disease, which killed 5,000 city residents in 1793 alone. Those who could afford to, simply fled the city.

Not Girard. When epidemics broke out, he stayed in Philadelphia, leading relief efforts, funding hospital operations, and providing care for individuals—even bathing and feeding the dying. He routinely put his personal and business affairs to the side during epidemics. "As soon as things have quieted down a little you may be sure I shall take up my work with all the activity in my power," he wrote to a friend in 1793. "But, for the moment, I have devoted all my time and my person, as well as my little fortune, to the relief of my fellow citizens."

> One of the five richest men in American history, Stephen Girard was known for his personal involvement in charitable efforts— like throwing himself into care for victims during periodic yellow-fever outbreaks at great personal risk.

But Girard is perhaps best remembered today for his final bequest. Composed five years before his death at age 81, it left $140,000 to family members, lifelong income to several household servants, and $800,000 for various civic improvements in Philadelphia. An additional $1 million was divided among many of the charities he had supported throughout his life. However, the largest share by far—some $7 million—was earmarked for the creation of "a college for poor white male orphans." (Many of the children he hoped to help had been left parent-less by the Yellow Fever epidemics.)

It was a project that had long been close to Girard's heart. There is evidence in his papers that Girard was planning the school as early as

1807—fully 24 years before his death. His painstaking instructions for the school suggest that considerable time and attention went into the plans. He spelled out a preference, for instance, that students be taught French or Spanish rather than Greek or Latin.

Girard's heirs challenged the validity of the will, arguing that it unlawfully excluded ministers from the college. The case went to the Supreme Court, where Justice Joseph Story ruled against the heirs. His opinion was a landmark ruling in the history of American philanthropy, which reaffirmed the principle of donor intent.

When Girard College opened its doors in 1848, its endowment was larger than that of any other educational institution. The school has since graduated 30,000 of the most vulnerable students imaginable. "For seven years," reflected one graduate in a 1997 *Wall Street Journal* op-ed, Stephen Girard "fed, clothed, sheltered, and educated me. He bought the milk and cereal, baked the casseroles and the cookies, provided the soap and toothbrushes, furnished the sneakers and baseball gloves, darned the socks and sweaters, sent me to the barber and the doctor, provided the books and lab supplies, and much more."

— Monica Klem

Further information

- ○ "The Father of Philanthropy," *Wall Street Journal* essay, girardcollege.edu/page.cfm?p=863
- ○ Cheesman Herrick, *Stephen Girard: Founder* (Girard College, 1923)
- ○ John McMaster, *The Life and Times of Stephen Girard, Mariner and Merchant* (J. B. Lippincott Co., 1918)
- ○ George Wilson, *Stephen Girard: The Life And Times of America's First Tycoon* (Da Capo Press, 1996)

EDWARD HARKNESS

Edward Harkness is one of the least well-known of the major American philanthropists of the first half of the twentieth century. His relative obscurity is all the more surprising given the scale of his charitable giving; he was among the very largest donors of his era. The John Rockefellers, father and son, each gave away over $500 million, while Andrew Carnegie's gifts amounted to $325 million. They were followed by a handful of contemporaries whose lifetime giving exceeded $100 million: James Duke, George Eastman, Nettie McCormick—and Edward Harkness.

Harkness inherited his wealth; he was the last surviving heir of a massive fortune created by his father's early investment in Standard Oil. His privileges

as a child did not prevent him from becoming a serious, orderly man. "A dollar misspent is a dollar lost," he often said. Harkness appeared to take his greatest pleasure in philanthropy, which was the principal occupation of his lifetime.

Biographer James Wooster estimates that Harkness gave away roughly $129 million before his death in 1940. (Wooster only counted gifts of more than $5,000, so Harkness's total was almost certainly higher.) Harkness dedicated his giving to three principal causes: fine arts, health care, and top educational institutions. Wooster concludes that Harkness is unknown today because his philanthropy was largely guided by a "passion for anonymity."

Born in 1874, Edward was the youngest of five children born to Stephen Harkness, a prominent Cleveland merchant who had success in distilled spirits. In 1867, Stephen agreed to invest $100,000 in a fledgling company headed by an ambitious young man named John Rockefeller. When Standard Oil offered its first 10,000 shares of stock, Rockefeller ended up with 2,667 shares to Harkness's 1,334. (After several recapitalizations, Harkness's ownership evened out at around 10 percent.) As Standard Oil boomed, Harkness remained a silent partner.

> Support for higher education and cultural institutions were central elements of the philanthropy of the Harkness family, heirs to Standard Oil money.

In 1888, Stephen Harkness died without a will, leaving a $150 million fortune. His wife, Anna, inherited a "widow's third," which was administered by two of her sons, Charles and Edward. Anna had for many years quietly supported local churches and charitable organizations, but eventually became a leading philanthropist in her own right. Edward's initial work in philanthropy came from serving as the manager of his mother's large-scale charitable giving.

When Charles died in 1916, Anna and Edward gave $3 million to Yale University for the construction of Memorial Quadrangle in his honor; four years later, they gave the college another $3 million to increase faculty salaries. Support for higher education and cultural institutions remained a central element of the family's philanthropy, with notable contributions to the Tuskegee Institute, Metropolitan Museum of Art, Museum of Natural History, New York Public Library, and New York Zoological Society. In 1922, Edward and Anna Harkness acquired a 22-acre site in Washington Heights and donated the land to Columbia-Presbyterian Hospital (later merged into New York-Presbyterian). As late as 1992, undeveloped land from this donation was being turned into

auxiliary facilities for the hospital.

Perhaps the most visible achievement of Edward and Anna Harkness was the creation of the Commonwealth Fund in 1918. Endowed with $10 million, the fund was chartered with the almost comically broad mandate of doing "something for the welfare of mankind." Among its first commitments was support for medical research, and the Commonwealth Fund supported the work of scientists pursuing (among other things) the causes of hypertension, the treatment and prevention of pneumonia, and the causes of tooth decay.

The Harkness family traced its roots to Dumfriesshire, and Edward retained a lifelong love of Great Britain. In 1925, Harkness set up a series of fellowships, administered by the Commonwealth Fund, to enable graduate students from Britain and its dominions to study in the United States. One of the first scholarships went to Alistair Cooke, who subsequently spent decades at the BBC explaining America to the British listening public. Harkness supported a range of other charities in the United Kingdom. In 1930, during the depths of the Great Depression, he donated £2 million to create the Pilgrim Trust, which to this day preserves historic sites, offers university scholarships, and funds treatment for those experiencing drug and alcohol addiction.

With encouragement from his wife, Mary Harkness, Edward became a leading patron of the Metropolitan Museum of Art. They were lifelong collectors of Egyptian art and antiquaries, and their contributions to the Met, begun in 1913, were rivaled only by those of J. P. Morgan. In 1917, they donated a ceramic turquoise hippopotamus from the Middle Kingdom; it has since been the museum's unofficial mascot, affectionately nicknamed "William."

Perhaps Harkness's most significant accomplishments were in the field of elite education. He was a benefactor of America's most prestigious secondary schools, including his alma mater St. Paul's, Lawrenceville, Taft, Hill, and especially Phillips Exeter. He grabbed headlines in 1930 with a $5.8 million donation to Phillips Exeter, a gift that capped class size at 12 students, all of whom were to share a common table with their instructor. The "Harkness Table"—with, as he put it, "no corners to hide behind"—remains a core element of the school's pedagogy.

The same concern for collegiality informed Harkness's extensive giving to higher education. (Beneficiaries included Harvard, Yale, Columbia, Brown, Oberlin, Connecticut College, and scores of others.) He saw American universities adopting the model of the large German research institutions, and feared that students were losing the sociability of collegiate life. Harkness's preferred solution was to promote the British model, in which a university was divided into smaller residential houses where students would

live, dine, study, and gather.

In 1926, having already endowed the drama school, he approached Yale, offering to donate $12 million to build a series of residential colleges on the Oxbridge model. After a year of negotiations, Yale declined. Harkness immediately met with Harvard president Lawrence Lowell, offering to fund a similar scheme of residential houses. "It took Lowell about 10 seconds to accept," Samuel Eliot Morison noted in a 1942 history of Harvard. "Thus a Yale man became the greatest benefactor to Harvard in our entire history." Harvard built seven residential houses with the Harkness gift—and Yale soon after accepted $15.8 million for the construction of eight residential houses, which remain an integral part of campus life.

"One of the most difficult tasks in the world is giving away money wisely," wrote Lowell, in a tribute shortly after Harkness's death, "and philanthropic multimillionaires usually, and quite correctly, avoid it by forming a board or committee to do the work for them. Not so Mr. Harkness."

~ Martin Morse Wooster

Further information

- Lewis Perry, "Edward and Mary Harkness" (*Bulletin of the Metropolitan Museum of Art*, October 1951)
- George Pierson, *Yale: The University College, 1921-1937* (Yale Press, 1955)
- James Wooster, *Edward S. Harkness* (Commonwealth Fund, 1949)

MILTON HERSHEY

Milton Hershey made milk chocolate a treat all Americans could afford, and in the process cooked up a great fortune. Hershey used his wealth to beautify his company's hometown and to build a remarkable orphanage that would take poor boys, give them a good home and sturdy lessons in character, and teach them to make their way in the world.

Hershey was born in Hockensville, Pennsylvania, in 1857. His parents had been raised as Reformed Mennonites, and young Hershey grew up among the devout, thrifty, and hardworking Pennsylvania Dutch. But his father was a dreamer and a drinker, and his family suffered from neglect. Young Milton grew up shoeless and hungry. Eventually his parents separated. Later in life, when asked about his gifts to orphans, Hershey would remind people, "I was a poor boy myself once."

Hershey took his first job at age 14, apprenticing with a small, German-language newspaper in Lancaster. He hated the work and promptly got himself fired. Then he took a job at Joseph Royer's Ice Cream Parlor,

where he learned the basics of candy-making. By the time he was 25, he had launched two businesses, a cough-drop company and a candy company. (Both failed.) His third attempt, Lancaster Caramel, was vastly more successful. By the early 1890s, he had 700 employees and three processing plants.

Everything changed in 1893. Hershey visited the World's Columbian Exposition in Chicago, where he first laid eyes on the industrial equipment of J. M. Lehmann of Dresden, Germany. Lehmann had built a full-scale chocolate-manufacturing plant, from roasting-oven for the cocoa beans to forming-presses for the molten chocolate. "The caramel business is a fad," Hershey declared, and he paid $20,000 to buy every single piece of equipment that Lehmann had on display. When he left Chicago, the machinery went with him.

Hershey began making chocolate alongside caramel, all the while systematically experimenting with new recipes. By 1900, he was confident he had a winning product, and he sold the caramel business for $1 million. With his new liquidity, he wanted to build a factory that could mass-produce milk chocolate. Three years later, he broke ground near Derry Church, right in the middle of Pennsylvania dairy farming country.

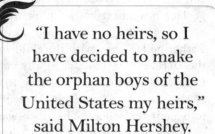

"I have no heirs, so I have decided to make the orphan boys of the United States my heirs," said Milton Hershey.

Hershey did not discover milk chocolate. What he discovered was how to make it affordable. He achieved the feat through gains from efficiency, populating his plant with the latest technology and designing the facility on the basis of Frederick Taylor's principles of industrial efficiency. The result was a steep cut in the per-unit cost of producing milk chocolate. Before Hershey opened his production lines, it was a delicacy. After Hershey, a milk chocolate bar could be enjoyed by anyone with a spare nickel.

Success came instantly. In its first year of operations, the company netted $1 million; five years later, with the introduction of the Hershey's Kiss, profits topped $2 million. As money poured in, Hershey worked to build a model city around his rural factory. He sponsored a nationwide contest to come up with a name for the town. (Entries included Ulikit, Etabit, Chocolate City, and St. Milton.) The winner was Hersheykoko, which the Post Office rejected as too commercial. So the town became Hershey, Pennsylvania.

Hershey oversaw most every aspect of the town's construction: tree-lined streets, handsome homes, extensive public transportation, and first-rate public schools. In 1907, he opened a park (today known as Hershey Park); in 1915, he built the nation's largest free private zoo. During the Great Depression, he launched a massive building campaign, something like a privately funded New Deal program. More than 600 men worked to build the Hershey Hotel, as well as a community building, sports arena, community theater, and high school.

As the Depression ground on, Hershey gave $20,000 to each of the town's five churches in 1935 to help them relieve the suffering of their congregants. That same year, he established the M. S. Hershey Foundation to support local educational and cultural charities. One of the foundation's first projects was creating the Hershey Gardens, a major botanical garden completed in 1942. The foundation also built (and still manages) the Hershey Theatre, the Hershey Community Archives, and a historical museum dedicated to the life and achievements of Milton Hershey.

Hershey's best-known philanthropic accomplishment, however, was his orphanage. Originally located on his homestead, it surrounded Milton and Catherine Hershey with the children they were never able to have. In 1909, the Hersheys executed a tightly constructed deed of trust for the Hershey Industrial School. In November 1918, they secretly placed all of his shares of the Hershey Chocolate Company into a trust whose sole purpose was to benefit the school. The stock was worth roughly $60 million; by way of comparison, notes biographer Michael D'Antonio, in 1918 Coca-Cola sold for $25 million.

Although Hershey made his gift in 1918, he did not reveal it until a 1923 interview with the *New York Times*. "I am 66 years old and do not need much money," Hershey said. "I have no heirs, so I have decided to make the orphan boys of the United States my heirs." Hershey explained that the Industrial School would provide "a thorough common school education, supplemented by instruction in the useful crafts"—blacksmithing, farming, the "rudiments of electrical work."

His interviewer then asked about college preparation for the students. "We do not intend to turn out a race of professors," Hershey replied, although he allowed that boys "of special promise" would be prepared for higher education. "The thing that a poor boy needs is knowledge of a trade, a way to make a living. We will provide him with the groundwork. Of what use is Latin when a fellow has to hoe a patch or run a lathe?"

Hershey was a constant presence at the school before his death in 1945. Since then, with an endowment worth $12 billion in 2017, the Milton Hershey

School has become one of the wealthiest educational facilities in the United States. It offers a superb boarding-school education to 2,000 elementary and secondary students, all from troubled backgrounds.

Hershey died with very little personal wealth, mostly his home and its furnishings. He had given away everything else during his lifetime. "I never could see," he once observed, "what happiness a rich man gets from contemplating a life of acquisition only, with a cold and legal distribution of his wealth after he passes away."

— Martin Morse Wooster

Further information

- Joel Brenner, *The Emperors of Chocolate: Inside the Secret World of Hershey and Mars* (Random House, 1999)
- Michael D'Antonio, *Hershey: Milton S. Hershey's Extraordinary Life of Wealth, Empire, and Utopian Dreams* (Simon and Schuster, 2006)
- Joseph Snavely, *The Hershey Story* (Privately published, 1950)

CONRAD HILTON

Conrad Hilton was born on Christmas Day, 1887, on the banks of the Rio Grande in the tiny frontier town of San Antonio, New Mexico Territory. Connie, as he was called, was the second child of eight, the oldest boy of A. H. "Gus" Hilton and Mary Laufersweiler Hilton.

From his father, Hilton learned the imperative of hard work. Gus Hilton was a trader and merchant, which in those days and in that place meant engaging any and all legitimate business that came his way. He sold goods behind the counter of his general store, at mining outposts, trappers' encampments, or the haciendas of old Spanish ranchers. As Hilton would later write of his father, work was "precisely as necessary to him as food and air, an ever present refuge in trouble.... He never connected it with the sweat of the brow nor the punishment of the sons of Adam. He was all for the joy of the thing." So it would be with the younger Hilton.

From his mother, a devout Catholic, Hilton came to view prayer as no less a necessity and no less a sanctuary than work. "Some men jump out windows, some quit," his mother told him during the Great Depression. "Some go to church. Pray Connie. It's the best investment you'll ever make." Even in the darkest, most difficult moments of his life, Hilton always found strength and consolation in his faith.

In 1912, New Mexico became the 47th state in the Union, and at age 23 Hilton was elected to the state's first legislature. But politics did not

much appeal to the budding entrepreneur, who decided two years later to try his hand at banking. That endeavor was interrupted by the start of World War I, throughout which he served as an Army officer. Then, with $5,011 to his name, he moved to the booming oil fields of Texas, where he hoped to buy a bank and resume his pre-war career. What he bought instead was the dilapidated Mobley Hotel in Cisco, Texas. It was Conrad Hilton's "first love."

In just 20 years, Hilton's hospitality business grew from small reclamation projects to newly constructed million-dollar high-rises. Like many entrepreneurs, his business acumen sprang less from acquisitiveness than from a spirit of ingenuity, creativity, and awe in the face of human possibilities. By 1929, he owned hotels all over Texas, with plans to expand beyond the Lone Star State.

The crash of 1929 nearly erased all of it. By 1933, Hilton retained only one hotel, and that barely. Yet he survived.

Recovery was slow at first: paying down debts and reacquiring lost properties. But as the Depression lifted, and the post-war boom started in earnest, the Hilton Hotel Company reached new heights. In 1946, a corporation was formed, and a year later, it became the first hotel traded on the New York Stock Exchange. In 1949, Hilton purchased the "Greatest of Them All": the Waldorf-Astoria. In 1954, Hilton Hotels Corporation acquired the Hotels Statler Company for $111 million, the largest real-estate transaction in history at that time. Hilton eventually owned 188 hotels, including the Palmer House in Chicago, the Mayflower in D.C., and both the Plaza and the Waldorf-Astoria in New York City. Hilton hotels could be found in 38 American cities and 54 locations overseas.

The Depression had taught Hilton humility, and reinforced in him the importance of faith. "When everything material failed," he wrote, "faith remained the only gilt-edged security." Moreover, the Depression impressed upon Hilton the trust and good will of those who had seen him through his most trying times. A man whose success had been made possible by so many others could not help but return the kindness.

In 1944, Hilton started the Conrad N. Hilton Foundation. The day after the fund was established, Hilton received a request from one of the Catholic Sisters of Loretto, who had taught him his catechism as a child in New Mexico. She was raising money to build a new gymnasium and hoped he might help. "Dear Sister," Hilton replied, "I received your letter of recent date. I am sure you have been praying extra hard, for your campaign has begun and ended." There would be more such letters to follow.

Over the next 35 years, the Conrad N. Hilton Foundation would award many small grants, with special solicitude for the work of Catholic sisters

and those who help children. Even more than through his foundation, Hilton gave generously from his personal wealth and talents. In his last will and testament, Hilton wrote:

> Be ever watchful for the opportunity to shelter little children with the umbrella of your charity; be generous to their schools, their hospitals, and their places of worship. For, as they must bear the burdens of our mistakes, so are they in their innocence the repositories of our hopes for the upward progress of humanity. Give aid to their protectors and defenders, the Sisters, who devote their love and life's work for the good of mankind, for they appeal especially to me as being deserving of help from the Foundation.

In addition to his support for Catholic education, Hilton was generous to charitable health-care providers, both Catholic and non-Catholic. He led the capital campaign for St. John's Health Center in Santa Monica, California. In 1972, Hilton committed $10 million to build a research center at the Mayo Clinic.

"Charity," wrote Conrad Hilton, is "the great channel through which the mercy of God is passed on to mankind."

Hilton was a staunch opponent of communism. As he bluntly told the National Conference of Christians and Jews in 1950: "The essence of communism is the death of the individual and the burial of his remains in a collective mass." Hilton firmly believed that his hospitality business could be an example of cooperation and goodwill in a perilously divided world. "Each of our hotels," Hilton said, "is a 'Little America,' not as a symbol of bristling power, but as a friendly center where men of many nations and of good will may speak the language of peace." Hilton also made sure his international hotels sourced local materials, and trained and hired local workers. Display the decency and goodness of American values in the communists' own backyard, Hilton thought, and the world would note the contrast.

Hilton believed that prayer was a vital force in what he called the "Battle for Freedom." On July 4, 1952, at the height of the Korean War, he published in magazines across the country a humble prayer for peace and forgiveness in a darkening world, titled "America on Its Knees." It received an overwhelming response, and a year later, Hilton hosted the first National Prayer Breakfast, alongside President Eisenhower. That event has become a Washington, and

national, institution.

When Hilton died in 1979, he left virtually his entire fortune to the foundation. "Charity is a supreme virtue," he wrote, "and the great channel through which the mercy of God is passed on to mankind. It is the virtue that unites men and inspires their noblest efforts."

ʙ Stephen White

Further information

○ Conrad Hilton, *Be My Guest* (Prentice Hall, 1958)

○ The Hilton Legacy, hiltonfoundation.org/images/stories/About/Publications/ LegacyBooks/Hilton_History_Book_Final.pdf

IMA HOGG

Ima Hogg ranks among the best-known and most admired philanthropists in the history of Texas. For much of her life, she was affectionately known as the "First Lady of Texas," owing to her family's long tradition of public service. Her grandfather helped write the Texas state constitution and her father, James "Big Jim" Hogg, went on to become the Lone Star State's first native-born governor. Her service to Texas was principally philanthropic—made possible by the discovery of large oil deposits beneath her family's plantation.

Born in 1882 in Mineola, Texas, Ima Hogg would spend most of her life contending with wisecracks that she had sisters named "Ura" and "Hoosa." (She didn't.) She had one older brother, William, and two younger ones, Michael and Thomas. At the age of 13, she cared for her mother as she died of tuberculosis, and ten years later nursed her father as he struggled unsuccessfully to overcome injuries sustained in a train accident. After her mother's death, she took over father's household and cared for her younger brothers. The Hoggs were a tight-knit family, and, for nearly 70 years, she was its head.

The inheritance Ima received upon her father's death in 1906 made her financially independent; he had made a small fortune through his work as an attorney, as well as investments in land and oil. But the Hoggs' philanthropic activity was greatly accelerated by the discovery of oil on the West Columbia property left to them by their father. In 1919, a supply of oil that would yield his children $225,000 per month was discovered.

Ima's first philanthropic efforts centered on fostering an appreciation for the arts in Texas. Early in her life she had hoped to become a concert pianist, and spent two years at the National Conservatory of Music in New York and two more in Vienna and Berlin studying piano. But she

returned to Houston in 1909, where she began teaching piano instead. Increasingly her interests centered on being actively involved in civic life. In 1913, she helped to found the Houston Symphony Orchestra, and in 1917 became president of its board. She continued to support the symphony for the rest of her life and worked to increase public exposure to music and the arts. When elected to the Houston Board of Education in 1943 she arranged symphony concerts for public school audiences, and increased the offerings of music and art classes.

The Hogg family's philanthropic efforts centered on their home state. An avid collector of early American antique furniture and decorative art, Ima declined to lend the pieces she acquired to East Coast exhibitions, saying, "They've got plenty of these things up there." She placed much of her collection at Bayou Bend, a house she built in 1927 as a home for herself and her brothers Will and Mike in the River Oaks neighborhood of Houston. Nearly 30 years later, after the deaths of both brothers, she decided to give the house to the Houston Museum of the Fine Arts, along with a $750,000 endowment. It opened as the MFA Bayou Bend Collection and Gardens in 1966.

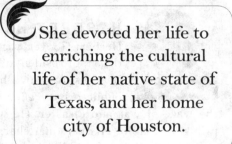

She devoted her life to enriching the cultural life of her native state of Texas, and her home city of Houston.

But of all the causes Ima supported, the one closest to her heart was probably the promotion of mental health. She had a lifelong concern for those who were then called "mentally disturbed," and, at a time and in a place where it was not especially popular, she promoted the study and treatment of mental illness. Her first major effort took place in 1929, when she founded the Houston Child Guidance Clinic. Open to people of all races and income levels, it represented a real advance in the field of child psychology. She would later say that, of all her endeavors, it was the one that satisfied her most.

When her brother Will died unexpectedly in 1930, he left $2.5 million to the University of Texas, but he was unclear about how the money ought to be used. In response, Ima and Mike put forward a plan for the Hogg Foundation for Mental Hygiene, which came into being in 1940. Administered by the University of Texas, its initial purpose was to provide mental-health education campaigns in small towns. In 1964, she founded the Ima Hogg Foundation, also administered by the University of Texas, to fund projects benefiting children's mental health in Harris County; it would eventually be the primary beneficiary of her will.

Ima also contributed to the preservation of Texas history. In 1953, she

helped to found and was appointed a member of what became the Texas Historical Commission. She lovingly restored and donated to the state of Texas several properties owned by her family.

Ima Hogg died in 1975 at the age of 93. A woman of unfailing poise, she once caught a burglar in her bedroom—and gave him the name and telephone number of a man who would give the thief a job. ("He didn't look like a bad man," she would later say.) A woman of great generosity, she devoted her life to preserving and enriching the cultural life of her native state, and to improving the education and mental health of Texan children and their families.

Monica Klem

Further information

○ Mary Kelley, *The Foundations of Texan Philanthropy* (Texas A&M University Press, 2004)

○ Gwendolyn Neeley, *Miss Ima and the Hogg Family* (Hendrick-Long Publishing Company, 1992)

HERBERT HOOVER

Herbert Hoover was an entrepreneur, philanthropist, and the 31st President of the United States. The humanitarian services for which he is perhaps best remembered were public-private efforts to relieve misery and suffering in the wake of war and disaster. He was also a significant philanthropist in his own right. His personal charitable giving centered on two areas: character-building for children, and creating one of the nation's oldest and most distinguished think tanks, the Hoover Institution on War, Revolution, and Peace.

Hoover was born in 1874 in the small village of West Branch, Iowa. Orphaned at a young age, he went to live with an uncle in Oregon. His character was shaped by the Quaker faith, from which he gained a strong sense of moral virtue, an appreciation for voluntary service, and a relentless work ethic. He enrolled in the inaugural class at Stanford University and was quickly fascinated by the study of geology. Years later, he authored the first English translation of *De Re Metallica*, Georgius Agricola's once-authoritative work on mining.

Soon after his graduation in 1895, Hoover found himself in Western Australia, where he applied new technologies to gold mining. His career soon took him to China, Russia, and South Africa. (Hoover and his wife mastered Mandarin Chinese during their years abroad, and would speak the language in the White House to keep aides from understanding their conversations.) One business success followed another and, according to George Nash, Hoover's

leading biographer, Hoover's net worth in 1913 was approximately $4 million.

On the eve of World War I, Hoover was working in England. When the conflagration began, he found himself on what he later called the "slippery slope of public life." Hoover was distraught over the suffering of civilians and organized the Commission for the Relief of Belgium. The effort fed millions of Europeans during and after the Great War; on two continents, Hoover was called the "Great Humanitarian." On the basis of his experience, write historians Richard Norton Smith and Timothy Walch, Hoover "developed a unique philosophy—one balancing responsibility for the welfare of others with an unshakable faith in free enterprise and dynamic individualism."

Throughout his life, Hoover would be called upon to assume the role of public humanitarian. In 1927, for example, the Mississippi River flooded, leaving 1.5 million Americans homeless. Although it did not fall under the jurisdiction of the Commerce Department, which Hoover then headed, six governors asked President Calvin Coolidge to put Hoover in charge of the relief effort. He marshaled a massive private-sector response. ("I suppose I could have called in the Army to help," he said years later, "but why should I, when I only had to call upon Main Street?") Two decades later, in the wreckage of postwar

Herbert Hoover, whose high character was shaped by his Quaker upbringing, is best remembered as a philanthropist for his work to relieve misery in the wake of war and disaster.

Germany, he led a similar effort to bring food and medicine to that devastated nation. He oversaw the distribution of 40,000 tons of emergency meals in what was a crucial precursor to the Marshall Plan.

But Hoover's involvement in public humanitarian projects (to say nothing of his political career) should not overshadow his generosity as a private citizen. With his wife, Lou Henry, he had a strong moral sense of responsibility for his fellow citizens. As many biographers have noted, however, Hoover had an equally strong moral sense that his private good deeds should be kept out of the public eye.

Even during the Great Depression, when Hoover was blamed for the worst economic crisis in American history, he never allowed his many charitable activities to be made public or politicized in any way. The nation, notes Smith,

"saw nothing of his private anguish, or the dozens of personal bequests he made to individuals in need." According to historian and biographer Glen Jeansonne, "Hoover did not simply save Belgium, much of Central Europe, and the Soviet Union from famine during the era of the Great War; he performed small acts of kindness virtually every day."

A central focus of Hoover's philanthropy was organizations that fostered character among young men. After leaving the Presidency, he became an active supporter of the Boys Club of America, including service as chairman. "The boy is our most precious possession," he wrote in 1937. But the life of the contemporary city boy meant "stairs, light switches, alleys, fire escapes" and "a chance to get run over by a truck." Through the Boys Club, he hoped to introduce young men to the wholesome pleasures of the great outdoors. Hoover, notes Smith, "devoted thousands of hours to the organization, building it up from 140 clubs to more than 600 at the time of his death."

Hoover was likewise committed to understanding the principles and policies that led to war or peace, deprivation or prosperity. In the aftermath of World War I, he donated $50,000 to Stanford University to begin collecting documents related to the issues and ideas that had caused the Great War. The Hoover Institution gathered materials on a variety of topics, but came to be a leading repository for scholarship on the dangers of communism. It soon became one of America's leading think tanks, defending the constitutional order and offering public-policy solutions rooted in the principles of liberty and limited government, wielding real influence on foreign and domestic policy throughout the twentieth century.

"Hoover," writes George Nash, "practiced the philanthropic virtues that he professed. As President, he declined to spend any of his salary on himself. Instead, he gave it away to charities or as income supplements to his associates. During their long marriage, he and his wife extended charitable assistance to countless needy recipients, usually anonymously and through surrogates. In the 1930s, Hoover's brother concluded that he had given away more than half of his business profits for benevolent purposes. Characteristically, however, Hoover concealed most of his benefactions, with the result that their full extent may never be known."

While in the White House, Hoover received a letter from a ten-year-old boy who was seeking advice on how to become President. His reply was revealing. "The first rule is just to be a boy getting all the constructive joy out of life," Hoover wrote. "The second rule is that no one should win the Presidency without honesty and sportsmanship and consideration for others in his character—together with religious faith. The third rule is that he

should be a man of education. If you follow these rules, you will be a man of standing in your community even if you do not make the White House. And who can tell? Maybe that also."

➤ John Hendrickson

Further information

○ Gary Best, *The Life of Herbert Hoover: Keeper of the Torch, 1933-1964* (Palgrave Macmillan, 2013)

○ Glen Jeansonne, *The Life of Herbert Hoover: Fighting Quaker, 1928-1933* (Palgrave, 2012)

○ George Nash, *The Life of Herbert Hoover* (W. W. Norton, six volumes, 1983-1996)

EWING KAUFFMAN

Ewing Marion Kauffman was a pharmaceutical entrepreneur and major Kansas City philanthropist and civic leader. Known for many philanthropic contributions related to K-12 education and human services in Kansas City, near the end of his life Kauffman discovered a new field for philanthropy: the promotion of entrepreneurship. Today, the Ewing Marion Kauffman Foundation is the largest foundation focused principally on fostering economic growth by supporting entrepreneurs.

Ewing Kauffman was born in 1916 into a farm family in western Missouri. As a boy, his salesmanship helped his strapped family to make ends meet. Kauffman sold eggs and magazines door-to-door and went "noodling"—diving into the Grand River's muddy underwater burrows to wrassle big catfish to the shore and sell them. When he was 11, a year of forced bed rest during a health crisis turned Kauffman into a lifelong speed-reader. Kauffman worked his way through junior college at a laundry service and continued there after graduating. He served in the Navy in World War II, and in the long stretches aboard ship, the shrewd poker player put away $90,000 in gambling winnings. His wife saved the money and invested in real estate, and when the war ended, Kauffman had the leisure to find the right job.

That job was in sales at the pharmaceutical firm Lincoln Laboratories. It didn't look like much—no salary, no benefits, only 20 percent commission—but Kauffman warmed to it immediately. He was a natural salesman, and by the end of his second year, he was earning more in commissions alone than Lincoln's president. The president cut Kauffman's commission and reduced the size of his territory, which naturally chafed at the star performer. He began planning his escape.

In June of 1950, Kauffman quit Lincoln and started Marion Laboratories in his basement. It was a pharmaceutical firm, a perhaps unusual choice for

a man who, in his own words, "had no pharmacy background and not very much scientific education." But Kauffman loved the unique challenge of selling to doctors.

Os-Cal was Kauffman's first big hit. A calcium supplement that included ground-up oyster shells, its success came through Kauffman's innovative marketing. "He was in a business that was rooted in science and fueled by research, and he had only a smattering of the former and could not afford the latter," writes one biographer. "He knew how to sell drugs, and he was confident he could learn the rest." In the 1950s, Marion Labs grew on Os-Cal variants and by licensing and bringing others' products to market. It reached sales of $1 million by 1959, and added new blockbusters in the 1960s, during which decade it went public.

"Mr. K," as Kauffman was known to his employees, was a popular boss. He offered a profit-sharing plan, stock options, and education benefits. By 1968, 20 of Marion's employees had become millionaires (including a widow in the accounting department). In 1989, when Marion merged with Merrell Dow, it had annual sales of over $1 billion—and hundreds of employees had become millionaires.

> Ewing Kauffman set up the largest U.S. foundation focused on fostering economic growth by encouraging entrepreneurs.

Through it all, Kauffman was a leading benefactor of Kansas City. In 1969, he bought a Major League Baseball expansion club: the Kansas City Royals. He initially had little interest in baseball; he acquired the team for the benefit of the city. Kauffman took to the sport quickly—and applied his vaunted marketing techniques to making the Royals a K.C. favorite. Kauffman propelled the Royals to a powerful decade starting with an American League division championship in 1976 and culminating in a World Series victory over the St. Louis Cardinals in 1985.

The Royals were not "a part of his financial portfolio," explains biographer Anne Morgan. The team "was a part of his civic philanthropy." As a final present to the region at his death, Kauffman donated the Royals to the Kansas City Community Foundation—with the stipulation that their proceeds from selling the team had to go to local charities, and that the buyer of the team had to agree to keep the Royals in Kansas City.

As soon as Marion Labs went public, Ewing and Muriel Kauffman began to engage in serious giving in Kansas City. They launched STAR, an evidence-based drug-abuse prevention program in Kansas City

schools; it reduced marijuana use by 43 percent compared to a control group. They also set up Project Choice, which used a carrot of college or vocational-training funds to incentivize high-school completion.

An entrepreneur to his fingertips, Kauffman learned from his mistakes. One of his first major philanthropic initiatives involved co-funding a campaign with Hallmark to underwrite home-heating bills for the poor. The campaign succeeded; nobody in town went without heat. But he decided not to participate again. After all, he observed, winter comes every year—and the program "didn't solve the problem. They just threw money at it." Kauffman preferred solutions-based giving.

"Even as he began to fund substance-abuse awareness and to offer postsecondary education to those who completed high school, he was always conscious of the need to create more and better paying jobs for those young people as they prepared to enter the workforce," observed Morgan. As a Kauffman Foundation report at that same time put it, "We've got to do something to help encourage the creation of jobs." That effort became the next act of the Kauffman Foundation.

In 1990, Kauffman directed his foundation to research what could be done to help entrepreneurs. He eventually created a Center for Entrepreneurial Leadership to train entrepreneurs, form networks, develop curricula, and foster research on entrepreneurship. The center's 1992 launch event would mark one of Kauffman's last public appearances. "We cannot finance everybody who wants to get into business," he explained. "But we have the capability of guiding them to the point where they can get seed money."

With this commitment, Kauffman set his foundation on a path of pioneering philanthropic specialization. With assets of more than $2 billion, Kauffman became the largest foundation in the country to focus on fostering entrepreneurship—and helping dreamers become the next generation of Ewing Kauffmans.

— Evan Sparks

Further information

○ Anne Morgan, *Prescription for Success: The Life and Values of Ewing Marion Kauffman* (Andrews McMeel, 1995)

Corbis

W. K. KELLOGG

Will Keith Kellogg invented corn flakes and stoked America's appetite for the convenience of dry breakfast cereal. His business became wildly successful. And from its profits, Kellogg poured a fortune into improving health care

and education for children.

Born in 1860, Kellogg was one of 14 children of a strict Seventh-day Adventist family. They observed the Sabbath on Saturday and abstained entirely from alcohol, tobacco, coffee, tea, and meat. Schooling for W. K. (as he was called throughout his adult career) ended at age 13, when he was apprenticed to his father's broom-making business. It was a childhood filled with work and responsibility. "As a boy," he later recalled, "I never learned to play."

W. K. worked for his father until he was 16 years old, at which time he was hired by his older brother John. In 1876, the newly minted physician Dr. John Kellogg was named superintendent of the Battle Creek Sanitarium in Battle Creek, Michigan. He hired W. K., eight years his junior, as a bookkeeper. Combining elements of the Seventh-day Adventist diet with insights from late-nineteenth-century medicine, the sanitarium was a sort of live-in spa where visitors could eat healthily, exercise vigorously, and rest soundly. For the next 30 years, it was where the brothers worked side by side.

> Kellogg's giving was a response to the poverty, strictures, and labor of his own boyhood.

It was not an easy relationship. John required W. K. to run beside him while he bicycled around the sanitarium, for example, and to take dictation while he used the toilet. John was a relentless self-promoter, who cajoled the great and the good to come to the sanitarium (a word he coined). Fascinated by holistic medicine, electrotherapy, and hydrotherapy, John became obsessed with digestion, administering frequent enemas of water (to flush the system) and yogurt (to supply healthy bacteria). He was also a rigid opponent of onanism, and prescribed a bland diet to ward off the temptations he associated with spicy and savory foods.

Food was a central concern at the sanitarium. Like many Seventh-day Adventists, the Kelloggs relied on a low-fat and low-protein diet that centered on fiber, whole grains, and nuts. In the mid-1890s, John told W. K. to develop a grain product more easily digestible than bread. W. K. started tinkering—boiling wheat, spreading the mixture on grinding rollers, and toasting it. Later he started using corn, and added salt and sugar. The flaked corn was served with cold milk and fruit, a far cry from the hot porridge or bacon and eggs that then greeted most Americans at the breakfast table.

The cereal was popular with patients, and the brothers started a small production and mail-order operation. John was too busy running the sanitarium and fighting degeneracy to notice the commercial potential of

corn flakes, but the upside was not lost on W. K. In 1904, a former sanitarium patient named C. W. Post launched a commercial line of cornflakes. W. K. could no longer stand by. In 1906, he founded the Battle Creek Toasted Corn Flake Company, which is known today as the Kellogg Company.

By the mid-1920s, W. K. Kellogg was the cereal king of America, and a very wealthy man. The final third of his life was dedicated to philanthropy. In 1923, he created the Fellowship Corporation, which quietly funded charities throughout Battle Creek and southern Michigan. In the late 1920s, as Kellogg was approaching 70, he wanted to create a more organized enterprise. This was the start of the W. K. Kellogg Foundation, which began operations in 1930.

Kellogg confined the foundation's giving to "the health, education, and welfare of mankind, but principally of children or youth…without regard to sex, race, creed, or nationality." In large part, this was a response to the poverty, strictures, and labor of his own boyhood. But there was another reason. In 1913, his grandson, a toddler named Kenneth Williamson, fell out of a second-story window. The boy nearly died, and was physically disabled for the rest of his life.

Kellogg was astounded that, despite his wealth, he could not find adequate medical care anywhere in southern Michigan. In a letter to a Battle Creek physician, Kellogg wrote that Kenneth's accident "caused me to wonder what difficulties were in the paths of needy parents who seek help for their children when catastrophe strikes, and I resolved to lend what aid I could to such children." A central focus of Kellogg's philanthropy would be children's health care.

A year after opening its doors, the Kellogg Foundation launched the Michigan Community Health Project. Focused on the seven counties of southern Michigan, the 17-year initiative built new hospitals in rural areas, helped organize public-health departments, and provided nurses and doctors for remote towns. In 1942, the State Department asked Kellogg to expand the program to Latin America as a wartime gesture of goodwill. Kellogg willingly complied. "In doing so," notes historian Joel Orosz, "the foundation curiously became international in scope before it became national."

Over the last 21 years of his life, Kellogg donated a total of some $66 million to the foundation. He initially funded its activities from his checkbook, refusing to endow the foundation until it had proven its effectiveness. (When he did endow the foundation, he gave it nearly all of his equity in the Kellogg Company—some 54 percent of the common stock.) Though glaucoma left him legally blind at age 80, he attended every board meeting, worked closely with his staff, and frequently visited with grantees, always accompanied by one of his faithful German shepherds, all of whom were descendants of Rin-Tin-Tin.

Through his foundation, Kellogg also created the Ann Kellogg School, named for his mother, one of the first elementary schools to teach children

with disabilities alongside children without disabilities. He likewise used his foundation to donate his Arabian horse farm to the University of California. In 1949, it became the home of California State Polytechnic, Pomona, which remains devoted to the teaching of technical arts and applied sciences. Although Kellogg conducted most of his philanthropy through his foundation, he funded a few projects from his checkbook, including his support for summer camps for low-income families, the creation of the Kellogg Bird Sanctuary, and the establishment of an experimental demonstration farm at Michigan State University.

"Dollars do not create character," W. K. Kellogg often said. But he knew that dollars could help in many other ways, and he charged his foundation, today one of the largest in the nation, with helping "children face the future with confidence, with health, and with a strong-rooted security in the trust of this country and its institutions."

Martin Morse Wooster

Further information

○ Gerald Carson, *Cornflake Crusade* (Rinehart, 1957)

○ Mary Cohen, *W. K. Kellogg Foundation, 75 Years of Philanthropy* (W. K. Kellogg Foundation, 2005)

○ Horace Powell, *The Original Has This Signature—W. K. Kellogg* (Prentice-Hall, 1956)

SEBASTIAN KRESGE

Sebastian Kresge was among the most successful retailers in American history. The founder of what would become the K-Mart chain of discount stores, he was also an accomplished philanthropist who focused on capital grants and building projects.

Kresge's background was the definition of "hardscrabble." Born in 1867 to ethnically German farmers, he was raised in rural Pennsylvania to be upright and God-fearing. His parents instilled lifelong habits of piety, thrift, and industriousness in their son, but hard work was no proof against crop failures and depression. When Sebastian was eight years old, his parents lost the family farm to foreclosure, victims of the Panic of 1873.

In his teens, Kresge set his sights on becoming a teacher. To finance his education, he struck a bargain with his parents: if they would pay his tuition, he would sign over his wages until age 21. In the meantime, he would live on the proceeds of his beekeeping business, which Sebastian had started as a boy.

Corbis

He kept the bargain, finished college, and spent one term teaching before he decided that his real interest was business. After a brief stint as a deliveryman and clerk in a Scranton hardware store, Kresge became an itinerant tin-and-hardware salesman, which brought him into contact with a group of men who would later become his mentors in the retail sales business: F. W. Woolworth, S. H. Knox, and John McCrory.

For an initial investment of $8,000, paid out of savings the young man had assiduously accumulated over the years, Kresge acquired two struggling five-and-dime stores. A dozen years later, he had spun his foothold in Detroit into 85 stores. Kresge was on his way to building the retailing empire that eventually became K-Mart.

Kresge's genius, most business historians agree, was in finding and occupying an unfilled retailing niche, the middlebrow space between low-cost five-and-dimes and more expensive brand-name retailers. He was personally involved in almost every aspect of his expanding empire, showing himself especially adept at finding cheap real estate, usually just months before the middle-class customers that were his bread and butter moved out to the newly built suburbs surrounding his shopping centers. Kresge was one of the first retailers to offer paid vacations, pensions, and profit-sharing. Eighty years after its founding, at

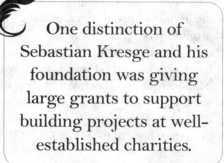

One distinction of Sebastian Kresge and his foundation was giving large grants to support building projects at well-established charities.

its 1979 high-water mark, K-Mart Corporation posted sales of $11.7 billion in 1,891 stores across the United States, Canada, and Australia.

Kresge was notoriously frugal—his two early marriages foundered because of his personal stinginess, and he gave up golf because he couldn't stand the lost balls. He was nevertheless profoundly generous to civic and charitable causes all his life. A lifelong Methodist, he was weekly to be found in the pews of a particularly austere country church in Monroe County, Pennsylvania, near his birthplace. Early on, he confided to fellow churchgoers that he hoped to give away his entire personal fortune. His philanthropic credo was simple. I want, he would say, "to leave the world a better place than I found it."

While simply derived, his approach was anything but simplistic. Befitting a man who created a whole new retailing niche, Kresge also developed a distinctive philanthropic identity. As a relatively young man, he became

known for his opposition to alcohol. Kresge was a lifelong teetotaler who abhorred the damage that liquor caused in the lives of the working poor. He supported anti-liquor groups long after the temperance movement ceased to be popular, and even after it became evident that Kresge's anti-liquor politics were hurting his bottom line.

When he funded the Kresge Foundation with an initial $1.3 million in 1924, he decided to focus on supporting mature charitable organizations like the YMCA and Girl Scouts, leaving to other foundations the task of identifying new approaches and groups. Not surprisingly for the man who founded a beekeeping operation before he turned ten, Kresge's foundation also focused on self-help charitable efforts that enabled the poor to lift themselves out of poverty. And driven by his devotion, Kresge favored religious organizations that without his support would be forced to rely on government funding—and the secularization that accompanied it.

Under Sebastian's close personal guidance—he remained an active member of the board until his death—the Kresge Foundation has especially distinguished itself in giving large grants to support major brick-and-mortar projects. The Kresge name is inscribed on the walls of many large universities, medical centers, and arts institutions. It has supported hospital expansions from Columbus to Fresno; built wings on museums and concert halls in Albuquerque and Indiana; and supported a medical school in Ann Arbor, a law library at Notre Dame, and a chapel at the Claremont Theological School in California. One of the Kresge Foundation's largest brick-and-mortar grants brought it back to the birthplace of the Kresge retailing empire, Detroit, where in 2002 the foundation donated a $50 million challenge grant to an ambitious downtown riverfront renovation.

Nearly 100 years old when he died in 1966, Kresge gave his foundation a total of $60,577,183 during his lifetime. That alone made him one of the largest donors in the country. And he almost achieved his wish to divest himself of the wealth he worked so long and intently to accumulate: when he died, his personal estate was worth less than a tenth of what he had given to the foundation that bears his name.

☞ *Justin Torres*

Further information

○ Stanley Sebastian Kresge and Steve Spilos, *The S. S. Kresge Story* (Western Publishing, 1979)

○ "The Pinch-Penny Philanthropist" (*Time*, October 28, 1966)

ELI LILLY

Eli Lilly transformed a sleepy family business into a pharmaceutical powerhouse, proving along the way that economic pragmatism and generosity are often complementary. Eli's namesake grandfather—called "Colonel Lilly" for his Civil War service—founded the family drugmaking business in Indianapolis in 1876. Lilly's father followed, starting as a bottle washer. After graduation from the Indianapolis public schools, grandson Eli was sent to school in Philadelphia to learn the pharmacy trade. All his life, Lilly would regret that he never received a fuller liberal education.

But Lilly grew the company in ways his father and grandfather never imagined. A practitioner of the scientific management techniques of Frederick Taylor, Lilly was named head of the company's newly created economics division. Lilly brought in industrial specialists to cut costs and increase production. Even more crucially, he moved the company away from its roots as a patent-medicines manufacturer and toward advanced pharmaceutical research.

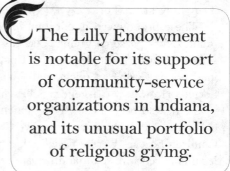

The Lilly Endowment is notable for its support of community-service organizations in Indiana, and its unusual portfolio of religious giving.

In the 1920s, this new focus paid off when Lilly & Company played a crucial role in the development of insulin for the treatment of diabetes. Lilly went on to equally instrumental roles in creating the polio vaccine and mass-producing penicillin, liver extract, and thimerosal, a preservative in medicines and vaccines. He retired as head of the company in 1948, but remained closely involved in its affairs until his death in 1977.

Lilly believed that it was the duty of the wealthy to support charitable causes. He brought to his many philanthropic efforts the same drive and attention to detail that made him successful in the drug business. But he also brought some pronounced personal passions.

Despite having assured financial success, thanks to the development of the insulin patents, Lilly was an unhappy man as he entered middle age. He was burdened with personal troubles: two sons died in infancy, his first marriage ended in divorce, and his daughter Evie suffered from mental instability and alcoholism throughout her life. Never a warm person—one of his closest friends, the president of Wabash College in Indiana, noted that Lilly used his

dry sense of humor and business acumen to keep people at arm's length—Eli could be harsh and short-tempered.

In 1927, though, Lilly remarried, and he and his wife, Ruth, were a much happier couple. They stayed together until her death in 1973. A buoyant Lilly then set out, as he wrote in a 1934 essay, "to broaden and brighten my life and surroundings." The mid-life turn started with a deliberate course of self-education in areas that were never broached in pharmacy school. Lilly became a learned autodidact in fields ranging from archaeology and historic preservation to Chinese art and comparative religion.

He began to publish books and monographs on topics of interest, making small but real contributions to various fields. Typical topics included "Prehistoric Antiquities of Indiana" and an interpretation of Lenape Indian pictographs. One of his personal heroes was Heinrich Schliemann, the amateur archaeologist who bested the "smug professionals," as Lilly put it in his article "Schliemann in Indianapolis," by discovering the site of ancient Troy in western Turkey.

These pronounced intellectual interests and personal enthusiasms would guide Lilly's personal giving. Like his grandfather and father before him, he supported historical and educational institutions in Indiana—like the liberal-arts institutions Earlham College and Wabash College, and the Indiana Historical Society. He was also a generous benefactor of Christ Church in Indianapolis, where he had been a choir boy as a child and where he attended services his entire life. He donated his extensive Chinese art collection to a local museum. Children's causes were especially dear to his wife Ruth, and Lilly supported a local children's museum and private religious groups that ministered to poor and needy children.

Unlike his father and grandfather, though, Lilly turned his philanthropy into a systematic activity. He had a keen eye for what we would today call "venture philanthropy"—a phrase that likely would have appealed to the man who once wrote a detailed manual for Lilly employees on the best way to fill gelatin capsules. Philanthropy, he told his daughter, "sounds easy, but the catch is that it takes lots of time and study" to learn what projects "are worthwhile and what are not."

Usually working anonymously, Lilly would seek out small organizations that seemed to be doing good work and could benefit from his giving. He was especially interested in character education, finding and supporting the work of Ernest Ligon, author of the popular mid-century character-education curriculum for religious schools called "A Greater Generation." With Lilly's support, Ligon founded the Character Research Project at Union College in upstate New York. Over more than a quarter century, Lilly supported

Ligon's work conducting research, writing articles, and convening youth congresses to study and advocate for character education.

In 1937, along with his father and brother, Eli founded the Lilly Endowment, comprised of Lilly stock and closely controlled by the Lilly family. It is still one of the largest philanthropies in the country. The Lilly Endowment is notable for its support of community-service organizations in Indiana and its unusual portfolio of religious giving, including support for scholars working on religious topics and financial aid to divinity and theology students. (For more information on Lilly's continuing work in support of religious communities, see "Placing the Call," *Philanthropy*, Spring 2010.)

Because he frequently made anonymous donations, it will never be possible to know the full extent of Eli Lilly's philanthropy. When he died in 1977, he left his estate of $165 million to be distributed to his and Ruth's favorite causes, including Wabash College, historical and religious institutions throughout Indiana, and community-service groups in the city of Indianapolis. Modest to the end, Lilly particularly requested that there be no eulogy at his funeral. So his bequests spoke for his life.

— Justin Torres

Further information

- E. J. Kahn, *All in a Century: The First Hundred Years of Eli Lilly & Co.* (Eli Lilly, 1976)
- James Madison, *Eli Lilly: A Life, 1885-1977* (Indiana Historical Society, 1989)

NICHOLAS LONGWORTH

Nicholas Longworth is best remembered, insofar as he is remembered at all, as the father of American winemaking. Longworth popularized the Catawba grape and created a widespread, if short-lived, enthusiasm for the sparkling wines of the Ohio River Valley. He was also a well-regarded attorney, a massively successful real-estate investor, and a tireless philanthropist who dedicated his enormous fortune to those whom he affectionately called "the devil's poor."

Longworth was born in Newark, New Jersey, in 1783, the son of a once-prominent merchant. Unfortunately for the family, his father had been a stalwart Loyalist during the American Revolution. After the war, virtually all of the family's property was confiscated. Nicholas spent his boyhood in poverty, bearing the stigma of his father's loyalty to the Crown. He learned hard work from an early age. For a while, he was apprenticed to a shoemaker; later, he was sent to clerk for a relative in South Carolina.

When he was 19 years old, he moved west, eager to distance himself from the shame and poverty of his youth. In 1804, he arrived in Cincinnati, Ohio, where he began to study law. His mentor was Jacob Burnet, a leading figure in Ohio politics—often called the "Father of Ohio's Constitution"—and one of Cincinnati's wealthiest men. In short order, Longworth passed the bar and began an energetic law practice. What money he made he used to buy real estate.

The investments proved immensely profitable. As Cincinnati boomed, the value of Longworth's property exploded. By 1819, he retired from his legal practice; his properties demanded his full attention. In 1850, Longworth paid more than $17,000 in taxes, the second-highest tax bill in the nation.

Retired from active business, Longworth was able to devote decades to his favorite pastime: experimental horticulture. His greatest success was the Catawba grape. In 1828, his friend John Adlum sent him specimens from Washington, D.C. They flourished along the banks of the Ohio River. Longworth pulled down his other vines, replacing them with the late-ripening, purplish-red grapes.

> He dedicated his enormous fortune to those whom he affectionately called "the devil's poor," the "wretched vagabonds that everyone else turns away."

With bumper crops of Catawba, Longworth began to make wine, employing armies of German immigrants and introducing the first large-scale winemaking operation in the New World. When a sparkling variant was created by accident, wine enthusiasts from San Francisco to Paris toasted the pink bubblies from Ohio. (In 1858, Henry Wadsworth Longfellow wrote an ode to "Catawba Wine" and dedicated the poem to Longworth.) By the time of his death, Longworth's vineyards were producing 150,000 bottles annually.

The great bulk of Longworth's wealth went to his idiosyncratic program of philanthropy. Longworth, explained an 1863 obituary in *Harper's Weekly*, "had a whimsical theory that those whom everybody will help were not entitled to any aid from him, and that he would confine his donations to the worthless and wretched vagabonds that everyone else turns away from." These, he would explain, were "the devil's poor." They were the beneficiaries of virtually all of his charitable giving.

Much about Longworth's giving is anecdotal, but the stories that remain are revealing. "A committee of Mormons, on a begging expedition,

was once sent to him by a friend," noted the *Harper's Weekly* obituary, "with a note intimating that, as these people were not Christians, and seemed to be abandoned by everybody that professed to be, they probably came within his rule, and he could consistently assist them. He did so without hesitation."

Every Monday morning Longworth was known to give away 10-cent loaves of bread to anyone who would ask for one; most weeks he reportedly gave away between 300 and 800 loaves. He built a four-story brick boarding house over his wine cellars, with 56 neatly appointed apartments that he rented below cost to poor laborers and their families. If a man could not afford the rent, Longworth would often allow him to stay, free of charge, for months and sometimes even years.

Unsurprisingly, "the devil's poor" often failed to reciprocate Longworth's good will. At one of his Monday morning distributions of bread, riots nearly broke out when the crowds realized that the loaves had been topped off with rye. (Told that the wheat "was running high"—meaning that the loaves were baking with large air pockets—Longworth had ordered the bakers to plump the bread with grain.) As for the boarding house, one of Longworth's biographers noted that the tenants were "most ungrateful and troublesome" and that they "used to annoy him incessantly, and frequently broke into the wine-vaults below and stole his choicest wine."

Despite the frustration, despite the ingratitude, Longworth persisted in his course of charitable giving. "Vagabonds, drunkards, fallen women, those who had gone far into the depths of misery and wretchedness, and from whom respectable people shrank in disgust, never appealed to him in vain," wrote James McCabe. "He would listen to them patiently, moved to the depths of his soul by their sad stories, and would send them away rejoicing that they were not utterly friendless. 'Decent paupers will always find a plenty to help them,' he would say, 'but no one cares for these poor wretches. Everybody damns them, and as no one else will help them, I must.' "

Longworth also made some more conventional philanthropic efforts. In 1842, he donated the land on which the Cincinnati Observatory was built. In his last public appearance, a 77-year-old John Quincy Adams traveled to Cincinnati to lay the cornerstone. When the institution opened in 1845, it was one of the finest facilities in the world. This project was unusual for Longworth, though; he preferred to help the poor—especially those who could not, or would not, help themselves.

Longworth died in February 1863 at 81 years old. Tributes poured forth, praising and honoring the son of a disgraced Loyalist. None, it seems

likely, would have moved Longworth so much as the sight of his funeral procession, with thousands of outcasts—drunkards and prostitutes, beggars and criminals—sobbing at the loss of this, their one true friend.

— Christopher Levenick

Further information

○ Clara Longworth Chambrun, *The Making of Nicholas Longworth: Annals of an American Family* (R. Long & R. R. Smith, 1933)

○ *American Studies* biographical essay, journals.ku.edu/index.php/amerstud/article/view/4203/3962

○ "The Late Nicholas Longworth" (*Harper's Weekly* March 7, 1863)

ALFRED LOOMIS

Alfred Loomis came from a philanthropic family. They created sanitariums for tuberculosis patients, funded medical research, and built up NYU, among other causes. The son and grandson of experimental physicians, young Loomis had a powerful scientific bent. He distinguished himself in mathematics at Yale, but after his father died while he was still an undergrad Loomis decided he needed a career that could support his family. So after graduation he enrolled at Harvard Law School.

Blood will tell, however, and soon the young Alfred Loomis found himself profoundly bored with the practice of law. He returned to his earlier fascination with science, befriending internationally prominent researchers and conducting his own quite-advanced investigations in garages and basements. Eventually concluding that he needed a fortune if he was going to experiment on a large scale, the restless genius made a plan. He would launch a Wall Street firm with his brother-in-law, pile up cash, and use it to pursue pure science.

Applying a mathematical approach, Loomis quickly built one of the largest investment banks in the country by financing rapid development of the brand-new electric-utility industry during the 1920s. From almost nothing, his firm grew to underwrite almost a sixth of all the securities issued in the U.S. Then Loomis became convinced that the stock market was overvalued and likely to collapse. In early 1929 he and his partner began transferring all their money into cash or Treasury bills. When Black Thursday hit in October of that year Loomis was not only safe, but well-positioned to bargain-shop. It is estimated that he made the modern equivalent of more than $700 million in the first years of the Depression,

MIT Museum

160

ending up one of the wealthiest and most powerful men on Wall Street, in a league similar to the Rockefellers and Morgans.

Now well able to subsidize high-level scientific research, Loomis cashed out in 1933 and threw himself into the work of the private lab he set up during the mid-1920s in a rehabbed mansion near his home north of New York City. The Loomis Laboratory became one of the world's great research institutes, better equipped than top academic or corporate labs, and visited by many of the world's leading scientists.

Loomis had a special ability to crash-study a new subject and quickly become expert. Throughout the 1920s and 1930s he used his fortune to conduct pathbreaking experiments, alone and with other scientists, on ultrasound, radiometry, the precise measurement of time, and many other subjects. He created the techniques for monitoring brain waves, discovered new sleep states, and co-invented the microscope centrifuge. He also funded scores of other researchers and built up the science departments at universities like MIT. When Yale gave him an honorary degree, the citation compared him to the American who had best combined science and philanthropy: "In his varied interests, his powers of invention, and his services to his fellow man, Mr. Loomis is the twentieth-century Benjamin Franklin."

Travels to Germany in the late '30s left Loomis disturbed over both the popularity of Hitler and the gathering technical might of the Germans. Biographer Jennet Conant summarizes his next dramatic move: "Long before the government moved to enlist scientists to develop advanced weapons, Loomis had assessed the situation and concluded it was critical that the country be as informed as possible about which technologies would matter in the future war. He scrapped all his experiments and turned [his lab] into his personal civilian research project, then began recruiting the brightest minds he could find to help him take measure of the enemy's capabilities and start working on new gadgets and devices for defense purposes."

Loomis put his main focus on using radio waves to detect and fix the location of objects—what eventually became known as radar. He immersed himself in the field, recruited academics, studied England's successes, then launched a series of intensive practical experiments. This work drew on several areas of science where Loomis personally was a scientific leader—wave behavior, electromagnetic-spectrum research, and precise measurement of time. Within a year the Loomis Radiation Laboratory had completed basic research, achieved breakthroughs in making radio-detection practical, and created a working prototype radar mounted in a converted diaper-delivery truck.

At just this point, bombs rained down on Pearl Harbor, kicking Loomis into overdrive. Back in World War I he had volunteered for service and been sent to test new weapons at the Army's Aberdeen Proving Ground. The experience left him amazed at the sluggishness and resistance to change within the military establishment, and within government generally. As this next, more terrible, war broke out, Loomis understood as few others did how important technical breakthroughs would be in determining the winner, and how much America's deep bench of scientists could contribute to victory. He made it his personal philanthropic mission to ensure that America's magnificently inventive industrial machinery would produce vital military innovations without getting gummed up by government bureaucracy.

In this, Loomis's leadership skills were even more essential to his success than his checkbook and his scientific perspicacity. When a small group of British scientists arrived in the U.S. on a covert mission to share their radar secrets in the hope that the Americans could make the technology more useable, precise, and widely available to Allied fighting forces, Loomis was the catalyst in instantly understanding their crucial breakthroughs, pressing U.S. military and civilian authorities to build on them, and then orchestrating important refinements and advances beyond the British technology.

> President Roosevelt described Alfred Loomis as second only to Winston Churchill in civilian contributions to victory in World War II.

He moved all of his valuable personal equipment and prototype findings to MIT, which had its own radar project (funded by him). When Congress was slow to approve the support needed to ramp up the MIT lab, Loomis began paying expenses out of his own pocket. Then he convinced MIT, on whose board he served, to advance the project $500,000, and he appealed to his friend John Rockefeller Jr. to advance another half million. (When government funding finally came through, MIT and Rockefeller were repaid.) Most importantly, Loomis and his close friend Ernest Lawrence, the Nobel-laureate physicist, used their credibility with many of America's top scientific minds to recruit them to drop everything and go to work in Loomis's new radar lab. Nearly all agreed.

"They had no official appointment from the federal government to do this. But Loomis got them all talked into doing it," one observer wrote later, "and it's a good thing they did." Loomis, who recognized

the power and efficiency of "American individualism and laissez-faire" and believed that most progress came from "free agency and freedom from politics," fiercely protected the scientists from interference in their work and encouraged them to follow their own individual and team judgments to make the fastest possible progress. One scientist described Loomis's laboratory as "the greatest cooperative research establishment in the history of the world." Lawrence later stated, "If Alfred Loomis had not existed, radar development would have been retarded greatly, at an enormous cost in American lives.... He used his wealth very effectively."

Very soon, the Loomis lab had not only mastered the science and technique of radar, but had designed nearly 100 different lifesaving and war-ending products. By June 1943, the Army and Navy had ordered 22,000 radar sets from the lab. These had many vital effects. Radar shot down Luftwaffe planes and kept the Germans from defeating England. Radar ended the U-boat menace, saving tens of thousands of lives and allowing the crucial output of American industry to be transported to our European allies. Radar negated Germany's leading technical breakthrough, the V-rocket. Radar gave our pilots and ship captains the ability to detect threats, to direct fire, and to survive bad weather and night conditions that would otherwise have thwarted or killed them.

Loomis also personally dreamed up the pioneering long-range navigation system called LORAN. Perfected in his lab over the original indifference of military agencies, its debut in combat changed everything for American and Allied wartime navigators. Until the recent arrival of satellite GPS, LORAN continued to serve for decades as the exclusive global positioning system. Fourteen years after World War II ended, Alfred Loomis was awarded patent #2,884,628 for inventing the original system of long-range navigation.

Contemporary observers concluded that "radar won World War II; the atom bomb ended it." As it happened, Alfred Loomis also had a lot to do with that latter triumph. He was a friend and important supporter of Enrico Fermi as Fermi led investigations into nuclear fission. And Loomis was the key champion and lead private funder of Ernest Lawrence's development of cyclotrons at the University of California, Berkeley. In addition to putting his own money behind Lawrence, Loomis made it his mission to convince other donors to back this highly speculative project—eventually sweet-talking a climactic $1.15 million contribution out of the Rockefeller Foundation.

As soon as Lawrence's cyclotron was funded, Loomis plucked off his philanthropist cap and donned his entrepreneur/financier hat in order to

beg and bully America's leading industrial corporations into finding the large quantities of iron, copper, electronics, and other war-constrained commodities needed to build the giant machine. Lawrence was astonished by the Wall Street titan's ability to marshal commercial cooperation. The cyclotron Lawrence and Loomis built together was subsequently used to laboriously purify the uranium for the first atomic explosions.

Loomis's broader contribution to the Manhattan Project was the modus operandi he pioneered in his private lab and then expanded on a large scale in the MIT radiation lab he oversaw during the war. The race to create the atomic bomb followed the Loomis formula to a tee: collect the best minds without regard to their immediate expertise, give them superb equipment and material support, guard their freedom to experiment, and encourage collegial exchanges of information and shared problem-solving. Nobel physicist Luis Alvarez, who worked in the radar lab and then created the A-bomb detonator for the Manhattan Project, credited Loomis's interventions for "the remarkable lack of administrative roadblocks experienced by…the builders of the atomic bombs."

Nearly all of Loomis's top hand-picked physicists were quietly pulled out of his radar lab when the Manhattan Project was launched, and sent to Los Alamos or one of the other project sites. Loomis acquiesced because he had long been pushing for exactly this crash program, alarmed as he was by military complacency that viewed atomic weapons as something to think about for "the next war," the dawdling pace of government research to that point, and the real possibility of German scientists being first to the bomb.

President Roosevelt later described Loomis as second only to Winston Churchill in contributions to Allied victory in World War II. After the war, Loomis helped institutionalize his entrepreneurial style of defense research by becoming an influential founding trustee of the RAND Corporation, a nonprofit established to apply the best scientific ideas to national defense. With funding from the Ford Foundation and other donors, RAND promoted multi-stage rockets, intercontinental missiles, magnetic-core computer memory, the building blocks of the future Internet, and many other innovations. The Loomis imprint can also be seen on DARPA, the Defense Advanced Research Projects Agency that picked up the mantle of the Loomis lab and carried it throughout the post-war era.

Alfred Loomis also left behind a flesh-and-blood embodiment of his whirlwind entrepreneurial giving. His great-grandson is Reed Hastings—who as CEO of the Internet pioneer Netflix, and one of the most influential

progenitors of the rise of charter schools, has been a huge game-changer in both business and philanthropy. (See 2000, 2005, and 2006 entries on our full list of Major Achievements in Education Philanthropy.)

⌁ Karl Zinsmeister

Further information

○ *Philanthropy* magazine reporting, philanthropyroundtable.org/topic/excellence_in_ philanthropy/donors_who_come_to_the_aid_of_their_country

○ Jennet Conant, *Tuxedo Park* (Simon and Schuster, 2002)

OSEOLA MCCARTY

Oseola McCarty was born into the world in 1908, and it was a raw start. She was conceived when her mother was raped on a wooded path in rural Mississippi as she returned from tending a sick relative. Oseola was raised in Hattiesburg by her grandmother and aunt, who cleaned houses, cooked, and took in laundry.

As a child, Oseola would come home from elementary school and iron clothes, stashing the money she earned in her doll buggy. The three women relied completely on each other, and when the aunt returned from a hospitalization unable to walk, Oseola dropped out of sixth grade to care for her, and take up her work as a washerwoman. She never returned to school.

"Work became the great good of her life," explained one person who knew her. "She found beauty in its movement and pride in its provisions. She was happy to have it and gave herself over to it with abandon."

McCarty herself put it this way: "I knew there were people who didn't have to work as hard as I did, but it didn't make me feel sad. I *loved* to work, and when you love to do anything, those things don't bother you…. Sometimes I worked straight through two or three days. I had goals I was working toward. That motivated me and I was able to push hard… Work is a blessing. As long as I am living I want to be working at something. Just because I am old doesn't mean I can't work."

And hers was not a standard-issue job. McCarty scrubbed her laundry by hand on a rubboard. She did try an automatic washer and dryer in the 1960s, but found that "the washing machine didn't rinse enough, and the dryer turned the whites yellow." After years of boiling clothes and then doing four fresh-water rinses, that wasn't good enough to meet her high standards. The machine was almost immediately retired, and she

went back to her Maid Rite scrubboard, water drawn from a nearby fire hydrant, and 100 feet of open-air clothesline.

Asked to describe her typical day, McCarty answered: "I would go outside and start a fire under my wash pot. Then I would soak, wash, and boil a bundle of clothes. Then I would rub 'em, wrench 'em, rub 'em again, starch 'em, and hang 'em on the line. After I had all of the clean clothes on the line, I would start on the next batch. I'd wash all day, and in the evenin' I'd iron until 11:00. I loved the work. The bright fire. Wrenching the wet, clean cloth. White shirts shinin' on the line."

This extraordinary work ethic, pursued straight through to her retirement at age 86, apparently produced results her customers appreciated. In 1996, Hattiesburg businessman Paul Laughlin wrote, "I know one person who still has several shirts that were last cleaned almost two years ago by Miss McCarty. He says that he does not intend to wear them; he just takes them out periodically to look at them and to enjoy the crisp fabric and its scent." McCarty, concludes Laughlin, was a walking object lesson "that all work can be performed with dignity and infused with quality."

"Hard work gives your life meaning," stated McCarty. "Everyone needs to work hard at somethin' to feel good about themselves. Every job can be done well and every day has its satisfactions…. If you want to feel proud of yourself, you've got to do things you can be proud of."

Shortly after she retired, McCarty did something that made many Americans very proud of her. She had begun to save almost as soon as she started working at age eight. As the money pooled up in her doll buggy, the very young girl took action. "I went to the bank and deposited. Didn't know how to do it. Went there myself. Didn't tell mama and them I was goin'."

"I commenced to save money. I never would take any of it out. I just put it in…. It's not the ones that make the big money, but the ones who know how to save who get ahead. You got to leave it alone long enough for it to increase."

Of course that requires self-control and modest appetites. "My secret was contentment. I was happy with what I had," said McCarty.

These sturdy habits ran together to produce McCarty's final secret. When she retired in 1995, her hands painfully swollen with arthritis, this washerwoman who had been paid in little piles of coins and dollar bills her entire life had $280,000 in the bank.

Even more startling: she decided to give most of it away—not as a bequest, but immediately.

Setting aside just enough to live on, McCarty donated $150,000 to the University of Southern Mississippi to fund scholarships for worthy but needy students seeking the education she never had. When they found out

what she had done, over 600 men and women in Hattiesburg and beyond made donations that more than tripled her original endowment. Today, the university presents several full-tuition McCarty scholarships every year.

Like a lot of philanthropists, McCarty wanted the satisfactions of giving while living. And she succeeded. The first beneficiary of her gift, a Hattiesburg girl named Stephanie Bullock, was president of her senior class and had supportive parents, but also a twin brother, and not enough family income to send them both to college. With her McCarty Scholarship, Bullock enrolled at Southern Miss, and promptly adopted McCarty as a surrogate grandmother.

Like a lot of philanthropists, McCarty felt a powerful impulse to act in her home region. When asked why she picked Southern Miss, she replied "because it's *here*." The campus (though she had never visited) was located just a couple blocks from her home.

Prior to making her gift, Oseola's one long trip had been to Niagara Falls. Here is her recollection: "Law, the sound of the water was like the sound of the world comin' to an end. In the evening we spread blankets on the ground and ate picnic dinners. I met people from all over the world. On the return trip, we stopped in Chicago. I liked it, but was ready to get back home. I missed the place where I belonged—where I was needed and makin' a contribution. No place compares to the piece of earth where you have put down your roots."

> "I can't do everything. But I can do something to help somebody. And what I can do I will do."

Like a lot of faithful philanthropists, Oseola McCarty was forgiving. Reminded that the university she was giving her money to had been white-only until the 1960s, she answered with equanimity: "They used to not let colored people go out there. But now they *do*. And I think they should have it."

Like a lot of philanthropists, McCarty had a strong and virtuous character and good habits. She lived frugally, walking almost everywhere, including more than a mile to get her groceries. When she stayed in a hotel for the first time after coming to public attention, she made the bed before checking out.

In addition to the dignity of work, McCarty's satisfactions were the timeless ones: faith in God, family closeness, and love of locale. One friend described McCarty's faith as "as simple as the Sermon on the Mount, and as difficult to practice." She was baptized at age 13, dunked in a local pond while dressed all in white (a mixed blessing for someone who washed her clothes by hand).

"I start each day on my knees, saying the Lord's Prayer. Then I get busy about my work," McCarty told one interviewer. "You have to accept God the best way you know how and then He'll show Himself to you. And the more you serve Him, the more *able* you are to serve Him."

"Some people make a lot of noise about what's wrong with the world, and they are usually blamin' somebody else. I think people who don't like the way things are need to look at themselves first. They need to get right with God and change their own ways…. If everybody did that, we'd be all right."

Like a lot of philanthropists, Oseola McCarty knew that giving is its own pleasure. When a journalist from *People* magazine asked her why she didn't spend the money she'd saved on herself, she smiled and answered that, thanks to the pleasure that comes from making a gift, "I am spending it on myself."

"I am proud that I worked hard and that my money will help young people who worked hard to deserve it. I'm proud that I am leaving something positive in this world. My only regret is that I didn't have more to give."

Like a lot of philanthropists, McCarty hoped to inspire others to similar acts. And she did. In addition to the local outpouring that more than tripled her endowment, cable TV mogul Ted Turner decided to donate a billion dollars to charity after hearing her story. He was quoted in the *New York Times* saying, "If that little woman can give away everything she has, then I can give a billion."

And like a lot of philanthropists, Oseola McCarty knew she didn't have to save the whole world. She cast her buckets down and fixed what was at hand. "I can't do everything. But I can do something to help somebody. And what I *can* do I *will* do."

……

Oseola McCarty deserves to be recognized not only for her own accomplishments, but as a representative of millions of other everyday Americans who give humbly of themselves, year after year. There are Oseolas all across the U.S.

Gus and Marie Salenske were a plumber and nurse who lived quietly in a small house in Syracuse, New York. Their one indulgence was weekly square dancing; other than that, they were savers. When they died, it was reported in 2012, this simple couple left more than $3 million to good causes, mostly their beloved Catholic church.

Anne Scheiber was a shy auditor who retired in 1944 with just $5,000 in the bank. Through frugal living and inspired stock-picking she turned this into $22

million by the time she died in 1995 at the age of 101. She left it all to Yeshiva University so that bright but needy girls could attend college and medical school.

Minnesota farmer Harvey Ordung consumed modestly, and invested prudently. When he passed on, he left $4.5 million to 12 charities in his home region of Rock County. The largest portion went to a program that gives college scholarships to local kids.

Elinor Sauerwein painted her own home, kept a vegetable garden, and mowed the lawn herself until she was in her 90s. She eschewed restaurants, cable TV, and other expenses as unnecessary luxuries. But when she died in 2011, she left $1.7 million to the local Modesto, California, branch of the Salvation Army. "Her goal for years and years was to amass as much as she could so it would go to the Salvation Army," reported her financial adviser.

Millicent Atkins earned a teaching degree in 1940 but eventually left that profession to help manage the family farm in South Dakota. She developed a keen eye for productive land, and an appetite for buying. She eventually owned 4,127 acres. When she died in 2012 she left $38 million to two nearby universities and her church.

Albert Lexie shined shoes in Pittsburgh for more than 50 years, and made a decision early on to donate every penny of his tips to the Free Care Fund of the Children's Hospital of Pittsburgh, which benefits families who can't afford treatment. From 1981 to 2013, Lexie handed over more than $200,000 to Children's Hospital—a third of his total earnings.

Gifts like these cumulate with millions of others from ordinary Americans in a powerful way. Between 70 and 90 percent of U.S. households make charitable contributions every year, with the average household contribution being $2,500. That is *two to 20 times* as much generosity as in equivalent Western European nations. In addition, a quarter to a half of all U.S. adults volunteer their time to charitable activities at some point in a year, giving billions of hours in total.

The result: A massive charitable flow of more than $360 billion per year, with 81 percent coming from generous individuals. Only 14 percent of all annual charity in the U.S. comes in the form of foundation grants. Just 5 percent is contributed by corporations.

One may quite accurately say that it is Oseola McCarty and similarly modest partners who make America the most generous nation on earth.

☞ *Karl Zinsmeister*

Further information

○ "Oral history with Miss Oseola McCarty," University of Southern Mississippi Center for Oral History and Cultural Heritage (1997), lib.usm.edu/legacy/spcol/coh/cohmccartyo.html

○ *New York Times* reporting, nytimes.com/1995/08/13/us/all-she-has-150000-is-going-to-a-university.html
○ *Oseola McCarty's Simple Wisdom for Rich Living*, edited by Shannon Maggio (Longstreet Press, 1996)

NETTIE MCCORMICK

Nancy ("Nettie") Fowler McCormick never expected to lead a life of ease. Orphaned at age 7, she learned early on to make the most of her days. Her firm moral purpose continued to steer her through life, even after her marriage to one of the wealthiest men in American history, Cyrus McCormick, inventor of the mechanical reaper.

Nettie was born in 1835, the youngest of three children. Her father was a dry-goods merchant in northwestern New York. After he died, her mother ran the business until her own death a few years later. At that point, the little girl was sent to live with her uncle and grandmother—both devout Methodists and generous givers in their community.

These early tragedies, combined with her subsequent upbringing, did much to shape her future philanthropy. Raised to be a faithful Methodist, she felt responsibility to God to be a good steward of her resources and time on earth. The young Nettie once wrote in her diary, "Usefulness is the great thing in life—to do something for others leaves a sweeter odor than a life of pleasure."

Her uncle Eldridge Merick's prosperity afforded new opportunities for young Nettie. His involvement in the church and community and his keen business sense had a prevailing influence on his niece, and his wealth provided her the opportunity for further education and training. Nettie attended Falley Seminary in Fulton, Emma Willard's Troy Female Seminary, and the Genesee Wesleyan Seminary in Lima, New York. As a student at Genesee Wesleyan, Nettie took on a leading role in the school's missionary society and was honored by the school as a lifetime member.

At the age of 21, while on a trip to visit friends in Chicago, Nettie met Cyrus McCormick, an inventor, businessman, and faithful Presbyterian. McCormick was over twice her age when the two began courting, and the couple married a year later, in 1858. Both were strong-willed individuals, and their marriage was by many accounts a challenging one. Nevertheless, it proved to be a formidable business partnership. Nettie was her husband's closest business associate.

She was also active in their joint philanthropic activities. They directed most of their charitable giving to religious organizations, usually churches and

schools. McCormick gave away $550,000 in his lifetime to the Presbyterian Church, McCormick Theological Seminary, and other church colleges.

In October 1871, the Great Chicago Fire destroyed the McCormick Harvesting Machine plant. Then aged 62, Cyrus was ready to retire. Nettie, however, devoted her considerable energy to rebuilding the business. She oversaw the construction of the new plant, and formed the reorganized International Harvester Company. She was the untitled director and president of the company until her husband's death in 1884.

Nettie McCormick faithfully followed the directions of her husband's will, which stated that she and Cyrus Jr. were to keep the estate intact for five years and make donations to charitable purposes that they believed Cyrus Sr. would have made if he was still living. Then she turned her attention to her own philanthropic causes.

She felt strongly that any gift she made should have a moral purpose, provide a spiritual or educational benefit, and enable the recipients to better themselves. Over time, her focus broadened to a greater variety of institutions but her pattern of giving to education, youth, and religious institutions remained. Orphanages, schools, colleges, hospitals, and relief agencies were all beneficiaries of her generosity, and she supported causes at home and abroad. She gave gifts to institutions such as Moody Bible Institute and Princeton University. She helped establish hospitals in Persia and Siam, and gave large gifts to religious colleges overseas, including Alborz College in Tehran and a theological seminary in Korea.

> McCormick held that any gift should have a moral purpose, provide a spiritual or educational benefit, and enable the recipients to better themselves.

Nettie carefully managed her giving and investments. At Tusculum College in Tennessee, she helped select faculty, devise curricular offerings, and appoint a new college president. Among her many charitable projects at the school, Nettie spearheaded the construction of a new women's dormitory, named for her daughter Virginia McCormick. Nettie gave specific stipulations as to how her money was to be spent on this project, and she oversaw the building process, even choosing the architect, to ensure that Tusculum had a fully modern facility for women. As a result, the school's enrollment of female students jumped from nine to 102. To this day, Tusculum holds a Nettie Fowler McCormick Service Day, focused on charitable works and improvement of the school grounds.

Upon her death in 1923, the obituary in the *Chicago Daily Tribune*, giving evidence of her private nature, grossly underestimated the scope of her philanthropy. It credited her with supporting six schools, whereas she is known to have been a major funder of at least 46 schools, and possibly more. Over the course of her life, Nettie McCormick gave away millions of dollars without expecting or wanting any recognition—in this life, at least.

※ Kari Barbic

Further information

○ Charles Burgess, *Nettie Fowler McCormick: Profile of an American Philanthropist* (State Historical Society of Wisconsin, 1962)

○ Stella Roderick, *Nettie Fowler McCormick* (Richard R. Smith Co., 1956)

ANDREW MELLON

Andrew Mellon was one of the most prominent financiers in American history. Mellon investments helped launch the aluminum, coke, and carborundum industries; by the 1920s, he paid the third-highest income tax in the United States. Mellon dedicated his fortune to several favored charitable causes, including the University of Pittsburgh and what became Carnegie Mellon University. But Mellon also loved art, and was, in effect, an artist in the field of philanthropy. Nowhere is this clearer than in his crafting of one of the world's great museums: the National Gallery of Art.

Mellon's key insight was that charity differs only somewhat from for-profit business. He therefore applied his own business principles to the shaping of his charitable gifts. Mellon principles were, in no particular order: Compete with the private sector, and honor it. Forget your ego. Ruthlessly exploit the mechanism of compounding. Always go up-market. To these fundamentals, Mellon added a final principle: When in doubt, make it marble.

After great success as a Pittsburgh banker and industrialist, Andrew Mellon came to Washington, D.C., in 1921, to serve as Secretary of the Treasury for President Warren Harding. Harding died in office, but Mellon stayed, serving first Calvin Coolidge and then Herbert Hoover as the Treasury Secretary. During this time, he settled on the contribution he wanted to make to the nation's capital: a grand art gallery.

The need was clear. Anyone strolling past the random ramshackle structures on Pennsylvania Avenue would see that Washington fell short of other national capitals in welcoming visitors with dignified edifices and inspiring attractions. Officials had ambitious plans for what we now know

as the Federal Triangle, where the National Mall was to be fringed with architecture that would elevate "the glory of Washington."

Mellon's aim was more than aesthetic. Many of the structures rising across Washington were monuments to government. Mellon thought private effort should help create a prominent landscape on the National Mall itself.

The art gallery Mellon envisioned would reinforce points he had made in his efforts at the Department of the Treasury. He warned that vigorous taxation snatched productive capital from the hands of private citizens who would have employed it to create compound gains. Leaving more cash in private coffers, he argued, would in the end benefit the public better than immediate federal outlays. The gallery would be a monument to the power of private investment, creation, and societal benefit.

In the 1930s, while President Franklin Roosevelt was assigning the private sector more blame than praise, Mellon offered the nation a gift from the fruits of private enterprise: a stunning assemblage of 152 works, with an offer to build a museum on the Mall worthy to house them. Construction began in 1937, and Mellon spent an extra $5 million on pink Tennessee marble—an order so large it constituted, in Depression time, an economic stimulus all by itself. Few other expenses were spared at the gallery, whose architectural details gave

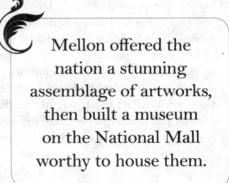

Mellon offered the nation a stunning assemblage of artworks, then built a museum on the National Mall worthy to house them.

much thought to citizen comfort. Understanding that some tourists would have difficulty handling stairs, for instance, Mellon kept his structure as horizontal as possible.

It was in amassing the content of the gallery that Mellon's intelligence and cunning most exerted itself. Crossing the globe with the opportunistic eye of an eagle, Mellon grabbed up value where he found it, including in Lenin's Bolshevik Russia. Some have said his large purchases from Petersburg's Hermitage Museum made Mellon more buzzard than eagle, but the Pennsylvania banker classed his acquisitions differently. Lenin and the communists stole art from owners and denigrated the processes that produced it, Mellon believed, so preserving and displaying the works respectfully in the United States for all people to enjoy was both wise and fair.

As with the construction materials, so with the content: Mellon chose only top paintings for his gallery, like the *Alba Madonna* of Raphael, and

Pietro Perugino's triptych. With fewer than 200 such objects meeting this standard, Mellon thus "had an art museum six blocks long on his hands, and enough paintings to decorate a good-sized duplex apartment," as critic S. N. Behrman quoted a Mellon friend saying. Mellon was wagering that if he gave samples of the highest quality work from many periods, he would provide the seeds for an eventual full collection. His gift would draw other gifts.

And he was right. By the time President Roosevelt dedicated the gallery in 1941, several other great business leaders—Samuel Kress, Joseph Widener, and Lessing Rosenwald—had already made major contributions. Mellon's inspiration eventually drew one donor who all philanthropists hope will follow them: his own son. Paul Mellon's 1999 bequest of 100 pictures and $75 million was the largest gift ever offered to the National Gallery.

The National Gallery was an immediate success. Ready by wartime, it provided a welcome refuge to soldiers on leave, and a haven to many seeking beauty and peace in a world lacking both. Even President Roosevelt, author of so many tax increases, could not hide his enthusiasm at Mellon's gift. "The giver of this building has matched the richness of his gift with the modesty of his spirit, stipulating that the gallery shall be known not by his name but by the nation's," said Roosevelt at the opening. "And those other collectors of paintings and of sculpture who have already joined, or who propose to join, their works of art to Mr. Mellon's…have felt the same desire to establish, not a memorial to themselves, but a monument to the art that they love and the country to which they belong."

↳ *Amity Shlaes*

Further information

○ David Cannadine, *Mellon: An American Life* (Alfred Knopf, 2006)
○ David Finley, *A Standard of Excellence: Andrew W. Mellon Founds the National Gallery of Art at Washington* (Smithsonian, 1973)
○ Amity Shlaes, *The Forgotten Man: A New History of the Great Depression* (Harper, 2007)

J. P. MORGAN

John Pierpont Morgan ranks among the preeminent financiers in American history. He was born in 1837 and raised in Hartford, Connecticut, heir to two of New England's most distinguished families. Educated in Boston, Switzerland, and Germany, he was groomed by his father for a career in international finance. In 1857 Morgan went to work in London at his father's bank. He moved to New York a year later, where he was based until his death in 1913.

Morgan was a central figure in many of the most important transactions of the Industrial Revolution. He was an active investor in railroads, reorganizing the Albany & Susquehanna (1869), the New York Central (1885), the Philadelphia & Reading (1886), and the Chesapeake & Ohio (1888). In 1892, Morgan arranged the merger of Edison General Electric and Thomson-Houston Electric, leading to the creation of General Electric. In 1901, he led the consolidation of Carnegie Steel Company with several other similar concerns, creating history's first billion-dollar corporation in U.S. Steel. When a financial panic gripped Wall Street in October 1907, Morgan took charge, convincing New York bankers and businessmen to pledge their own assets to provide liquidity to the faltering financial system. Thanks to his intervention, the crisis was averted, and by November financial markets returned to relative stability.

Morgan was among the most maligned of the so-called "robber barons." He is remembered as a beefy, red-faced bully, fierce and lonely, possessed of small ideas and consumed by enormous greed. All of this is deeply unfair to Morgan. Recent biographers—most notably Jean Strouse—have looked at Morgan with fresh eyes, finding a much more subtle and interesting character than his caricature would allow. He was a genuine polymath, fluent in French and German, steeped in literature and the arts, whose aptitude for mathematics prompted one of his professors at the University of Göttingen to encourage him to consider an academic appointment. He was remarkably generous, and devoted his considerable wealth and energy to a few favored causes.

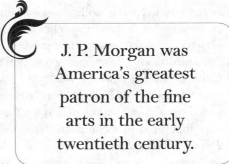

J. P. Morgan was America's greatest patron of the fine arts in the early twentieth century.

At the turn of the century, Morgan was America's greatest patron of the fine arts. He began collecting art while touring Rome, not long after finishing at Göttingen at the age of 19. It was the start of a lifelong love affair. He was the driving force behind the rise of the Metropolitan Museum of Art, serving as president and donating extensively from his personal acquisitions. His reputation, however, was established by a bitter enemy, the artist and critic Roger Fry. Fry belonged to the Bloomsbury Set, and had once been a curator of paintings at the Met. He suspected—not without reason—that Morgan was behind his firing. "A crude historical imagination," Fry icily pronounced, "was the only flaw in his otherwise perfect insensibility."

As Strouse notes, the letters Fry wrote to his wife during a purchasing tour of Europe in 1907 tell a rather different story. They praise at surprising length the artistic sensibilities of the "Big Man." Contemporary critics increasingly agree with this pre-embittered assessment. "Almost single-handed, Morgan turned the Metropolitan from a merely notable collection into one of the three or four finest anywhere," writes historian Paul Johnson. "Morgan obviously employed experts…but it is astonishing how few mistakes he allowed them to make on his behalf."

Morgan was a man of truly catholic charitable interests. In addition to his lifelong engagement with the arts, he was deeply interested in the natural sciences. A trustee of the American Museum of Natural History for 44 years, Morgan served on the board from the museum's opening in 1869 until his death in 1913. He was often the museum's lead donor—frequently giving under condition of anonymity—and he served at various times as vice president, treasurer, and finance committee chairman. Among his many contributions to the museum, notes Strouse, were "collections of minerals, gems, meteorites, amber, books, prehistoric South American relics, American Indian costumes, fossil vertebrates, skeletons, and the mummy of a pre-Columbian miner preserved in copper salts."

Third among Morgan's great philanthropic interests was the Episcopal Church. Throughout his working life, he set aside three weeks every third year to meet with Episcopalian bishops and discuss theology. He served as treasurer and senior warden at St. George's Episcopal Church. In 1886, he was appointed to a committee responsible for revising the *Book of Common Prayer*, which, writes Strouse, "he knew practically by heart." He quietly underwrote the salaries of scores of Manhattan clergymen and contributed heavily—$500,000 in 1892 alone—to the construction of Manhattan's (as-yet unfinished) Cathedral of St. John the Divine.

Morgan was born in 1837, a year after the Second Bank of the United States lost its charter; he died in 1913, a few months before the creation of the Federal Reserve Bank. In his lifetime, there was no central bank. That role was filled, with considerable moral seriousness, by Morgan himself. Perhaps the least noted but most enduring testament to his public-spiritedness was how little he abused that trust. When Morgan died, the newspapers estimated the value of his estate at about $80 million (or about $1.7 billion in 2011), a fraction of the wealth of the businessmen he financed. ("And to think," marveled John Rockefeller upon learning the news, "he wasn't even a rich man!") For Morgan, finance and philanthropy were different, but never opposite, forms of service.

↜ *Christopher Levenick*

Further information

○ Jean Strouse, *Morgan: American Financier* (Random House, 1999)

○ Ron Chernow, *The House of Morgan: American Banking Dynasty and the Rise of Modern Finance* (Atlantic Monthly Press, 1990)

○ Frederick Lewis Allen, *The Great Pierpont Morgan* (Harper Brothers, 1949)

JOHN OLIN

John Olin was an entrepreneur and industrialist who went on to become one of the twentieth century's most influential philanthropists in public policy.

Olin was born in 1892, in Alton, Illinois, the son of a businessman who owned a gunpowder mill. He attended Cornell University, majoring in chemistry. Upon his graduation in 1913, Olin joined the family business, which had grown into the Western Cartridge Company, a maker of ammunition.

Early on, Olin showed a flair for developing new products. Twenty-four patents bear his name, all for arms and ammunition manufacture and design. His best-known innovation was the Super-X shotgun shell, which extended firing range and became popular among hunters.

Olin's real genius, however, was in finance and executive leadership. During the Depression, his company acquired Winchester Repeating Arms. In 1938, Olin helped build the large St. Louis Ordnance Ammunition Plant. When the Second World War erupted, his family firm, rechristened Olin Industries, became a major provider of ammunition to U.S. and Allied forces.

After the war, the company expanded into chemical production and other areas. Olin was fiercely competitive: "Show me a good loser and I'll show you a loser," he liked to say. In 1957, *Fortune* ranked Olin and his brother Spencer at #31 on its list of the wealthiest Americans, estimating their net worth at $75 million.

In his spare time, Olin was an avid sportsman. He was featured as a hunter on the cover of the November 17, 1958 edition of *Sports Illustrated*. In 1974, his horse, Cannonade, won the Kentucky Derby.

The John M. Olin Foundation was started in 1953. For several years, it was a conventional rich man's philanthropy, supporting the Cornell University Alumni Fund and several other causes. By 1973, however, Olin decided on a special mission: "I would like to use this fortune to help to preserve the system which made its accumulation possible in only two lifetimes, my father's and mine," he told Frank O'Connell, a company employee who coordinated foundation activities in the 1970s. Olin decided to deploy his money to defend America's tradition of free enterprise and individual liberty, and bring its benefits to as many Americans as possible.

Over the next three decades, the Olin Foundation dispensed hundreds of millions of dollars to scholars, think tanks, publications, and other entities. Its savvy underwriting shaped the direction and aided the growth of the modern conservative movement that first sprang into visibility in the 1980s. Perhaps more than any other philanthropist of the modern era, Olin succeeded by clearly defining a mission (he was as clear about what he did *not* want to do as what he hoped to achieve), establishing a timeline, and carefully selecting dedicated partners who shared his vision.

In 1977, Olin stepped down as his foundation's president. William E. Simon, the former U.S. Secretary of the Treasury, replaced him, leading the foundation until his death in 2000, when he was succeeded by James Piereson, the foundation's longtime executive director. Another executive director, Michael Joyce, influenced the foundation in its early years, before joining the Lynde & Harry Bradley Foundation, which became a significant force with many of the same goals as the Olin Foundation. Irving Kristol, the neoconservative writer and intellectual, was an important influence on all of these men.

> Olin decided to use his fortune to defend America's tradition of free enterprise and individual liberty.

One of the Olin Foundation's signal achievements was the establishment of law and economics centers at major colleges and universities. A brand-new discipline that brought empirical rigor and clear-eyed assessment to the understanding of governance and the solving of social problems, programs in law and economics gained firm footholds after the foundation started devoting more resources to that cause than any other. The law schools at the University of Chicago, Harvard, Stanford, Virginia, and Yale started law and economics centers in Olin's name.

In 1982, the Olin Foundation sponsored a seminal academic conference for law students and professors that gave rise to the Federalist Society, a membership organization of conservative and libertarian law students, lawyers, judges, and professors. The Federalist Society would go on to transform legal education and shape the federal judiciary.

Olin also became a backer of alternative campus newspapers at colleges where right-of-center perspectives of various sorts were missing, or even blocked, from public debate. The foundation also supported pioneering researchers, journalists, and public intellectuals in producing influential new arguments and books. These included Allan Bloom (author of *The Closing of*

the American Mind), Linda Chavez (*Out of the Barrio*), Dinesh D'Souza (*Illiberal Education*), Milton Friedman (*Free to Choose*), Francis Fukuyama (*The End of History* and *The Last Man*), Samuel Huntington (*The Clash of Civilizations*), Richard John Neuhaus (*The Naked Public Square*), and Michael Novak (*The Spirit of Democratic Capitalism*). Olin funding was often aimed more at generating constructive debate than in promoting particular points of view: Fukuyama and Huntington, for instance, were friendly rivals on vital questions about the nature of global conflict.

Organizations that relied on Olin support as they grew into important roles in American intellectual life and policy debates included the American Enterprise Institute, Center for Individual Rights, Heritage Foundation, Hoover Institution, Manhattan Institute, National Association of Scholars, *New Criterion*, The Philanthropy Roundtable, and many others. Olin research funding was crucial in launching new analyses that ended up driving consequential national reform movements in areas like school choice, welfare reform, and colorblind public policy.

Olin was also distinctive in how he organized his philanthropy. Before he died in 1982, he instructed his foundation to spend itself out of existence within a generation of his passing. Having observed the spectacle of the Ford Foundation turning against what many took to be the purposes of its founding family, Olin wanted to make sure his own foundation remained true to its mission. He believed a preordained lifespan was the best protection against wandering goals at a foundation, and a disconnection from the donor's intent.

Robust investment gains complicated Olin's objective of dispersing all of its funding relatively quickly. At the same time, this endowment growth and the determination to move all money out the door in a limited timespan gave the foundation the means to have an even larger effect during its operating years. This was magnified by a disciplined focus on doing a limited number of things very well in the realm of public policy, and a decision to support a limited number of the most effective entities, rather than dispersing grants far and wide.

By early in the twenty-first century, the Olin Foundation was issuing a series of large "termination grants" to proven recipients. In 2005, the foundation held its final board meeting, completed its last round of grantmaking decisions, and closed its doors.

⇀ John J. Miller

Further information

○ John J. Miller, *A Gift of Freedom: How the John M. Olin Foundation Changed America* (Encounter Books, 2006)

RAYMOND ORTEIG

Raymond Orteig was an early twentieth-century French-American hotelier, aviation enthusiast, and philanthropist. The scale of his charitable giving was not especially impressive, but Orteig's philanthropy was enormously consequential. He funded an innovative incentive prize that inspired Charles Lindbergh to make the first New York-to-Paris airplane flight. Decades later, it would directly inspire other incentive prizes, including the one that launched a new era of non-governmental manned space flight.

Born in 1870 in a shepherd community in the French Pyrenees, Orteig immigrated to the United States at the age of 12. He took a job as a bar porter in New York City, making $2 per week, and soon found work at the Hotel Martin in Greenwich Village. Orteig worked his way up in the hotel, serving as waiter, head waiter, and hotel manager, and by 1902 he had saved up enough money to buy the hotel. He renamed it the Hotel Lafayette in honor of the Marquis de Lafayette, the young French nobleman who served as George Washington's aide-de-camp. Soon thereafter, he acquired a second property, the Brevoort Hotel in Greenwich Village.

Orteig's properties were jovial places, overseen by the short and bald bon vivant. They were particular favorites of French airmen who steamed over to the United States in the years after the First World War. Aviation was a young and risky field, and Orteig was captivated by the aviators' war stories. "He developed a serious passion for aviation, dreaming of the good that air travel could do and wanting to find a way to help progress along," write Peter Diamandis and Steven Kotler. In 1919—inspired by news of a nonstop flight from Newfoundland to Ireland and impassioned by the fellow-feeling among American and French flying aces—Orteig wrote to the Aero Club of America: "Gentlemen, as a stimulus to courageous aviators, I desire to offer, through the auspices and regulations of the Aero Club of America, a prize of $25,000 to the first aviator of any Allied country crossing the Atlantic in one flight from Paris to New York or New York to Paris, all other details in your care."

The distance, 3,600 miles, was twice that of the longest previous nonstop flight. At first, Orteig's prize seemed impossible. After five years it remained unclaimed; Orteig renewed his offer. But the incentive prize spurred technological improvements, and aviators were determined to capture the purse. (Six men died in various failed attempts.)

On May 20, 1927, Charles Lindbergh took off from Roosevelt Field on Long Island in pursuit of the award. Some 33 hours later, he landed the *Spirit*

of St. Louis at Paris's Le Bourget airfield. Orteig was vacationing in France and rushed immediately to Paris, where he met Lindbergh and arranged for the purse to be awarded. He later treasured the endorsed and canceled check as one of his proudest possessions.

To be sure, the idea of an incentive prize was not unprecedented. In 1714, the British Parliament created a Longitude Prize, to be awarded to anyone who devised a simple method by which ships at sea could determine their longitude within 60 nautical miles. But Orteig's was among the first incentive prizes offered by a private individual. And it encouraged enormous innovation. By some estimates, the purse sparked $16 of investments in new technologies for every dollar the giver had offered.

"The Orteig Prize captured the world's attention and ushered in an era of change," write Diamandis and Kotler. "A landscape of daredevils and barnstormers was transformed into one of pilots and passengers. In 18 months, the number of paying U.S. passengers grew thirtyfold…. The number of pilots in the United States tripled. The number of airplanes quadrupled."

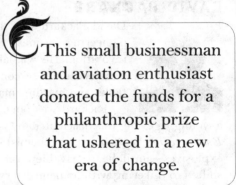

This small businessman and aviation enthusiast donated the funds for a philanthropic prize that ushered in a new era of change.

"Orteig-inspired madness" is how historian Joe Jackson dubbed the 12 years of extraordinary aviation progress after Lindbergh won the Orteig Prize. Hawaii was reached by an airplane in 1927. The U.S.-to-Australia route was flown in 1928. Amelia Earhart became the first woman to fly solo across the Atlantic in 1932. Patents were awarded for jet engine designs, and rocket-fueled aviation was tested. Delta and American Airlines date to this era. In the summer of 1939, Pan Am launched the first regular passenger service from the U.S. across the Atlantic on its Boeing "flying boats."

Although Orteig himself flew regularly in the U.S., he never flew across the Atlantic. He made his annual summer sojourn to his native France by ship. Twenty years after he helped launched a new era in travel and innovation, the hotelier died in 1939.

Orteig's incentive prize, however, has outlived him in influence. His achievement was the direct inspiration for the X Prizes created by Peter Diamandis. The initial X Prize, funded by the Ansari family, offered $10 million to the first non-governmental team to launch a reusable three-person manned spacecraft into space twice within two weeks. With funding from

Microsoft co-founder Paul Allen, Burt Rutan's *SpaceShipOne* took home the X Prize in 2004.

In the 1920s, Raymond Orteig's philanthropy opened the skies over the Atlantic. Nearly 80 years later, its echo opened the heavens to private spaceflight. Thus did the one-time porter inspire a new generation of humans to go aloft.

⤳ Evan Sparks

Further information

○ Richard Bak, *The Big Jump: Lindbergh and the Great Atlantic Air Race* (John Wiley, 2011)

○ Peter Diamandis and Steven Kotler, *Abundance: The Future Is Better Than You Think* (Free Press, 2012)

○ Joe Jackson, *Atlantic Fever: Lindbergh, His Competitors, and the Race to Cross the Atlantic* (MacMillan, 2012)

DAVID PACKARD

David Packard was the co-founder of Hewlett-Packard, a pioneering business that accelerated America's computer revolution. He was also a prominent public servant, and a major funder of conservation efforts, public-policy think tanks, and his alma mater, Stanford University.

Packard was born in Pueblo, Colorado, in 1912. From a young age, he was fascinated by science. Relying on the *World Book Encyclopedia*, he dabbled in chemistry, cooking up his own homemade explosives—until he nearly blew off his left thumb. Young David then shifted to tinkering with homemade crystal-radio sets. By the time he was in high school, the six-foot-five Packard stood out for his athletic prowess—he lettered in football, basketball, and track—and his academic achievement.

In 1930, Packard began his freshman year at Stanford University. (During the lean years of the Great Depression, his father managed the quarterly tuition of $114 thanks to one of the era's few steady jobs: bankruptcy referee.) At Stanford, Packard had a remarkably rounded college career. He won three varsity letters in his first year. He studied engineering under Fred Terman, a relentless innovator whose research on vacuum tubes, circuits, and radios helped establish the field of electrical engineering. Under Terman's mentorship, Packard dropped basketball and track (but not football, he later explained, because of "peer pressure") and devoted most of his attention to his studies.

Packard excelled academically, and met his future business partner at Stanford, William Hewlett, another of Terman's students. He also met his future wife, Lucile Salter, while he was washing dishes at the Delta Gamma sorority. They married in 1938, forming a bond that lasted until her death in 1987, producing

one son and three daughters. After graduation, Packard worked briefly for General Electric in Schenectady, New York, before returning to Stanford to earn a master's degree in electrical engineering in 1938.

Just as some American presidents were born in one-room log cabins, so too have some iconic American corporations been launched in one-car garages. One of the greatest of these is Hewlett-Packard, a pioneer in personal and business computers, and among the largest manufacturers of electronics in the world. It was founded in 1939 in Palo Alto, California, by Hewlett and Packard with an initial investment of $538. When the company incorporated in 1947, they tossed a coin to decide its name. Packard won the toss and put Hewlett's name first. It was that sort of partnership.

Having set up business in Packard's garage, Hewlett and Packard's first product was an innovative audio oscillator, a device for testing and synchronizing sound equipment. At the time, precision audio oscillators sold for over $200, but they introduced a temperature-dependent resistor that greatly improved stability. The two amateur history buffs decided to charge $54.40, after the 1844 Democratic rallying cry, "Fifty-four Forty or Fight!" Walt Disney bought eight of the oscillators for use in the production of *Fantasia*. The partners never looked back. In 2014, the company's net revenue was $111

The Packards became generous givers, and then left the bulk of their $4 billion estate to philanthropy.

billion, with 302,000 employees and an estimated 1 billion customers worldwide.

Hewlett concentrated on the product side of the business while Packard tended to the business side, where he ran a famously tight ship. (When Hewlett-Packard went public in 1961, several executives missed the ceremony at the New York Stock Exchange because they got lost on the subway on the way down from their midtown hotel. Their expense accounts didn't cover taxis, let alone limousines.) Packard stayed with the company he founded the rest of his life, except for two years (1969-1971) when he served as Deputy Secretary of Defense. He remained remarkably forward-looking throughout his business career; it was Packard who decided in 1986 to register the domain name HP.com, fully a decade before the Internet became commercially important.

Packard's contributions to corporate America are well-known; his beneficence as a philanthropist, perhaps less so. That is unfortunate, not least because of the scale of his giving. He and his wife established the David and Lucile Packard Foundation, to which he left the bulk of his $4 billion estate. Moreover, the

Packards were notable givers during their lifetimes.

Environmental conservation in general, and marine conservation in particular, was a lifelong concern for Packard. Perhaps the most conspicuous result of Packard's conservation giving is the Monterey Bay Aquarium, visited by 1.8 million people annually. Located on the site of an old California sardine cannery that had been featured in two of John Steinbeck's novels, it ranks among the world's largest aquariums. At the 1984 opening, Packard credited two of his daughters who studied marine biology—Nancy and Julie (Julie remains executive director of the aquarium)—with fanning his interest in the project.

Packard invested himself in the aquarium. Before beginning, he studied other successful models. "What we learned," he explained in a 1985 interview, "was that most aquariums are built on a fixed budget, and they made short cuts." Not so Packard. ("The result was that the aquarium cost us $40 million instead of $10 million," he added.) The aquarium has spectacular exhibits, including a live California kelp forest, made possible by pumps that circulate 2,000 gallons per minute of ocean water from Monterey Bay. Naturally, Packard designed the wave machine that keeps the kelp undulating. "My children thought we shouldn't charge admission so that poor people could come," he later said. "I said we weren't going to do it that way. If what we did was right, people will pay for it. If it wasn't right, we shouldn't have done it."

David Packard, who flourished so abundantly in the American capitalist system, was a firm believer in the power of free markets to enrich society as a whole. He served for years on the boards of the Hoover Institution, the Herbert Hoover Foundation, and the American Enterprise Institute. He was an enthusiastic patron of each, reported *Philanthropy* magazine in 2000, "donating his time, talents, and fortune to their success." When AEI hit financial trouble in the early 1980s, Packard "helped very significantly with his finances and his advice," according to former AEI president Christopher DeMuth. "He bailed us out. He was a hands-on trustee, a great man."

The third principal recipient of the Packard family's generosity was Stanford University. In 1986, David and Lucile Packard donated $40 million to found the Lucile Packard Children's Hospital located in Palo Alto, which opened in 1991, four years after her death. It is regarded as one of the best pediatric hospitals in the country, with a physician staff of 650. In 1996, it merged with the Stanford Medical Center.

Packard funded three professorships at his alma mater, in engineering, marine science, and literature. He also funded everything from sports facilities

to the Terman Fellowships—named in honor of his old Stanford mentor to provide financial support to young science and engineering professors. In 1994, Packard partnered with Hewlett to donate $77 million to the school to build the David Packard Electrical Engineering Building next to the William Hewlett Teaching Center.

Altogether Packard and Hewlett, jointly and separately, donated more than $300 million to Stanford. As the university put it on his death, "Dave Packard, along with his wife, Lucile, and his partner, Bill Hewlett, have shaped and nurtured this university in ways that can only be compared to the founders, Jane and Leland Stanford."

"Everywhere I look I see the potential for growth, for discovery far greater than anything we have seen in the twentieth century," reflected David Packard in 1995, a year before he died. All mankind needed, he believed, was determination. "The state of change is proportional to the level of effort expended."

John Steele Gordon

Further information

◦ *Philanthropy* magazine article, philanthropyroundtable.org/topic/excellence_in_philanthropy/the_new_packard

◦ David Packard, *The HP Way: How Bill Hewlett and I Built Our Company* (HarperBusiness, 1995)

◦ Christophe Lécuyer, *Making Silicon Valley: Innovation and the Growth of High Tech, 1930-1970* (MIT Press, 1996)

GEORGE PEABODY

George Peabody is often referred to as the "father of modern philanthropy." It is believed that Peabody gave away about $8 million of his $16 million fortune within his lifetime. Peabody's generosity was hailed as an example for his contemporaries, and later generations of philanthropists have continued to invoke it.

Peabody was born in 1795, the third of eight children in a working-poor family from Danvers (since renamed Peabody), Massachusetts. His family could only afford to give him four years of formal schooling; at age 11, he was sent to apprentice at a general store. In 1811, his father died, in debt, forcing the sale of the family home and many of its belongings. George and his brothers had to feed, house, and clothe their mother and sisters. "I have never forgotten," he once reflected, "and never can forget the great privations of my early years."

Peabody moved south to Washington, D.C., where he opened a dry-goods store in Georgetown. He served in the Army during the War of 1812, where he met an older merchant named Elisha Riggs Sr. The two men hit it off, and Riggs offered to make Peabody, then 19 years old, a partner at his business, importing wholesale dry goods. The business flourished, and within three years, Peabody was worth $40,000, repaying his father's debts and providing a more comfortable life for his family.

In 1816, Peabody left D.C. and moved to Baltimore, where he spent the next two decades. Trusted for his fairness, Peabody prospered as a wholesale-goods merchant, and by 1827 was traveling to London to negotiate the sale of American cotton in Lancashire. In 1835, he established George Peabody & Co., a merchant bank offering securities in American enterprises—railroads, canals—to British and European investors.

His bank became one of the most important of his era, channeling much-needed British and European capital into promising ventures in the booming U.S. Given his rising stature among international bankers and London's unmatched centrality in the world of finance, Peabody moved to that city in 1837. Except for three visits back to the States, he remained in England for the rest of his life.

> Both in the scope of his giving and in the care and precision with which he targeted it, George Peabody was the "father of modern philanthropy."

But there was never any mistaking his first loyalties. His Fourth of July parties were a highlight of the London social calendar. But Peabody's patriotism went deeper than that. He put his reputation on the line during the Panic of 1837, pledging creditors that the states he represented would not default on their loan obligations—even securing an emergency $8 million loan to save Maryland's credit. Peabody refused the $60,000 commission for his services. The Maryland state treasury, he insisted, needed to pay bondholders first. When several states did default, Peabody moved heaven and earth to persuade their legislatures to resume payment, with interest.

George Peabody never quite escaped the marks of his boyhood poverty. He routinely worked ten-hour days, every day of the week, and during one 12-year stretch he never took off three consecutive days. He was frugal to the point of absurdity. His partner, Junius Morgan (father of J. Pierpont Morgan, who began his distinguished career in finance at the New York office of George Peabody), once found him standing in a drenching London rain. Morgan knew that Peabody had left the office 20 minutes earlier and

stated, "Mr. Peabody, I thought you were going home." "Well, I am, Morgan," Peabody replied, "but there's only been a twopenny bus come along as yet and I am waiting for a penny one." At the time, Peabody had more than £1 million to his name, according to Ron Chernow.

In the early 1850s, Peabody's interests began to turn to philanthropy. For his Massachusetts hometown's 1852 centennial celebration he announced his plans to build the first Peabody Institute Library. The gift was followed by a number of similar benefactions throughout the United States. In 1857, he founded the Peabody Institute of Baltimore, which included a music conservatory, art gallery, lecture hall, and reference library. (It remains one of America's great music schools.) He built other Peabody Institute Libraries in Massachusetts, Vermont, and Washington, D.C. After a favorite nephew began teaching paleontology at Yale, Peabody funded a museum of archaeology and ethnology at Harvard and a museum of natural history at Yale.

In 1862 Peabody wrote a letter to the *Times* of London announcing his intention to create an endowment, initially stacked with £150,000 of his money, to "ameliorate the condition of the poor and needy of this great metropolis, and to promote their comfort and happiness." The Peabody Donation Fund (since renamed the Peabody Trust) was chartered to build affordable housing for the workingmen of London. With gas lights, running water, subsidized rent, and smartly appointed dwellings, the resulting structures were vastly superior to the housing otherwise available to the laboring poor. Peabody ensured that tenants were deserving, demanding punctual rent payments, instituting a nighttime curfew, and enforcing a morals code.

The gift was an instant sensation. Queen Victoria sent an adoring letter of thanks, enclosing a miniature portrait of herself and offering him a baronetcy or knighthood. (Peabody, a one-time infantryman who had borne arms against the British, declined the titles.) Peabody, proclaimed Prime Minister William Gladstone, "taught men how to use money, and how not to be its slave." He was the first American to be made Freeman of the City of London, and his statue was erected at the Royal Exchange. The gift "has repaid me for the care and anxiety of 50 years of commercial life." Peabody was so pleased with the results of his Donation Fund that, shortly before his death in 1869, he increased his total contribution to £500,000.

From 1866 to 1867, Peabody visited the United States and toured the American South. He was shocked by the war wreckage he found. Eager to help, he later announced the creation of the Peabody Education Fund, endowed with $2.1 million and charged with restoring primary and secondary education in West Virginia and 11 states of the former Confederacy. Peabody

offered school seed grants to counties and districts, requiring local leaders to provide matching funds and charter the schools under state legislation. The Peabody Education Fund worked for 47 years, promoting and sustaining public schools and funding teacher-training institutes throughout the South.

Peabody's generosity endeared him to British and Americans alike, and at his death in 1869 he was honored on both sides of the Atlantic. A grave was prepared for him at Westminster Abbey—the first American to receive such honors—and it was made clear that the royal family wished to bury him in England. It was not to be. Peabody's dying words ("Danvers—Danvers! Don't forget!"), combined with the explicit instructions of his will, deprived London of his remains. Peabody was returned to his native land by a joint squadron of British and American naval vessels, where the flags of former enemies were matched at half-mast, reflecting two nations united in mourning, and in admiration.

↳ *Kari Barbic*

Further information

○ Phebe Hanaford, *The Life of George Peabody* (B. B. Russell, 1870)
○ Muriel Hidy, *George Peabody: Merchant and Financier, 1829-1854* (Arno, 1978)
○ Franklin Parker, *George Peabody: A Biography* (Vanderbilt Press, 1995)
○ Robert Charles Winthrop, *Eulogy, Pronounced at the Funeral of George Peabody* (John Wilson & Son, 1870)

THOMAS PERKINS

Thomas Perkins was a wealthy Boston merchant who became one of the great patrons of early nineteenth century Boston. He supported dozens of local causes and was a founder of the Massachusetts General Hospital, the Bunker Hill Monument, and the Boston Athenaeum. But he is perhaps best remembered as the benefactor of the Perkins Institution for the Blind, a school that revolutionized education for the physically handicapped.

Perkins was born in Boston in December 1764, the sixth of eight children to one of the colony's most successful wine merchants. Not long after his fifth birthday, young Thomas crouched inside his father's shop as the Boston Massacre raged outside. It marked the beginning of a turbulent time. Thomas's father died in 1773, forcing his mother, Elizabeth, to provide for the family. She opened her own merchant house, trading china, glass, and wine. She scratched together enough to send her three sons to preparatory school, hoping that they would all attend Harvard.

Thomas, however, "was strongly inclined by temperament to active life," according to a biographer. He apprenticed with Messrs. Shattuck, one of

Boston's busiest counting houses. There he remained until he turned 21, at which point he joined a partnership with his two brothers, managing commerce between Boston and Santo Domingo. In February 1789, he sailed aboard the *Astraea* to the recently opened port of Canton, where he traded a cargo of cheese, lard, wine, and iron for tea and silk cloth. He threw himself into the maritime fur trade, acquiring sea otter skins from the Pacific Northwest and selling them in China. Perkins set up a trading house in Canton, from which he entered the highly profitable opium trade.

His commercial enterprises produced adventures. While fording a stream on the island of Java, Perkins saw a dozen crocodiles brush by his knees. He gambled on cock fights in Malaysia. Shortly after the Reign of Terror, Perkins was in France, where James Monroe, Minister of the United States, asked him to perform a service for the nation. Would he, asked Monroe, smuggle the Marquis de Lafayette's son, George Washington Lafayette, to the United States? Perkins cheerfully did so, and was promptly invited to Mount Vernon where he was thanked by Washington himself.

After the turn of the nineteenth century Perkins began to spend less time abroad and more time managing his affairs from Boston. With his growing wealth came increasing civic responsibilities. He was named president of the Boston branch of the First Bank of the United States, elected to the Massachusetts State

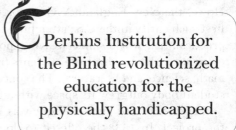

Perkins Institution for the Blind revolutionized education for the physically handicapped.

Senate, and made a colonel in the state militia. "Colonel Perkins," wrote Freeman Hunt, always took "a lively interest in all that concerned the welfare of the community in which he lived." He was an active supporter of the Mercantile Association of Young Men in Boston, the McLean Asylum for the Insane, and the Boston Museum of Fine Arts.

His first great philanthropic achievement was helping to found the Massachusetts General Hospital. In 1811, the Commonwealth granted a charter for the hospital that would take effect once the effort had raised $100,000. Perkins and his brother James each donated $5,000. By 1813, the full amount was raised and ground was broken. Perkins served on the board until 1827, including stints as president, vice president, and chairman.

Perkins was also a driving force behind the creation of the Bunker Hill Monument Association. In 1823, he hosted a breakfast at which William Ticknor suggested the memorial, and by June 1825 the Marquis de Lafayette laid the cornerstone. To haul granite from the quarry to barges on the Neponset, Perkins

organized the Granite Railway, the first commercial railroad in the United States. Insufficient funds frequently interrupted construction, but Perkins guided the project until the capstone was erected in July 1842.

Perkins was not a founder of the Boston Athenaeum, but he supported it with funds and with items from his own collection. At two critical junctures, he offered donations that would allow the library and gallery to keep its doors open. In 1826, when $30,000 was needed, Perkins and his nephew each stepped forward with $8,000. Then, in 1853, after the Athenaeum incurred enormous expenses while building its current home at 10½ Beacon Street, Perkins offered to retire whatever debt remained at the end of the year. His offer proved unnecessary (an unexpected bequest covered the shortfall) but to this day, a full-length portrait of Perkins adorns the Long Room in the ground floor entrance of the grateful Athenaeum.

Thomas Perkins may have had his biggest effect building up the Perkins School for the Blind. European schools for the blind fell into one of two camps: either vocational or academic. Under the leadership of Samuel Gridley Howe, the New England Asylum for the Blind, chartered in 1829 as the first such entity in the U.S., attempted to combine the two models: providing practical, real-world skills (weaving, pottery, and basket-making) while also cultivating the minds of the students (reading by "raised letters," as well as math, science, and literature). The concept was immediately popular, and the student body outgrew its space within a year.

Perkins, whose own eyesight was declining, took a special interest in the project. In 1833, he offered to donate his mansion on 17 Pearl Street, on one condition: that the school raise $50,000 within 30 days. The funds were collected, and the school moved into its new home, where it tripled its enrollment within six years. By 1839, it was clear that the school would need still more space. Perkins arranged the sale of the Pearl Street mansion and the purchase of the Mount Washington Hotel in South Boston, where the school remained for the next 75 years. Thankful for his sustained generosity, the school renamed itself the Perkins Institution for the Blind.

When Perkins died in 1854, a choir from the Perkins Institution sang the requiem. "Their high regard for his memory was seen," reported one newspaper, "in gleams of pleasure lighting their faces."

~ Christopher Levenick

Further information

○ Thomas Cary, *Memoir of Thomas Handasyd Perkins, Containing Extracts from His Diaries and Letters* (Little, Brown, 1856)

○ Freeman Hunt, *Lives of American Merchants* (Derby & Jackson, 1856)

○ Carl Seaburg, *Merchant Prince of Boston: Colonel T. H. Perkins* (Harvard, 1971)

J. HOWARD PEW

John Howard Pew was a successful oil entrepreneur who dedicated his philanthropy to serving the Presbyterian Church, funding higher education, and advancing the principles of a free society. Born into a devout family in 1882, the second son of the Sun Oil Company founder, Howard graduated from Grove City College at age 18. He studied at MIT, then joined his father and older brother at Sun Oil.

Pew was a talented engineer. His father assigned him to find a use for the unwanted black residue from refining Texas crude. "The young scientist didn't disappoint his father," writes a historian of the Pew Charitable Trusts. "He developed a lubricating oil with an extremely low cooling point; it became an international success under the name Sun Red Stock. Howard's laboratory work also yielded the first commercially successful petroleum asphalt, called Hydrolene."

In 1912, Howard took over the company along with his younger brother after their father died. For 35 years, Howard presided over Sun's rise to national prominence in the oil business. Under his leadership, the firm vastly extended its interests, eventually including refineries, pipelines, oilfields, shipbuilding, and mining.

Pew had a natural instinct for anticipating current events. He prepared for the Depression's market crashes, and was proud that no Sun Oil employee was laid off or given a pay cut during the 1930s. Sensing another war in Europe, in 1933 Pew started to sell off Sun's investments on the Continent. In 1937, Pew opened the world's first large-scale, commercial catalytic cracking plant. During World War II, Sun's shipbuilding plants turned out 250 vessels—40 percent of America's tankers.

The Pews' conservative views were strengthened by the Supreme Court's 1911 decision to break up the Standard Oil Company under the Sherman Anti-Trust Act. "It reinforced their conviction that industry thrives best when markets and competition are free," writes one historian. Pew held free-market convictions throughout his life. The austere man would bristle, however, if anyone suggested that his beliefs were anything less than disinterested. He vigorously criticized the New Deal as a "government cartel" worse than any "private cartel," but he insisted that his "attack on the New Deal has not been prompted by materialistic considerations, but rather a desire to preserve in America an opportunity for coming generations." After World War II, Pew also opposed price controls, arguing that "free prices are the regulators of American industry."

To that end, Pew became involved in organizations that promoted free-market causes. He was a board member of the Foundation of

Economic Education, led by Leonard Read (famous for his "I, Pencil" story that illustrates the working of the invisible hand). In joining FEE, Pew became part of the nexus of conservative and libertarian funders, organizations, and thinkers who helped to challenge the New Deal economic and political consensus. Pew didn't always agree with FEE's positions—he tussled with the board over FEE's anti-tariff perspective—but he found what biographer Mary Sennholz has called "a remnant of kindred souls...who shared with him a great concern about the future of individual freedom and the private property order." Pew also supported emerging conservative think tanks, such as the Hoover Institution and the American Enterprise Institute.

Pew's philanthropy extended to other causes as well—in particular education and civic organizations. But his "most enduring object of philanthropy," as Sennholz puts it, was Grove City College, his alma mater. "I hardly remember a time when I did not know Grove City College," Pew reminisced. He joined its board in 1912, and served until his death—including four decades as chairman. Pew visited frequently, funded numerous projects on campus, and celebrated Grove City's conservative principles and reputation for independence. "To teach this appreciation of our liberty and the recognition of the forces that threaten it, will always be the foremost mission of this college," he said. Pew supported dozens of other colleges as well, especially a number of historically black universities.

> Pew helped fund organizations and thinkers who challenged the New Deal, built evangelical religious institutions, and taught the tradition of liberty on campuses.

After he left the helm of Sun Oil in 1947, Howard devoted more of his time and money to religious organizations. "In the years that followed World War II," writes historian Kim Phillips-Fein, "his most abiding preoccupation was rescuing the Protestant church in America from what he saw as the dangerous influence of liberal ministers."

A lifelong member of the mainline Presbyterian Church, Pew had a multi-pronged approach to his religious philanthropy. First, he participated in church debates, serving as president of the church's board of trustees and chair of the National Lay Committee, and opposing what he called "the

same ideological mistake as was made by communism: that of attempting to change society by changing man's environment." Inspired by the Reformed doctrine that church councils should not take up secular causes, he fought church resolutions to endorse collective bargaining, promote birth control, and oppose capital punishment.

Pew also funded the then-emerging "parachurch" institutions of the evangelical movement. He gave millions to merge two seminaries to create Gordon-Conwell Theological Seminary, which is today actively evangelical and the largest seminary in the Northeast. He contributed $150,000 to launch *Christianity Today* magazine. He supported Billy Graham's ministry, the National Association of Evangelicals, and the International Congress on World Evangelization.

Finally, Pew sought to educate Christian ministers about the perils of left-wing politics, and encouraged church leaders to focus on mission and evangelizing. He helped to build up Spiritual Mobilization, which sought to counterbalance the New Deal surge toward centralization and redistribution of income. It involved business executives in lay church leadership and distributed books like F. A. Hayek's *The Road to Serfdom* to clergymen. Pew later helped to found (and contributed millions to) the Christian Freedom Foundation, which sent the *Christian Economics* newsletter twice a month to 180,000 ministers.

Pew did not achieve to his own satisfaction the goal of saving the Presbyterian Church from further decline. In his ecumenical work, however, he helped to create an evangelical infrastructure, from seminaries to publications, that would support new churches and soon eclipse the mainline in membership.

Pew and his wife, Helen, lived simply. They are said to have given 90 percent of their income away. In addition to the gifts they made during their lifetime, Pew and his brother and sisters contributed shares of Sun Oil to create the Pew Memorial Foundation, which would be dedicated to their ideals and in memory of their parents. In subsequent years, family members would establish separate funds under the umbrella of the family trust; the J. Howard Pew Freedom Trust was created in 1957. These together became known as the Pew Charitable Trusts. When Howard died in 1971, nearly all of his remaining $100 million was given to the Freedom Trust, which joined the $900 million (at the time) then held in the various other Pew trusts.

Pew gave a very specific mandate to his Freedom Trust:

> To acquaint the American people with the evils of bureaucracy and the vital need to maintain and preserve a limited form of

government in the United States as intended by our forebears and expressed by them in the Constitution and the Bill of Rights—to point out the dangerous consequences that result from an exchange of our American priceless heritage of freedom and self-determination, for the false promises of socialism and a planned economy…. and to inform our people of the struggle, persecution, hardship, sacrifice and death by which freedom of the individual was won.

To acquaint the American people with the values of a free market—the dangers of inflation—the need for a stable monetary standard—the paralyzing effects of government controls on the lives and activities of people….

To promote recognition of the interdependence of Christianity and freedom and to support and expound the philosophy that we must first have faith in God before we can enjoy the blessings of liberty—for God is the author of liberty….

This charter was honored to the letter for the first few years after Pew's death, but starting in 1977 it was quickly eroded in pursuit of more conventional and left-leaning goals. Recently, the head of the Pew Charitable Trusts could only say that Howard "was a man of strong convictions and his successors on our board are following in his tradition by having strong convictions," adding that "times are different now and I don't think we really know how Howard Pew's views would have played out."

And so, despite his clear statement of philanthropic purposes, the funds Pew placed in trust are being applied to very different aims.

ⓑ *Evan Sparks*

Further information

○ Joel Gardner and Sue Rardin, *Sustaining the Legacy: A History of the Pew Charitable Trusts* (Pew Charitable Trusts, 2001)

○ Mary Sennholz, editor, *Faith and Freedom: A Biographical Sketch of a Great American* (Grove City College, 1975)

○ Martin Morse Wooster, *The Great Philanthropists and the Problem of "Donor Intent"* (Capital Research Center, 2007)

HENRY PHIPPS

Henry Phipps was a lifelong friend and business partner of Andrew Carnegie. The second-largest shareholder in Carnegie Steel, he had a brilliant mind for finance and accumulated one of the 100 largest fortunes in American history. With that wealth, Phipps built extensive public parks and conservatories throughout his hometown of Pittsburgh. He funded research into the treatment, prevention, and cure of tuberculosis, an effort which led him to create reduced-cost housing for the working poor. Perhaps most notably, he funded the creation of the country's first medical faculty in the field of psychiatry.

Born in 1839, Phipps grew up in Pittsburgh. "Harry," as he was universally called, dropped out of school at age 14, taking work as a jeweler's apprentice for $1.25 per week. At 17, he borrowed 25¢ from his brother and placed an ad in the *Pittsburg Dispatch*. It read: "A willing boy wishes work." Dilworth and Biddle, a company that made iron and railroad spikes, offered him a job as an errand boy.

"There was no holding back a boy like that," Andrew Carnegie later reflected in his autobiography. Phipps spent five years taking night courses in accounting, during which time he was made bookkeeper and not long after, partner. Thomas Miller, another childhood friend, lent Phipps $800 to invest in a new railroad equipment company, headed by Andrew Kloman. The partnership flourished and was soon investing in steel mills. In 1865, it caught the eye of Andrew Carnegie, who bought out Kloman and Phipps. It was then that Harry decided to work for his boyhood pal—a job he would hold for the next 36 years.

Phipps handled corporate finance—"he's my money-getter," Carnegie often said. Known for his calm demeanor, Phipps was a diplomat among and negotiator between increasingly fractious shareholders. (More than anyone else, Phipps ensured that Carnegie Steel held together until its merger into U.S. Steel.) When Carnegie and his partners sold the business in 1901, Phipps held 11 percent of the company's stock, second only to Carnegie's 58 percent. (Phipps's full statement to reporters: "Ain't Andy wonderful!") Phipps netted between $40 and $50 million from the sale—yet it would prove the basis for only part of his wealth. In 1907, he created a family office to oversee his fortune, which in time evolved into Bessemer Trust, now one of the nation's leading wealth managers.

Phipps dedicated the majority of his money to charity, although the full extent of his gifts will never be known. He refused all interview requests and chose to keep most of his gifts private. "Unlike Carnegie, Harry shunned all publicity about his personal life and philanthropies," notes his granddaughter.

Phipps began his efforts to beautify the city of Pittsburgh in the 1880s, donating to public parks, baths, playgrounds, and gardens. He is perhaps best

remembered for creating the Phipps Conservatory in 1893, which remains to this day one of America's leading botanical gardens. In his dedication, Phipps made clear his desire to "erect something that will prove a source of instruction as well as pleasure to the people." In an unusual stipulation, he required that the conservatory be open on Sundays, so that workingmen and their families could visit on their day of rest. Local ministers denounced the proposal, but Phipps insisted on it—and ultimately won the argument.

"For my part," wrote Andrew Carnegie in *The Gospel of Wealth,* "I think Mr. Phipps put his money to better use in giving the working-men of Allegheny conservatories filled with beautiful flowers, orchids, and aquatic plants, which they, with their wives and children, can enjoy in their spare hours, and upon which they can feed their love for the beautiful, than if he had given his surplus money to furnish them with bread."

After the sale of Carnegie Steel, some of Phipps's first philanthropic projects involved improving the quality of health care for the poor. His first target: tuberculosis. In January 1903, he funded a new clinic in Philadelphia dedicated to the study, treatment, and prevention of tuberculosis. The institute, which eventually merged with the University of Pennsylvania, made special efforts to reach African Americans afflicted by the disease. Later that year, Phipps created another such institute in Baltimore, under the

> Phipps's most enduring accomplishment may be his help in launching the academic discipline of psychiatry.

auspices of the Johns Hopkins Hospital. In both cases, reported the *New York Times,* "All money needed will be furnished by Mr. Phipps."

Once involved in the fight against tuberculosis, Phipps became increasingly interested in ways to improve housing for the urban working poor. In 1905, he donated $1 million to a new nonprofit to build homes for the poor in New York City. Now known as the Phipps Houses Group, this nonprofit has constructed over 6,000 apartments and for more than a century been among the city's leading affordable-housing developers.

Phipps's most enduring accomplishment may be his help in launching the academic discipline of psychiatry. In May 1908, while visiting the tuberculosis institute he had founded at the Johns Hopkins Hospital, he struck up a conversation with William Welch, dean of the medical faculty, who gave Phipps a copy of Clifford Beers's *A Mind That Found Itself.* A month later, Phipps sent Welch a letter, offering $825,000, plus $60,000 annually

for a decade, to endow the Henry Phipps Psychiatric Clinic. "I understand that the building will be used both for treating and studying insanity," wrote Phipps, "and this study of dethroned minds by our finest physicians may result in great works." He remained committed to the school, funding it for the rest of his life, including a $1 million challenge grant in 1923 to improve faculty compensation and recruitment.

Phipps is one of the least-remembered great philanthropists of the early twentieth century. He sought no recognition for his philanthropy; he never endowed a foundation. But his charitable giving did real and lasting good, improving Pittsburgh civic life, exploring new ways to fight poverty, advancing medical research, providing health care to the poor, and inspiring other donors. Long before his death in 1930, he was widely admired for his decency and kindness. James Bridge, the muckraking author of a caustic account of Carnegie's rise, observed in a 1902 profile that Phipps's career "is without parallel for a man as successful as he has been: he never made an enemy, nor lost a friend."

— *Martin Morse Wooster*

Further information

○ Peggie Phipps Boegner and Richard Gachot, *Halcyon Days: An American Family Through Three Generations* (Harry Abrams, 1986)

○ James Bridge, *The Inside History of the Carnegie Steel Company: A Romance of Millions* (Aldine Book Company, 1903)

ENOCH PRATT

Enoch Pratt was one of nineteenth-century Maryland's most prominent businessmen. Today he is perhaps best remembered for creating a system of free lending libraries in Baltimore—a pioneering effort that set a model for his contemporaries, not least Andrew Carnegie.

Pratt was born in 1808 to a respectable middle-class family in Massachusetts, the second of eight children. His father was a successful businessman who left farming to manage a sawmill, a general store, and later a wholesale hardware business. Young Enoch learned to make nails at the little smithy in the Pratt's family kitchen.

After completing his education at Bridgewater Academy, Enoch announced himself ready for a life of business. "I suggest I am old enough to do considerable business," the 15-year-old wrote to a close family friend. "My school will be out in a fortnight and I do not want to stay at home." His friend helped young Enoch

secure his first job: clerking at a wholesale hardware store. Pratt diligently saved his money, looking forward to the day when he could start his own business. At age 23, with just $150 to his name, Pratt opened a wholesale hardware business in Baltimore, the city he would call home for most of his life.

Pratt's iron business met with great success. As his fortune grew, Pratt expanded his portfolio, serving as vice president of the Philadelphia, Wilmington, & Baltimore Railroad; president of the National Farmers' and Planters' bank of Baltimore; and controlling stockholder in the Maryland Steamboat Company. Pratt matched success in business with domestic felicity. In 1837, he married Maria Hyde. It was a happy match, even though the couple was unable to have children of their own.

Pratt's philanthropy began with gifts to his church. A faithful Unitarian, he shouldered much of his church's financial burdens—paying off significant debts, buying a new organ, and remodeling the building. For more than 40 years, Pratt served as a church trustee, and on occasion as a delegate to national Unitarian conferences.

> **Pratt created a superb free public library that became the finest in the country, inspiring other donors (including Andrew Carnegie) to likewise bring books and learning to everyday Americans.**

Much of Pratt's early philanthropy was similarly personal, escaping the notice of the larger public. It was a common practice, notes his biographer Richard Hart, for Pratt to come to the aid of hardworking young men "with money and good advice." He was patron to sculptor Edward Bartholomew, funding his study abroad under Italian master Ferrero. Pratt purchased many of Bartholomew's works and commissioned him to create busts and memorials throughout the city, perhaps most notably the statue of George Washington in Druid Hill Park, Baltimore's largest city park.

Later in life, Pratt became more focused on his philanthropy, with the majority of his gifts centered on the city of Baltimore. In 1870, he donated Cheltenham, a 752-acre tract of land in Prince George's county, to be used as a reform school for African-American boys. Pratt was president of the school's board for several years, and would regularly hire men who had been trained at Cheltenham to work on the grounds at his country home, Tivoli.

Education was Pratt's great, lifelong interest—but, like many self-made men of his era, he did not equate education with schooling. He wanted to support those who wanted to learn, but he realized that few

working people could afford to take the time to study in a formal, structured environment. For aspiring autodidacts, he found an elegant solution: the free lending library.

In 1865 Pratt expanded a school library in Massachusetts and opened it to all local citizens. He later came to believe that "a free circulating public library open to all citizens regardless of property or color" was the greatest need in his city of Baltimore. To address that need, in 1882, he offered the city his plan for a library with many local branches, plus a million-dollar endowment to operate it.

"For 15 years, I have studied the library question, and wondered what I could do with my money so that it would do the most good," he explained. "I soon made up my mind that I would not found a college—for a few rich. My library shall be for all, rich and poor without distinction of race or color, who, when properly accredited, can take out the books if they will handle them carefully and return them."

Pratt's funding established a central headquarters and four branches, and the interest on his endowment maintained the entire system. He remained an actively involved donor, took great pride in his libraries, and would frequently visit the branches. He personally escorted fellow philanthropist Andrew Carnegie on a tour of the central Baltimore library.

Andrew Carnegie took great interest in the Pratt library system, which became a model for his own program of building free lending libraries in Pittsburgh and beyond. "Many free libraries have been established in our country, but none that I know of with such wisdom as the Pratt Library in Baltimore," Carnegie wrote in *The Gospel of Wealth*. "By placing books within the reach of 37,000 people…. Mr. Pratt has done more for the genuine progress of the people than has been done by the contributions of all the millionaires and rich people to help those who cannot or will not help themselves."

Pratt's final gift to his adopted hometown was a $2 million bequest (of his remaining $2.5 million) to the Sheppard asylum, because he was so impressed with how that institution's trustees had handled their responsibilities. "They are the only board of trustees in Baltimore who have carried out exactly the directions of the founder," said Pratt. Pratt's bequest expanded the pioneering mental hospital and helped make it, now the Sheppard Pratt Health System, the largest mental-health institute in Maryland.

⁓ Kari Barbic

Further information

○ Richard Hart, *Enoch Pratt: The Story of a Plain Man* (Enoch Pratt Free Library, 1935)

JOHN ROCKEFELLER SR.

After starting life in humble circumstances, John Rockefeller came to dominate the burgeoning petroleum industry by the time he was 40 years old. He became the richest man of his time, and indeed has a good claim to perhaps being the richest self-made man who ever lived. At its peak, Rockefeller's net worth was around 1.5 percent of the country's total annual economic output—the equivalent of about $280 billion today, or about three times the wealth controlled by Bill Gates.

He was equally distinguished as a philanthropist. A natural businessman with a strong moral sense and intense religious convictions, he dedicated unprecedented resources to charity. Within his lifetime, Rockefeller helped launch the field of biomedical research, funding scientific investigations that resulted in vaccines for things like meningitis and yellow fever. He revolutionized medical training in the United States and built China's first proper medical school. He championed the cause of public sanitation, creating schools of public health at Johns Hopkins and Harvard, and helped lead major international public-health efforts against hookworm, malaria, yellow fever, and other maladies. He vigorously promoted the cause of education nationwide, without distinction of sex, race, or creed. He created the University of Chicago, virtually from scratch, and within a decade turned it into one of the world's leading universities.

Born in upstate New York in 1839, Rockefeller was the son of a strait-laced, deeply devout Baptist mother and a boisterous, fun-loving father who called himself a traveling salesman but was really a flimflam man. (Amid his many long business trips, Rockefeller's father would eventually contract a bigamous second marriage and have a second family while still returning periodically to his first.) The young Rockefeller, serious and somewhat humorless by nature, was much more influenced by his mother. A lifelong adherent of the northern Baptist church, he neither drank nor smoked.

As a boy, his family moved frequently. In 1853 they settled in Strongsville, Ohio, a suburb of rapidly expanding Cleveland. Rockefeller attended a local high school and took a ten-week course in bookkeeping. At age 16 he got his first job, keeping ledgers at a brokerage of fresh produce. From the very beginning of his work life, he gave 6 percent of his salary (which at first was a mere 50¢ per day) to charity. He was soon tithing to the Baptist church.

In 1859, Edwin Drake drilled the first oil well, in northwest Pennsylvania, and one of the world's greatest industries was born. That year Rockefeller and a partner opened a brokerage of their own, Rockefeller and Clark, that traded not only lettuces and tomatoes and other produce but petroleum products

as well. Cleveland, with its proximity to the Pennsylvania oil fields and its excellent transportation network, quickly became the center of petroleum refining. In 1863, Rockefeller and partners opened their own refinery.

In 1865 Rockefeller bought out his partners and established a new firm with the chemist Samuel Andrews. Needing capital, he approached Stephen Harkness, who invested $100,000 and became a silent partner in the firm, requiring that his relative, Henry Flagler, be taken in as a partner to oversee the Harkness interests. Flagler proved an inspired choice, with organizational and creative business skills that neatly matched Rockefeller's careful money management.

In 1870, Flagler convinced Rockefeller to transform the partnership of Rockefeller, Andrews, and Flagler into a corporation named Standard Oil. Standard Oil expanded rapidly, both horizontally by buying up other oil refining companies, and vertically by acquiring oil wells and transportation routes and selling products at the retail level. Standard Oil pursued a monopoly position, using techniques—such as secret rebates from railroads and predatory pricing—that are today illegal, but were not then. It also invented the trust form of organization in order to circumvent out-of-date incorporation laws. It paid a fair price for the companies it wanted to acquire, often doling out Standard Oil stock and taking in useful executives. By 1880, Standard Oil controlled 90 percent of the oil business in America.

> One of the richest men in history, with a strong moral sense and intense religious convictions, John Rockefeller dedicated unprecedented resources to charity and dramatically improved many social ills.

Rockefeller had a clear conscience about how he won his fortune. "God gave me the money," he often said. Believing that, he felt a profound obligation to put the money to good use. By the early 1880s, he was receiving thousands of letters a month asking for help. Rockefeller regularly gathered his family after breakfast to review the merits of the petitions. "Four fifths of these letters," Rockefeller noted years later, were "requests of money for personal use, with no other title to consideration than that the writer would be gratified to have it."

In these first years of large-scale philanthropy, Rockefeller favored a few causes close to his heart. He was the single most generous donor to the

northern Baptist conventions, and he underwrote the work of missionaries and relief workers at home and abroad. He also took a deep interest in higher education for African Americans. In 1882, he began a series of gifts to the Atlanta Baptist Female Seminary, a struggling school for African-American women. As Rockefeller's contributions grew, the school took the maiden name of Rockefeller's wife: Spellman. Similar gifts were soon directed to two other black colleges—the Tuskegee Institute and Morehouse College.

"About the year 1890 I was still following the haphazard fashion of giving here and there as appeals presented themselves. I investigated as I could, and worked myself almost to a nervous breakdown," Rockefeller noted in his 1909 memoir. "There was then forced upon me the necessity to organize and plan this department of our daily tasks on as distinct lines of progress as we did with our business affairs." It marked an important turning point in his career as a philanthropist.

Rockefeller made his fortune through canny consolidation, careful cost management, and economies of scale. Those instincts were reflected time and again in his charitable giving. Rather than make thousands of small, scattershot contributions, he preferred to make large donations to institutions that he believed had great promise. "The best philanthropy," he wrote, "is constantly in search of finalities—a search for a cause, an attempt to cure evils at their source."

Higher education was the first major beneficiary of Rockefeller's more focused philanthropic efforts. A project of lifelong interest to him was the creation of a distinguished Baptist university. Rockefeller considered several options before pairing with William Harper to establish the University of Chicago. In 1890, he made his first contribution—for $600,000—to the school. Over the rest of his life, he would give it a total of $35 million, making it possible for the upstart school to instantly rank among the world's leading institutions of higher learning. Rockefeller insisted that his name not be used anywhere on campus, even rejecting an image of a lamp on the university seal, lest it be taken as a suggestion of the influence of Standard Oil. The University of Chicago, he later said, was "the best investment I ever made."

At the urging of Frederick Gates, perhaps his most trusted philanthropic adviser, Rockefeller became increasingly devoted to medical research. In 1901, he funded the Rockefeller Medical Research Institute in New York City. Modeled on the Institut Pasteur in France and the Robert Koch Institute in Germany, it was the country's first biomedical institute, soon on a par with its European models. The results were dramatic. Within a decade, it created a vaccine for cerebrospinal meningitis and had supported the work of America's first winner of a Nobel Prize in medicine. Today, known as

Rockefeller University, it is one of the leading biomedical research centers in the world. Twenty-four Nobel Prize winners have served on its faculty.

Like many wealthy industrialists of his era, Rockefeller was scandalized by the poverty and deprivation that still afflicted the American South nearly half a century after the conclusion of the Civil War. He created the General Education Board in 1902, charging it with a ranging mission that included improving rural education for both whites and blacks, modernizing agricultural practices, and improving public health, primarily through efforts to eradicate hookworm, which debilitated many Southerners and dragged down productivity of all sorts. The General Education Board helped establish hundreds of public high schools throughout the South, promoted institutions of higher education, and supported teacher-training efforts for African Americans.

Rockefeller's work to eliminate hookworm was part of a broader effort to improve public health generally. Starting in 1913, the smashing success against hookworm in the U.S. was exported globally. It was soon followed by similar efforts against malaria, scarlet fever, tuberculosis, and typhus, all under the auspices of the Rockefeller-funded International Health Commission. Rockefeller created the first school of public health at Johns Hopkins University in 1918, which he then duplicated at Harvard in 1921. In all, he spent $25 million introducing public-health programs at scores of universities across the globe. Rockefeller took a special interest in China (second only to the United States as a destination for his funding), and the China Medical Board he created can be credited with first introducing the country to modern medical practices.

Throughout the first decade of the twentieth century, Rockefeller was thinking seriously about founding a perpetual grantmaking foundation. By 1909, he had given away $158 million of personal funds to various causes. That year he donated 73,000 shares of Standard Oil, worth $50 million, as a first installment to establish what would become the Rockefeller Foundation. It was not the first such foundation, but it quickly became the largest. It was chartered by New York State in 1913 with a mission "to promote the well-being of mankind throughout the world."

The benefactions of the Rockefeller Foundation have been many and varied, from funding the research that led to the yellow-fever vaccine, to the Montreal Neurological Institute, to a new building that holds five million books at Oxford's Bodleian Library. The foundation was a pioneer funder of the Green Revolution, which dramatically increased agricultural yields across the developing world, and may have saved as many as one billion lives. For decades, the Rockefeller Foundation distributed more foreign aid than the entire U.S. government.

As impressive as the legacy of the Rockefeller Foundation is, however, it is not clear that it has yet caught up with the accomplishments of its founding donor. John Rockefeller gave away (unadjusted for inflation) $540 million before his death in 1937 at the age of 97. With that money, he created two of the world's greatest research universities, helped pull the American South out of chronic poverty, educated legions of African Americans, jumpstarted medical research, and dramatically improved health around the globe. It is not surprising that his biographer Ron Chernow concluded that Rockefeller "must rank as the greatest philanthropist in American history."

— John Steele Gordon

Further information

∘ Ron Chernow, *Titan: The Life of John D. Rockefeller, Sr.* (Random House, 1998)
∘ Raymond Fosdick, *The Story of the Rockefeller Foundation* (Transaction Publishers, 1989)
∘ John D. Rockefeller, *Random Reminiscences of Men and Events* (Doubleday, 1909)

JOHN ROCKEFELLER JR.

John Rockefeller Jr. was the only son and principal heir of the founder of Standard Oil. Much of the younger Rockefeller's working life was dedicated to philanthropy— first as an agent of his father and later with his own inherited funds. His principal philanthropic interests included conserving natural landscapes, preserving historical landmarks, collecting fine art, fostering international cooperation, and promoting the cause of Protestant Modernism.

Born in 1874, "Junior" (as he was known within the family) was earnest and devout, a dutiful son who labored conscientiously to reflect well on the family. After graduating from Brown, he went to work in his father's office, with unspecified responsibilities but an expectation that his time would be devoted to both business and philanthropy. He soon discovered he lacked his father's aptitude for profitmaking. After a nervous breakdown in 1904, Junior decided to devote himself almost exclusively to charitable giving.

Working alongside Frederick Gates, one of Rockefeller's key aides, Junior helped launch some of his father's most important philanthropic enterprises: the Rockefeller Institute for Medical Research (1901), the General Education Board (1903), the Sanitary Commission for the Eradication of Hookworm (1909), and the Rockefeller Foundation (1913). Junior won his father's respect with his hard work and commitment to the work he was given.

Junior rose to national prominence in 1915. The United Mine Workers had been striking against the Rockefeller-controlled Colorado Fuel and Iron,

and in April 1914 the Colorado National Guard was sent in to keep order. A firefight broke out, in which two women and 11 children were killed. The "Ludlow Massacre" made John Rockefeller one of the most hated men in America. Junior stepped forward, reaching out to the union, speaking to the press, and testifying before the U.S. Commission on Industrial Relations. He charmed everyone. Even the *Masses*, a leading left-wing journal, called him "apparently frank," "gentle," and "Christianish."

Impressed by his son's leadership during the crisis, Senior began transferring his fortune to Junior. Between 1916 and 1922, Junior received gifts of approximately $450 million. By 1920, his net worth hovered around $500 million. This gave him independence in his charitable giving.

As a philanthropist in his own right, Junior remained famously self-effacing. In the late 1920s, for example, he decided to visit Versailles. He had recently contributed $2 million to the restoration of the palace and its grounds, but arrived at closing time, and the guards, not recognizing him, turned him away. He thanked them politely and returned to his hotel. This became "headline news in France," notes one biographer, "and no action on his part could have so endeared him to the French people."

The younger Rockefeller was an ardent conservationist, best remembered for his leadership in creating Grand Teton National Park in Wyoming and his contributions to Acadia National Park in Maine. In both cases, he bought tens of thousands of acres and donated them to the National Park Service; in Maine, he paid for the construction of 57 miles of auto-free "carriage roads," where visitors could enjoy the park's beauty at the speed of a horse instead of a car.

In all, it is estimated that Junior gave about $45 million to various conservation efforts, leading one expert to call him "the most generous philanthropist in the history of conservation." He put up $10.3 million to preserve parkland in northeastern New Jersey, donated funds to buy land and build a museum in Yosemite National Park, and underwrote the purchase of land for California's Humboldt Redwoods State Park. He helped create Shenandoah National Park, Mesa Verde National Park, and the Great Smoky Mountains National Park.

The same conservative impulse that inspired Junior's conservation efforts also animated his interest in historic preservation. In 1926, Junior visited Williamsburg, Virginia, then little more than William and Mary College surrounded by a few crumbling churches. Rockefeller began to restore the venerable town one building at a time, insisting on scrupulous historical accuracy, in what ultimately became a $60 million gift. It was a labor of love—"I really belong in Williamsburg," he once said. He later took up a similar effort to restore sections of the historic Hudson Valley.

Junior's conservation projects spanned the globe. He funded the restoration of Notre-Dame de Reims, a thirteenth-century French cathedral that was devastated by shellfire in World War I. When an earthquake destroyed the main library of Tokyo Imperial University (now Tokyo University), Junior paid for its reconstruction. Grants to the American School for Classical Studies helped archaeologists excavate the Ancient Agora of Athens. With a $2 million gift, he launched the Palestine Museum (now the Rockefeller Museum), the first institute in Jerusalem devoted to archaeological preservation.

Junior's taste in art was traditional, as evidenced by his close involvement in the creation of the Cloisters in New York City. In the 1920s, Junior began working with George Barnard, a sculptor who collected pieces from the great cathedrals of medieval France. Junior decided to combine Barnard's collection with the medieval works he had collected—most notably the seven "Hunt of the Unicorn" tapestries. To house one of the world's great collections of medieval art, Rockefeller funded the creation of a building that incorporates parts from five French cloistered abbeys, taken apart and shipped to northernmost Manhattan, where they were assembled between 1934 and 1938. Surrounding land was landscaped in styles recorded in medieval manuscripts and images.

> Lacking his father's aptitude for money-making, John Rockefeller Jr. devoted himself to guiding the most important charitable enterprises started by his father.

Junior's wife, Abby Aldrich Rockefeller, had entirely different tastes in art. She fell in love with modern art quite early, and was given an allowance by her husband to pursue that interest. With those funds and some inheritance she acquired works by young, struggling artists. Later, she organized other donors and created New York's Museum of Modern Art. In 1934, Junior loosened the purse strings and allowed his wife to spend what she pleased on contemporary works. When she died in 1948, he honored her memory with gifts to the Museum of Modern Art that ultimately totaled over $6 million, despite his lifelong distaste for contemporary art.

Junior also used his philanthropy to promote the cause of international harmony. He gave a library to the League of Nations, and later contributed the Manhattan real estate that allowed the United Nations building to

be constructed there rather than abroad. He was a founder and major contributor to the Council on Foreign Relations. He funded dozens of International Houses, residential facilities on college campuses intended to enable graduate students from different countries to live together. He created the International Education Board and provided $28 million to fund graduate studies and institutions in 39 countries.

The largest component of Junior's philanthropy—totaling some $72 million altogether—was directed to churches and religious causes. Every year between 1919 and 1933, he was the largest single contributor to the Northern Baptist denomination, contributing as much as 13 percent of its annual budget. During the 1920s, as Modernist and Fundamentalist factions increasingly came into conflict, Junior sided squarely with the Modernists. His friend and family pastor was Harry Emerson Fosdick, a leading light among the Modernists; Fosdick's brother Raymond was a longtime Rockefeller employee (and Rockefeller Foundation president) and Junior's first biographer.

In 1922, Junior paid for the distribution of Fosdick's sermon "Should the Fundamentalists Win?" to every Protestant minister in the United States. He funded the nondenominational Riverside Church, contributing $32 million to its construction between 1925 and 1928. He supported the theologically liberal faculty at the University of Chicago Divinity School and gave millions to the Interchurch World Movement, an ecumenical effort to unite the Christian denominations.

Historians estimate that John Rockefeller Jr. gave away $537 million during his lifetime. Although one of the nation's most accomplished philanthropists, Junior always subordinated himself to his father. When the Virginia legislature formally honored him for the creation of historic Williamsburg, he was invited to deliver a few remarks. At one point, he looked up, departing from his prepared text. "How I wish my father were here," he said, his voice choking. "I am only the son."

— Martin Morse Wooster

Further information

○ Raymond Fosdick, *John D. Rockefeller, Jr.: A Portrait* (Harper, 1956)

○ John Harr and Peter Johnson, *The Rockefeller Century* (Scribner, 1988)

○ Suzanne Loebl, *America's Medicis: The Rockefellers and Their Astounding Cultural Legacy* (Harper, 2010)

JULIUS ROSENWALD

Julius Rosenwald, who was born in 1862 while Abraham Lincoln was president, in a house just one block from the liberator's own home in Springfield, Illinois, eventually played his own towering part in reinforcing the unity of America, elevating its black citizenry, and moving the nation closer to fulfilling the promises of its founding.

A child of German immigrants, Rosenwald dropped out of high school after two years to apprentice with his uncles, who were major clothing manufacturers in New York City. By his 30th birthday he had achieved moderate success running his own business that made ready-to-wear men's suits. Then came his big break.

Richard Sears, a gifted advertising writer but chronically disorganized entrepreneur, had a tiger by the tail as he struggled to fill mail orders at his booming new company Sears, Roebuck. Julius got a chance to buy a quarter of the company, and soon he was imposing order on the shipping-room chaos.

Sears was the Amazon.com of its day, and Rosenwald had to take extraordinary measures to keep up with its growth. He put 7,000 laborers to work day and night building a huge warehouse. Special machines were made that could open letters at the rate of 27,000 per hour. A system of conveyor belts, pneumatic tubes, and color-coded tags shunted merchandise through the vast new plant. Henry Ford reportedly visited and absorbed ideas for his future assembly line. Management expert Peter Drucker later characterized Rosenwald as "the father…of the distribution revolution which has changed the world economy in the twentieth century and which is so vital a factor in economic growth."

When the dust settled around the end of 1908, Sears was one of the most popular enterprises in the country, with millions of customers and tens of thousands of employees, and Rosenwald was its president and a multimillionaire. With the company on an even keel, his attention turned rapidly toward philanthropy. Soon he was giving away money with at least as much gusto as he poured into earning it.

A deep root of Rosenwald's generosity was the fact that he was a secure and grounded individual, lacking in ego. In a 1916 article, young journalist B. C. Forbes (who founded his own business magazine the next year) profiled Rosenwald this way:

> The most notable thing about Julius Rosenwald is not any superhuman business ability, nor any phenomenal smartness in seeing and seizing mercantile opportunities…. *The greatest thing about Julius Rosenwald is not his business but himself, not what he has but*

what he is, his character, his personality, his sincerity, his honesty, his democracy, his thoughtfulness, his charity of heart, his catholicity of sympathy, his consuming desire to help the less fortunate of his fellow creatures.

Religious motivations were an immediate spur for Rosenwald's philanthropy. His rabbi, Emil Hirsch, taught him that "property entails duties." Hirsch introduced Rosenwald to many people who inspired him to donate.

During the summer of 1910, Rosenwald read the autobiography of the great black educator Booker T. Washington, and was strongly affected. Within a year, Rosenwald and Washington were building a relationship that included visits to each other's homes. Rosenwald's first speech introducing the educator to Chicago's business leaders described Washington as "helping his own race to attain the high art of self-help and self-dependence" while simultaneously "helping the white race to learn that opportunity and obligation go hand in hand, and that there is no enduring superiority save that which comes as the result of serving."

In 1912, Rosenwald made a dramatic entry into large-scale philanthropy. He announced he would be celebrating his 50th birthday by giving away close to $700,000 (about $16 million in current dollars), and encouraged other wealthy individuals to support good causes of their own. "Give While You Live" was his slogan.

> When government neglected its duties at the height of the Jim Crow era, Rosenwald's philanthropic grants built the schools where 27 percent of all black children in America got their education.

One of Rosenwald's birthday gifts was $25,000 to Washington's Tuskegee Institute. Washington shrewdly set aside part of it to launch a new experiment which he expected might interest his donor—a $2,100 effort to build new schools in parts of Alabama where little or no education was being offered to rural blacks. Washington documented progress on the schools with photos and careful accounting, including descriptions of the community enthusiasm the erection of the new schools created among locals of all races. Pride in the fresh facilities often overflowed into newly painted houses, improved roads, and expanded cooperation among residents.

Rosenwald was captivated. Only 5 percent of slaves had been literate. And during the Jim Crow era, educational offerings to African Americans (and many residents of the rural South in general) were miserably inadequate. Soon Rosenwald and Washington were ramping up their program, eventually building schools all across the South over more than 20 years. There were correlated efforts to train teachers to serve in the new schools, and funds to provide libraries and workshops for students. These facilities would never have materialized absent this aggressive philanthropy, and they had both immediate and deeply enduring effects.

By 1932, the year Julius died, an astonishing 4,977 Rosenwald schools, and 380 complementary buildings, had been erected in every Southern locale with a significant black population. Fully 35 percent of all black children in the South (and 27 percent of black children period) were educated that year in a Rosenwald school. A 2011 study by two Federal Reserve economists found that children with access to a Rosenwald school advanced more than a year ahead of other students, and that the Rosenwald schools were a huge factor in equalizing the educational levels of black and white students in the South. America would be a very different, and lesser, nation absent this philanthropic inspiration (which outflanked a scandalous dereliction of duty by a variety of governments).

In the rural-school program and all the rest of his giving, the *way* in which Rosenwald made his philanthropic investments was often as inspired as his underlying cause. For sheer canniness in donating resources, Julius Rosenwald may have been America's most innovative and influential donor ever.

In the school-building program, for instance, he insisted right from the beginning that his donation would only be made if it was matched by local residents (most of whom were poor blacks who skeptics said could never come up with adequate funds). He also craftily maneuvered local and state governments into participating, overcoming their historical dismissal of black education with the lure of outside manna.

These decisions reflected Rosenwald's disdain for unconditioned largesse, and his insistence that beneficiaries do their own large part in improving their lot. And despite their limited resources, thousands of rural black communities succeeded in pulling together the funds to match Rosenwald's gift. Poignant stories have been recorded of black laborers emptying bags of old coins, representing years of savings, to underwrite these schools. Sharecroppers set aside a "Rosenwald Patch" when they planted their cotton. Innumerable pie sales and fried chicken suppers were organized to raise matching funds. During construction, many black families donated materials or invested sweat equity via their labor. Local whites also contributed, encouraged by the uplift the new schools offered their towns.

Retrospective calculations show that, in the end, black families contributed slightly more than Rosenwald to the schools—16 percent of total costs, versus 15 percent from his fund. And leveraging the remainder from state and county education authorities was a game-changing triumph. Booker T. Washington credited Rosenwald with starting the entire program of state funding for black education in the South. And during this segregated era, that in turn initiated additional resources to improve substandard white schools.

Rosenwald was totally opposed to handouts, which he believed caused enervation and corruption of incentives. The only lasting help was self-help, he believed. He thus proclaimed that in his philanthropy he was looking for "opportunities for self-improvement, for education and recreation, for the acquisition of spiritual, moral, mental, and physical strength, that makes for manhood and self-reliance."

Rosenwald also pioneered other innovations in the mechanics of giving. Perhaps foremost, he urged that successful men and women should give not just of their money but of their time and expertise. When Rosenwald "became involved in a project, he did not merely accept the idea, write the checks, and hand the project over to someone else," notes biographer Peter Ascoli. Instead, he became deeply involved, contributing his wisdom, management expertise, and personality as well as his funds.

Rosenwald had well-developed and savvy ideas about use of the donor's name. He did not believe in giving anonymously, because he thought the visible support and credibility lent by a gift was often even more valuable to a receiving institution than the immediate cash. At the same time, he fought aggressively to keep his name from being affixed prominently to buildings and projects—not just out of his genuine humility, but in keeping with his idea that if a donor could get beneficiaries to take ownership of a project themselves and become emotionally invested in it, the undertaking is likelier to thrive and endure. "If no name is used it will belong to the people," was Rosenwald's encapsulation.

He also was a path-breaker in insisting on follow-up, evaluation, and accountability. He sent architects out to check on the construction of schools built with his money, demanded careful financial records, and followed outcomes. "Benevolence today has become altogether too huge an undertaking to be conducted otherwise than on business lines," he argued.

Rosenwald also combined business and philanthropy in novel ways, devising stock-purchase, profit-sharing, and health-and-welfare programs that benefited Sears employees. He created one of the first corporate foundations in history, the Sears, Roebuck Foundation, and built it to substantial size. To reduce the risk of

bureaucracy and falling into complacent ruts, he was a trailblazer in encouraging term limits on trustees at foundations (six years in the case of his own fund).

Rosenwald was adamantly opposed to setting up foundations to exist forever, dribbling out only a small fraction of their money each year. He insisted this would lead inevitably to a focus on staff sinecures and the perpetuation of assets, rather than getting things done. Instead, he believed, foundations should urgently attack national problems with their best resources right now, use up their funds within a reasonable time, and leave future challenges to future donors. He insisted his own foundation should spend energetically so as to close up shop within 25 years of his death, and thus avoid the sclerosis he was already observing in permanent endowments. His was the first major foundation in American history to voluntarily "sunset" itself out of existence, in order to have better immediate results.

One of Rosenwald's most unusual and bold philanthropic innovations was his willingness to pledge his own fortune (more than once) to protect Sears employees and even preserve the company during the periodic financial panics that wracked the U.S. in the early decades of the twentieth century. Most dramatically, when the sudden recession after World War I pushed Sears to the brink of bankruptcy, Rosenwald bailed out the firm while he was president by pledging $21 million of his personal wealth (the equivalent of $288 million today) in a combination of gifts and loans. This stunned Rosenwald's fellow business executives, and deeply impressed the country. Business writer C. W. Barron, who later fathered *Barron's* magazine, hailed the move as "business philanthropy."

Julius Rosenwald left a powerful imprint on numerous causes. He brought the inspirational science and technology museum to America by single-handedly funding the Museum of Science and Industry in Chicago. He gave many millions to Jewish interests, including saving thousands of victims of the Russian Revolution. He was a generous backer of black colleges. He funded the construction of 22 YMCA/YWCA community centers and urban dormitories for blacks during the segregated era. And he funded a third of the litigation costs of the *Brown v. Board of Education* case that ended school segregation. He was for many years also the largest donor to the University of Chicago, located within a mile of his home, and spawned its medical school among many other worthy intellectual projects.

While Julius Rosenwald never possessed the assets of his contemporaries Rockefeller and Carnegie (in current dollars Rosenwald's total donations amounted to something under $2 billion) he got an enormous bang for his buck. This was due to his philanthropic vision and his determination to pump his fortune quickly into ameliorative projects rather than locking it up in permanent trusts.

In addition to changing the country, Rosenwald changed philanthropy. Together, this combination of the lives he directly transformed, and his many innovations in the practice and execution of giving which inspired other wealthy individuals to become more effective givers, set him apart. That he is largely unknown—thanks to his principles like keeping his name off projects and limiting the life of his foundation—is only a further tribute to his good motives.

~ Karl Zinsmeister

Further information

○ Peter Ascoli, *Julius Rosenwald: The Man Who Built Sears, Roebuck and Advanced the Cause of Black Education in the American South* (Indiana University Press, 2006)

○ Joseph Hoereth, "Julius Rosenwald and the Rosenwald Fund: A Case in Non-Perpetual Philanthropy," Loyola University Chicago, 2007

○ Julius Rosenwald, "The Principles of Public Giving" (*Atlantic Monthly*, May 1929)

BENJAMIN RUSH

"Be indulgent to the poor." Those were the last words of Benjamin Rush, spoken to his son. An appropriate coda for a man who may have had the deepest altruistic streak of any of our nation's founders.

"More benevolent, more learned, of finer genius… more honest." That was Thomas Jefferson's comparison of Rush to other signers of the Declaration of Independence. Jefferson's political rival John Adams was equally admiring: "He has done more good in this world than Franklin or Washington."

One of Rush's many small philanthropic acts was to catalyze a late-in-life reconciliation between Adams and Jefferson, whom he called "the North and South Poles of the American Revolution." Rush cajoled the two old lions, who had been close collaborators before they became bitter rivals, into resuming a correspondence. As a result, when they died within hours of each other on July 4, 1826—the 50th anniversary of the Declaration—they were once again good friends.

The only physician to take a prominent role in the establishment of our nation, it was Rush who pressed Thomas Paine to write *Common Sense*, gave the book its title, and shaped the drafts as Paine read them aloud. The political doctor hosted George Washington for dinners, and helped get the Virginian selected to head the Continental Army. Ben Franklin treated the animated conversationalist and fellow Pennsylvanian like a son, sponsoring bits of his scientific education while Rush was a star medical student in Scotland, and introducing him to some of Europe's leading thinkers.

213

Rush was a fascinating combination of soft and hard, of humanitarianism and patriotism. He revered his first ancestor who had relocated to America—his great-great-grandfather John, a commander of horse troops in Cromwell's army who in his 60s refused to conform to the Church of England. "He fought for liberty, and migrated into a remote wilderness in the evening of his life in order to enjoy the privilege of worshipping God according to the dictates of his own conscience," wrote Rush. The kind doctor hung over his bed a sword he had inherited from John, describing it to his wife as "dyed…with the blood of the minions of arbitrary power."

Rush's grandfather and father were similar mixes of vinegar and honey, both being known equally as ingenious gunsmiths and as intensely religious Presbyterians. Benjamin's own service during the Revolutionary War was dualistic. After Britain cut off gunpowder imports to the recalcitrant colonies, he (then a professor of chemistry) devised the formulas for substitute homemade explosives. Meanwhile, as an army surgeon he dispensed mercy on battlefields to friend and foe alike.

In debates leading up to the rupture with Britain, Rush was a fire-breather. While attending an oration in London where one speaker dismissed American demands by noting they possessed no cannonballs, Rush leapt to his feet and shouted that his countrymen would remedy the deficiency "by digging up the skulls of those ancestors who had courted expatriation from the old hemisphere under the vivid hope of enjoying more ample freedom in the new one!" In the Continental Congress, Rush was a stubborn advocate for full self-governance, arguing that war and even deadly defeat would be preferable to loss of liberty. He later recollected the "pensive and awful silence that pervaded the house" as the Declaration of Independence was signed, since the signatories knew it might "be our own death warrant."

Among his fellow seekers of freedom, though, Rush was a force for cooperation and comity. As the former colonies struggled to unify in the Articles of Confederation, he told other delegates that "when I entered that door, I considered myself a citizen of America." While later helping put the U.S. Constitution in place to end the wrangling and drift of the early republic, he commented approvingly that "while the nations of Europe have waded into order through seas of *blood*, you see we have traveled peaceably into order only through seas of *blunders*."

Rush's vision for his nation was that it must be a moral society, not just a political power. During his schooling in Edinburgh he was impressed by the way his host city mixed Enlightenment wisdom with Presbyterian ethics. "The churches were filled on Sundays…. Swearing was rarely heard… drunkenness was rarely seen…. Instances of fraud were scarcely known….

I once saw the following advertisement pasted up at the door of the play house: 'The gentleman who gave the orange-selling woman a guinea instead of a penny last night is requested to call at the check office for it.'" He was less impressed with London, "of alehouses and taverns and gin swigging, of elegant lords and their ladies and liveried footmen, of dim street lights and vice and cruelty and grime and public hangings."

After completing the best-available medical training abroad, Rush immediately began to apply his knowledge to improving and softening life for his fellow Americans. When he returned to Philadelphia and became the first professor of chemistry in America at the age of 23, he simultaneously opened a private medical practice ministering almost exclusively to the poor. Rush had "a natural sympathy with distress of every kind," and afflicted health was a heartbreak he knew well. Three of his siblings died as youths, and he and his wife themselves lost four children in infancy, and others to adult afflictions. Diseases like yellow fever, diphtheria, typhus, and tuberculosis descended with grim regularity in his day, sometimes almost depopulating entire villages and neighborhoods.

In 1786, Rush provided expertise and resources, and raised additional money from others, to open the Philadelphia Dispensary—the first free walk-in health clinic in the United States. House calls for indigents too sick to leave home were also provided. Rush was famous for his inquisitive and kindly bedside manner, which he offered to citizens modest and mighty without distinction. An on-site apothecary compounded medicines of all sorts, which were given away at no charge along with the advice of the attending physicians. Rush did all of his work at the Dispensary for free, even though the thousands of patients he ministered to there required him to reduce his private practice by a fourth. (The charity treated 8,000 patients in just its first five years.) With Rush's encouragement, the model of the Philadelphia Dispensary subsequently spread to other cities, and this kind of clinic became for generations our primary means of providing health care to the urban poor.

Rush also practiced medicine at the Pennsylvania Hospital, which had been established with a large personal donation from Benjamin Franklin and then sustained by him and other donors as the first U.S. institution of its kind, devoted to restoring sick residents to active life, regardless of their means. When Rush joined the charity he put a particular emphasis on "care of lunatics." Recognizing that most mental disorders were organic illnesses, he created a new ethic of respect and tenderness for sufferers who had mostly just been locked away before. He separated the insane from criminals, improved their housing and caretaking, and set them to productive work.

Out of this experience, Rush wrote one of the first books on mental illness, which became influential internationally and caused him to be known as "the father of American psychiatry."

Rush also offered extraordinarily popular medical lectures at the University of Pennsylvania. He is estimated to have taught 3,000 medical students, and thereby spread updated understandings of the healing arts all across the U.S. Historians note that nearly every prominent physician in America during our first hundred years was trained either by Rush or by one of his pupils.

Physicians in that era, including Rush, had few effective tools, and sometimes harmed as much as they helped, via their bleedings and dosings and primitive understandings of biological processes. But Rush was better than most—a pioneer at introducing scientific method into health care, he improved our knowledge of many diseases, and showed strong instincts for cause and effect. He was particularly helpful in advancing preventative medicine and public-health practices. "Obviating diseases is the business of physic as well as curing them," he wrote. In his day, the poor seldom washed, and the wealthier generally did so only in warmer weather. Street gutters served as open sewers, and lice, flies, and mosquitoes were everywhere. He knew these problems well from his many house calls on sick patients in Philadelphia's most wretched neighborhoods.

To improve conditions, Dr. Rush held classes for women on the importance of keeping houses clean, cool, and insect-free. He encouraged the use of soap, wearing fresh clothing, and eating healthy food. He circulated one of the first pamphlets encouraging daily exercise as an essential contributor to health. He and a few friends formed a Society for Inoculating the Poor which provided immunizations without charge. And Rush recognized that tooth decay can cause other infections and problems.

He was a very early and persistent campaigner for temperance, warning that hard liquor had many pernicious effects on the human body and on social life, a position he got endorsed by the College of Physicians in Philadelphia. He promoted "simple, healthy, and frugal drinks" as alternatives to alcohol. Our first practical temperance societies grew out of his work.

He did merciful duty in military medicine. In most wars, he noted, "a greater proportion of men perish with sickness…than fall by the sword." So he urged military leaders to pay attention to camp locations and sanitation, along with the diet, cleanliness, and dress of their soldiers. "If it be criminal in an officer to sacrifice the lives of thousands by his temerity in a battle, why should it be thought less so to sacrifice twice their number in a hospital by his negligence?" The Continental Army sponsored pamphlets to bring Rush's advice out to fighters in the field.

In addition to the humane ideas, abundant pro bono work, and personal donations that he brought to medicine, Benjamin Rush was a pioneering philanthropist in many other fields. He organized and became president of the first anti-slavery society in America. His heavily circulated *Address... Upon Slave-keeping* urged in 1773 that the traffic in persons be shut off, and that until such time as all slaves were set at liberty and given the same "privileges of freeborn British subjects" they should "be educated in the principles of virtue and religion...taught to read and write...and instructed in some business, whereby they may be able to maintain themselves." Rush poured his own money and energy into raising up the most prominent black Christian fellowship in America, the African Methodist Episcopal Church.

Dr. Rush was also famous for his prison philanthropy. Instead of public punishments, he called for placing criminals in private confinement in hygienic facilities, with labor, solitude, religious instruction, and correction as necessary. His paper "An Enquiry into the Effects of Public Punishment upon Criminals, and upon Society" earned him another accolade of intellectual parentage—the "father of penal reform."

As an education philanthropist, Rush organized and raised the funds to create Dickinson College, bringing "the light of science and religion" to students in backwoods Pennsylvania who were poor and of dissenting faiths. He led a similar effort to set up Franklin College (now Franklin & Marshall) so that German youths living distant from the capital could likewise have access to education. Germans made up about a third of his state's population, he noted, and "fill the treasury with their taxes" while "their blood was shed liberally" in the war for independence, yet few from those families headed into "the learned professions, or possess office."

Rush was also a persistent advocate for the education of women. He established and encouraged a variety of female schools. There were numerous years when he poured more of his time into raising money, setting up classes, and gathering books and staff for these colleges and schools than he devoted to his own medical practice. In addition, Rush was president of the Philadelphia Humane Society—which strove to save the lives of drowners, both accident victims and attempted suicides.

Benjamin Rush synthesized empiricism and faith in fascinating ways that influenced his philanthropy. He was a scientist whose first love was chemistry, the producer of 85 serious articles and books, a true evidence-seeking, open-minded observer. A person anxious at all times to "add to my stock of ideas upon all subjects," he studied Laplanders, disease in China, and Persian diets. He looked into Hinduism and Orthodox Judaism. He urged his students, according to historian and fellow Revolutionary-era physician and

congressman David Ramsay, "to think and judge for themselves, and would freely, and in a friendly manner, explain his principles, resolve their doubts, listen to their objections, and either yield to their force, or show their fallacy."

Yet Rush rejected the extreme rationalism of the Enlightenment. He concluded that God was the primary cause of all things, and the ultimate source of benevolence in human behavior. He worshiped frequently and with great piety at numerous churches in the many neighborhoods his house calls took him to.

By the end of his life, both medicine and politics had disappointed Rush. Philadelphia's horrific yellow-fever epidemics near the close of the eighteenth century killed up to 10 percent of the population in each outbreak. Rush was one of the few physicians to stay in the city during these panics, attending to more than 100 patients a day (even while suffering from yellow fever himself

> Benjamin Rush was a fascinating combination of soft and hard, of humanitarianism and patriotism, of faith and science.

during the 1793 outbreak). Despite his heroic efforts to stanch suffering, Rush was attacked viciously for his ineffectiveness at saving lives, leading eventually to a boycott that cost him nearly all of the paying customers of his medical practice and estranged him from his home city.

Rush was also distressed by the terrible squabbling among the former colonies, particularly during what he called the "lost decade" after the Revolution and before ratification of the U.S. Constitution. This showed him that even the best-intended political ventures would always be hobbled by foolish, fearful, selfish human nature.

So, "strongly impressed with a sense of divine things" and "animated by a hope in God's mercy," as he put it, he fell back on the Gospel truths to guide him through his later adult life. It was his spiritual vision more than anything else that drove Benjamin Rush's powerful benevolence, And in this way a medical doctor spread across America the noble virus of charitable profusion.

> ⌐ *Karl Zinsmeister*

Further information

○ Alyn Brodsky, *Benjamin Rush: Patriot and Physician* (St. Martin's Press, 2004)
○ Amanda Moniz, *From Empire to Humanity* (Oxford Press, 2016)

OLIVIA SAGE

Margaret Olivia Sage—Olivia to those who knew her—was the widow of Russell Sage, among the greatest Wall Street investors of the 1800s. When the 89-year-old financier died in 1906, he instantly made her one of the wealthiest women in the country. She in turn used her inheritance to become one of the nation's most notable philanthropists, a patroness of higher education for women, and a leading figure in the effort to apply social science to the root causes of large-scale social problems.

"One should remember," wrote Sage in her only published work, "that in America what is called 'blue blood' is distributed through both classes—with a preponderance of it, perhaps, among the unmoneyed class." It was a fact she was keenly aware of: though the Slocum and Sage families were both of distinguished stock, when she had married Russell Sage in 1869, at the age of 41, she left behind the life of a school teacher and governess struggling to support herself.

Sage was born in 1828 in Syracuse, New York, to Margaret and Joseph Slocum. Her father, a businessman who had benefited from the economic boom in central New York sparked by the Erie Canal, suffered tremendous losses in the Panic of 1837. Having received a private education to that point, Olivia was able to borrow money from an uncle to attend Troy Female Seminary, the first institution of higher learning for women. Her introduction to the school's founder, Emma Willard, would have a lifelong influence. Though Willard called suffragists "hyenas in petticoats," she was deeply committed to the cause of female education, and her school produced moral and cultural leaders who championed women's causes in many ways.

Upon her 1847 graduation from the Troy Female Seminary, Olivia praised "our distinguished inhabitants who spend their wealth in deeds of charity," giving evidence of the ideals she had acquired at the institution. But her family's worsening finances caused her to spend the next 22 years working hard, first as a teacher in Syracuse and then as a governess in Philadelphia.

In 1869, her fortunes seemed to change dramatically when Russell Sage made her an offer of marriage. He was a former Congressman and the partner of hated businessman Jay Gould. Sage was himself a tight-fisted miser, and 20 years earlier, he had swindled her father. But she accepted his proposal.

Though her married life was one of financial abundance, she was not able to pursue the charitable activity that she had admired even as a student. Russell Sage was notoriously stingy. A 1902 letter to the editor of the *New York Times* thanked the paper for the amusement it provided in chronicling his

miserliness, seldom allowing "a week to pass without furnishing a new story about 'Uncle Russ,'" for instance, "how he permits his lawn grass to grow into hay for his horses." In the 37 years of their marriage, Russell and Olivia Sage were to make only three major donations: to the Troy Female Seminary, the Women's Hospital, and the American Seamen's Friend Society, totaling approximately $220,000. In the years after Russell's passing, however, Olivia made up for lost time.

Ruth Crocker, Sage's most recent biographer, refers to the period of her marriage as one of "performative philanthropy." In 1890, she helped to found and became the president of the Emma Willard Society, the alumni association of the Troy Female Seminary. In 1898 she made possible the publication of *Emma Willard and her pupils; or, Fifty years of Troy female seminary, 1822-1872*. She volunteered significant amounts of time working as a "lady manager" of the New York Women's Hospital. And by 1894 she was sponsoring women's suffrage meetings, motivated in part by the news that the governor of New York had vetoed the appointment of four women to Troy Female Seminary's board of trustees.

> Though her husband was a notorious miser, Olivia Sage used his money after his death to do much good in education and in studying social problems.

When Russell Sage died in 1906, he left a fortune of $75 million to his wife. She proceeded to give away approximately $45 million in the next dozen years before her own death in 1918. Her donations went to a wide variety of causes, the bulk of them in relatively small amounts. Much of her philanthropy was directed towards educational institutions—including large building and program grants to Syracuse University, Cornell, Princeton, and a founding grant for Russell Sage College—but she also invested significantly in the work of religious organizations and women's causes.

Olivia Sage is best remembered today for launching the Russell Sage Foundation for Social Betterment, which she endowed with $10 million in 1907. Her open-ended instructions were that "the income thereof [be] applied to the improvement of social and living conditions in the United States of America." The foundation gave modest amounts directly to poor people. Its much stronger focus was to employ experts in the emerging "social sciences" to study societal problems and devise systemic, "root causes" solutions.

The Russell Sage Foundation dramatically increased the influence of the social sciences in the nation's large foundations, and in America generally. Over many following decades it was a pioneer in encouraging the new tools of social science. In addition to supporting research and analysis, Russell Sage occasionally put social science into action in attempts to solve particular problems. For instance, as an experiment in municipal planning, it purchased a large expanse of land in Queens, now known as Forest Hills Gardens, to create a model suburb following the methods of the English garden-city movement. Olivia herself put $2.75 million into the project, with a hope that it would spur many similar projects where families of modest incomes could live comfortable lives near major cities.

In 1916, together with the head of the Troy Female Seminary (now known as the Emma Willard School) Olivia Sage founded Russell Sage College, a women's liberal arts college offering preparation for a variety of professions. Located in the buildings that the Emma Willard School had vacated six years earlier, it granted degrees under the auspices of the Willard School until it was granted its own charter in 1927.

When Olivia Sage died in 1918, a total of 19 educational institutions received equal allotments of approximately $800,000. Other organizations—including the Women's Board of Foreign Missions of the Presbyterian Church, the Emma Willard School, and the Metropolitan Museum of Art—received more than $1 million. The Russell Sage Foundation received a bequest of $5 million.

A "woman is responsible in proportion to the wealth and time at her command," she wrote in a 1905 *North American Review* article. "While one woman is working for bread and butter, the other must devote her time to the amelioration of the condition of her laboring sister. This is the moral law." And as soon as she had the independence to make her own choices, Olivia Sage followed those dictates of her conscience with obedient generosity.

Monica Klem

Further information

o Ruth Crocker, *Mrs. Russell Sage: Women's Activism and Philanthropy in Gilded Age and Progressive Era America* (Indiana University Press, 2008)

o David Hammack, *The Russell Sage Foundation: Social Research and Social Action in America, 1907-1947* (UPA Academic Editions, 1988)

o Margaret Olivia Sage, "Opportunities and Responsibilities of Leisured Women" (*North American Review*, November 1905)

ELLEN SCRIPPS

Ellen Browning Scripps, whose fortune derived from the Scripps family's newspaper empire, is not well known outside of southern California, largely because she confined her extensive philanthropy to local causes. Indeed, when she was approached in 1914 and offered the opportunity to support an effort in Cleveland, Ohio, she declined with the simple response: "Charity begins at home."

She was born in London to James Scripps and his second wife in 1836. When she was seven years old, three years after her mother had died, the Scripps family left England for the United States, where they settled in Illinois. Her father then married again and had five more children, bringing the number of his children to 13. Ellen was 19 years older than her youngest stepbrother, Edward Willis (known as E. W.), and had a particularly formative influence on him.

As a child, Ellen took full advantage of her father's library, and she continued her pursuit of knowledge longer than any of her siblings did. After spending two years teaching—and saving—she was able to enroll at Knox College in 1856. She spent three years at Knox before returning to teaching, but soon her brothers' increasing involvement in the newspaper business led her to work first as a copy editor and then as a columnist.

In 1873, when her brother James founded the *Detroit Evening News*, she invested her savings from teaching; when the paper was incorporated, she received a large number of shares. Consequently, she was able to provide assistance to E. W. when he founded *The Penny Press* in Cleveland, in 1878. Her investments in her brothers' businesses, which would expand steadily, provided her with financial independence. The Scripps family's successes led, however, to many difficulties. Ellen once wrote to E. W. that she wished she could be "where the air that I breathe will not be tainted, nor my ears polluted with the foul smell and sound of money, and the baseness of spirit it engenders."

It had occurred to Ellen that California might provide something like that respite. She had never visited the state before 1890, when she traveled to see her sister Annie who, in search of healing for rheumatoid arthritis, had established herself in a utopian community in Alameda. Her stepbrother Fred toured the state with her. They ended their trip in San Diego, which Ellen admired and which Fred was fascinated by, imagining it beneficial to his health and as offering him new financial beginnings. When they left California, Fred decided to buy a ranch there. His more successful sibling E. W. realized that he would have to finance Fred's project if it were ever to come to pass, so he went to San Diego to see it for himself.

By 1891, E. W. had purchased property and Fred had established himself in southern California. Within a few months, E. W. and Will, their wives, and their mother followed him, and they began construction on a house that was meant to be a home for the entire family. After the extended family had lived in the complex they called Miramar for a year, Ellen found herself discontentedly asking E. W., "Are there any two of us as a family who could live happily and contentedly together?" Shortly thereafter Will and Fred moved to properties of their own.

In 1896, Ellen bought land in La Jolla and had a house built on it, which she named South Moulton Villa after the street on which her family had lived in London. She rapidly became immersed in the life of the town, joining numerous clubs and going to lectures and concerts. In her conscious effort to enjoy the simplicity of life in the small town, she contributed to its becoming known as an active yet unpretentious place "where you could wear out your old clothes."

When George Scripps died in 1900, he left the bulk of his estate to his sister. Ellen wanted to use the money in a way that would honor him. In 1903, she and E. W. decided to assist William Ritter, a Berkeley biologist, in founding the Marine Biological Association of San Diego. Ellen gave it a sizable endowment, and the Scripps family provided its entire operating budget until it was taken over by the University of California at San Diego and renamed the Scripps Institution of Oceanography.

Believing that "charity begins at home," Ellen Scripps concentrated her giving in the San Diego area.

Ellen had been an early supporter of better education for women. In 1909, the bishop of the Episcopal diocese of Los Angeles approached her to ask for help in founding a college preparatory school for girls. She initially donated land for the Bishop's School and commissioned its first building; for years afterward, she remained one of its most important supporters. And in 1926, she endowed what would become Scripps College, a part of the Claremont Colleges, which she had helped to found. She also commissioned the La Jolla Women's Club's headquarters, the building that would become the La Jolla Community Center, and the country's first public playground.

In 1911, Ellen became a member of the Egypt Exploration Fund; she began providing support for its expeditions in 1919. (Her efforts resulted in the San Diego Museum's Ancient Egyptian collection.) She also worked to preserve the

area that would become Torrey Pines State Natural Reserve, and helped finance the new headquarters of the San Diego Natural History Museum. In 1923, she gave the San Diego Zoo an aviary and an animal research hospital. And in 1922, she founded the Scripps Memorial Hospital and the Scripps Metabolic Clinic, prompted by dissatisfaction with the care she received for a broken leg.

Education was a central focus of Ellen Scripps's philanthropic work. From her youth until her death in 1932 at the age of 95, she saw herself primarily as an investor in human capital rather than as an almsgiver. The charity she launched "at home" in southern California fulfilled her sense of familial and civic duty to help persons and causes she believed would prove beneficial to all.

Monica Klem

Further information

○ Molly McClain, "The Scripps Family's San Diego Experiment" (*Journal of San Diego History*, Winter 2010)

○ Charles Preece, *E. W. and Ellen Browning Scripps: An Unmatched Pair* (BookCrafters, 1990)

○ Frances Hepner, *Ellen Browning Scripps: Her Life and Times* (San Diego State College, 1966)

WILLIAM SIMON

William Simon was a successful banker, public servant, and noted philanthropist. He was a bond trader and a pioneer of leveraged buyouts. He served as Secretary of the Treasury in the Nixon and Ford administrations, and led the U.S. Olympic Committee during the 1984 summer games. He gave generously of his own wealth and became a trustee of some of America's most influential philanthropic organizations.

Born in New Jersey in 1927, Simon volunteered for the Army and served as a private. After he was discharged, he attended Lafayette College. With graduation approaching, Simon was married and in debt, with one young son and another on the way. He camped out in the offices of Union Securities on Wall Street until he landed a $75-per-week job in the mailroom. Within two years, he made partner and was heading the firm's municipal bonds trading desk.

He moved to Salomon Brothers, where he became famous for his 16-hour days, standing beside his desk, guzzling gallons of ice water, and barking orders to his traders. He was a senior partner, member of the firm's executive committee, and sat on the board that oversaw federal mortgage giants Fannie Mae and Freddie Mac when, in 1973, he left Salomon to become chief deputy to George Shultz at the Treasury Department.

As Shultz's deputy and later as Secretary of the Treasury in the Ford administration, many of Simon's most cherished initiatives—tax reform,

a balanced budget—would languish. In an ironic twist, the principled free-marketer was asked to head the government's price-control program for gasoline. He would later joke that he was the guy who "caused all the lines at gas stations."

After his government service, Simon returned to private life and found himself near-bankrupt. Inflation and losses in his blind trust had eviscerated his net worth. He quickly rebuilt his fortune, though, through a series of leveraged buyout deals. Most famously, with his partner Ray Chambers he purchased Gibson Greeting Cards for $80 million (all but $1 million of which they borrowed). They revitalized it, and took it public again for $290 million. In later years, Simon turned his attention to building a Pacific Rim merchant banking house with his sons, Bill and Peter.

From 1980 to 1984, Simon was president of the U.S. Olympic Committee. Under the leadership of Simon and Pete Ueberroth, the 1984 summer games in Los Angeles turned a profit of $225 million. These were the first profitable games since 1932.

> Simon required all members of the board of his personal foundation to perform 150 hours per year of hands-on service to the poor.

At the time, U.S. Olympic athletes were struggling under confusing regulations governing their amateur status and what kind of resources they could use to train. Soviet-bloc countries skirted the rules by bringing their athletes onto state payrolls, an option unavailable to American athletes. Simon used a large part of the 1984 profits to create the U.S. Olympic Foundation, an elegant solution to the dilemma facing American Olympians. American athletes would no longer be handicapped because their government did not subsidize their training. Instead, private citizens would offer the funds that would ensure American Olympians could afford to prepare as needed. "It was really all Bill's doing," said hockey executive William Tutt.

Simon could be charming, but he was also—in the admiring words of Ed Feulner, head of the Heritage Foundation—a "mean, nasty, tough bond trader who took no B.S. from anyone." To an interviewer who suggested that he didn't suffer fools gladly, Simon barked, "Do you?" If his teenage sons slept late, he woke them up by dumping ice water over their heads.

But Simon had a softer side, which made his philanthropy deeply personal. Simon and his family often visited the homeless teens at Covenant House,

playing games with them and working in the kitchen. Later in life, Simon became a eucharistic minister of the Catholic Church, taking Communion to the sick, lonely, and dying. He required all members of the board of his personal foundation to perform 150 hours per year of hands-on service to the poor.

Simon was also tapped to serve other philanthropists. John Olin asked him to lead his foundation after Simon left the Ford administration. Olin wanted his funds to be used to strengthen the American free-market system, and Simon was a natural ally. Under Simon's direction, Olin funded what Simon called "the counter-intelligentsia," the scholars and organizations who became the intellectual infrastructure of modern conservatism and libertarianism. Because Olin had a particular concern with the impact of law on public policy and culture, Simon also supported a host of academic programs that developed the law and economics movement at top-flight schools around the country, including Harvard, Chicago, Columbia, and Virginia.

Simon's commitment to Olin's donor intent was forged by Henry Ford II's departure from the board of the Ford Foundation in frustration at its direction in 1977—and by his own experience serving on the board of the John D. and Catherine T. MacArthur Foundation from 1979 to 1994. Catherine MacArthur had read his book *A Time for Truth* and wanted her foundation "to have the same mandate as the Olin Foundation." It was not to be: Catherine's stepson, Rod MacArthur, quickly steered the foundation his own way. New board members from academia and government were elected, and without a clear mandate in the foundation's incorporating documents, they picked causes they cared about—many of which Simon believed would have infuriated the MacArthurs. "As a result," Simon later said, "the MacArthur Foundation lost its ability to do what its founder wanted it to do."

Simon carried on Olin's program of research and organization-building through his own William E. Simon Foundation, which funds programs that support free markets, faith, and strong families. The foundation has striven to build the capacity of the poor and needy to help themselves, and promulgated its founder's support for one-on-one service. It has funded scholarship programs for poor children in Catholic schools, Bible literacy programs, retirement funds for priests and religious workers, mentoring programs, homes for runaway youth, and aid to victims of domestic violence.

Simon died in 2000, and his foundation is in the process of spending itself out of existence, like Olin's before it. That was an easy choice for Bill Simon. He believed that the capitalist system produced, in his words, "the greatest prosperity, the highest standards of living, and most important,

the greatest individual freedom ever known to man"—and would soon enough bring forward new wealth, new philanthropists, and new ideas for improving America.

⊷ Justin Torres

Further information

○ *Philanthropy* magazine article, philanthropyroundtable.org/topic/excellence_in_ philanthropy/simon_says

○ William Simon, *A Time for Reflection: An Autobiography* (Regnery, 2004)

ROBERT SMITH

Robert Smith was a prominent real-estate developer in the Washington metro area, best known for leading the development of Crystal City in Arlington, Virginia. He was also a leading benefactor of prominent institutions in the national capital, with significant donations to the National Gallery of Art, the University of Maryland, and regional sites of historic importance like Mount Vernon, Montpelier, and Abraham Lincoln's summer cottage.

Born in 1928 to a family of newly immigrated Jews, Smith spent his earliest years in New York City. During the Second World War, his father, a homebuilder and property manager, moved the family to Washington, D.C. Robert Smith graduated from the University of Maryland in 1950, and immediately went to work for his father's company. He expanded the portfolio of the Charles E. Smith Company, adding commercial properties to its existing stock of residential properties.

In 1961, Smith inked what came to be his signature deal: a 99-year lease on 20 acres of rundown land near Washington National Airport. In exchange for 3 percent of gross profits, he had the rights to the land on which Crystal City was built. Six years later, his father retired, and Robert, with his brother-in-law Robert Kogod, took charge of the company. One successful deal followed another. Shortly before a 2002 merger, the Charles E. Smith Company managed over 15 million square feet of office space and more than 30,000 residential units in D.C., Maryland, Virginia, Florida, Chicago, and Boston.

In 1952, Smith married a painter named Clarice Chasen. She taught him to appreciate art, and helped assemble the couple's superb collection of Renaissance-era bronze sculpture. In 1972, they made their first major donation to the National Gallery of Art. They befriended Paul Mellon, son of the gallery's founder, Andrew Mellon. When Paul Mellon retired from the board, he asked that Smith replace

Brian Smale

him as a trustee. Smith accepted, and soon was leading a $123 million fundraising campaign; from 1993 to 2003, he served as president of the board. In 2008, the Smiths announced their intention to donate their entire collection to the National Gallery.

In the mid-1990s, the University of Maryland approached Smith about a business-school donation, and he asked for a concrete, multi-year strategy for raising the school's stature. He gave the business school a $15 million gift in 1997, and the Robert H. Smith School of Business has since shot up in the rankings—reaching the top 20 nationwide, and the top five among public schools. The Smiths later gave the University of Maryland another $15 million to complete the 318,000-square-foot Clarice Smith Performing Arts Center. Another $30 million was offered in 2005, making the family the largest benefactor of public education in Maryland's history.

But their patronage of higher education extended beyond College Park: the Smiths were the lead donors to the Wilmer Institute at Johns Hopkins University, which is intended to become the nation's leading treatment and research center for eye diseases. At Hebrew University in Jerusalem, whose board Smith chaired from 1981 to 1985, they made major gifts for plant science and agricultural genetics research, and for expanding interdisciplinary research among those disciplines and animal sciences, biochemistry, nutrition, and environmental studies.

> "One who has forgotten to be thankful has fallen asleep in the midst of life."

But Smith is perhaps best remembered for his leadership in preserving sites of historic interest. In the mid-1990s, he was asked to help fund an archaeological survey at Montpelier, the bucolic plantation home of James Madison. Smith had been reading biographies of the Founders, and felt a great respect for Madison, co-author of the *Federalist Papers*, driving intellect behind the Constitution, and fourth President of the United States. Smith helped fund the dig, and then led an effort to conserve 200 acres of old-growth forest on the property. He put up a $10 million challenge to increase the capacity of the Constitutional Village, a facility at Montpelier that hosts weeklong seminars on the Constitution.

In 2000, Smith took on another preservation project: Mount Vernon. His donations helped build theaters and auditoriums, endowed a senior curator position, created a book-publishing fund, and redesigned Mount Vernon's website. He conceived and underwrote the "big tree program," in which 65 mature trees (some over 40 feet tall and weighing four tons) were planted to create a natural barrier between newly constructed facilities and the historic

grounds. The trees are species that existed in eighteenth-century northern Virginia: elm, maple, tulip poplar, oak, beech, and American holly. Most recently, the Smiths played an instrumental role in preparing for construction of the Presidential library for George Washington.

Smith also took charge of restoring the Benjamin Franklin House in London, which opened on Ben Franklin's 300th birthday in 2006. It was at 36 Craven Street that Franklin served as deputy postmaster for the British colonies and befriended many of the most important political and intellectual leaders in the empire. Smith not only re-created the townhouse but funded a scholarship center to encourage research into Franklin.

When Abraham Lincoln's summer cottage in northern Washington, D.C., was reopened to the public in 2008, the Smiths had paid for more than $7 million of the $15 million restoration. At Monticello, they permanently endowed a center for Jefferson studies with $15 million. Smith was a major benefactor of Gettysburg National Military Park, and helped fund renovations at the New York Historical Society. The list goes on.

Arguably America's most important recent preserver of historic sites associated with the Founders, Smith explained his support as a token of his gratitude. "My family has had tremendous opportunities because we live in this free, democratic society, for which I am thankful," Smith said when President George W. Bush awarded him a National Humanities Medal. "One who has forgotten to be thankful has fallen asleep in the midst of life."

— *Christopher Levenick*

Further information

- *Philanthropy* magazine article, philanthropyroundtable.org/topic/excellence_in_ philanthropy/build_hold_give
- David Smith, *Conversations with Papa Charlie: A Memory of Charles E. Smith* (Capital Books, 2000)

JAMES SMITHSON

James Smithson was a Briton who died in Italy in 1829 at the age of 75. Six years later, the primary beneficiary of Smithson's will died, and urgent letters were sent to Washington, D.C. It emerged that Smithson's estate, worth an estimated £100,000, had devolved "to the United States of America, to found at Washington, under the name of the Smithsonian Institution, an Establishment for the increase & diffusion of knowledge

among men." It was the first time a private individual had made such a gift to the new nation, and added new contours to American philanthropy.

Smithson was born in 1754, the illegitimate son of Elizabeth Macie and Hugh Smithson, the first duke of Northumberland. During his years in Pembroke College at Oxford University, he became interested in the natural sciences, particularly chemistry. His research so impressed his colleagues and mentors that within a year of graduating from Oxford he was admitted as a fellow of the Royal Society of London.

Deprived of the right to his father's titles, Smithson set out to establish his name respectably and quickly gained the regard of his peers. Though he would call London home, he spent many years traveling the world to obtain samples of minerals and meteorites, study geography, and examine the mining and manufacturing processes.

> James Smithson's gift to a people and a country he did not know personally grew out of his interest in a "culture of improvement" and a belief that the U.S. would play an important role in future human progress.

Smithson's interests were broad: he investigated improved methods for making coffee and tea, wrote a paper on "Some improvements of lamps," and was said to have once held a small container to a woman's face in order to capture her tear, take it to his study, and analyze it. While doing much for his romantic reputation, the story has a note of plausibility; the majority of Smithson's work was dedicated to studying the chemical composition of compounds.

His methods were scrupulously careful, and he acknowledged the importance of detail in scientific work. At the end of a paper on the element fluorine he wrote that "measuring the importance of the subject by the magnitude of the object" might lead some people to "cast a supercilious look on this discussion; but the particle and the planet are subject to the same laws, and what is learned of the one will be known of the other." He advocated for publication of even marginal advances in scientific investigation, rather than withholding them on the assumption that they were insufficiently important.

It is not entirely clear how Smithson acquired his fortune. It seems to have been inherited, although biographers split on whether it resulted from a combination of inheritances from several relatives, or if it was Smithson's own careful investment of his mother's estate. In any case, by the time Smithson wrote his will in 1826 he was a wealthy man.

After providing an annuity for his servant, Smithson left his estate to a nephew, and in the event of his death to his children. But in the event Smithson's nephew had no children, the estate would transfer to the U.S. and the broad pursuit of knowledge.

Why America remains a mystery. Despite his world travels, Smithson had never visited the United States. He is not known to have been in regular communication with any Americans, and his papers—other than his will—never mention the U.S. The question of why Smithson chose to deed his estate to the citizens of a nation he seemingly had no connection to may never be satisfactorily answered. Heather Ewing, author of the most recent and comprehensive biography of Smithson, suggests that his donation reflected the late-eighteenth century's interest in a "culture of improvement," and a widespread belief that the United States would play an important role in advancing the arts and sciences.

A handwritten note later discovered among Smithson's papers suggests his decision was partly motivated by a bastard son's search for legitimacy, perhaps immortality. "The best blood of England flows in my veins," Smithson lamented, "but this avails me not." He hoped that his quests in the world of science might help his name "live in the memory of man when the titles of the Northumberlands and the Percys are extinct and forgotten."

Regardless of Smithson's motivation, the bequest flummoxed our government. President Andrew Jackson was unsure of the constitutional propriety of accepting the gift, and turned the matter over to Congress. Former President John Quincy Adams, then a Representative from Massachusetts, championed the gift as being consonant with "the spirit of the age." Senator John Calhoun of South Carolina vigorously disagreed, proclaiming it "beneath the dignity of the United States to receive gifts of this kind from anyone." Adams won that argument, and in 1836 Congress sent an envoy to London to secure the funds.

It took two more years of paperwork and promising that the stipulated institution would be built, but eventually our representative carried 11 boxes of gold coins back to the U.S. mint. The sovereigns were recast into $508,318 worth of hard currency—a sum equivalent to 1/66 of the federal budget. After nearly an additional decade of wrangling over what shape it should take, Congress formally established the Smithsonian Institution in 1846.

Since then, the Smithsonian has robustly achieved the ambitious goal set by its donor. The institution is today the world's largest museum complex, and a prominent center of research. James Smithson established a powerful precedent that individuals, acting voluntarily, can wield private gifts to

achieve public benefits, even ones as grand as "the increase & diffusion of knowledge among men."

⟿ *Monica Klem*

Further information

○ Heather Ewing, *The Lost World of James Smithson: Science, Revolution, and the Birth of the Smithsonian* (Bloomsbury Publishing USA, 2007)

○ Nina Burleigh, *The Stranger and the Statesman: James Smithson, John Quincy Adams, and the Making of America's Greatest Museum: The Smithsonian* (Harper Collins, 2004)

○ William Rhees, "James Smithson and His Bequest," Smithsonian Miscellaneous Collections, Vol. XXI (Smithsonian Institution, 1881)

LELAND STANFORD

Leland Stanford built his railroad wealth in an era of rough-and-tumble politics and crony capitalism. He translated his riches into an institution that brought elite education west of the Rockies, became one of the world's most highly regarded universities, and incubated many of the twentieth century's technological triumphs.

Born in 1824 and raised in the Mohawk River valley near Albany, New York, A. Leland Stanford never used his given name of Amasa. He studied in the small town of Cazenovia, apprenticed at law in Albany, and went west in 1845 to open a legal practice in the new state of Wisconsin. Stanford spent seven years there, and married Jane Lathrop. But his firm faltered, and after a fire consumed his law office and library he turned his eyes farther west. In 1852, he followed his five brothers to California.

Stanford started off in ancillary businesses of the California Gold Rush, keeping a grocery store then a wholesale shop in Placer County. He participated in the founding of California's Republican Party, and was eventually elected governor in 1861. That same year, he became one of the four principal investors in the Central Pacific Railroad, which Congress authorized in 1862 to build the eastbound section of the first transcontinental railroad.

The transcontinental railroad was a remarkable feat of engineering, especially the Central Pacific's herculean efforts to carve tracks through the heights of the Sierra Nevada. Stanford, as president, enjoyed the triumph of driving the "golden spike" at Promontory Summit, Utah, in 1869 and for the rest of his life Stanford would remain one of California's best-known figures. From 1868 to 1890, he headed a second railroad, the Southern Pacific, which later merged with the Central Pacific. In 1885, he was elected to the U.S. Senate.

Political maneuvering made Stanford a very rich man. He participated in the worst practices of the Gilded Age: stock watering, kickbacks, rebates, bribes, collusion, monopoly. There is no acquitting Stanford on this front; his participation in such schemes is amply recorded in his letters.

Stanford is best remembered today, however, not for corruption but for a tribute to his only child. Leland DeWitt Stanford was born in 1868, and eventually came to call himself Leland Stanford Jr. On a trip to Europe in 1884, Leland Jr. died of typhoid fever. His parents were beside themselves. In their grief, the Stanfords pledged to themselves that "the children of California shall be our children."

What the children of California needed, they determined, was a modern university. They traveled through the East, visiting colleges along the Atlantic seaboard. They learned about the practical education and applied sciences taught at new land-grant institutions like Cornell. And they were impressed by the modernizing curricular reforms taking place at many of the old, elite schools like Harvard.

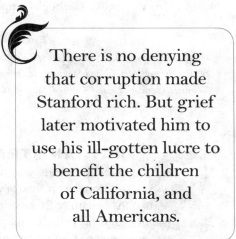

There is no denying that corruption made Stanford rich. But grief later motivated him to use his ill-gotten lucre to benefit the children of California, and all Americans.

In 1885, they founded the Leland Stanford Junior University. It would be private, coeducational, non-sectarian, and tuition-free. It would offer an education designed to "fit the graduate for some useful pursuit"—focusing on engineering, agriculture, and other practical disciplines in addition to the liberal arts and core sciences. It was consciously aimed to break higher education from its northeastern stranglehold, bringing a great university to the shores of the Pacific.

The Stanfords were intimately involved in virtually all aspects of planning the school. They located it on their stock farm in Palo Alto and hired Frederick Olmsted to lay out the grounds. For the design of the school they settled on a quadrangle of facilities made from local materials that reflected the nearby California landscape.

With total giving that would amount today to half a billion dollars, Stanford personally funded the operations of the university during its early years. When he died in 1893, his estate was frozen by federal lawsuits over loan repayments on Central Pacific construction funds. During the lawsuit's six years, Jane kept the university afloat via creative transfers of her personal living funds.

Stanford University immediately attracted excellent students; Herbert Hoover was in its first class. It opened professional schools in business, engineering, medicine, and law, and soon resoundingly achieved its founders' goal of making top-flight higher education a truly national rather than regional enterprise. Then in 1939, two Stanford alumni—Bill Hewlett and David Packard—opened an electronics business in their Palo Alto garage, spawning what is now called Silicon Valley, and turning Stanford University into ground zero for some of the most creative entrepreneurship of the digital age.

"Perhaps the greatest sum ever given by an individual for any purpose is the gift of Senator Stanford," wrote Andrew Carnegie in 1889, "who undertakes to establish upon the Pacific coast, where he amassed his enormous fortune, a complete university." Impressed by Stanford's skill and determination in bringing his gift to life, Carnegie simply concluded: "He is to be envied."

᠁ *Evan Sparks*

Further information

○ Hubert Bancroft, *History of the Life of Leland Stanford: A Character Study* (Biobooks, 1952)
○ Bertha Berner, *Mrs. Leland Stanford: An Intimate Portrait* (Stanford, 1935)
○ Norman Tutorow, *Leland Stanford: Man of Many Careers* (Pacific Coast Publishers, 1971)

NATHAN STRAUS

Nathan Straus was one of the greatest retail merchants in American history, a co-owner of the Macy's and Abraham & Straus department-store chains. He used his fortune to help the poor in New York City, fund Jewish causes at home and abroad, and create safe milk at a time when milk was the leading killer of children. One of the most successful businessmen of his time, Straus gave away almost all of his money during his lifetime. For Straus, it was a point of principle. Invoking a Jewish proverb, he wrote in his will: "What you give for the cause of charity in health is gold, what you give in sickness is silver, and what you give in death is lead."

At the age of 18, Nathan Straus launched a glass and china import business with his brother and father. In 1874, L. Strauss & Son began to operate the china and glassware department at Macy & Co. Within a few years, they had the highest profits of any department and accounted for 18 percent of the total gross at Macy's. By 1898, the Straus family owned both Macy's and the Brooklyn store Abraham & Straus.

Nathan Straus had an instinct for merchandising. He was the first to offer depository accounts, against which customers could draw as they shopped. He was at the forefront of bargain sales, demonstrations, and store exhibitions. Perhaps most importantly he opened a lunch counter at Macy's—not to mention public restrooms—making shopping into something more than an errand. He helped turn it into a recreational activity, a way for middle-class women to spend part of a day.

All of this brought the Straus family great wealth. Nathan and his brothers were instilled with a sense of civic duty, and this was expressed by serving in public office. Nathan was Parks Commissioner of New York from 1889 to 1893, and was offered the Democratic nomination for mayor. (He declined.) Other times the brothers exercised civic leadership in a private capacity. During the Panic of 1893, for example, Straus saw firsthand the widespread human suffering. In New York City alone, over 39,000 families found their breadwinners without work. Thousands of homeless men wandered the streets, searching for work or food.

Nathan Straus did all he could to alleviate misery. As the terrible winter of 1893–94 blanketed the city, he provided 1.5 million buckets of coal to the poor. The following year, he supplied 2 million tickets for coal, food, and lodging at shelters he established. When coal was selling for 20¢ per pail, he supplied it at 5¢ to those who were poor, and gave away 2,000 tons for free to those who were desperate.

> It is estimated that the efforts of Nathan Straus directly saved the lives of 445,800 children.

Straus undertook many other charitable initiatives. During the Spanish-American War, Rabbi Joseph Krauskopf alerted him of the need for pure water for the American troops in Santiago de Cuba. Straus sprang into action, buying a water distillation plant with a daily capacity of 20,000 gallons for the soldiers. In 1909, he led earthquake-relief efforts in Italy. When the Great War triggered widespread layoffs, he provided more than a million 1¢ meals for the unemployed. He paid for the construction of dozens of tuberculosis clinics from coast to coast—as well as a Catholic Church in Lakewood, New Jersey.

But the great philanthropic crusade of his life was providing safe milk for the nation's children. Before the Industrial Revolution, the overwhelming majority of babies were breast-fed. And most older children had access to fresh cow's milk because they lived on farms. But as the population moved increasingly to cities, the milk supply became a problem. Rich urbanites could keep a cow in their stables, but the less affluent had to depend on "swill milk."

Produced by cows kept by brewers and distillers to eat up their agricultural waste, it was of the poorest quality imaginable.

The railroads changed the situation in some ways, allowing fresh milk to be brought quickly to cities. It looked and tasted wholesome, but all too often it was not. Cows were milked by unwashed hands, and the milk was poured into unsterilized containers and transported long distances from farms to cities, without refrigeration. Along the way microorganisms multiplied quickly. Typhoid, diphtheria, and cholera can all be contracted from contaminated milk, even when there is no sign of spoilage. In New York in the 1850s, fewer than half all children born lived to see their fifth birthday, and bad milk was one of the biggest culprits.

Straus knew there was a scientific solution to this problem: pasteurization. He set to work both to provide pasteurized milk to needy children, and to have the process legally mandated for all milk sold. He set up milk stations in poor areas in New York City to give away pasteurized milk, and proof of the efficacy of his program was not long in coming. In 1891, fully 24 percent of babies born in New York City died in their first year. But of the 20,111 children fed on pasteurized milk supplied by Nathan Straus over a four-year period, only six died.

In 1898 Straus served as president of the city's Board of Health. He immediately donated pasteurization equipment to the city's orphan's asylum, located on what is now Roosevelt Island in the East River, which was run by the board. Straus established, at his own expense, 297 milk stations in 36 other cities. The national death rate for infants fell from 125 per thousand in 1891 to 16 in 1925. Altogether it is estimated that the efforts of Nathan Straus directly saved the lives of 445,800 children.

Straus's interest in eradicating disease and alleviating poverty extended beyond the shores of America. In 1912, he and his wife, Lina, traveled to Europe to attend the International Tuberculosis Conference in Rome. (His brother and sister-in-law went on the same trip, but sailed home aboard the *Titanic* and famously refused seats offered to them in the lifeboats.)

Before the conference, Nathan and Lina stopped in Palestine, which was ravaged at the time by disease and famine. The couple opened up a soup kitchen, and founded a health department there. Straus became active in the movement to create a Jewish state. He served as chair of the American Jewish Congress Committee and fought for the organization to adopt a stronger Zionist stance. The town of Natanya on the Mediterranean was named after him.

Straus returned to Palestine many times and his support would never waver—he gave over $1.5 million during the course of his life. He offered one of the first major gifts to Hadassah, the Zionist women's organization,

for the support of a medical mission to Israel. He funded the construction of the Nathan and Lina Straus Health Center in Jerusalem, which he said was to be for all the inhabitants of the country, irrespective of race or creed. In 1927, after a great earthquake shook Palestine, Straus wired $25,000 to Jerusalem to help alleviate the suffering. At the age of 80, he served as the honorary chairman of the New York United Palestine Appeal, to which he donated $100,000. In 1931, Straus passed away at the age of 82, having expended most of his fortune on good causes.

"Candidly, as a Jew," Straus once reflected in the *Christian Herald*, "I have often felt that I owed this apology or explanation to my co-religionists, for the fact is that I have done a great deal more for Christians than I have for Jews. But when, as a Jew, the impulse has come to me to do more for my own people, the controlling thought has been that the God of all mankind does not draw any racial or religious lines in the distribution of his bounties."

— Naomi Schaefer Riley

Further information

○ *Philanthropy* magazine article, philanthropyroundtable.org/topic/excellence_in_ philanthropy/the_milk_man

○ June Hall McCash, *A Titanic Love Story: Ida and Isidor Straus* (Mercer University Press, 2012)

○ Lina Gutherz Straus, *Disease in milk: the remedy, pasteurization—the life work of Nathan Straus* (E. P. Dutton, 1917)

ARTHUR AND LEWIS TAPPAN

Never mind the Wright brothers. Ignore the Kennedys. Forget the Kochs. Arthur and Lewis Tappan had a bigger transformative effect on America than any other brothers in our history.

Highly successful Wall Street merchants and energized evangelical Christians, the Tappan brothers mastered both sides of the philanthrocapitalist formula. Amid the popular revival known as our Second Great Awakening, their organizing, giving, and undaunted leadership powered a flurry of influential culture reforms. The America they left behind was profoundly different from the Jacksonian society in which they came of age—in large measure thanks to their philanthropic action.

Arthur and Lewis grew up in a middle-class home in small-town western Massachusetts, thoroughly immersed in Puritan culture and religion. They were introduced as young men to the writings of British philanthropist

and politician William Wilberforce, recommended by their uncle for three qualities: his "ardent piety," his "patriotism," and his "philanthropy."

The boys' mother was kin to Ben Franklin, and in their marriages they connected themselves to other public-spirited American families. Lewis's father-in-law was a famously kind, religious, and locally beloved physician in Brookline, Massachusetts, who saved many lives from smallpox and other afflictions. Arthur's bride grew up in the New York City home of Alexander Hamilton. Her father had been one of Hamilton's closest friends during the Revolution, so when both of her parents died while she was a toddler, Hamilton stepped in as surrogate father and raised her like one of his own offspring.

As young men, Arthur and Lewis pitched in on a variety of charitable causes. Arthur supported many churches in lower Manhattan. He campaigned for businesses to give their workers Sunday off as a day of rest. He founded missionary groups, and battled sex trafficking. He was a director of the Seaman's Friend Society that offered aid to elderly sailors. Lewis volunteered as a counselor with a temperance group, and donated and raised money to support the Deaf and Dumb Asylum, Hospital for the Sick, Asylum for the Insane, and Asylum for Indigent Boys. He supported the American Bible Society, and helped start the Boston Provident Institution—one of the very first banks created to help the poor accumulate wealth.

> **Though they were excoriated in the partisan press, physically attacked, and eventually financially ruined through business boycotts, the Tappans never blanched from their culture-change philanthropy.**

After the textile business Lewis had built to success became overextended and went bankrupt, he went to work as a partner in Arthur's silk-importing firm. The two labored hand-in-glove for much of the rest of their lives. Arthur was already making a remarkable array of potent donations, establishing new charities, and offering them managerial expertise. When he saw up close the life his brother had carved out as a Christian businessman and philanthropist in Manhattan, Lewis was deeply impressed.

Arthur had also built his faith right into his merchant practices. He viewed stiff interest charges as un-Christian, so eschewed the common trading practice that joined high prices with easy credit and

usurious borrowing rates. Instead, he built his firm on a new pattern of consistently low cash prices, high transparency and fairness, and sterling honesty—yielding heavy sales volumes that made his low-margin model work financially. Arthur used his own funds to boost up libraries, chapels, meeting rooms, and decent rooming houses where young apprentices newly relocated from countryside to city could live, improve themselves, and socialize away from the corrupting streets. He gifted money to many of his former employees to set them up in business, knowing that most would end up competing with him in the same markets.

Looking over his brother's profoundly ambitious experiment in Christian living, Lewis marveled that "this is enjoying riches in a high degree…in the good he achieves while living." For both brothers, moral considerations became a centerpiece of their commerce and philanthropy alike. Lewis eventually created (with Arthur as a partner) the first firm for rating the honesty and reliability of businesses and businessmen. It "checks knavery, and purifies the mercantile air," said Lewis, and eventually evolved into Dun & Bradstreet. It was an ethical and economic two-for-one, because by cleaning up business practices it also reduced the corporate collapses that were then so common, and put national growth on a firmer footing.

Though they labored in close parallel for decades, and agreed on nearly all matters of principle and practice, Arthur and Lewis Tappan had contrasting personalities, and achieved their good works in quite different ways. Arthur was taciturn, sensitive, and a bit forbidding. He kept no guest chairs in his small office because he believed they only encouraged visitors to tarry, distracting him from getting things done.

Lewis was much more social, indeed a tireless extrovert, and a compelling public speaker. He "performed the muscular work" that allowed the brothers' business ventures and philanthropic projects to thrive. He was a master strategist and natural leader, and showed repeated brilliance at turning current events into object lessons for the American public.

Even at the peak of their business careers and philanthropic leadership, both Lewis and Arthur always made time to join small prayer meetings, visit the sick, and hand out Bibles in the sterile countinghouses lining Wall Street or the dank taverns that sprouted like mushrooms along the East River wharves. There were occasions where they charged into grim brothels "to pluck fallen women from roaring lions who seek to devour them," placing their rescues in homes with food and clothing, mentoring, and training for respectable employment.

For most of their lives, Arthur was much wealthier than Lewis, and a far heavier donor. (But then, he was a heavier donor than perhaps anyone

else in his half century.) Arthur was abstemious and frugal, spending almost nothing on himself, and modestly on his family. He viewed his money as a resource entrusted to him by Providence, to be used accountably to improve life on earth and lift men's eyes to higher goals. In typical seasons he gave away the lion's share of his yearly income.

Arthur Tappan had a razor-sharp philanthropic vision and the courage to put down large sums for difficult or unpopular work. He was one of the first American philanthropists to act on a "comprehensive" scale—launching new organizations when they were wanting, sticking with recipient groups through thick and thin over decades, making huge investments in particular charities as they hit a crossroads, pursuing long-term goals.

Almost without exception, Arthur left speaking and writing to others. He made his contributions by volunteering his managerial expertise behind the scenes, soliciting fellow members of his New York City merchant class to pitch in for charitable causes, and making heavy gifts of his own (even when his business and income were tottering). Arthur Tappan's main means of expressing himself, as one biographer put it, was "the metallic eloquence of his money."

And that was a huge contribution. "Our great benevolent system owes its expansion and power to his influence," observed one contemporary. "His example inspired the merchants of New York…leading them to give hundreds and thousands where before they gave tens or fifties." By the 1820s Arthur was known as the most generous donor in New York City, and is estimated to have donated roughly $50,000 every year for decades. (As a fraction of the national economy, that is the current-day equivalent of distributing more than half a billion dollars annually.) John Pintard, a formidable businessman and Christian philanthropist in his own right, marveled in 1830 that "he is truly a wonderful benefactor.… I wish we had more Arthur Tappans."

The Tappan brothers were linchpins in building up the so-called Benevolent Empire—a thick web of thousands of local and national charitable groups established in the first half of our nineteenth century to ameliorate a host of social problems plaguing the nation. About half of American children, for instance, were not attending school at that point. So the Tappans, and many allies, fueled the Sunday-school movement—which created tens of thousands of free schools starting in the 1820s, and became the nation's major source of improved literacy as well as character training.

The Tappans were also stalwarts of the temperance movement. When they began their work, alcohol consumption was shockingly high in the U.S.—three to four *times* current per capita levels. They subsidized and spread

across our land many local programs of education, voluntary persuasion, and peer support that eventually reduced drinking dramatically (which in turn improved family life, public safety, work productivity, and other indicators of societal health).

The brothers planted new churches in New York City and brought in popular pastors like Charles Finney and Lyman Beecher to inspire personal transformations and Christian service. They supported Bible societies, and missions aiding blacks, Indians, poor people overseas, and others. They established several schools and colleges—like Oberlin, which they insisted be open to African Americans and women at a time when that was unknown, and even illegal in many places.

Fired by their deep Christian convictions, the Tappan brothers built the then-controversial cause of abolishing slavery into a popular national movement. Arthur was the lead funder and visionary and Lewis the vital organizer behind the American Anti-Slavery Society. Starting from nothing in 1833, it quickly became the largest and most effective culture-change organization in American history, initiating a massive shift in public sentiment on the most contentious issue our nation has ever faced.

Arthur dispatched 70 talented orators to spread the anti-slavery message all across the countryside. Lewis set up and circulated magazines and journals that could reach everyone from children to pastors to judges. They paid for legal defenses of journalists, teachers, and others who ran afoul of laws perpetuating enslavement. A large grant from Arthur helped put more than a million pieces of anti-slavery literature into the U.S. mail. Lewis brilliantly made a cause célèbre of the trial of some Africans who had taken over their slave ship, the *Amistad*. The brothers hired interpreters and tutors, engaged a crack legal team that included former President John Quincy Adams, fed daily updates to the national newspapers, and used the incident as a teachable moment that turned many citizens against human bondage.

For sparking the abolition movement in these ways, the Tappans were excoriated in the partisan press, physically attacked, and eventually financially ruined through business boycotts. Vandals destroyed Lewis's home, trashed Arthur's store, and wrecked churches established by the brothers. When the Tammany Hall political machine turned a blind eye, this marauding by slavery apologists turned into a seven-day riot that ended only when martial law was declared in Manhattan. Vilification of the Tappans then went national. President Jackson and his underlings encouraged vigilantes to break into post offices and destroy the abolitionist literature mailed by Tappan-supported charities. The brothers were hung in effigy in many cities, and large bounties were offered across the South for their assassination.

Very soon, the liberties of all Americans were imperiled by this backlash against charitable efforts to make the nation understand the true nature of slavery. While "we commenced the present struggle to obtain the freedom of the slave," commented William Jay, son of first U.S. Supreme Court chief justice John Jay, "we are compelled to continue it to preserve our own. We are now contending, not so much with the slaveholders of the South about human rights, as with the political and commercial aristocracy of the North for the liberty of speech, of the press, and of conscience."

Arthur and Lewis Tappan never blanched in the face of this pressure. It did eventually cost them their livelihoods. But thanks to their efforts, the hearts and minds of many middle-class Northerners were won over to the cause of emancipation. For the first time in our history, abolition developed a wide popular following. The most consequential social change in the history of the United States had begun, and two philanthropist brothers were at the center of it.

☞ *Karl Zinsmeister*

Further information

○ *The Life of Arthur Tappan*, Lewis Tappan (General Books, 1870)
○ *What Comes Next?*, Karl Zinsmeister (Philanthropy Roundtable, 2016)

JOHN TEMPLETON

One of the world's most successful mutual-fund managers, John Templeton eventually dedicated much of his money and energy to research into the overlap between two of his deepest fascinations: science and religion.

Born in 1912 in Winchester, a small town in rural Tennessee, Templeton was a straight-A student whose parents encouraged his healthy curiosity. They let him buy dynamite to dispose of backyard tree stumps, and gunpowder to manufacture his own fireworks. They took him on cross-country road trips in the early days of automobiles.

He studied at Yale and Oxford (the latter as a Rhodes Scholar), then took a job on Wall Street. His investing strategy was guided by the principles of thrift and positive thinking. "Bull markets are born on pessimism, grown on skepticism, mature on optimism, and die on euphoria," he said. "The time of maximum pessimism is the best time to buy, and the time of maximum optimism is the best time to sell." In 1939—on the eve of World War II, a time of maximum pessimism—Templeton purchased $100 worth of every publicly traded stock available to him that was trading for less than a dollar.

He bought into 104 companies, only four of which never panned out. After an average holding period of four years, that portfolio had returned 400 percent. Templeton often mentioned that he wished he had held those particular stocks longer.

Templeton developed a methodical investment philosophy based on his own valuations of companies. "Templeton's basic formula is to divide the total value of a company by the number of shares the company has distributed," wrote biographer William Proctor. "This calculating will give you the true value of a company's stock, and if the market price is lower, it's a bargain." This method was used to operate the Templeton Growth Fund, opened in 1954. It was spectacularly successful, with the fund producing an annualized return of 14 percent over several decades. A $10,000 investment in 1954 would have been worth $2 million in 1992, when Templeton sold the fund.

Templeton attributed his success in part to his diligent research and in part to his relocation to the Bahamas in 1968, where he felt insulated from the groupthink on Wall Street. Templeton also attributed his success to the blessings of God, with whom he felt a closeness and unity. Throughout his life, Templeton was inspired by religious idealism.

As he grew financially successful, Templeton began to dabble in philanthropy. He built on his boyhood interests in science, philosophy, and religion. One of his first philanthropic initiatives was the Templeton Prize for Progress in Religion, which he created in 1972 out of the conviction that Alfred Nobel's prizes neglected

> **Templeton believed that material, social, and religious progress were bound together.**

metaphysical wisdom, and specifically the role of religion in progress. He offered a purse calculated to be larger than that of the Nobel Prizes, and stipulated that the award was to be ecumenical, with at least one judge from each of the five major religions "so that no child of God would feel excluded." To maximize attention to the winners, Templeton arranged for Prince Philip, the Duke of Edinburgh, to award the Templeton Prize at Buckingham Palace.

The first honor was given to Mother Teresa of Calcutta, who six years later would win the Nobel Peace Prize. Other notable Templeton laureates have included Frère Roger, Cicely Saunders, Billy Graham, Aleksandr Solzhenitsyn, Stanley Jaki, Baba Amte, Charles Colson, Michael Novak, Freeman Dyson, and the Dalai Lama. Since 2000, laureates have tended to be philosophers, physicists, or biologists with insights that bear on religion.

Templeton believed that material, social, and religious progress were bound together, and that society advanced when these spheres moved together in unity. Templeton denied that there was any fundamental conflict between science and religion, and believed that each field has ground-breaking insights to share with the other. He wrote: "Is our human consciousness only a tiny manifestation of a vast creative consciousness that is often referred to by...names such as God, Allah, Spirit, Yahweh, Brahman, or the Creator? Has our human concept of this creative source been too small?...How can we learn to encourage progress and discovery in ways that tap the deep symphonies of divine creativity and involve us in God's purposes? Perhaps future generations will use scientific methods to speed up the search."

In 1987, Templeton established the John Templeton Foundation as a philanthropic vehicle for these inquiries. Through the foundation, he funded ventures ranging from an essay contest inviting youngsters to explore the spiritual principles of life, to an "honor roll" for character-building at universities, to a new college at Oxford University. Today the foundation has an endowment exceeding $2 billion, and funds research in four areas related to Templeton's "big questions": science (in particular math, physics, biology, psychology, and sociology), character development, free enterprise, and genetics. Speeding the pace of religious inquiry so that it might match the progress in science is a particular interest.

Templeton remained closely involved with the Templeton Prize and his foundation until his death in 2008 at age 95. He was married and widowed twice, and had three children, and as he aged he felt an urgency in his philanthropic work. "Evidence indicates that the rate of spiritual development is accelerating," he wrote. "Throughout the 200,000 years of our history as a species, there have been periods of gradual growth, followed by rapid development.... Now, a new vision of our place and purpose in the cosmos is unfolding. Possibly, we may be setting the stage for a giant leap forward in our spiritual understanding."

Templeton received many honors and awards during his lifetime, including a knighthood from Queen Elizabeth II. But the man known for his humility and belief in unity might well have preferred the Biblically inspired tribute offered by Princeton Theological Seminary: "There was a man sent from God whose name was John."

⊯ Evan Sparks

Further information

○ Robert Herrmann, *Sir John Templeton: Supporting Scientific Research for Spiritual Discoveries* (Templeton Press, 2004)

○ William Proctor, *The Templeton Touch* (Templeton Press, 2012)

JUDAH TOURO

Judah Touro was a leading merchant and philanthropist during the early days of our nation, known for benefactions throughout the country, but especially in Louisiana and Rhode Island. Born in 1775 in Newport, Rhode Island, Touro was the second son of Rabbi Isaac Touro, leader of Newport's synagogue.

Constructed in 1763, and now known as the Touro Synagogue due to the gifts and service of the Touro family, the Newport assembly was the recipient of a famous 1790 letter on religious liberty from George Washington. "The government of the United States," wrote Washington, "which gives to bigotry no sanction, to persecution no assistance, requires only that they who live under its protection should demean themselves as good citizens…. May the children of the stock of Abraham, who dwell in this land, continue to merit and enjoy the good will of the other inhabitants."

As a boy, Judah and his brother were apprenticed to their uncle, one of Boston's leading Jewish merchants. Judah fell in love with his cousin Catherine, but Judah's uncle disapproved. In 1801, his hopes of marriage firmly blocked, Judah left for the burgeoning port of New Orleans.

There, he opened a store handling consignments and shipments for colleagues in Boston. His timing was fortuitous. Touro established himself just before the Louisiana Purchase added New Orleans to the growing republic. The young man was ideally positioned to capitalize on the subsequent commercial boom. He traded in soap, candles, codfish, and other goods sent by his contacts in New England, and then invested his profits in ships and New Orleans real estate.

Touro's assets grew handsomely in value as the Crescent City expanded into one of America's preeminent urban centers. Within a decade, he was one of the wealthiest men in the entrepot. During the War of 1812, Touro volunteered as a private in the Louisiana Militia. He was seriously wounded in the Battle of New Orleans, and required more than a year to recover from injuries that his doctors initially assumed would be fatal.

Touro remained a devout Jew, although for most of his life he was without a synagogue. When he arrived in New Orleans, his co-religionists in the city could be counted on two hands; as late as 1826, there were no more than a few hundred Jews in all of Louisiana. In 1828, Touro supported the founding of New Orleans's first synagogue, which after some years divided into separate congregations in the Ashkenazi and Sephardic traditions. Touro, by then quite wealthy, gave generously to both congregations and attended the Sephardic gathering. (In 1881, the synagogues merged, and today the

combined congregation is named for its benefactor.) Touro also created and funded numerous Jewish relief agencies and Hebrew schools in New Orleans.

Touro gave liberally and ecumenically. In 1824, he erected a free public library. He purchased a Christian church building and assumed its debts, while allowing the congregation to use the building rent-free in perpetuity. When a friend suggested the property might be valuable if sold for commercial purposes, Touro responded, "I am a friend to religion and I will not pull down the church to increase my means!" He founded a home for the poor, and during a yellow-fever epidemic, he established a hospital. After his death, it became known as Touro Infirmary, and it remains the only nonprofit, faith-based community hospital in New Orleans. Influenced by the abolitionist views of his former Boston employer, he would also purchase slaves in order to manumit them.

> More than 200 years ago, this religious Jew started helping Americans of every religion and state of life, in multiple ways that continue to have positive effects today.

Touro's generosity also extended to his early hometowns of Newport and Boston. In 1840, he gave $10,000 anonymously to complete the long-languishing Bunker Hill Monument. (By nature somewhat bashful and retiring, he briefly considered withdrawing his gift when his anonymity was compromised.) At the dedication ceremonies in 1843, Daniel Webster, antebellum America's greatest orator, praised Touro and fellow funder Amos Lawrence in verse that is usually credited to Oliver Wendell Holmes:

Amos and Judah! Venerated names!
Patriarch and prophet press their equal claims.
Like generous coursers running "neck to neck,"
Each aids the work by giving it a check.
Christian and Jews, they carry out one plan
For though of different faith, each is in heart a man.

Touro died in 1854. In his will, he bequeathed $500,000 to institutions around the country—more than half of which went to non-Jewish causes. (As a percentage of GDP, these gifts would approximate $2 billion today.) The will includes Touro Synagogue and Touro Infirmary; various benevolent

societies and hospitals; orphanages, almshouses, and asylums; libraries and schools; and relief for Jews overseas. According to one contemporary observer, "he gave ten times more than any Christian in the city to aid the cause of Christians in the land of Judaea."

He also gave thousands of dollars each to 23 Jewish congregations in 14 states—especially the Newport synagogue, where he endowed the cemetery in which he was laid to rest, the final surviving member of the Touro family line. "The last of his name," reads his tombstone, "he inscribed it in the Book of Philanthropy to be remembered forever."

☞ Evan Sparks

Further information

○ Leon Huhner, *The Life of Judah Touro* (Jewish Publication Society of America, 1946)

○ Max Kohler, *Judah Touro, Merchant and Philanthropist* (American Jewish Society, 1905)

WILLIAM VOLKER

William Volker made his fortune manufacturing home furnishings, and dedicated the overwhelming majority of that fortune to charity. He gave generously to causes and institutions throughout his adopted hometown of Kansas City. To the best of his ability, he gave anonymously.

At one point, Volker partnered with Kansas City public officials, hoping to increase the effectiveness of his giving. To his horror, he discovered that city leaders saw charity not as a way to help people help themselves, but rather as a form of patronage that would help them retain power. The experience led Volker to a deeper appreciation for private initiative, and a desire to fund the study and promotion of classical liberalism.

Born near Hanover, Germany, in 1859, William Volker was taught early in life to work hard and love God. His father entrusted him with responsibility beyond his years, as when he charged the five-year-old boy with feeding the family's cows. His mother, pious and kind, provided religious instruction, and William read the Scriptures every day for the rest of his life. When he was 12 years old, war broke out between France and Prussia; fearing William would be conscripted, his family left Germany. They immigrated to the United States, settling in Chicago just days after the Great Fire of 1871.

Volker departed Chicago at age 23, having saved enough capital to start a small business in Kansas City, Missouri. William Volker & Company sold home furnishings—picture frames, window shades, moldings. After a few difficult years, the business thrived; it posted profits every year except for 1930-31. By 1906, at the age of 47, Volker was a self-made millionaire. He

would have acquired his first million sooner had he not made it his lifelong practice to give away, by one estimate, about one-third of each year's income.

Early every morning after Volker arrived at work, he made himself available to employees, friends, and callers facing problems. He gave many thousands of small gifts to people with immediate needs—a pair of new dentures for an elevator operator, tuition for a hardworking college student. So personally involved was he that he wrote out every check himself, so that each gift could be kept confidential. While he tried to ascertain that there was a real need of assistance before offering aid, Volker would give a person the benefit of the doubt. He never wanted to risk denying help to someone in true need.

Deeply invested in the civic life of Kansas City, Volker supported scores of institutions and causes, building a research laboratory, diagnostic clinic, and nurse's residence at the Research Hospital, acquiring a collection of Chinese art for the Nelson-Atkins Museum—even purchasing two camels for the Swope Park Zoo. Perhaps his most visible contribution was to the University of Kansas City. Volker was the principal driver behind the creation of the school, donating 40 acres for the campus and endowing it with millions of dollars to fund the university's library, president's house, and science building.

> From disappointing experience, Volker concluded that government should "be restricted to those activities which can be entrusted to the worst citizens." For more idealistic and selfless improvement, society depended on personal generosity.

Between 1908 and 1915, Volker worked closely with the city government. In 1908, he helped found the Kansas City Board of Pardons and Paroles, which oversaw the process of releasing prisoners. He made it a condition of parole that employment was arranged before release—"no job, no parole"—and that parolees agree to garnished wages, with the deducted funds deposited into a savings account. Impressed with the success of this program, he began to look for other ways to partner with local authorities.

In 1910, Volker led the creation of the Board of Public Welfare, the first municipal-welfare department in the country. Excited about continuing his philanthropy through the new agency, Volker was surprised to learn that the city failed to adequately fund its commitments. He quietly contributed $50,000

to make up the difference. Almost immediately, local politicians—most notably, Tom Pendergast, the machine boss in Kansas City—began using the funds to further their partisan interests. After Volker retired in 1918, the board became a barely veiled political enterprise. The episode taught Volker, he later explained, that "political charity isn't charity." He concluded that "government must be restricted to those activities which can be entrusted to the worst citizens, not the best."

Volker returned to his extensive program of private philanthropy, which he continued until his death in 1947. When Friedrich von Hayek's *The Road to Serfdom* was published in 1944, Volker discovered a thinker who made sense of his experience. Disillusioned by government failures, he began funding scholars, writers, and teachers who could champion the cause of free enterprise, individual initiative, and limited government. He started supporting free-market and libertarian institutions, including the Foundation for Economic Education, the Institute for Humane Studies, and what became the Intercollegiate Studies Institute. He underwrote Hayek's salary at the University of Chicago, and paid a stipend that enabled Ludwig von Mises to teach at New York University.

Perhaps the most consequential check William Volker ever wrote was dated May 7, 1945. Made to Friedrich Hayek for $2,000, it underwrote the travel expenses for 17 American scholars to attend the first meeting of the Mont Pelerin Society. Volker did not live to see all of the Mont Pelerin Society's accomplishments, but with that small boost to a group of penurious writers and scholars, he helped launch an international network that distinguished itself in defending freedom in the West during the last half of the twentieth century.

Mont Pelerin Society members periodically gather and debate to refine their ideas and encourage one another. Eight members eventually won the Nobel Prize in economics—four of whom, thanks to Volker, attended the first meeting. According to Nancy Hoplin and Ron Robinson, 22 of the 66 economic advisers to Ronald Reagan's 1980 presidential campaign were members. In Western Europe, three members of the Mont Pelerin Society became heads of state.

Closer to home, the people of Kansas City continue to honor Volker today. There is a Volker Elementary School, a Volker Memorial Fountain, and a Volker Boulevard. The University of Missouri-Kansas City Volker Campus is named for him, as is the Volker Neighborhood Association. This local outpouring, in the face of his diligent efforts to adhere to the Biblical precept that "alms…be in secret," is a testament to William Volker's remarkable generosity.

↝ *Monica Klem*

Further information

○ David Boutros, "William Volker and Company," Kansas City Public Library (July 2007)

○ Herbert Cornuelle, *Mr. Anonymous: The Story of William Volker* (Caxton Printers, 1951)

○ Nicole Hoplin and Ron Robinson, *Funding Fathers: The Unsung Heroes of the Conservative Movement* (Regnery, 2008)

MADAM C. J. WALKER

Madam C. J. Walker ranks among the greatest African-American philanthropists in history. When she died in 1919, Walker was widely eulogized as the first woman to become a self-made millionaire. The assumption may not have been correct; the estimated value of her remaining estate at the time of her death was $600,000 (about $8 million in today's dollars). Nonetheless, several generations of African Americans looked upon her as proof that dramatic economic success was possible for blacks as well as whites.

Born in 1867 as Sarah Breedlove, her first years were spent on the Louisiana plantation where her family had worked as slaves. She was the first in her family to be born free. Her parents died when she was a young child, leaving her to live with her sister. Ill treatment by her cruel brother-in-law motivated 14-year-old Sarah to leave the household and marry Moses McWilliams. Seven years later McWilliams died, and Sarah and her three-year-old daughter, Lelia, moved to St. Louis, where three of her brothers lived.

She took up work as a washerwoman. She remarried in 1894, and soon found herself supporting a drunkenly abusive and openly unfaithful husband. Determined to provide her daughter with a better life, she managed to send Lelia to Knoxville College in Tennessee. In 1903, she left her husband and took a job as a sales agent for Annie Pope-Turnbo, a St. Louis businesswoman who produced products that claimed to stimulate hair growth.

After two years, Sarah moved to Colorado. Her success as Pope-Turnbo's Denver sales agent suggested that she might begin selling hair products of her own. She created her own line of hair-care products, made specifically for African-American women. C. J. and her third husband, Charles Walker, spent a year traveling through the South, building the foundations of a mail-order business. By 1908, she had trained hundreds of sales agents. A visit to Indianapolis in 1910 convinced the Walkers that it would be a good location for a permanent headquarters.

An Indianapolis campaign to build a new YMCA recreation facility in a black neighborhood provided her first opportunity for public philanthropy. She explained her $1,000 gift saying, "If the association can save our boys, our girls will be saved, and that's what I am interested in." As her reputation for generosity grew, Walker was inundated with requests for help. Initially inclined to help individuals who showed a desire for self-improvement, the focus of her charitable giving gradually shifted away from individuals (due to a series of bad experiences) and toward organizations and causes instead.

In 1910, she created the Madam C. J. Walker Manufacturing Company of Indiana, putting up the necessary capital herself. (She had adopted "Madam" as a first name, to preclude being called "Auntie" by whites.) Walker traveled extensively, going as far as the Caribbean and Central America to increase the distribution of her products and train new agents. In 1916 she created the Madam C. J. Walker Benevolent Association, staffed by employees of her company, arguing that the beneficial publicity that flowed from charitable work was good for business.

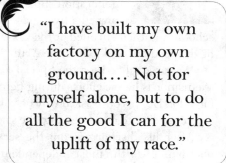

"I have built my own factory on my own ground.... Not for myself alone, but to do all the good I can for the uplift of my race."

Walker was devoted to improving the lives of African Americans. She was a major funder of anti-lynching programs run by the NAACP and the National Association of Colored Women. She led the effort to preserve the home of Frederick Douglass in the Anacostia neighborhood of Washington, D. C. When she passed away in 1919, Walker left the bulk of her estate to charity.

"I am a woman who came from the cotton fields of the South," summarized Walker in a speech to the National Negro Business League Convention a few years before her death. "From there I was promoted to the washtub. From there I was promoted to the cook kitchen. And from there I promoted myself into the business of manufacturing.... I have built my own factory on my own ground."

"I am in the business world, not for myself alone," she told Booker T. Washington in 1912, "but to do all the good I can for the uplift of my race." She worked toward that goal not only through her philanthropic activity, but by giving thousands of African-American women well-paying and dignified jobs as commissioned sales agents. As the *New York Post* acknowledged following her death, Walker's rags-to-riches life demonstrated that the American dream of personal success—and then sharing that success with one's fellows—applied

to blacks as well as whites, and that talented and generous citizens of any color "may rise to the most distinctive heights of American achievement."

↣ *Monica Klem*

Further information

○ Beverly Lowry, *Her Dream of Dreams: The Rise and Triumph of Madam C. J. Walker* (Vintage Books, 2003)

○ A'Lelia Bundles, *On Her Own Ground: The Life and Times of Madam C. J. Walker* (Washington Square Press, 2001)

JOHN WALTON

John Walton was a son of Walmart founder Sam Walton who used his multibillion-dollar inheritance to champion some of the most effective educational reforms of the last generation. Born and raised in Arkansas where his father owned a five-and-dime store, John attended the local public schools and then enrolled at the College of Wooster in Ohio. After two years he dropped out and joined the Army in 1966.

Walton qualified for the Special Forces, and served as a combat medic in Vietnam. His heroic efforts during fierce fighting in Laos won him a Silver Star for valor. He was once asked why he volunteered for the Green Berets. "I figured if you're going to do something," he said, "you should do it the best you can."

After his discharge from the service, Walton decided to strike out on his own. "He's the most independent of the bunch," his father later wrote. John tried his hand at crop dusting in Texas and Arizona. He launched a boat-building business in California. He joined the board of Walmart in 1992. Seven years later he founded True North Partners, a venture-capital fund that invested in high-technology companies.

Walton's philanthropy was principally focused on improving K-12 education in the United States. In 1983, he read *A Nation at Risk*, with its ominous warnings about the failings of public education. He circulated it among family members, prompting a number of discussions about ways to improve education. Sam Walton announced, "I'd like to see an all-out revolution in education."

In many ways, John Walton spent his life trying to bring that "all-out revolution" to schoolhouses. It was a more daunting task than he originally anticipated. "Our family followed the usual course of education giving," he explained in 2002. "You begin to support programs you hope will address the problems, and you see some improvement. But the improvements are

transitory, lasting only as long as the heroes making them work are on the job. When the heroes go away, the programs become ineffective."

To create lasting change, Walton came to realize, the structure of the nation's public education would have to change. "If you look at it in terms of power," he explained, "you will 'follow the money.' The money in education comes from the top, filters its way down, and various interest groups and factions pull off their share into what they think is important. The customers at the bottom just take what they're given." Public schools would only improve, he believed, if "customers"—parents—had the power to leave ineffective schools and take the money with them.

In 1998, Walton and financier Ted Forstmann created the Children's Scholarship Fund. Each of the two donors pledged $50 million to underwrite scholarships that would enable low-income students to attend private schools. Their $100 million was able to fund 40,000 scholarships. In CSF's first season, an astonishing 1.2 million applications came in. Walton and Forstmann were right in guessing that low-income parents all over the country were eager to have better alternatives for their children's education, and would act if given any opening.

> John Walton believed public schools would only improve if "customers"—parents— had the power to leave ineffective schools and take the money with them.

The initial donation was an experiment, and nothing was promised beyond a four-year period of support. But CSF's early results were so impressive—and the demand for its scholarships so intense—that the board and founders not only continued but greatly extended the program, which continues to flourish today. Through 2015, CSF has provided $645 million in scholarships to 152,000 low-income children. The great majority of CSF families are African-American, Latino, or recent immigrants. CSF serves a large number of single mothers, and grandparents who are raising their grandchildren.

Walton believed it was important to offer immediate help to children and parents who are struggling with failing public schools today. That was stage one. He also understood that it was necessary to change public education itself, to reduce the future ranks of ill-served kids.

Walton was an early backer of charter schools as an essential response to the long-term problem. As public schools that operate independent

of district bureaucracies, charter schools enjoy a degree of autonomy in exchange for a measure of accountability. Recognizing the potential of charter-school successes to refute the defeatist notion that poverty and other factors make inner-city children unteachable, Walton drove his family's effort to seed effective charter schools across the country. Under his leadership, the Walton Family Foundation provided startup grants of $250,000 to hundreds of charter schools. Other support was offered to groups that organize and encourage charter-school growth, and cultivate and train administrators, principals, and teachers.

The Walton Family Foundation has watered those initial seeds by supporting venture-philanthropy groups like the NewSchools Venture Fund. Founded in 1998, NewSchools raises capital from a variety of donors and then invests it in promising charter-school networks so they can replicate their successful educational formulas in additional schools and fresh cities. This early funding for educational entrepreneurs has proven crucial in the expansion of impressive charter-school networks like KIPP, Uncommon Schools, Aspire Public Schools, Achievement First, and others, which collectively now operate hundreds of exemplary schools in scores of American cities.

John Walton further realized that large-scale school reform could not be accomplished without changing public policy. He founded the American Education Reform Foundation in 1991, which ultimately merged into today's American Federation for Children, which advocates for mechanisms that allow parents and children to choose schools matching their needs. As part of this public-policy work, Walton helped fund the legal defense of Cleveland's school voucher program, which in 2002 was constitutionally validated by the U.S. Supreme Court.

John Walton died in a plane crash in 2005, when he was 58 years old. The year before, *Forbes* estimated his fortune at $18 billion. But such great wealth never seemed to affect him. Not long after a new charter school opened in San Diego, Walton made an unannounced visit, asking how he could be of service. The school's founder didn't recognize him, and told Walton that the bathrooms needed cleaning. Walton simply asked, "Where's the mop?" The fourth-wealthiest person in America then spent 25 minutes swabbing the floors, happy to help.

↳ *Naomi Schaefer Riley*

Further information

- *Philanthropy* magazine article, philanthropyroundtable.org/topic/excellence_in_ philanthropy/the_carnegie_of_school_choice
- Sam Walton and John Huey, *Made in America: Sam Walton* (Doubleday, 1992)
- "A Tribute to John Walton" (*Education Next*, Fall 2005)

GEORGE WASHINGTON

George Washington was well described as "first in war, first in peace, first in the hearts of his countrymen." What is much less known is that Washington was also first among the philanthropists of his generation. Throughout his life he was generous toward the poor; as he approached death he was revealed as the era's greatest patron of higher education.

The achievements of George Washington are without parallel in American history. Without his leadership, it is unlikely the Continental Army would have survived eight years of brutal war. Without his endorsement, the Constitution would probably never have been ratified. Without his guidance at innumerable points, our great experiment in republican government might have faltered. He was, in the elegant summation of one of his most perceptive biographers, the "indispensable man."

The brilliance of his public service sometimes blinds us to Washington's considerable achievements in private life. He was a self-made man who rose from relatively humble origins to acquire one of the largest fortunes in American history. Washington refused a salary even for his years as commander of the Continental Army. His wealth was all acquired in the private sector.

The basis of Washington's fortune was land. A surveyor in his youth, he had an eye for promising acreage, and owned property throughout Virginia, Maryland, Pennsylvania, Ohio, and Kentucky. This he collected by inheritance, purchase, and marriage—the widowed Martha Custis was the wealthiest woman in Virginia, and her marriage to Washington added some 17,000 acres to his holdings. Liquidity, however, was often a problem. Like many of his fellow planters, Washington was often poor-in-cash relative to his wealth of land.

Washington's early charitable giving reflected his upbringing in colonial Virginia. Life in the Northern Neck was built on reputation and hierarchy, British North America's closest approximation to the mores of the English country. Charitable giving was rarely institutional, but rather centered on a personal relationship between patrons and beneficiaries.

In 1769, for example, Washington offered his friend William Ramsay a sum of £25 annually so Ramsay's son could attend college at Princeton. "No other return is expected or wished for this offer than that you will accept it with the same freedom and good will with which it is made," he wrote, "and that you may not even consider it in the light of an obligation, or mention it as such; for be assured from me that it will never be known."

When Washington left Mount Vernon to assume command of the Continental Army, he left instructions to the groundskeeper that reflected a

Virginian's sense of liberality. "Let the Hospitality of the House, with respect to the poor, be kept up," he wrote. "Let no one go hungry away. If any of these kind of People should be in want of Corn, supply their necessities, provided it does not encourage them in idleness; and I have no objection to your giving my Money in Charity, to the Amount of forty or fifty Pounds a Year, when you think it well bestowed. What I mean, by having no objection, is, that it is my desire that it should be done."

Many biographers have observed that the Revolutionary War changed Washington's perspective. After eight years campaigning in the states of the mid-Atlantic and New England, his outlook became much more nationalistic. His politics and mores became closer to those of a Philadelphian than a Virginian.

This transition of his Revolutionary years was reflected, to some extent, in Washington's charitable giving. He grew more inclined to give as a donor than as a patron, to provide money for a cause rather than a cousin. While in New York and Philadelphia, President Washington made hundreds of gifts to churches and charities, many of which were offered under condition of anonymity and were only discovered after the publication of his papers.

> "No other return is expected or wished for this offer than that you will accept it with the same freedom and good will with which it is made."

"Washington," writes biographer Ron Chernow, "had particular sympathy for those imprisoned for debt, and gave generously to an organization—later called the Humane Society of the City of New York—that was formed to assist them." He often sent surplus food from the Presidential mansion to a nearby prison; when he made his Thanksgiving Day proclamation, Washington made a personal donation of beer and hot meals to persons imprisoned for debt. It was a rare instance in which he allowed his contribution to be made public, presumably because he thought it appropriate to set an example for the rest of the country.

Another favored cause for the childless Washington was the care and education of orphans. He contributed to orphanages in several states, but reserved his largest donations for the Alexandria Academy, established only a few miles from Mount Vernon.

In 1796, three years before he died, Washington offered a gift to Liberty Hall Academy of Lexington, Virginia: 100 shares of the James River and

Kanawha Canal Company, worth at the time approximately $20,000. It was then the largest contribution to higher education in American history. Grateful for the gift, the school's trustees immediately renamed the college Washington Academy; today it is known as Washington and Lee University. By one estimate, roughly $12 of every current student's tuition is underwritten by the generosity of George Washington.

Generosity was an obligation to Washington. It was a virtue to be practiced constantly and liberally. "One thing more and I will close this letter," Washington once advised his step-grandson, George Washington Parke Custis, who was then attending college at Princeton. "Never let an indigent person ask, without receiving something, if you have the means; always recollecting in what light the widow's mite was viewed."

— Christopher Levenick

Further information

○ James Flexner, *Washington: The Indispensable Man* (Little, Brown, 1974)

○ Leonard Helderman, *George Washington: Patron of Learning* (Century, 1932)

○ Writings of George Washington, etext.virginia.edu/washington/fitzpatrick

ISAIAH WILLIAMSON

Isaiah Williamson was the son of devout Pennsylvania Quakers, one of eight children, a farm boy who learned early on the value of industry, frugality, and honesty. At the age of 15, he apprenticed himself at a nearby country store. Within seven years, Williamson had saved $2,000—enough money to move to Philadelphia and open his own dry-goods business. By 1838, with assets worth about $2 million today, he retired, spending the next few years touring Europe.

But Williamson was unsuited for the life of a dilettante. He returned to Philadelphia, where he began investing his money in real estate and promising enterprises. By the 1880s he was known to be one of the wealthiest men in the commonwealth, with an estimated fortune of $20 million (approximately $500 million today). He was equally famous for his thrift, and was known throughout the city for making a meal of bread crusts, and keeping one suit for decades.

As he entered the last decades of his life, philanthropy engaged more and more of Williamson's attention. Determining the extent of his generosity is difficult, as virtually all of his donations were made in strict secrecy or under the pseudonym "Hez," but he is known to have

handed off millions of dollars. Throughout the Delaware River basin he supported scores of asylums and orphanages, hospitals and benevolent societies, libraries, seminaries, colleges, and universities. As his close friend John Wanamaker—himself a philanthropist and entrepreneur as founder of the Wanamaker department store—wrote in the only book-length biography of Williamson: "He was invariably strongly moved to help the man who was trying to help himself, however humble the effort. But for mere beggars, low or high, he had little sympathy."

As early as the 1850s, Williamson had begun thinking of a plan for a school that would bear his name. As he told Wanamaker, "It was seeing boys, ragged and barefooted, playing or lounging about the streets, growing up with no education, no trade, no idea of usefulness, that caused me to think of founding a school where every boy could be taught some trade free of expense." In 1888, he unveiled his plan. "He had to be wheeled from his carriage in a rolling chair," wrote Wanamaker, "but his spirit was alert and joyful."

> Williamson gave a huge gift for a school where poor boys would learn a trade, because "In this country, every able-bodied, healthy young man who has learned a good mechanical trade, and is truthful, honest, frugal, temperate, and industrious, is certain to succeed in life."

Williamson committed $2.1 million (roughly $50 million in present value) to the project for the purchase of a 211-acre site near Media, Pennsylvania, where the Williamson Free School of the Mechanical Trades would be opened in 1891.

In considering admission to the school, "preference shall always be given to the poor," Williamson stipulated. To this day, the school recruits young men from the region's toughest areas, working closely with ministers, guidance counselors, coaches, and other mentors to find promising young men who would benefit from learning a trade. The school still provides a full scholarship for all of its students, not one penny of which comes from public sources. Programs are offered in carpentry, masonry, landscaping, machine tools, painting, and power-plant technology. All students are required to live on campus in supervised dormitories, attend a daily chapel service, and conform to the dress code.

"In this country," Williamson explained, "every able-bodied, healthy young man who has learned a good mechanical trade, and is truthful, honest,

frugal, temperate, and industrious, is certain to succeed in life, and to become a useful and respected member of society." Isaiah Williamson did his part in keeping that wholesome pattern alive.

ɞ Christopher Levenick

Further information

○ *Philanthropy* magazine article, philanthropyroundtable.org/topic/excellence_in_ philanthropy/a_useful_and_respected_member_of_society

○ John Wanamaker, *Life of Isaiah V. Williamson* (J. B. Lippincott, 1928)

MAJOR ACHIEVEMENTS
of
AMERICAN PHILANTHROPY
1636-2017

The full-length version of *The Almanac of American Philanthropy* contains a thousand thumbnail profiles on the major achievements of private giving in the U.S. These accomplishments begin in 1636 and extend right up to the present and are grouped into nine categories —listed on the tabs to the right.

To give you a flavor of these extremely rich and varied entries, we have included here a sample of just the most recent listings.

For the comprehensive collection of donor achievements over more than 380 years of our national existence, in categories stretching from health to hometown life, please consult the longer version of *The Almanac of American Philanthropy* in print or online at PhilanthropyRoundtable.org/Almanac

MEDICINE

EDUCATION

ARTS

NATURE

PROSPERITY

RELIGION

POLICY

OVERSEAS

LOCAL

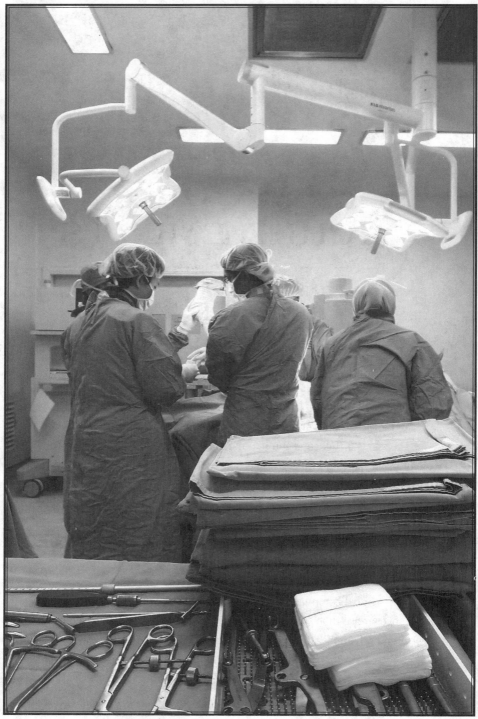

MAJOR ACHIEVEMENTS OF AMERICAN PHILANTHROPY

MEDICINE & HEALTH

Medical philanthropy has a long history in the United States—from the founding of our first charity hospital in 1735 (by a common businessman acting in a remote frontier town that had only been in existence for 18 years) to the development of therapies that have saved hundreds of millions of lives. Charitable giving has been crucial in catalyzing many of the most far-reaching advances in medicine, such as penicillin, insulin, hookworm control, the polio vaccine, kidney transplants and dialysis, and much of today's success against cancer. Philanthropists established most of America's best medical schools and research institutes. They have endowed professorships, created labs, and built clinics. Philanthropy has been vital in carrying improved health measures out into communities—from the Rockefeller Foundation's heroic campaign against yellow fever right up to today's Gates Foundation battles against malaria, leprosy, polio, and other neglected diseases. With the last generation's explosion of private-industry research and government spending on health care, private philanthropy now comprises only a small portion of total funding for medical research and public health, yet because it tends to be flexible, risk-tolerant, fast-moving, and offered without the onerous red tape of government grants, philanthropic funding is especially prized by medical researchers, and continues to have a powerful impact on the field, as you will learn in the pages following.

   Section research provided by Karl Zinsmeister, Cindy Tan, and Thomas Meyer

2017

MAJOR BONUS FOR MICROBIOME

The Chicago-area Duchossois family had previously donated $37 million to the medical school of the University of Chicago. But in 2017 they made an especially interesting gift of $100 million, aimed not just at treating disease, but at understanding how the body fends off invaders and keeps itself well. Specifically, they funded work to deepen understanding of human "microbiomes"—the large collection of healthy bacteria and other microorganisms that exist inside all of our bodies, which we have recently learned are crucial to balancing our nutrition and body weight, immunizing us against environmental threats, and influencing how effectively we metabolize the drugs we take to cure problems.

Chicago sciences dean Conrad Gilliam called the Duchossois family's decision to focus on the microbiome "prescient." He noted it now "appears that the microbiome affects nearly every organ and possibly every disease. So…we liked the family's idea that rather than try to go after each disease, let's focus on how the microbiome can be manipulated to maintain a person's health."

Another innovative twist to the family's gift is that they have connected it to business spinoffs to make it self-sustaining. Their new program will link with the university's center for entrepreneurship to bring scientific discoveries to the health-care market in partnership with businesses. All money made in this way will be reinvested into the institute's work. The $100 million of philanthropy will last ten years, by which time revenue from the commercial spinoffs is intended to support future investigations.

Further information

○ *Chicago Tribune* reporting, chicagotribune.com/business/ct-duchossois-gift-university-chicago-0524-biz-20170523-story.html

2017

MARCUS INSTITUTE FOR
BRAIN HEALTH HEALS VETERANS

Training accidents, sports injuries, and battlefield blasts put military servicemembers at risk for concussions and brain injuries. Most of these heal with standard medical treatment and time, but some are persistent and disruptive. Getting treatment for these can be difficult and frustrating.

When Home Depot co-founder Bernie Marcus found that out, he went to work. He was on a 2007 visit to Shepherd Hospital, a top destination for neurological care, when he met a young brain-injured servicemember who had recently regained his ability to walk after military doctors wrote him off as paralyzed for life. In talking to the young man and then learning about the relatively high prevalence of concussions and brain injuries in the military today, he decided to launch a private clinic to provide attention to difficult cases. With his $2 million grant to Shepherd Hospital, the SHARE Program was born, offering specialized care that is time-consuming and expensive, but doesn't cost a dime for those injured in service.

After registering successes, Marcus offered to work closely and collaboratively with the Department of Veterans Affairs and Department of Defense, but was quickly frustrated by the bureaucracy and territorial posturing of the government agencies. So he pushed the SHARE program forward on its own, intensively treating around 40 patients per year. But Marcus knew the potential and the need were far greater.

In 2014, he hired a young Army officer to help him expand his philanthropy for veterans, and particularly to launch a wider effort in concussion treatment. They recruited a leading expert who had founded the Fisher-family-funded National Intrepid Center of Excellence and considered what private-sector care for brain-injured veterans might look like. They zeroed in on diagnosing underlying causes of different symptoms, recruiting doctors from a wide range of specialties, developing detailed treatment plans that involve family members, and ensuring that veterans transition home with ongoing care.

With this plan and a $38 million grant from Bernie Marcus, the University of Colorado Anschutz Medical Campus became the first site for the Marcus Institute for Brain Health. Marcus will next develop other sites around the country to build a network of care. By early 2017, he had already committed over $70 million to veterans' causes, making him one of the most generous donors to this population.

Further information

- *Denver Business Journal* reporting, bizjournals.com/denver/news/2017/05/12/cu-anschutz-medical-campus-gets-38m-gift-for-brain.html
- Thomas Meyer, *Uniform Champions* (The Philanthropy Roundtable, 2017)

2017

RE-ENGINEERING HEALTH CARE

When he was five years old and seriously ill, Robert Kern received charitable medical treatment at the Mayo Clinic—under a program for helping the children of religious workers like his father, a Baptist pastor. The child recovered, grew to be an engineer and inventor, and built his company making portable generators into a billion-dollar enterprise. Then he paid back the Mayo Clinic's kindness. More generally, he began to apply his engineering instincts to upgrade medical education and care.

Robert and Patricia Kern donated $20 million to Mayo in 2011 to establish the Center for the Science of Health Care Delivery. It uses scientific assessments to improve the effectiveness, safety, and value of patient treatments, and then shares proven models with other doctors and hospitals around the country. The Kerns followed up with an additional grant of $67 million in 2013. This brought their total giving to the Mayo Clinic to $100 million (they have also supported neuroscience there).

Then in 2017 the Kerns made their latest gift aimed at re-engineering medical care for improved outcomes. They donated $38 million to the Medical College of Wisconsin to establish an institute that will coordinate a group of top medical schools as they explore new approaches for improving doctor training. For instance, the Medical College of Wisconsin (to which the Kerns had previously given $10 million) recently established new satellite campuses to school physicians who want to practice in rural areas and smaller cities that currently lack doctors, or go into specialties like primary care and psychiatry where there are occupational shortages. These refinements will benefit lots of Americans—including needy five-year-olds.

Further information

○ *Milwaukee Journal-Sentinel* reporting on 2017 gift, jsonline.com/story/money/business/2017/06/08/largest-gift-medical-college-wisconsins-history/379860001/

○ Mayo Clinic news from 2013, newsnetwork.mayoclinic.org/discussion/kern-family-gives-100-million-to-mayo-clinic-signaling-confidence-in-mayo-to-transform-health-care/

2016

SHARPENING VISION AT THE CLEVELAND CLINIC

Thanks to donor support, the Cleveland Clinic's institute for eye and vision problems went from a hole in the ground to one of the top programs in the

country in only about 15 years. That kind of meteoric rise is unusual in the medical world. But success can also cause problems. Board member Jeffrey Cole (who ran one of the world's largest companies selling eyeglasses) discovered that the vision clinic had reached the capacity of its building, and thus could no longer accept more patients, or expand into additional areas of research. So he provided $31 million to fund a new building that will provide needed space. As planning for the building began in 2017, the eye institute had a staff of 100 physicians and researchers who carried out more than a quarter-million patient visits and 13,000 annual surgeries.

Further information

○ Cleveland Clinic announcement, newsroom.clevelandclinic.org/2016/11/29/jeffrey-
patricia-cole-donate-31-million-cleveland-clinic-cole-eye-institute/

2016

BIG MONEY, FRESH APPROACHES, BOLD METHODS

From his Facebook proceeds, Sean Parker donated $250 million in 2016 to found an unusual cancer institute. It will focus tightly on using the body's own immune system to fight tumors. Until very recently, notes Parker, immunology was "the red-headed stepchild of the oncology world. There was a dedicated band of scientists who were convinced that the immune system played an important role in cancer, but they were essentially refugees from the cancer establishment." Now they'll have a chance to pursue their theories.

Even more than the huge pile of money Parker put up, or the bleeding-edge science he is supporting, it is likely to be the business-like philanthropic method he applied that separates his efforts from others. Parker insisted that all scientists receiving his money must coordinate their work in order to avoid duplication, and speed practical progress from research lab to treatment clinics. Neither bureaucracy nor prima donna personalities will be allowed to encumber transfer of information among the 40 labs in six institutions (ranging from UCLA to Penn to the M. D. Anderson Cancer Center). The cooperative network Parker set up will propose research agendas, collect and share data on results, establish the necessary clinical trials, and handle all licensing of useful technologies and ideas so companies can bring them to market quickly. The network is also establishing direct partnerships with 30 companies....

☞ *To see the rest of this collection of Major Achievements in Medicine, with entries dating back to our national founding, please consult the full-length version of* The Almanac of American Philanthropy *(online or in print).*

MAJOR ACHIEVEMENTS OF AMERICAN PHILANTHROPY

EDUCATION

More philanthropic donations are channeled into education than to many other sector of American society except religion. That's been true since we were just a collection of settlements and not yet a nation. Our first college, donor-supported, was created in 1636—nearly as early as our first permanent towns. America's initial public schools for children, funded by private investors who wanted to make "New Amsterdam" attractive to additional residents, opened in the 1640s. American philanthropy created many of the greatest libraries in the world, beginning when we were a mere colony. From the seventeenth century right into the twenty-first, from preschool through independent research institutions, private giving has catalyzed many of our best educational innovations, deepened knowledge, and enhanced its sharing across our nation.

Section research provided by Karl Zinsmeister, Connor Ewing, Scott Walter, and Evan Sparks

2017

PUBLIC COLLEGES, PRIVATE GIFTS

Even state-operated colleges now depend on private gifts. Indeed, public institutions like the University of Virginia and University of California, Berkeley now receive more money in a given year from individual donors than they do from the states that run them. And 2017 saw the arrival of the largest private contribution ever made to public higher-ed in the state of California. Bill Frost, who earned a degree in biochemistry from Cal Polytechnic, San Luis Obispo then founded the company Chemlogics, offered $110 million to his alma mater to strengthen its hands-on teaching of math and science. Cal Poly is a 21,000-student campus known for its "learn by doing" instructional method.

Further information

○ *Los Angeles Times* reporting, latimes.com/local/lanow/la-me-cal-poly-slo-donation-20170502-story.html

2017

MEETING DEMAND FOR COMPUTER SCIENCE IN SEATTLE

At the University of Washington in Seattle (the city that is home to Microsoft, Amazon, and many other technology companies), computer science is the most sought-after major among the more than 30,000 undergraduates. In a country with a serious shortage of trained computer-science professionals, that's an encouraging trend. Problem is, U.W. has to turn away most of those potential majors for lack of facilities. Only about a third of the students who apply get into the computer department.

Microsoft co-founder and major philanthropist Paul Allen has been helping with that problem for many years. He gave the lead $14 million gift that created the main building where U.W.'s computer training has been based since 2003. Then in 2017 he donated $40 million (with Microsoft kicking in an additional $10 million in Allen's honor) to endow the department and turn it into a full-fledged school within the university. A major new building is under construction (mostly funded through philanthropy), and important enhancements of the student body and faculty are unfolding.

Allen is not a Washington graduate. Like many other technology titans he dropped out of (a different) college. He and Bill Gates did, however, get

hooked on computers by sneaking into the U.W. computer lab while they were high-school students. He has since paid for those seminal trespasses with more than $100 million of total gifts to the University of Washington.

Further information

○ University of Washington news release, washington.edu/news/2017/03/09/paul-g-allen-school-of-computer-science-and-engineering/

○ *Seattle Times* reporting, seattletimes.com/seattle-news/education/paul-allen-gives-40-million-to-uw-computer-science-regents-name-school-after-billionaire/

2017

CHAPMAN RISES IN SOUTHERN CALIFORNIA

Dale Fowler graduated from Chapman University, located in Orange County, in 1958 with a degree in economics, then became a successful real-estate developer in southern California. In 2017 he and his wife Sarah Ann pledged $45 million to establish a new engineering school at Chapman. Campus officials announced that they hoped to start granting advanced technical degrees in 2019 or 2020.

Back in 2013, the Fowlers had given $55 million to Chapman to bolster its law school. Philanthropy also brought another big expansion to campus in 2016, when a new 1,044-seat performance hall opened, funded entirely by private donations. Donors Paul and Marybelle Musco footed $39 million of the $82 million cost.

Further information

○ *Orange County Register* reporting on the Fowlers, ocregister.com/articles/university-744957-school-chapman.html

○ *Los Angeles Times* reporting on the Muscos, latimes.com/entertainment/arts/la-et-cm-musco-center-opening-20160316-story.html

2016

MUSIC FROM NOTRE DAME

Joseph O'Neill is a Notre Dame graduate who went on to serve his alma mater on many boards. His sister Helen and brother-in-law Charles Schwab honored that service in 2017 with a $25 million gift to the university that provided lead funding for the new six-story building housing Notre Dame's department of music. The new structure includes a recital hall, many soundproof practice rooms, a music library, and organs and other special

facilities to support Notre Dame's program in Sacred Music.

Further information

○ *Notre Dame News*, news.nd.edu/news/notre-dame-receives-25-million-gift-for-oneill-hall/

2016

SCHOOLED IN SCIENCE, OUTSIDE OF SCHOOL

"People often remember the first teacher to have a profound impact on their lives. For me, that teacher was the Boston Museum of Science," states philanthropist Michael Bloomberg. "I went every Saturday…. Those mornings were the highlight of my weeks. I learned to ask questions, to recognize just how much there is to learn about the world."

In his autobiography, Bloomberg describes taking a bus and train to attend classes and lectures at the museum, starting when he was ten and continuing through high school. "I sat spellbound as an instructor brought snakes, porcupines and owls for us to hold; demonstrated the basic laws of physics with hands-on experiments; and quizzed us on every museum exhibit." The museum "changed my life…in ways that traditional school didn't do," says Bloomberg—who went on to study engineering at Johns Hopkins University and then founded a company for computerizing financial data that eventually gave him a net worth in the neighborhood of $40 billion.

In 2016, Bloomberg made his fourth, and largest, gift to the museum that had been so important to his boyhood. He donated $50 million to increase the institution's endowment by nearly 40 percent. The earnings will be used specifically to support education programs, at which the museum excels. The Boston Museum of Science has hosted 11 million school children and 122,000 teachers in the last decade, and produces an engineering curriculum for elementary students that is one of the most used in the country.

Further information

○ *Boston Globe* reporting, bostonglobe.com/business/2016/10/17/museum-science-changed-michael-bloomberg-life-gives-back-with-million-gift/SFj5KnsTQfma3v0VWcLIqO/story.html

2016

SCALIA SCHOOL OF LAW

Two major donations—a $20 million anonymous gift, and a $10 million grant from the Charles Koch Foundation—raised ambitions at a Washington, D.C.-

area law school that has a tradition of cross-training lawyers in economic analysis, property rights, limited government, and individual liberty. At George Mason University in suburban Virginia, the gifts will establish new scholarships for students and new positions for legal faculty. And the law school will be named for recently deceased U.S. Supreme Court Justice Antonin Scalia, one of the most influential judicial minds of his generation.

Further information

○ Antonin Scalia Law School, law.gmu.edu/about/program_highlights

---

2016

EXPANDING THE BEST
CHARTER NETWORK IN NEW YORK

Success Academy Charter Schools were ten years old in 2016. And they celebrated the date with $10 million of donations from a variety of New York City philanthropists, plus a $25 million capstone gift from hedge-fund pioneer Julian Robertson. The $35 million total will be used to expand the school network from its current 34 campuses to a total of 100 over the next several years. And Robertson's gift in particular will be used to ramp up the Success Academy Education Institute, an online portal where the school shares its innovative curriculum and potent teacher-training methods with any other schools who want to make use of them. Robertson was one of the major backers who funded creation of the Institute some years ago, as a means of sharing the techniques of New York state's most successful schools.

Though it accepts almost entirely low-income and minority students by random public lottery, Success has outperformed schools in even New York's most affluent communities—ranking in the top 1 percent statewide in math, and the top 3 percent in reading. Despite Success's rapid growth, close to ten times as many children want to attend as can be enrolled through the annual lottery. In the latest year, a heartbreaking 17,000 families put themselves on a waiting list for open seats. Thus the importance of the major expansion funded by Robertson and other donors, including New York financier John Paulson, who offered $8.5 million back in 2015.

Further information

○ Success Academies, successacademies.org

↝ *To see the rest of this collection of Major Achievements in Education, with entries dating back to our national founding, please consult the full-length version of* The Almanac of American Philanthropy *(online or in print).*

MAJOR ACHIEVEMENTS OF AMERICAN PHILANTHROPY

ARTS & CULTURE

D espite its comparatively short history, the United States has become one of the most artistically and culturally rich societies in the world. It is largely private philanthropy that has done this. And unlike in some other nations, it continues to be philanthropy and audience support (rather than state funding) that creates and sustains most artistic activity today.

Consider symphony orchestras. Fully half of their income currently comes from donations (33 percent from annual gifts, 16 percent from revenue off of endowments given previously). Paid concert revenue comes to 42 percent of their total income. Only 6 percent of symphony funds come from local, state, or federal governments.

The story is about the same for other creative fields. Nonprofit arts institutions in the U.S. as a whole currently get 45 percent of their budgets from donors. Eliminate philanthropy and our lives immediately become duller, flatter, darker, more silent.

Arrayed by year below you will find examples of some of philanthropy's significant contributions to our national artistic life: musical performance and creation, museums, architecture, historical preservation, arts education, libraries and the book arts, living history, poetry, TV and film, dance and theater, and more.

Section research provided by Karl Zinsmeister and Brian Brown

2017

A PERFORMANCE SPACE IN A
NEW NYC NEIGHBORHOOD

Perhaps the largest private urban redevelopment in the U.S. is taking place today in New York City, where about 40 blocks of previously unavailable Manhattan real estate are being turned into homes, offices, retail, and entertainment facilities—by decking over and building on top of the Hudson Yards parking and maintenance area for rail cars. This new neighborhood will include an arts facility, known as The Shed, created via a $500 million fundraising campaign. The building has been designed to flexibly accommodate everything from theater plays for 500 people, to museum shows, to outdoor concerts with audiences in the tens of thousands. The largest gift, among the many donors, was $75 million from Michael Bloomberg.

Further information

○ *New York Times* reporting, nytimes.com/2017/05/24/arts/design/michael-bloomberg-gives-75-million-to-shed-arts-center.html?_r=0

2017

LUCAS CELEBRATES POPULAR STORYTELLING ART

George Lucas made billions of dollars exploring the public appetite for popular morality tales—stories of good and evil, youth versus age, the joy of friendship, the pleasures of ordinary life, and the power of religious faith. Lucas understood that good art doesn't have to hold itself apart from, and above, the everyday masses of people. In fact, some of the very greatest art is great precisely because it strikes universal chords via broadly accessible images and language.

So when he wasn't creating his own works like the Star Wars, Indiana Jones, and American Graffiti films, Lucas was collecting potent popular art such as the paintings and drawings of Norman Rockwell, N. C. Wyeth, Jessie Wilcox Smith, Maxfield Parrish, and Alberto Vargas. He also accumulated thousands of pieces of film memorabilia; posters; magazine illustrations; landmark animations, cartoons, and comics; and other artifacts of mass storytelling.

Lucas is unabashed in his defense of art that meets and speaks to the public. "You know, so many artists have a tendency to paint without emotion, without any connection to the audience," he once told CBS News. "Both Steve Spielberg and I are diehard emotionalists. We love to connect with the audience. Rockwell loved to connect with the audience."

To crystallize and share his attachment to storytelling artistry, Lucas and his wife Mellody Hobson announced a gift totaling more than a billion dollars to create a Museum of Narrative Art. The donation will include all costs of a spectacular 275,000-square-foot building (the latest plans look a bit like a hovering space vessel), a cash endowment of a least $400 million to operate the museum, and more than 10,000 pieces of art that Lucas has collected over decades, including his important Rockwell stash. After abortive wrangles with regulators in San Francisco and Chicago, it was decided that the museum will be built in Los Angeles, at a site near 100 public schools, the University of Southern California, the Coliseum, and three other major museums, to encourage public access. The founding president will be Don Bacigalupi, who helped Alice Walton launch her similarly ambitious (and similarly non-snobby) grand museum in Bentonville, Arkansas. (See 2011 Crystal Bridges entry in the full-length *Almanac*.)

Further information

○ L.A. siting announcement in *Los Angeles Times*, latimes.com/entertainment/arts/la-et-cm-la-wins-lucas-museum-20170110-htmlstory.html

○ Lucas Museum of Narrative Art, lucasmuseum.org

2016

A PEARL OF A MUSEUM GROWS BIGGER, QUICKLY

The Albright-Knox Museum in Buffalo, New York, is one of America's superb art museums, with a particular strength in 7,000 modern works. But it has been desperately short of space in which to exhibit its deep collection. Until a prominent bond trader solved that problem in very short order with an innovative matching-grant donation. Jeffrey Gundlach used a $43 million donation to inspire $41 million of other private gifts. And he made this happen at breakneck speed.

The museum announced in June that it had selected the architect for a major building expansion, and intended in September to gradually roll out a multi-year capital campaign to raise the necessary money. Instead, Gundlach made his $43 million offer right away and pushed the institution to wrap up the fundraising "by Labor Day, because these things lose momentum." He asked that museum leaders raise a match to his money, beginning with a blitz of the board members—who quickly kicked in $21 million. Within an astonishing 12 weeks of starting from nothing, Albright-Knox had raised $103 million—"probably the fastest capital campaign in U.S. history," in the words of gallery director Janne

Sirén. (At that point the museum expanded its fundraising goal from the original $80 to $125 million, which will allow its endowment to be doubled at the same time the new campus is created.)

"When I was young, I was dragged there," explained Gundlach, who grew up in Buffalo and now lives in Los Angeles, so "I've always had a belief in and fondness for the Albright-Knox." In addition to loyalty, his decision to give to his hometown was based on a desire for effect. "I tend to do things not with teaspoons, but to try to make a difference." If he had donated $43 million to New York City's Metropolitan Museum of Art, Gundlach suggested, "you wouldn't be able to find it with a microscope." Instead, this donor allowed a grand expansion of a great museum to be fully funded before its managers even expected to start their fundraising.

Further information

○ Albright-Knox expansion history, albrightknox.org/campus-expansion/about-ak360

2016

PRIVATE FUNDING AT A SMITHSONIAN

The latest in the ever-expanding empire of federal museums on the Washington, D.C., mall—the National Museum of African American History and Culture—opened in 2016. And the majority of the funds that went into creating this latest Smithsonian branch came from private donors. Of the $500 million building cost, $265 million came from charitable contributors. Large givers included the Lilly Endowment, Oprah Winfrey, investor Robert F. Smith, Chuck Feeney's Atlantic Philanthropies, Carlyle co-founder David Rubenstein, Colin Powell, the Rhimes family, and the Gates, Ford, Rockefeller, and Mellon foundations. Among the individuals who gave $1 million or more, three quarters were African Americans.

Museum director Lonnie Bunch believed "it was important to show average people owned this project," so to complement these large gifts the museum carried out a broad grassroots fundraising campaign. Months before the museum even opened, more than 100,000 people had already pledged $25 a year to become members. This is the largest member base of the Smithsonian museums.

Individuals also donated many of the artifacts that are featured in the collection. Shirley Burke offered her enslaved great-grandfather's violin. T. B. Boyd gave the printing press his grandfather used to support himself after slavery. Robert Hicks provided a white shirt he wore when he became the first black supervisor at a factory in his town. David Rubenstein loaned

two documents signed by Abraham Lincoln: a copy of the Emancipation Proclamation, and a copy of the 13th Amendment ending slavery.

Further information

○ *Philanthropy* magazine, philanthropyroundtable.org/topic/excellence_in_philanthropy/
briefly_noted83

LIVE PERFORMANCE IN A ONCE-DEAD PLACE

A decade and a half after the terrorist destruction of the World Trade Center, the site had rebounded remarkably. Dramatic new office towers had occupants, a much-improved transportation hub was operating, an affecting museum was in place, and the streetscape of the neighborhood was more efficient and attractive than ever before. Only one piece was still missing: a proposed performing-arts center. A major theater had been included in the 2003 master plan for bringing the dead neighborhood back to life, but that got delayed amidst the many other demands of the massive project.

Then in 2016, businessman Ronald Perelman ponied up $75 million to jumpstart the project. Soon plans were in place for a technologically advanced structure that could seat an audience of 1,200—or be easily subdivided into three smaller theaters. Music, dance, drama, and an annual film festival will animate the space throughout the year. Perelman, who is known as a hands-on, high-energy donor, was reported at the time of his donation to be taking a particular interest in making sure the theater has advanced media capabilities so its performances can be shared around the world via Internet streaming.

Further information

○ Perelman Center, theperelman.org/artistic-vision

ARTS

☞ *To see the rest of this collection of Major Achievements in Arts, with entries dating back to our national founding, please consult the full-length version of* The Almanac of American Philanthropy *(online or in print).*

NATURE, ANIMALS, AND PARKS

Many of America's most iconic natural attractions are the products of philanthropy. Hundreds of national parks, urban green spaces, zoos and aquariums, wildlife protections, gardens, and arboretums have been created or bolstered by private givers. The Rockefeller family alone established or enlarged parks like Grand Teton, Great Smoky Mountains, Virgin Islands, Yosemite, Big Bend, Rocky Mountain, Acadia, Olympic, Grand Canyon, Glacier, Haleakala, Redwood, Lassen Volcanic, Mesa Verde, Shenandoah, Antietam, Big Hole, Fort Donelson, various state parks, the Marsh-Billings farm, the Blue Ridge Parkway, numerous historic sites and monuments, and local parks. Small donors and grassroots philanthropic efforts have been even more important, helping save creatures like the peregrine falcon, swift fox, wild turkey, wolf, snowy egret, bluebird, whooping crane, and numerous fish, creating outdoor oases for everyday citizens to enjoy, conserving rare trees and plants, uncovering fresh solutions to ecological dilemmas, and pushing the boundaries of natural science through privately supported research.

> ☛ *Section research provided by Karl Zinsmeister,*
> *Brian Brown, Evan Sparks, and Justin Torres*

2017

TAKING FOUNTAINS TO NEW HEIGHTS

Longwood Gardens was the prize creation of donor Pierre du Pont. It offers visitors 1,000 acres of formal landscaping, forest, and greenhouses. But its centerpiece is a grand fountain garden that du Pont created after studying classic European examples for years.

Opened in 1931, Longwood's liquid displays, stonework, and integrated plantings were in serious need of repair when the institution's directors decided that the right way to honor du Pont's love of water parks would be to upgrade theirs to today's state of the art. So rather than simply redoing the 85-year-old existing layout they launched a $90 million renovation that increased the number of fountain jets from 380 to 1,719 (with some reaching a height of 175 feet), added propane flames to certain water columns, and choreographed the displays, via computer, to pieces of music—so that every show varies according to what is being heard.

Grand fountains have been a centerpiece of landscape design for centuries, but perhaps nowhere else in the world have they taken as spectacular a form as at this well-endowed park outside Philadelphia.

Further information

○ Longwood Gardens, longwoodgardens.org

2016

SEPARATING BIKERS AND PEDESTRIANS IN CHICAGO

Chicago's Lakefront Trail is the busiest in the country, with more than 100,000 locals walking or rolling down the 18-mile path on peak days. The fact that bikers and pedestrians have to share the existing trail is a serious problem at present, with frequent near-misses and collisions. At the end of 2016, Chicago financier Ken Griffin solved that difficulty with a $12 million pledge that will allow creation of separate trails for those on foot and those who are riding. "Our lakefront is unparalleled," said Griffin in announcing the donation. "On a beautiful day, the Lakefront Trail should be a place where cyclists, runners, and walkers can enjoy their activities without having to navigate around one another."

Further information

○ Report on plan for split trails, dnainfo.com/chicago/20161221/downtown/lakefront-trail-path-separate-bicycles-runners

2015

A GOLDEN AGE FOR PARKS

"Throughout much of the country, this is a golden age for signature urban parks. From Boston to Houston, New York to San Francisco, Atlanta to Pittsburgh, St. Louis to Detroit, beautiful old destination parks are being renewed and some great new ones are being created." That's the conclusion of a 2015 report from the Trust for Public Land, which looks closely at the use of private, donor-powered conservancies to manage public parks. The report finds that since the first experiment in 1980—the Central Park Conservancy which has since raised more than $700 million to burnish that New York City treasure—roughly half of all major cities now rely on at least one nonprofit to manage and fund crucial parks. A majority of these have been created just since 2000.

Further information

○ Trust for Public Land Study, tpl.org/sites/default/files/files_upload/ccpe-Parks-Conservancy-Report.pdf

2014

HEALING HORNED OWLS AND BREEDING BUGS

Oracle software chief Larry Ellison has long shown philanthropic interest in wildlife. Now he is taking an active role in sustaining threatened animals. He is making a major donation, estimated in the range of $55 million, to create a center near San Jose, California, that will rehabilitate about 8,500 injured creatures annually, and also operate an advanced breeding and rehabilitation facility focused on local species—particularly on unflashy reptiles, amphibians, and insects. It is hoped, for instance, that Ellison's breeding program can have a role in rebuilding the population of Lange's metalmark butterfly, down to an estimated 45 individuals at last count. U.S. Fish and Wildlife officials say they would welcome the help of a donor-organized effort that might someday allow the creature to be removed from the endangered species list.

Further information

○ *San Jose Mercury News* report, mercurynews.com/saratoga/ci_27336567/saratoga-cutting-edge-wildlife-facility-works-courtesy-oracles

NATURE

2014

NATURAL-HISTORY EDUCATION

Over a 20-year period, investor Richard Gilder donated more than $125 million to the American Museum of Natural History in New York City. He also devoted much time and brainpower—for instance in spearheading the museum's expansion of its Hayden Planetarium into the more ambitious Rose Center for Earth and Space (described in a 1999 entry in the full-length *Almanac*). His most interesting gift, however, may have been the one that established the Richard Gilder Graduate School right within the museum—where scientists can now earn Ph.D.s in biology, and teachers can complete master's degrees in science instruction. Building on this unusual pedagogical capacity within the museum, Gilder announced his latest and largest gift in 2014: $50 million to kick off a six-story addition that will particularly provide space for the museum's growing education programs. The new wing will also accommodate additional research by staff, and help the museum cope with its jump in visitors—from 3 million annually during the 1990s to 5 million per year in 2015.

Further information

∘ *New York Times* report, nytimes.com/2014/12/11/arts/design/american-museum-of-natural-history-plans-an-addition.html

2014

A PARK ON THE WATER

The Hudson River Park Trust is a nonprofit charged with converting four miles of abandoned piers and industrial lots strung along the lower west side of Manhattan into nature spaces and entertainment venues. In 2014, the trust proposed one dramatically different park that had emerged from its discussions with philanthropists Barry Diller and Diane von Furstenberg. Asked to contribute funds for a simple pier rebuilding along the decayed Hudson waterfront around 13th Street, Diller urged something more ambitious. He hired a prominent architect to design an undulating wooded and grassy area that hovers above the river on 300 mushroom-shaped concrete columns. The suspended island would be reached by two gangways, and would feature open amphitheaters where a range of ambitious live performances would be scheduled.

In addition to offering these ideas and promising a $113 million donation to build the park, Diller recruited top theater and entertainment impresarios to

advise on the cultural programming, and created an independent foundation to take responsibility for carrying it out. The proposal enjoyed wide endorsement from New York leaders. But this being New York City, some activists were politically and environmentally annoyed by the notion of a privately funded park, requiring piers driven into a river. Lawsuits were launched in 2015 to try to stop the project, and had managed to halt all work on the endeavor by mid-2017.

Further information

○ Project design, pier55.com

○ News archive at Curbed, ny.curbed.com/pier-55

2014

$350 MILLION FOR A CITY PARK IN TULSA

Tulsa, Oklahoma, offers a good example of how local philanthropy enriches American lives. This small city has generous individual donors and independent foundations along with a community foundation endowed with $3.8 billion in assets. Now a new donor-funded park is taking shape along the Arkansas River that runs through town, placing a fresh green crown on Tulsa's head. In the summer of 2014 local oilman and banker George Kaiser made a $350 million gift—the largest for a public park in U.S. history—to create what will be known as "A Gathering Place." The park will wind through the heart of the city and total nearly 100 acres when complete.

Drawing on suggestions collected in public meetings, it will connect four riverside sites into a cohesive recreation area with amenities like bike trails, boating, tennis courts, open lawns and gardens, playgrounds, a skate park, water features, and public meeting spaces. The Kaiser Foundation donated most of the land, as well as design, engineering, and construction plans, plus $50 million to operate and maintain the park once it is open. Supplementing Kaiser's $200 million were funds from other private donors, companies, and foundations like those created by the Chapman, Schusterman, Murphy, and Helmerich families. The local government will own the property, but a private conservancy established by the Kaiser Foundation will manage and program it, following the philanthropic model which has been so successful in other parts of the country....

To see the rest of this collection of Major Achievements in Nature, with entries dating back to our national founding, please consult the full-length version of The Almanac of American Philanthropy *(online or in print).*

PROSPERITY

Fighting poverty is one of the oldest charitable imperatives. This in turn often requires battling syndromes that lead to poverty—like family breakdown, alcohol and drug abuse, or economic obstructions. Philanthropists often act to make their fellow citizens more prosperous, and to spread economic flourishing broadly among all Americans. Private donors were helping Indians, African Americans, ethnic minorities, refugees, and women become educated and productive many decades before government agencies got in the act.

Donors have often been motivated in this work by religious impulses. Many entries on the list that follows could just as easily have been filed on our roster of Major Achievements in Religious Philanthropy. Likewise, many charities that might have been included here because of their success in spreading prosperity among Americans—like the Salvation Army, Habitat for Humanity, Goodwill Industries, etc.—are featured instead on our Religious Philanthropy list.

On top of efforts to extend economic success to widening circles of citizens, interventions that encourage economic flourishing generally have been almost as popular among philanthropists. Many donors believe that expanding our economic pie over the long run is the very best way to ensure that everyone eventually earns a generous slice. Gifts to economic research and the hard sciences, for example, are usually made in this hope of increasing general prosperity. Nearly a third of the funds available for science research at America's top 50 universities currently come from private donations. Top lab directors like Eric Lander and Leroy Hood have energetically explained how important philanthropy is as a form of risk capital that lets scientists explore unconventional, unusually hard, or very early-stage problems. Many technical breakthroughs that later bear economic fruit in abundance are powered by donations. Even defense-related innovations like artificial intelligence, rocketry, code-breaking, and radar that we think of as classic government responsibilities have been initiated by philanthropy.

Section research provided by Karl Zinsmeister,
Scott Walter, Jo Kwong, and Thomas Meyer

2017

BATTLING BAD SCIENCE

By 2017, the Laura and John Arnold Foundation had already donated more than $80 million to fix a problem the rest of the world was just becoming aware of: a large fraction of all scientific research today is badly flawed, impossible to reproduce, and inaccurate. When it comes to improving the quality of science, says science watchdog John Ioannidis, "the Arnold Foundation has been the Medici."

One beneficiary has been the Reproducibility Project, launched by a University of Virginia professor to test how many of the studies published in top psychology journals could be repeated with the same experimental result by other scientists. Only about four out of ten, it turned out. With Arnold funding, this has led to new efforts to improve the quality and integrity of research by helping, and pressing, scientists to post their raw data for public study and otherwise be more open about their procedures and assumptions.

Similar critiques and reform projects supported by the foundation helped expose the arbitrary and incomplete nature of many of today's scientific pronouncements on nutrition, and flaws in much of the research that produces pharmaceutical drugs. This single-handed work by the Arnolds helped convince a majority of scientists themselves that current research is plagued with biases and "reproducibility" flaws. A 2016 investigation by the journal *Nature* found that more than 70 percent of researchers have tried and failed to reproduce another scientist's experiments, and more than half have failed to reproduce their own experiments.

The Arnold Foundation has made long-term commitments to continue airing this problem, and funding potential solutions built on better and more open research methods, for decades to come.

Further information

○ Reporting in *Wired* magazine, wired.com/2017/01/john-arnold-waging-war-on-bad-science/

○ Survey of scientists by *Nature*, nature.com/polopoly_fs/1.19970!/menu/main/topColumns/topLeftColumn/pdf/533452a.pdf

2017

EMBRACING DATA SCIENCE

The new field of "data science" trains people in how to sift, clean, organize, and make practical use of the huge new mounds of information now being produced by computer networks. It involves not just analysis but also new techniques like machine learning and advanced visualization that help find the patterns in giant data dumps, and then turn them into understandings that can drive actions that will be useful to society. For instance: a data scientist might analyze the millions of requests for rides made by Uber users to discover the most efficient places to stage drivers, or build future roads, or establish mass-transit pickups, or site new residences. An epidemiologist might use data science to find commonalities in patients experiencing a rare disease. The economic value of new insights and discoveries made through data science can be very large.

Like many new intellectual fields, data science is just starting to develop consistent understandings and ways of working, and its practitioners are fitfully separating themselves from related areas of knowledge like statistics, information technology, mathematics, and graphic arts. University programs are doing most of this exploration at the frontiers of today's data explosion, and San Diego donor Taner Halicioglu is making the University of California, San Diego one of the leaders in this area.

A UCSD graduate himself, Halicioglu was the first full-time hire of Facebook when he joined the firm as a software engineer, and subsequently became wealthy as the firm mushroomed. After leaving Facebook and becoming a lecturer back at his alma mater, he made a $2 million gift to the UCSD computer department in 2015. Then in 2017 he announced a $75 million gift specifically focused on building up a data-science institute at the university that can become a leader in the field.

Further information

○ *San Diego Union Tribune* reporting on $75 million gift, sandiegouniontribune.com/news/
science/sd-me-ucsd-fundraising-20170320-story.html

2017

MAKING OFF-CAMPUS LEARNING UNIVERSAL
FOR STUDENTS

Recognizing that there is a "world beyond the academy" where college students can and should learn important lessons that might be hard to internalize on

PROSPERITY

campus, donor Andrew Davis gave $25 million to Colby College in Maine to create DavisConnects. The staff assigned to this new program will work with students starting in their first year to plan out a series of work experiences, internships, independent research, and travel abroad that can "complement their core academic program." In addition to providing the staff and campus building where this out-of-classroom learning can be mapped out, Davis's gift also provides all necessary funds for living stipends and travel costs so that students of modest incomes can partake of unpaid research or internships or study abroad just as higher-income students are able to.

Further information

○ Reporting in the *Kennebec Journal*, centralmaine.com/2017/04/19/colby-receives-25-million-from-davis-family-foundation-to-guarantee-every-student-an-experience-abroad/

2016

COLLABORATING FOR CHILD PROSPERITY

Led by the Edna McConnell Clark Foundation, about a half dozen living donors and another half dozen foundations have joined forces in a cooperative calling itself Blue Meridian Partners that will deliver major, long-term support to a limited number of proven charities serving children. The group intends to collectively donate at least a billion dollars over the next decade. With this large, reliable, long-term funding stream directed to organizations that have proven their ability to improve life courses, hundreds of thousands of youngsters may enjoy a better future.

As of 2017, eight supporters had pledged to spend at least $50 million each in this coordinated way: living donors Stanley Druckenmiller (who will chair the board), Steve Ballmer, Sergey Brin, Arthur Samberg, George Kaiser, and David Tepper, plus the Duke Endowment and Edna McConnell Clark Foundation. An interesting governance structure gives each of these "general partners" a vote on the dispersal of funds. The effort also has four "limited partners" who committed at least $10 million to the joint effort: the Hewlett, JPB, Packard, and Schusterman Family foundations. These contributors will not vote, but by riding on the effort's coattails will benefit from its research, grantee assistance, technical assessment, and other services.

As of 2017, six charities had been selected to receive the pooled funding. Each will receive both money and assistance with planning and management. This will allow them to dramatically expand their successful programs.

The Nurse-Family Partnership (which brings nurses into the homes of low-income mothers as they bear their first child, almost always out of

wedlock) will receive $33 million to expand its services, which have been demonstrated to improve both the development of children and the economic self-sufficiency of mothers.

The signature adoption-assistance program of the Dave Thomas Foundation, Wendy's Wonderful Kids, was promised $35 million over four years. That will fund the first phase of a 12-year plan to move many hard-to-place foster children (those with disabilities, siblings, advanced age, etc.) into families.

Youth Villages (which operates 11 group homes for teens and young adults with behavioral, emotional, and criminal problems) got a commitment from Blue Meridian Partners for $36 million over four years.

Year Up, an organization that shepherds poor youngsters into jobs and community colleges, will receive $40 million in expansion funding over four years. Two medical charities that will receive smaller grants complete the initial investments of the partnership.

Further information

○ Blue Meridian Partnership, emcf.org/our-strategies/blue-meridian-partners/penny_knight_will_giv.html

—————————— 2016 ——————————

PROSPERITY

UNEXPECTED SOCIAL-WORK RICHES

No donor had ever given a social-work school a gift as large as $60 million. The previous high was the $50 million that Constance and Martin Silver donated to New York University's social-work school back in 2007. But what made 2016's record-setting benefaction to the University of Southern California School of Social Work doubly surprising was that it came from someone who is a prominent social worker herself. "Wealthy social worker" is not a phrase that gets typed often in newsrooms. Yet in addition to her work within her main profession, Suzanne Dworak-Peck was able to accumulate a fortune through real-estate investments in southern California, and a consultancy that advised film and media producers on how to portray social problems in entertainment.

The USC social-work department to which she directed her gift is the largest such school in the world. It has an enrollment of 3,500 students, and produces one out of every 20 graduate-level social workers in the....

▷ To see the rest of this collection of Major Achievements in Prosperity, with entries dating back to our national founding, please consult the full-length version of The Almanac of American Philanthropy *(online or in print).*

RELIGION

America's major faiths put great emphasis on charitable giving. Christians are taught to look out for those with the least, to be good stewards, and to tithe (or donate ten percent of their income). Jews have the obligation of *tzedakah*, and Muslims the duty of *zakat*. In all cases the motivation is to improve the well-being of others, to share bounty with fellow creatures of God, to express devotion. Religious giving is a pillar of belief and conformity with divine intentions, and a means of expanding the community of faith and bringing enlightenment to new corners.

Religiously motivated generosity combines with American wealth and cultural norms to create potent charitable flows in the U.S., especially compared to other nations. In 2016 Americans donated $123 billion to religion-related causes. That was 32 percent of all charitable giving, and more than twice as big as the next favorite cause, education. The deep religious convictions of Americans are a leading reason that we give at a rate two to ten times higher than other developed nations.

In addition to supporting good works at home, there is a 200-year tradition of U.S. Christians sending donations overseas. This is actually an original aspect of the faith: Christian witness has always moved restlessly toward the weak and unwanted—from ancient Jerusalem to forsaken Greece, then Italy and north Africa during their pagan centuries, next to Dark Ages Europe, eventually over to frontier America, and now across the developing world.

Interest among U.S. Christians in carrying good works and the Gospel to people in poor lands has clearly risen in recent years. Today's developing world is thought to be where needs are most urgent, where people are most receptive, where opportunities for improving both external and internal life are most open. This migration of mission work is one reason the number of Christians in Latin America, Asia, and Africa is currently rising ten times faster than population growth. A milestone was passed within the last few years: the majority of the globe's Christians now live in the less-developed world. As said by one evangelical, poor countries "are where God is really working" right now.

God is also at work—in partnership with millions of faithful givers—in a great many communities across America, as documented below.

☛ *Section research provided by Karl Zinsmeister, Connor Ewing,*
Evan Sparks, and Liz Whyte

RELIGION

293

———— 2017 ————

MUSEUM OF THE BIBLE

In 2015, a $400 million construction project was launched by the Green family to create a highly visible, philanthropically created Museum of the Bible in Washington, D.C. Located three blocks from the National Mall and U.S. Capitol, the building will house the Green Collection of Biblical Artifacts (see 2011 entry), attractions like specialized films and a reconstruction of first-century Nazareth, a 500-seat performing-arts theater, and a large scholarly wing with a reference library, artifact research labs, and academic conference center. A flight simulator will allow guests to soar over Washington, then swoop down and read the Biblical inscriptions that adorn so many of its landmarks. Textured bronze panels at the street entrance, custom stained-glass work, and a 200-foot LED-panel ceiling will display artistic interpretations of Biblical themes.

"The Bible has had a huge impact on our world today—from culture and politics, to social and moral justice, to literature, art and music, and more," explains philanthropist Steve Green, chairman of the Museum of the Bible, and president of Hobby Lobby, which his family founded and owns privately. "Our family has a passion for the Bible and we are excited to be part of a museum dedicated to sharing its impact, history, and narrative with the world." The museum opened in 2017.

Further information

○ Steve Green interviewed in *Philanthropy*, philanthropyroundtable.org/topic/excellence_in_ philanthropy/interview_with_steve_green

○ *Architectural Record* on the museum design, archrecord.construction.com/ news/2015/02/150220-Hobby-Lobby-Owners-Break-Ground-on-Bible-Museum.asp?WT. mc_id=rss_archrecord

———— 2017 ————

MUSLIM DONORS, CATHOLIC UNIVERSITY

Rafat and Zoreen Ansari are not extraordinarily wealthy, but they are both physicians earning good salaries, and have lived modestly during full careers in a suburb of South Bend, Indiana. And they are grateful for the opportunities they have enjoyed in America after leaving Pakistan. "We came as immigrants, and this country has given us so much," said Mrs. Ansari.

After mulling ways they could share their good fortune in lasting ways, the Muslim donors announced they would give $15 million to the Catholic

university nearby, Notre Dame, to create an institute where the religious traditions of Christianity, Judaism, Islam, and other faiths can be studied, with an eye toward their interactions and their influence on behavior, changes in culture, and world events. Notre Dame president John Jenkins says the institute will focus on the human effects of the religions, rather than viewing them through a political or social lens.

Mr. Ansari told the *New York Times* that this money would have gone to their children, but after explaining they wanted to leave a positive legacy to their adopted nation and to all people, their daughters and son were supportive. "It's better to do something good with this. It's better to give it," said daughter Sarah Ansari.

Further information

○ Reporting in the *South Bend Tribune*, southbendtribune.com/news/education/granger-couple-gives-million-to-notre-dame-for-religion-studies/article_13d7f52c-0b2c-11e7-8c55-07cf19209b67.html

---

2016

RECORD GIFT FOR JEWISH EDUCATION

Hillel is a charity that provides services and instruction in Judaism to college students. With chapters on 550 campuses in the U.S. and Canada, and 56 more abroad, it is the largest such group in existence. As such, it is the largest employer of rabbis, faith instructors, and other religious professionals, many of whom go on to lead synagogues and other Jewish charities after their work at Hillel.

In 2016, Hillel received its largest gift ever: $38 million from Home Depot co-founder Bernie Marcus and his wife Billi. The grant launched a new effort to find, train, and retain excellent leaders for the group's outreach to students. This followed on another large donation, of $16 million, made the year previous by the Jim Joseph Foundation, also aimed at deepening and expanding the group's religious education for young Jews.

Further information

○ Hillel International, hillel.org

2016

EXPLORING RELIGION AND ART THROUGH JOURNALISM

Fieldstead and Company, the philanthropy operated by Howard and Roberta Ahmanson, has a special interest in the intersection between religion and

RELIGION

art, and often funds exhibitions, creation, research, and journalism on this topic. In 2016 the group made a two-year grant to the Religion Newswriters Foundation to encourage in-depth coverage of the ways that faith spurs artistic production. The money will fund new directories listing experts on religion and the arts, for free use by all journalists. And it will underwrite production of 30 news stories, with photo or video illustration, on "the ways art, both historic and contemporary, is inspired by sacred texts, the faith of artists, ritual practice, private devotion." These stories, on a topic described by the Religion Newswriters Foundation as "underreported in the mainstream media," will be distributed nationally through the Religion News Service, which was founded in 1934 and is located at the University of Missouri's School of Journalism. This donation followed on two 2015 gifts to the journalism school at USC also aimed at improving religion reporting: a $1 million gift from the Lilly Endowment, and a smaller grant from the Henry Luce Foundation.

Further information

○ Religion Newswriters Foundation press release, rna.org/news/276486/RNF-receives-grant-to-explore-influence-of-religion-on-visual-arts.htm

2015

A RECORD FOR CATHOLIC-SCHOOL SCHOLARSHIPS

In September 2015, the Inner-city Scholarship Fund run by the Archdiocese of New York announced the largest-ever U.S. gift to Catholic schooling. Christine and Stephen Schwarzman gave a record $40 million to an endowment that will provide 2,900 New York City children per year with scholarships. The Schwarzmans started contributing money in 2001 to this cause. "We've met so many impressive young women and men who have benefited greatly from the values provided by a Catholic-school education," stated Christine, who also serves as a trustee of the Inner-city Scholarship Fund. The fund combines contributions from New York business leaders and church donors, and provided tuition assistance to nearly 7,000 Catholic-school students in 2015, prior to the Schwarzman gift. The church has pledged to match the Schwarzman gift, and to raise an additional $45 million from other donors to increase the fund's scholarship endowment by $125 million in total.

Further information

○ Andy Smarick and Kelly Robson, *Catholic School Renaissance: A Wise Giver's Guide to Strengthening a National Asset* (The Philanthropy Roundtable, 2015)

A FUND TO SEED NEW CATHOLIC SCHOOLS

B. J. Cassin has taken the venture-capital model that made him wealthy and applied it to his Catholic-schooling philanthropy. He was a key funder in building Chicago's acclaimed Cristo Rey Jesuit High School from a single site in 2000 to a network of 32 schools in 22 states today, with more on the way. These Catholic schools now serve 10,700 low-income students each year, with excellent educational results (90 percent of graduates go to college, compared to 61 percent of similar low-income students, and 86 percent of high-income students), affordable tuition, an acclaimed program for placing every student in a work-study job at one of 2,525 partner businesses, and a sustainable economic model.

Now Cassin is seeking to amplify this success. He is part of a group of Catholics seeking new models for financing religious schools, whose enrollments as a proportion of the entire U.S. student body have declined by a third over the past half century. He and two colleagues have launched a philanthropic venture called the Drexel Fund that will invest in carefully selected academies, education entrepreneurs, and school networks with the intention of "transforming" and expanding faith-based schooling. The fund will raise $85 million from a variety of wealthy individuals and use it as venture capital to create tens of thousands of new seats in excellent, sustainable schools—most of them Catholic, but also including other religious orientations and some secular private schools.

"There are a lot of interesting new models in faith-based and especially Catholic schools, but we don't have a platform to replicate the most successful ones," Cassin says. "That's where the idea of Drexel came from." It seeks to do for religious schools what the NewSchools Venture Fund and the Charter School Growth Fund have done for charters: provide capital to scale up successful existing institutions and start promising new networks. Cassin gave $1 million in seed money and recruited several other donors, allowing the effort to launch in six states where tax credits or vouchers also help parents afford religious and private schools—Arizona, Florida, Indiana, Louisiana, Ohio, and Wisconsin.

By 2024, Drexel's funders aim to create 125 new schools, grow six to eight school networks, and cultivate 40 new school entrepreneurs....

☛ *To see the rest of this collection of Major Achievements in Religion, with entries dating back to our national founding, please consult the full-length version of* The Almanac of American Philanthropy *(online or in print).*

RELIGION

PUBLIC-POLICY REFORM

Donating money to modify public thinking and government policy has now taken its place next to service-centered giving as a constructive branch of philanthropy. Many donors now view public-policy reform as a necessary adjunct to their efforts to improve lives directly. From school choice to creation of think tanks of all stripes, from tort reform to gay advocacy, donors have become involved in many efforts to shape opinion and law.

This is perhaps inevitable given the mushrooming presence of government in our lives. In 1930, just 12 percent of U.S. GDP was consumed by government; by 2012 that tripled to 36 percent. Unless and until that expansion of the state reverses, it is unrealistic to expect the philanthropic sector to stop trying to have a say in public policies.

Sometimes it is not enough to pay for a scholarship; one must change laws so that high-quality public schools exist for scholarship recipients to take advantage of. Sometimes it's not enough to build a house of worship; one must erect guardrails that protect the ability of citizens to practice their faith freely.

Because public-policy philanthropy has only become common recently, this list has more entries dating from the latest generation, compared to our other lists of U.S. philanthropic action. And since one man's good deed is another man's calamity when it comes to giving with political implications, we have included policy advocacy of all sorts on this list.

Not all public policies split neatly into "Left" or "Right" variants. But for those that do, the reality is that much more philanthropic money has been deployed leftward than rightward. Detailed quantification in the book *The New Leviathan* showed that 122 major foundations with total assets of $105 billion provided $8.8 billion of funding for liberal causes in 2010. That same year, 82 foundations with total assets of $10 billion provided $0.8 billion for conservative causes. In other words: there is eleven times as much foundation money going into public-policy philanthropy that aims left as aims right. (Individual donors are more evenly split, though still predominantly on the left.) The *Washington Post* once observed that the Ford Foundation alone has given more to liberal causes in one year than donor Richard Scaife (sometimes called the Daddy Warbucks of the Right) gave to conservative causes in 40 years.

Section research provided by Karl Zinsmeister and John Miller

POLICY

PROTECTING CHILDREN WHERE GOVERNMENT DIDN'T

The troubled city of Flint, Michigan, shifted in 2014 to a new public water source that ended up exposing between 6,000 and 12,000 children to unhealthy levels of lead. After this was discovered, dysfunctional governments proved unable to move quickly to protect the youngsters from harm. Ten charitable organizations rapidly stepped into this void—pledging a combined $125 million for water testing, health care, and various kinds of short- and medium-term relief for households.

"There are needs out there that just can't wait for the state to appropriate the money and wait for the bureaucratic channeling of funds," stated Eric Lupher of the Citizens Research Council of Michigan. "If you live in the city of Flint you don't want to wait for the money to show up. You want to take your kids to the doctor now."

The Charles Stewart Mott Foundation, which is based in Flint, provided $50 million to the recovery effort for immediate use in the first year. Other philanthropies among those pitching in included the FlintNOW, Kellogg, Kresge, and Skillman foundations.

Further information

○ *Detroit Free Press* reporting, freep.com/story/news/local/michigan/flint-water-crisis/2016/05/11/foundations-pledge-nearly-125m-to-flint-recovery/84180758/

2016

NONPROFIT NEWSPAPERS

The newspapers in Philadelphia, as in every city, have struggled mightily over the last decade to find a viable business formula in the era of Internet news. To save them from collapse, Philadelphian and prominent national philanthropist Gerry Lenfest some years ago purchased the *Philadelphia Inquirer* (America's third-oldest newspaper) and the *Philadelphia Daily News*, plus the companion website Philly.com.

In 2016, Lenfest donated all three properties, along with a $20 million endowment, to a nonprofit entity. The notion is that the publications will continue to operate as for-profit businesses, adapting as necessary to balance their bottom lines, but that there will be no pressure on them to make money, and special projects can be funded with earnings from the endowment. So

far, endowment grants have been applied to improving the use of technology by the papers. The one other major newspaper in the U.S. that operates as a for-profit under a nonprofit umbrella is the *Tampa Bay Times*, owned by the Poynter Institute.

In 2017, the nonprofit that owns the Philadelphia publications announced it had supplemented Lenfest's original $20 million endowment with an additional $27 million raised from other donors. Lenfest then announced that if $40 million more in gifts could be raised, he would match that amount. That would leave the nonprofit trust with an endowment exceeding $100 million.

Given that declining circulation knocked the value of the Philadelphia newspapers down from $515 million in 2006 to under $50 million in less than a decade, it's clear that even with these funds they'll have to make many adjustments to their operations. But the executive director of their nonprofit trust says the philanthropic support will subsidize "a test lab for local news innovation."

Further information

○ Lenfest Institute for Journalism, philafound.org/OurWork/
TheLenfestInstituteforJournalism.aspx

○ *Philanthropy* magazine special issue "Can Philanthropy Save Journalism?,"
philanthropyroundtable.org/magazine/spring_2014

— 2016 —

NEW TOOLS FOR FAMILY REVIVAL

Like other Americans, donors have worried about the direction of family trends since the 1960s, when mushrooming divorce, illegitimacy, father absence, and other problems began to expose children to new risks. It is widely understood that family breakdown is a major contributor to other social problems like rising poverty, criminal behavior, schooling lags, and health issues. But few charities have showed much success at re-knitting families together. And culture wars surrounding family issues scared many donors away from even trying.

Then in 2015 The Philanthropy Roundtable began convening major donors and encouraging them to contribute to a kitty of at least $30 million to be used to support fresh efforts at bolstering family integrity. This "Culture of Freedom" initiative particularly proposed to borrow new techniques from the business and technology worlds and adapt them into tools to be used by churches and local nonprofits in low-income communities where family decay is dragging down incomes, child welfare, and adult happiness. Things like demographic micro-targeting of social

POLICY

301

services, social-media promotion of family-reinforcement programs, app-based support for healthy home habits, and so forth. The initiative chose three cities in which to test services: Jacksonville, Dayton, and Phoenix. An initial drop in divorces in Jacksonville and spike in family church attendance in Dayton gave donors and service providers hope, early in 2017, that some of these new techniques may hold national promise.

Further information

○ *Philanthropy* magazine reporting, philanthropyroundtable.org/topic/philanthropic_freedom/closing_the_marriage_gap

---

2015

GESTATING AN IRAN DEAL

President Obama's 2015 decision to end sanctions on Iran in return for promises of increased nuclear accountability did not emerge on its own. It grew directly out of years of quiet activity by the Rockefeller Brothers Fund. After the 9/11 attacks demonstrated that al-Qaeda had become the most urgent Islamic threat, the fund began to convene meetings to explore the possibility of some U.S.-Iran rapprochement. Its Iran Project, given $4.3 million, funded a group of former U.S. diplomats to develop a relationship with Mohammad Javad Zarif and other Iranian officials, and begin to get them engaged with influential Americans. Zarif is now Iran's chief nuclear negotiator and the godfather of the Iran-Obama plan. The Rockefeller Brothers Fund also paid for most of a $4 million campaign launched in 2010 by the Ploughshares Fund, a San Francisco-based peace group, to build support among liberal think tanks and activists for pressure on behalf of an Iran deal.

Further information

○ Bloomberg reporting, bloomberg.com/politics/articles/2015-07-02/how-freelance-diplomacy-bankrolled-by-rockefellers-has-paved-the-way-for-an-iran-deal

---

2015

INDEPENDENCE PROJECT FOR VETERANS

With almost predictable regularity over recent years, the Department of Veterans Affairs has become embroiled in repeated scandals combining failed services with mushrooming backlogs. A root of the problem is an explosion in the number of former servicemembers who are now defined as disabled. Only 11 percent of all World War II veterans received disability payments. Among those

who served in Vietnam, 16 percent got checks. But among the men and women who served after the 9/11 attacks, a whopping 45 percent have already applied for disability compensation after leaving the service, and that ratio will increase as this cohort ages.

Not only do close to a majority of former servicemembers now call themselves disabled, but under what has come to be known as the "disability-compensation escalator," those on the rolls tend to ratchet up their official degree of disability every few years. Recipients can claim additional disabilities at any time, and it is very common for someone who goes on the books at "30 percent disabled" to later be re-rated at 40 percent, then 60 percent, etc.

The vastly increased recourse to disability checks, and the constant upward drift of benefits, combine to create terrible disincentives against work and independence. This hurts participants in many ways. Veterans who work not only have much higher income than those on the dole, they are also more likely to recover from their afflictions and have better mental health, much bigger social networks, deeper self-esteem, and more stable family lives. So the disability "aid" increasingly pumped out by the federal government correlates with more joblessness, and less wealth, health, and happiness among veterans.

On top of these ill-effects for vets, the existing system is bad news for taxpayers. The cost of the veterans disability program more than tripled from 2000 to 2015, to an annual charge of $65 billion, and is still rising fast. The budget of the Department of Veterans Affairs is now ballooning more rapidly than any other major department of the federal government.

Despite all this, efforts to create a more humane and effective system for assisting wounded warriors have failed in Congress. There are simply too many interest groups with a stake in the status quo. To get around this public-policy gridlock, donors launched a bold effort in 2015 to find a better way of operating. Their privately funded experiment will turn disability benefits on their head—instead of trickling a lifelong stream of small monthly checks to vets that keep them in low-income dependency, the program will make heavy upfront investments in veterans with mild to moderate injuries so they can acquire the skills for their dream jobs, start businesses or trades, and otherwise upgrade their lives to the point where they can then support themselves in dignity. A wide variety of medical, technical, motivational....

POLICY

To see the rest of this collection of Major Achievements in Policy, with entries dating back to our national founding, please consult the full-length version of The Almanac of American Philanthropy *(online or in print).*

enviromantic / istockphoto.com

OVERSEAS

For more than two centuries, Americans have sought to be helpful to fellow human beings beyond their own borders. They have carried literacy, knowledge, and technology to remote places, battled medical suffering, and alleviated poverty and misery of all sorts. From the first Christian missionaries in the nineteenth century, to the bold overseas projects of Rockefeller and Carnegie, to the 8 million lives saved in the developing world by the Gates Foundation in just its first two decades of existence, to the disaster assistance and many relief organizations powered by small gifts from millions of citizens, Americans have built a record as the most charitable of neighbors.

It's a powerful but little understood fact that our private giving actually dwarfs the official humanitarian aid sent overseas by the U.S. government. The latest calculations from the indispensable *Index of Global Philanthropy and Remittances* show that $44 billion of private philanthropy was invested in developing countries in 2014, while individual Americans (mostly immigrants) sent an additional $109 billion abroad to support relatives and friends in foreign lands. Meanwhile, official development assistance from the U.S. government that year totaled $33 billion.

And it isn't just the quantity of aid that matters, but also the quality. From creating new lifesaving vaccines to constructing major universities, from promoting property rights to battling terrorism and nuclear proliferation in fresh ways, American philanthropists are pursuing many inventive initiatives overseas. Not only the content but also the forms of giving are being rapidly refined—with for-profit mechanisms, e-giving, entrepreneurial methods, and other new means reshaping the efficiency and effectiveness of philanthropy in lands where bureaucracy and corruption are constant risks.

Many additional examples of overseas philanthropy in specific areas like medicine and religion can be found on our companion Major Achievement lists devoted to those topics.

↳ Section research provided by Karl Zinsmeister,
Christopher Levenick, and Evan Sparks

OVERSEAS

305

OVERSEAS GIVING BY U.S. CHURCHGOERS

American Christians have actively donated to charitable work overseas for more than 200 years. And there is evidence that the level of foreign donations by U.S. Christians has risen briskly during the past decade.

American churches contributed about $13 billion to relief and development abroad in the latest year. (This totals both direct mission work and giving to other aid groups.) That religious giving compares to $5 billion sent overseas by foundations, $8 billion from secular relief organizations, and $11 billion donated internationally by U.S. corporations. The $13 billion in religious overseas philanthropy also compares impressively to the $33 billion of official development aid handed out by the federal government that same year.

One indicator of the sharp rise in overseas giving by U.S. churchgoers is the *Mission Handbook* compiled by the Billy Graham Center. It cumulates the budgets of prominent Protestant groups that are providing international aid—like World Vision, Compassion International, Heifer International, and Opportunity International. Between the years of 1992 and 2008, those budgets more than doubled (in constant, inflation-adjusted dollars).

Further information

○ *Philanthropy* magazine reporting, philanthropyroundtable.org/topic/excellence_in_ philanthropy/unto_the_nations

○ The 2016 *Index of Global Philanthropy and Remittances*, hudson.org/research/13314-index- of-global-philanthropy-and-remittances-2016

○ Linda Weber, editor, *Mission Handbook* (Billy Graham Center, 2010)

2016

BUILDING UP ISRAEL'S YOUNGEST UNIVERSITY

Howard Marcus was a dentist who left his native Germany when Hitler came to power. He and his wife Lottie lost to the Nazis most of their family members who remained behind. While Mrs. Marcus was working as a secretary on Wall Street, she became friends with a very young investor named Warren Buffett. They put much of their savings in his hands, never sold a share, lived thriftily their whole life, and ended up with hundreds of millions of dollars. In 2005 they shared their blessings by donating $200 million to Israel's youngest and fastest-growing university, Ben-Gurion.

Howard lived to 104, and Lottie died a year later at 99. In 2016 their estate announced a posthumous gift to Ben-Gurion University of an additional $400 million—believed to be the largest single philanthropic grant to any Israeli institution. Ten percent of the gift will be directed to one of the university's specialties and a special interest of the Marcuses: research on water use in desert areas. The rest will more than double the college endowment.

Further information

° Ben-Gurion University release, in.bgu.ac.il/en/Pages/news/marcus_donation.aspx

GATES DOUBLES SPENDING AGAINST HUNGER

In 2015, Melinda Gates announced that the foundation she and her husband steer would double its investments against hunger in the developing world. "Malnutrition is the underlying cause of nearly half of all under-five child deaths," she noted, promising that the Gates Foundation would spend $776 million over the next six years to help change that. Malnutrition is now concentrated in a small number of countries where Gates will focus its efforts—India, Ethiopia, Nigeria, Bangladesh, and Burkina Faso. Emphasis will be placed on improving the nutrition of women and girls as soon as they become pregnant, educating mothers on infant feeding, encouraging breastfeeding, increasing sanitation to reduce energy-sapping infections, fortifying purchased foods with nutrients known to be underconsumed, and focusing on keeping children fed from birth to age two, when neurological development and other crucial growth is most rapid.

Further information

○ News report, trust.org/item/20150603143702-53fbj/?source=fiOtherNews2

○ Gates Foundation nutrition strategy, gatesfoundation.org/What-We-Do/Global-Development/Nutrition

2014

A CHINESE RHODES SCHOLARSHIP

Stephen Schwarzman, co-founder of the Blackstone investment company, has focused his giving on learning. In the U.S. he is a long-time supporter....

☞ *To see the rest of this collection of Major Achievements Overseas,
with entries dating back to our national founding, please consult the
full-length version of* The Almanac of American Philanthropy *(online or in print).*

OVERSEAS

LOCAL PROJECTS

Fantom: I despise a narrow field. O for the reign of universal benevolence. I want to make all mankind good and happy.

Goodman: Dear me! Sure that must be a wholesale sort of a job. Had you not better try your hand at a town or neighborhood first?

Fantom: Sir, I have a plan in my head for relieving the miseries of the whole world…. I would alter all the laws, and put an end to all the wars…. This is what I call doing things on a grand scale….

Goodman: One must begin to love somewhere; and I think it is as natural to love one's own family, and to do good in one's own neighborhood…. If every man in every family, village, and county did the same, why then all the schemes would be met, and the end of one village or town where I was doing good would be the beginning of another village where somebody else was doing good….

Fantom: Sir, a man of large views will be on the watch for great occasions to prove his benevolence.

Goodman: Yes, sir; but if they are so distant that he cannot reach them, or so vast that he cannot grasp them, he may let a thousand little, snug, kind, good actions slip through his fingers in the meanwhile. And so between the great thing that he cannot do and the little ones that he will not do, life passes, and nothing will be done.

McGuffey's Reader, 1844

LOCAL

"When I became serious about philanthropy, it was easiest to determine the needs in my own community. When you start working in your own community, there are a lot of positives. You've already got relationships. The programs you support are accessible and visible. You can go see them, talk with them, get a feel for them. And you get lots of affirmation. There are many reasons why people give locally."

David Weekley, Philanthropy, *Winter 2009*

As a simple matter of fact, more donors agree with the rhetorical Mr. Goodman and the very real Mr. Weekley (winner of the 2015 William E. Simon Prize for Philanthropic Leadership) than with the more abstract and grandiose Mr. Fantom. A study out of Indiana University's Lilly Family School of Philanthropy showed that of all gifts of a million dollars or more made during the years 2000-2011, two thirds went to organizations in the same region as the giver. If you add in all the gifts of less than a million dollars, the proportion of American philanthropy that takes place locally is overwhelming.

In addition, a great many of the most effective national charities in America—Goodwill, the Boy Scouts, the Salvation Army, Habitat for Humanity, the Union Gospel Missions, KIPP schools, and many more—provide their local affiliates with a powerful degree of operational autonomy. When donors give to these groups built on decentralized chapters, they are effectively supporting a neighborhood or regional group more than a national entity.

By definition, most local, small-scale giving is not visible to outsiders, so it's easy to miss. The cases we present below are merely examples—a kind of tip of the U.S. iceberg. Our intent is simply to remind everyone interested in philanthropy that, each day in this country, scads of close-to-home acts of support take place. It's easy to think that these local philanthropies are too small, too uncoordinated, too limited to generate "fundamental change." But piece together a scholarship program here and an inspiring museum there, a rural dental program in this town and an "Alice's Integrity Loan Fund" in another, and soon you see the outlines of a living, thousand-armed mechanism that responds to millions of local needs and longings, marshaling tens of billions of dollars. And every one of our hometowns is made more livable, richer, safer, and more interesting by the gifts rained down by this organic process of sharing bounty among neighbors.

Section research provided by Karl Zinsmeister, Brian Brown, Caitrin Keiper, and Bill Kauffman

FLORIDA LAKE, LAND, PARK (LAKELAND)

Located halfway between Tampa and Orlando, Lakeland, Florida, is a city with a population of 100,000, but is headed toward a million in its fast-growing metro region within a generation. One local family, the Barnetts—who built up the Publix Super Market chain—recognized that their hometown lacked the parkland needed for an urban area of that size. So they invested energy and money into sparking a major new recreation area for the region. The Barnetts and local allies announced acquisition of 160 acres, and creation of a plan for building a $50-60 million urban escape there, without any money from government. The property is about half attractive woods and lakefront, and half industrial land that will need to be reclaimed. Nature trails, playgrounds, gardens, bike paths, and other amenities will be constructed, and a private nonprofit will provide popular programming for the public, all within walking distance of downtown. The philanthropic sponsors are aiming for an opening around 2020.

Further information

° Reporting in the *Lakeland Ledger*, theledger.com/news/20170206/barnetts-to-introduce-vast-urban-park-in-lakeland

° Park plan, lkldnow.com/organizers-detail-plans-massive-bonnet-springs-park/

HELPING THOSE LEFT BEHIND BY THE TECH BOOM (SILICON VALLEY)

While the computer revolution has turned Silicon Valley into a boomtown, it has also made that region into one of the most expensive places in the country to live, squeezing many local families. And the local foundations built on tech fortunes give only about 7 percent of their funds to charities in their own San Jose/Palo Alto/Santa Clara/San Mateo area. But real-estate developer John Sobrato, who became rich creating campuses for Apple, Yahoo, and other firms, is giving away money with a strong focus on helping local residents left behind by the tech expansion.

Expanding schools and teaching programs that help the area's Spanish-speaking children has been one major emphasis. The Sobrato family founded a Cristo Rey Catholic high school, supported numerous other schools, and developed a new way of teaching English to non-native speakers that has now spread to 39,000 students.

LOCAL

The Sobratos have also built up office complexes in San Jose, Redwood City, and Milpitas where about 70 charities are provided with free headquarters space. This allows them to avoid the notoriously high rents in the region. It also gives them a proximity to learn from each other and collaborate on projects.

The family has made multi-million-dollar gifts to the local children's hospital and the Valley Medical Center, and to the National Hispanic University and the Jesuit-run University of San Francisco. In 2017 they announced their largest gift ever: $100 million to Santa Clara University to allow it to unify and strengthen its science and math training for students. That ranked as the second-largest gift ever to a Catholic college. It brought the family's total charitable contributions to about $380 million over the last 20 years. And six months later the Sobrato gift was bolstered by an additional $30 million from the Leavey Foundation (big supporters of Catholic causes, education, and medicine) for Santa Clara University's expansion into science and math.

Further information

○ Santa Clara University release, scu.edu/news-and-events/press-releases/2017/january-2017/100-million-gift-from-john-a-and-susan-sobrato-launches-sobrato-campus-for-discovery-and-innovation-at-santa-clara-university-.html

○ Report on Silicon Valley giving, static1.squarespace.com/static/579ea07b414fb51257607b72/t/580e9b90e6f2e1af3c27c429/1477352344309/GivingCode_full_download_102516.pdf

REPAYING HIS EYE DOCTORS (SACRAMENTO)

Ernest Tschannen noticed in 2000 that his eyesight was failing, so he visited an eye clinic at the University of California at Davis, and later underwent successful surgery. In gratitude, he donated $25 to the university. But in addition to being a soft-spoken engineer, Tschannen proved to have a gift for investing. He made millions of dollars buying real estate (though he continued to live in a modest apartment even after becoming wealthy). So he was later able to give UC Davis $1.5 million so it could hire an optic-nerve specialist. And then in 2016, the 91-year-old donated $37 million so the university could unite all of its eye programs—which treat 55,000 local patients annually—in one new facility.

Further information

○ University announcement, ucdavis.edu/news/record-generosity-385-million-uc-davis-vision-science

INVESTIGATING METABOLIC DISEASE (INDIANA)

In 2013, Indiana bioscience companies donated $25 million, matched by a state appropriation, and announced plans to establish a center in Indianapolis that would research metabolic diseases like diabetes and heart trouble, and their connection to nutrition. But it took an $80 million gift from the Lilly Endowment and a $20 million grant from the Eli Lilly company foundation to make the proposal real three years later. The center broke ground in 2016 on a freestanding facility that is expected to bolster the Indianapolis downtown in addition to improving medical understanding.

Further information

○ Reporting in the *Indianapolis Star*, indystar.com/story/news/2016/02/24/new-biosciences-institute-gets-100m/80794292/

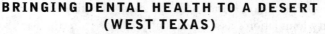

BRINGING DENTAL HEALTH TO A DESERT (WEST TEXAS)

West Texas and the U.S.-Mexico border have been a bit of desert when it comes to dentistry. The dental school closest to El Paso is more than 500 miles away, and in El Paso County the number of dentists per population is only half the state average. A majority of the local population do not visit a dentist at all in a typical year. Thanks to Woody and Gayle Hunt, that problem is about to improve. The family, which operates a cluster of businesses in the region centered around real estate, construction, and finance, donated $25 million to open the first new dental school in Texas in nearly 50 years.

Further information

○ Texas Tech University announcement, eptechview.ttuhsc.edu/ttuhsc-el-paso/25-million-gift-establishes-new-dental-school-in-el-paso/

A YANKEE GIVES BACK (VERMONT)

Robert Larner grew up in Vermont, one of seven children of a roofer. After winning a state debate championship, he attended the University of Vermont on a scholarship. Then he attended UVM's medical school. After serving in

LOCAL

World War II he built a medical practice in southern California. His practice was successful, but what made him wealthy was his knack for making commercial real-estate investments in the booming Los Angeles region.

He never forgot his Vermont roots, and indeed made UVM his main beneficiary when he became a generous philanthropist. In 2015-2016, Larner earmarked $95 million to the university that minted his career. This inspired Vermont to name its medical school for him. It was the first time a med school has ever been named for an alumnus.

Further information

○ University of Vermont announcement, uvm.edu/~uvmpr/?Page=news&&storyID=23418

———————— 2015 ————————

TRIPLING A COMMUNITY FOUNDATION (SAN ANTONIO)

John Santikos owned 11 cinemas, some shopping centers, and open land in San Antonio and southern Texas. When he died, he left those assets, worth more than $605 million, to the San Antonio Area Foundation. This was the largest single charitable gift on record in that city, and the largest philanthropic donation nationwide in 2015. It will more than triple the community foundation's assets. Annual proceeds from the Santikos gift will mostly be distributed to a wide variety of local charities, bolstering people in need, students, cultural institutions, and medical treatment. However, the immigrant from Greece—whose family suffered through the Greek civil war—also specified that two non-San Antonio nonprofits should each get 10 percent of the annual donations from his estate: Doctors Without Borders, and International Orthodox Christian Charities.

Further information

○ Reporting in the *San Antonio Express-News*, expressnews.com/business/local/article/ Santikos-gift-tops-600-million-6698709.php

———————— 2015 ————————

RECYCLING ABANDONED HOMES (INDIANAPOLIS)

The foremost spending priority of the Lilly Endowment is development of its home region around Indianapolis. It has, for instance, awarded $172 million to the Indianapolis Neighborhood Housing Partnership since the creation of that nonprofit in 1988. Indeed, Lilly has recently covered $5.3 million of the organization's annual budget of $9.5 million. INHP funds are mostly used to

help moderate-income buyers purchase residences in the city—where vacant homes and blight have been a problem. The *Indianapolis Star* found in 2015 that there were 6,800 abandoned houses in the urban area, stressing some neighborhoods.

The Housing Partnership has long wanted to have a fund it could use to buy up these houses when they become available, keep them from falling into disrepair, and then recycle them to new residents as they become qualified to buy. What's really needed, says the nonprofit's president, is "flexible, patient capital" that can be used to gradually transform neighborhoods.

In 2015, that wish came true. The Lilly Endowment made a special $27 million grant to INHP, above and beyond its annual support, for the charity to use as a property-acquisition fund in an anti-blight campaign.

Further information

○ Reporting in the *Indianapolis Star*, indystar.com/story/money/2015/12/08/266m-lilly-endowment-grant-targets-blight-indianapolis/76977566/

2015

AN HONORS COLLEGE TO HONOR THE HOME STATE (KENTUCKY)

Tom Lewis got his graduate degree at UNC Chapel Hill. He lived nearly all his adult life—and made his fortune as a homebuilder—in Arizona. But in 2015 he donated $23 million to the University of Kentucky (its largest gift ever), so a new honors college could be created on campus. Asked why, Lewis invoked the kind of personal connection that drives much voluntary giving. His aim, he said, was to "honor the history of our family in Kentucky." It turns out all 16 of his great-grandparents were Kentuckians. He spent his own childhood there as well, a seventh-generation resident of the state.

Lewis's gift allowed the university to build a new hall where top students can reside, hire a dean and ten new staff members, and create special curricula that will challenge their most intellectually serious enrollees. By attracting more of the state's very brightest students to remain in Kentucky for their education, Lewis said he hoped more of them would end up living in the state and "contribute to its growth and prosperity."…

☞ To see the rest of this collection of Major Local Achievements, with entries dating back to our national founding, please consult the full-length version of The Almanac of American Philanthropy *(online or in print).*

LOCAL

GREAT
QUOTATIONS

on

PHILANTHROPY

The human impulse to voluntarily give away resources,
with the aim of boosting people who are falling short of their
God-given potential, is a bit mysterious, quite inspiring, and
particularly strong in American breasts. Here are some of the
pithiest observations that have been offered over the years on
the causes, effects, and essential elements of charitable giving.

It is one of the most beautiful compensations of life that no man can sincerely try to help another without helping himself.
▸ Ralph Waldo Emerson

Most people think that Americans are generous because we are rich. The truth is that we are rich, in significant part, because we are generous.
▸ Claire Gaudiani

As I grow older, I pay less attention to what men say. I just watch what they do.
▸ Andrew Carnegie

Don't just think, do.
▸ Horace

If you would help another man, you must do so in minute particulars.
▸ William Blake

It is easy to love the people far away. It is not always easy to love those close to us…. This is where our love for each other must start.
▸ Mother Teresa

No one has ever become poor by giving.
▸ Anne Frank

To love the little platoon we belong to in society is the first principle (the germ as it were) of public affections. It is the first link in the series by which we proceed towards a love to our country, and to mankind.
▸ Edmund Burke

Don't judge each day by the harvest you reap, but by the seeds you plant.
- *Robert Louis Stevenson*

Every charitable act is a stepping stone toward heaven.
- *Henry Ward Beecher*

Charity is the great channel through which the mercy of God is passed on to mankind.
- *Conrad Hilton*

Blessed is the influence of one true, loving human soul on another.
- *George Eliot*

It is in giving that we receive.
- *Francis of Assisi*

What I did was help myself by learning to help others. You only keep what you have by giving it away.
- *Sean MacMillen*

That best portion of a good man's life: His little, nameless, unremembered acts of kindness and of love.
- *William Wordsworth*

Do all the good you can. By all the means you can. In all the ways you can. In all the places you can. At all the times you can. To all the people you can. As long as you ever can.
- *John Wesley*

When I do good, I feel good; when I do bad, I feel bad.
☞ *Abraham Lincoln*

If you want to feel proud of yourself, you've got to do things you
can be proud of.
☞ *Oseola McCarty*

The raising of extraordinarily large sums of money, given voluntarily
and freely by millions of our fellow Americans…is truly a jewel of
an American tradition.
☞ *John Kennedy*

There are only four things you can do with your money. You can
give it to the government. You can spend it. You can give it to your
kids to their detriment. My three sons understand this. I never want
to deprive them of the wonderful feeling of making it on their own.
I don't think you do your kids a favor by leaving them a lot of money,
or letting them think they're working with a net. And the fourth
thing you can do with your money is create something good with it.
I think it's incumbent on everybody with any amount of funds at all
to start thinking like that.
☞ *James Kimsey*

Let no one go hungry away. If any of the kind of people should be
in want of corn, supply their necessities, provided it does
not encourage them in idleness.
☞ *George Washington*

Charity is injurious unless it helps the recipient to become
independent of it.
☞ *John Rockefeller*

The best way of doing good to the poor is not making them easy in poverty, but leading or driving them out of it.
☞ *Benjamin Franklin*

Neither the individual nor the race is improved by almsgiving. The best means of benefiting the community is to place within its reach the ladders upon which the aspiring can rise.
☞ *Andrew Carnegie*

What the poor need is not charity but capital, not caseworkers but co-workers.
☞ *Millard and Linda Fuller*

The proper aim of giving is to put the recipients in a state where they no longer need our gifts.
☞ *C. S. Lewis*

There are eight levels of charity…. The highest is when you strengthen a man's hand until he need no longer be dependent upon others.
☞ *Maimonides*

The best philanthropy is constantly in search of the finalities— a search for a cause, an attempt to cure evils at their source.
☞ *John Rockefeller*

To get the best long-term results the foundation should not only provide grants to help competent men do their best work, but should also seek to increase the supply of competent men.
☞ *1949 Ford Foundation report*

I wanted to give my children enough money so that they would feel they could do anything, but not so much they could do nothing.
☞ *Warren Buffett*

I was trained from the beginning to work, to save, and to give.
☞ *John Rockefeller Jr.*

It is more blessed to give than to receive.
☞ *Acts 20:35*

Cast your bread upon the waters, for after many days you will find it again.
☞ *Ecclesiastes 11:1*

Each man should give what he has decided in his heart to give, not reluctantly or under compulsion, for God loves a cheerful giver.
☞ *St. Paul*

A bit of fragrance always clings to the hand that gives roses. If you are generous, you will gain everything.
☞ *Confucius*

Help your brother's boat across, and your own will reach the shore.
☞ *Hindu proverb*

We make a living by what we get, we make a life by what we give.
☞ *Winston Churchill*

You take nothing with you that you gained—only what you gave away.
☞ *Francis of Assisi*

Never doubt that a small group of thoughtful, committed citizens can change the world. Indeed, it is the only thing that ever has.
ᵇ⁻ *Margaret Mead*

No one need wait a single moment to improve the world.
ᵇ⁻ *Anne Frank*

It is prodigious the quantity of good that may be done by one man, if he will make a business of it.
ᵇ⁻ *Benjamin Franklin*

It's better to tell your money where to go than to ask where it went.
ᵇ⁻ *Farmer's Gazette*

When we do any good to others, we do as much, or more, good to ourselves.
ᵇ⁻ *Benjamin Whichcote*

I absolutely believe in the power of tithing. My own experience is that the more I give away, the more that comes back. That is the way life works.
ᵇ⁻ *Ken Blanchard*

Whoever sows sparingly will also reap sparingly, and whoever sows bountifully will also reap bountifully.
ᵇ⁻ *St. Paul*

What we do for ourselves dies with us. What we do for others and the world remains and is immortal.
ᵇ⁻ *Albert Pine*

Every man goes down to his death bearing in his hands only that which he has given away.
☞ *Persian proverb*

It is by spending oneself that one becomes rich.
☞ *Sarah Bernhardt*

A man there was, though some did count him mad, the more he cast away, the more he had.
☞ *John Bunyan*

As I give, I get.
☞ *Mary McLeod Bethune*

It is more difficult to give money away intelligently than to earn it in the first place.
☞ *Andrew Carnegie*

If you want to lift yourself up, lift up someone else.
☞ *Booker T. Washington*

The best philanthropy is not just about giving money but giving leadership. The best philanthropists bring the gifts that made them successful—the drive, the determination, the refusal to accept that something can't be done if it needs to be—into their philanthropy.
☞ *Tony Blair*

If you want happiness for a year, inherit a fortune. If you want happiness for a lifetime, help someone else.
☞ *Confucius*

As the purse is emptied the heart is filled.
☞ *Victor Hugo*

The charitable give out the door and God puts it back through
the window.
☞ *traditional proverb*

To give away money is an easy matter and in any man's power. But to
decide to whom to give it and how large and when, and for what
purpose and how, is neither in every man's power nor an easy matter.
☞ *Aristotle*

I can testify that it is nearly always easier to make $1,000,000
honestly than to dispose of it wisely.
☞ *Julius Rosenwald*

I resolved to stop accumulating and begin the infinitely more
serious and difficult task of wise distribution.
☞ *Andrew Carnegie*

Different philanthropists have different views about what makes
society better off. One of the things that I think is wonderful about
the non-accountability of philanthropy is that it allows for multiple
versions of what makes society better off. The U.S. is unique in
supporting those multiple versions of the good.
☞ *Paul Brest*

At the head of any new undertaking where in France you would
find the government, or in England some great lord, in the
United States you are sure to find an association.
☞ *Alexis de Tocqueville*

In America, communities existed before governments. There were
many groups of people with a common sense of purpose and a feeling
of duty to one another before there were political institutions.
ɞ Daniel Boorstin

Philanthropic leaders genially speak of complementing
government, not competing with it—as if monopoly were good
and competition destructive—thus unwittingly conspiring
against the public interest.
ɞ Richard Cornuelle

Some writers have so confounded society with government as to
leave little or no distinction between them; whereas they are not
only different, but have different origins.
ɞ Thomas Paine

Governments don't really like organizations which are outside their
control. There is much talk today in the voluntary sector of a
"compact" with the state. This could turn out to be the sort of
compact which the oysters had with the Walrus and the Carpenter:
it ends up with one party getting eaten by the other.
ɞ Robert Whelan

There's no substitute for rolling up your sleeves and working
with the people who can make a difference. They get the benefit of
your participation and you gain a direct understanding of the real
problems and potential solutions.
ɞ Michael Milken

To say or imply that the foundation exists only on the sufferance of
government is to reason from the untenable notion that the citizen and
all his institutions are creatures of the state, not the other way around.
ɞ Richard Cornuelle

Donors represent a private version of the legislative process—
a deliberative process that selects goals, sets values, and
allocates resources…. an alternative vehicle for getting things done.
☛ *Paul Ylvisaker*

Society is produced by our wants, and government by our
wickedness. The former promotes our happiness positively by
uniting our affections, the latter negatively by restraining our vices.
The one encourages intercourse, the other creates distinctions.
The first is a patron, the last a punisher.
☛ *Thomas Paine*

It is calculated that a certain amount of revenue is lost to the
government because a private college is tax exempt. The logic
is that all of society's wealth really belongs to the government
and that the government should therefore be able to determine how
wealth exempted from taxation should be used. This implication is
incipiently totalitarian.
☛ *Peter Berger and Richard John Neuhaus*

Rich men are neither better nor worse than all other humans.
They contribute to greatness or mediocrity, strength of character
or weakness in exactly the same proportion as persons in all other
walks of life do.
☛ *Julius Rosenwald*

No person was ever honored for what he received. Honor has been
the reward for what he gave.
☛ *Calvin Coolidge*

Never respect men merely for their riches, but rather for their
philanthropy; we do not value the sun for its height, but for its use.
☛ *Gamaliel Bailey*

One of the great movements in my lifetime among educated people is the need to commit themselves to action. Most people are not satisfied with giving money; we also feel we need to work.
☛ *Peter Drucker*

Men who leave their money to be distributed by others are pie-faced mutts. I want to see the action during my lifetime.
☛ *George Eastman*

No one is useless in this world who lightens the burdens of another.
☛ *Charles Dickens*

A man wrapped up in himself makes a very small bundle.
☛ *Benjamin Franklin*

Any good that I can do or any kindness that I can show to any human being, let me do it now. Let me not defer or neglect it, for I shall not pass this way again.
☛ *Mahatma Gandhi*

I feel called to help individuals, to love each human being. I never think in terms of crowds in general but in terms of persons. Were I to think about crowds, I would never begin anything.
☛ *Mother Teresa*

Do what you can, with what you have, where you are.
☛ *Theodore Roosevelt*

Do your little bit of good where you are; it's those little bits of good put together that overwhelm the world.
☛ *Desmond Tutu*

No act of kindness, no matter how small, is ever wasted.
✒ *Aesop*

Let no one be discouraged by the belief that there is nothing one person can do against the enormous array of the world's ills…. Each of us can work to change a small portion of events. And in the total of all those acts will be written the history of a generation.
✒ *Robert Kennedy*

If you can't feed a hundred people, then feed just one.
✒ *Mother Teresa*

It is not our part to master all the tides of the world, but to do what is in us…uprooting the evil in the fields that we know, so that those who live after may have clean earth to till. What weather they shall have is not ours to rule.
✒ *J. R. R. Tolkien*

The man who dies rich dies disgraced.
✒ *Andrew Carnegie*

Your Giving Pledge has a loophole…permitting pledgees to simply name charities in their wills. Some billionaires hate giving large sums of money away while alive and instead set up family-controlled foundations to do it for them after death. And these foundations become, more often than not, bureaucracy-ridden sluggards.
✒ *Robert Wilson replying to Bill Gates's invitation to sign the Giving Pledge*

I particularly dislike people saying, "I'm going to leave it in my will." What they're really saying is, "If I could live forever, I wouldn't give any of it away."
✒ *Jon Huntsman Sr.*

Where charity keeps pace with gain, industry is blessed.
☞ *William Penn*

Every right implies a responsibility; every opportunity, an obligation; every possession, a duty.
☞ *John Rockefeller Jr.*

My theme for philanthropy is the same approach I used with technology: to find a need and fill it.
☞ *An Wang*

If your aims as a donor are modest, you can accomplish an awful lot. When your aims become elevated beyond a reasonable level, you not only don't accomplish much, but you can cause a great deal of damage.
☞ *Irving Kristol*

Benevolence today has become altogether too huge an undertaking to be conducted otherwise than on business lines.
☞ *Julius Rosenwald*

The highest use of capital is to make money do more for the betterment of life.
☞ *Henry Ford*

As the furnace purifies the silver, so does charity rid wealth of its dross.
☞ *William Downey*

If you combine all the spectral rays into a single beam, you get white light; and if you combine all the virtues into a single beam you get charity.
☞ *Austin O'Malley*

Men have committed murder for jealousy's sake, and anger's sake, and hatred's sake, and selfishness' sake, and spiritual pride's sake; but no man that ever I heard of ever committed a diabolical murder for sweet charity's sake.
☞ *Herman Melville*

Nothing contributes more to make men polite and civilized than true and genuine charity.
☞ *Wellins Calcott*

Charity is a universal remedy against discord, and a holy cement for mankind.
☞ *William Penn*

Charity is the note that resolves the discord.
☞ *Austin O'Malley*

A bone to the dog is not charity. Charity is the bone shared with the dog, when you are just as hungry as the dog.
☞ *Jack London*

When the crumbs are swept from our table, we think it generous to let the dogs eat them; as if that were charity which permits others to have what we cannot keep.
☞ *Henry Ward Beecher*

If life happens to bless you with talent or treasure, you have a responsibility to use those gifts as well and as wisely as you possibly can.
☞ *Bill and Melinda Gates*

I have always believed that most large fortunes are made by men…
who tumbled into a lucky opportunity. Hard work and attention to
business are necessary, but they rarely result in achieving a large
fortune. Do not be fooled into believing that because a man is rich,
he is necessarily smart. There is ample proof to the contrary.
* Julius Rosenwald*

Gain all you can without harm to mind or body, your own or your
neighbor's, by honest industry and by common sense.
Save all you can to keep yourself, as well as your children from
prodigal desires….
And, finally, as God placed you here not as a proprietor, but a
steward, give all you can.
* John Wesley*

We must be knit together in this work as one man, we must
entertain each other in brotherly affection, we must be willing to
abridge ourselves of our superfluities, for the supply of other's
necessities….We must delight in each other, make others' conditions
our own…always having before our eyes our community as members
of the same body.
* John Winthrop at the founding of the Massachusetts Colony*

What do we live for, if it is not to make life less difficult for each other?
* George Eliot*

The true friend of the people should see that they be not too poor,
for extreme poverty lowers the character of the democracy.
* Aristotle*

When wealth is centralized, the people are dispersed.
When wealth is distributed, the people are brought together.
* Confucius*

The political maturity of a country is measured by what citizens willingly do for themselves and one another.
Frank Prochaska

A large part of altruism…is grounded upon the fact that it is uncomfortable to have unhappy people about one.
H. L. Mencken

Let your heart feel for the afflictions and distresses of everyone, and let your hand give in proportion to your purse. It is not everyone who asks that deserves charity. All, however, are worthy of the inquiry, or the deserving may suffer.
George Washington

Charity begins at home, but should not end there.
Francis Bacon

God sends us the poor to try us…. And he that refuses them a little out of the great deal that God has given, lays up poverty in store for his own posterity.
William Penn

When I talk to young people who seem destined for great success, I tell them…concentrate on your family and getting rich (which I found very hard work). Don't forget that those who don't make money never become philanthropists.
Robert Wilson

No one would remember the Good Samaritan if he'd only had good intentions—he had money as well.
Margaret Thatcher

I believe the power to make money is a gift from God…to be developed and used to the best of our ability for the good of mankind.
⁄ *John Rockefeller*

Historically, Americans did not raise funds by appealing to donors' guilt, or by urging them to "give back" to society. Instead, they appealed to their fellow citizens' ideals and aspirations, their religious principles, and their desire to create.
⁄ *Adam Meyerson*

I'm not doing my philanthropic work out of any kind of guilt. I'm doing it because I can afford to do it, and I believe in it.
⁄ *George Soros*

The ultimate achievement is how you feel about yourself. And giving your wealth away to have an impact for good does help with that.
⁄ *Gerry Lenfest*

The only ones among you who will be really happy are those who will have sought and found how to serve.
⁄ *Albert Schweitzer*

Think of giving not only as a duty but as a privilege.
⁄ *John Rockefeller*

The best recreation is to do good.
⁄ *William Penn*

Not what we give, but what we share,
for the gift without the giver is bare.
⁄ *James Russell Lowell*

Leisure is time for doing something useful.
✍ *Benjamin Franklin*

Many persons have a wrong idea of what constitutes true happiness. It is not attained through self-gratification but through fidelity to a worthy purpose.
✍ *Helen Keller*

Too often, a vast collection of possessions ends up possessing its owner.
✍ *Warren Buffett*

In the modern era, government has been seen as society's problem-solving agency, the place people go to address every conceivable need. This assumption of government omnipotence has profoundly influenced the evolution of philanthropy. It becomes the principal function of a philanthropic group to interest government in carrying out its goal, rather than solving problems in its own right.
✍ *James Payne*

It is a misconception that corporate or government support has ever provided the majority of arts funding....The real stars of arts giving are individual donors, who give more to arts than corporations and government entities combined.
✍ *Beth Nathanson*

Many people are alienated by faceless bureaucracy and what they see as an erosion of participatory democracy. Consequently, there has been a revival of interest in charitable service.
✍ *Frank Prochaska*

Community is a consequence. It results when people come together to accomplish things that are important to them and succeed. People who are uninvolved cannot feel this connection.
☞ *Richard Cornuelle*

The more government takes the place of associations, the more will individuals lose the idea of forming associations and need the government to come to their help. That is a vicious circle of cause and effect.
☞ *Alexis de Tocqueville*

How about no income tax at all on people over 65? People would continue working, remain healthier, not be an economic and social drain on society. Then the elderly would also have more disposable income to help charitable activities.
☞ *John Templeton*

I was fortunate to get a scholarship when I went to Lehigh University and Princeton.... Somebody was kind enough to spend their money to educate people that they would never get to know. That's what I think philanthropy is about.
☞ *Lee Iacocca*

The spirit of community will be revived as we succeed in devising ways to reinvolve people in solving the perplexing problems they see about them, not just in talking about them, and certainly not in petitioning government to solve them.
☞ *Richard Cornuelle*

Giving frees us from the familiar territory of our own needs, by opening our mind to the unexplained worlds occupied by the needs of others.
☞ *Barbara Bush*

When you give to the needy do not announce it with trumpets...
to be honored by others.... Your Father, who sees what is done in
secret, will reward you.
☞ *Jesus*

Do not give, as many rich men do, like a hen that lays her egg and
then cackles.
☞ *Henry Ward Beecher*

Let him that hath done the good office conceal it; let him that
received it disclose it.
☞ *Seneca*

Speeches by businessmen on social responsibility may gain them
kudos in the short run. But it helps to strengthen the already too
prevalent view that the pursuit of profits is wicked.... There is one
and only one social responsibility of business—to engage in open
and free competition without deception or fraud.
☞ *Milton Friedman*

A certain amount of corporate philanthropy is simply good business
and works for the long-term benefit of the investors.
☞ *John Mackey*

Remember, you don't live in a world all your own.
☞ *Albert Schweitzer*

Life's persistent and most urgent question is "What are you doing
for others?"
☞ *Martin Luther King Jr.*

A man of humanity is one who…desiring attainment for himself, helps others to attain.
Confucius

The value of a man resides in what he gives.
Albert Einstein

The greatest use of life is to spend it for something that will outlast it.
William James

The most useful and influential people in America are those who take the deepest interest in institutions that exist for the purpose of making the world better.
Booker T. Washington

Real generosity toward the future lies in giving all to the present.
Albert Camus

If you want to do something for your children and show how much you love them, the single best thing—by far—is to support organizations that will create a better world for them and their children.
Michael Bloomberg

I cannot think of a more personally rewarding and appropriate use of wealth than to give while one is living…. Interventions have greater value and impact today than if they are delayed.
Charles Feeney

The true measure of a man is how he treats someone who can do him absolutely no good.
↳ *Samuel Johnson*

Earlier in this century, philanthropy often flowed from the wills of dead industrialists. In recent decades, it's as likely to have come from a very alive business leader.
↳ *Michael Milken*

Philanthropists enjoy the freedom to experiment and take risks—risks that business and government entities cannot, or will not, accept. In this way, philanthropy has served as society's "risk capital."
↳ *Tom Tierney and Joel Fleishman*

The foundation is an instrument forged by citizens who transfer profit from the commercial sector and put it directly to work as risk capital for the general betterment of the society.
↳ *Richard Cornuelle*

For scientific researchers, charitable donations are enormous engines of new opportunities, of starting in directions that wouldn't have been possible to fund by conventional sources.
↳ *Leroy Hood*

Show me a person who never made a mistake, and I will show you a person who never did anything.
↳ *William Rosenberg*

The world is moving so fast these days that the one who says it can't be done is generally interrupted by someone doing it.
↳ *Harry Emerson Fosdick*

STATISTICS

on

U.S. GENEROSITY

The most important numbers in American philanthropy.

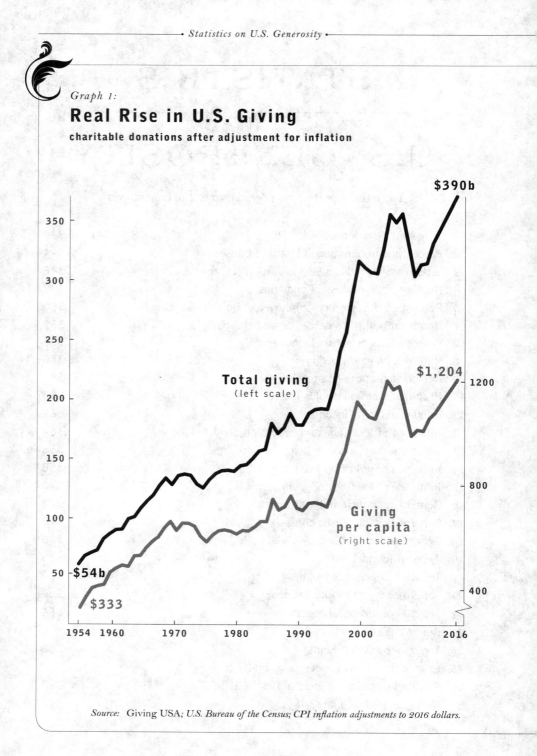

Graph 1:

Real Rise in U.S. Giving

charitable donations after adjustment for inflation

$390b

350

300

250

Total giving
(left scale)

$1,204

1200

200

150

800

Giving per capita
(right scale)

100

50 **$54b**

$333

400

1954 1960   1970   1980   1990   2000   2016

Source: Giving USA; U.S. Bureau of the Census; CPI inflation adjustments to 2016 dollars.

After adjusting for inflation, charitable giving by Americans was close to seven times as big in 2016 as it was 62 years earlier.

Of course, one reason total giving went up is because the U.S. population almost doubled. But if we recalculate inflation-adjusted charitable giving on a *per capita* basis, we see that has also soared: by 3½ times. Charitable causes are very lucky to have a remarkably expansive American economy behind them, and a standard of living that refuses to stagnate.

What if we calculate charitable giving as a proportion of all national production (GDP)? The math reveals that over the last 60 years, donations as a proportion of our total annual output increased—but only very slightly. For most of the last lifetime, giving has hovered right around 2 percent of our total national treasure.

Two percent of GDP is a huge sum, particularly in comparison to other countries (see details on that at Graph 27). But it's interesting that even as we have become a much wealthier people in the post-WWII era, the fraction we give away hasn't risen. There seems to be something stubborn about that 2 percent rate.

Graph 2:

Percentage of U.S. Donations Going to Various Causes

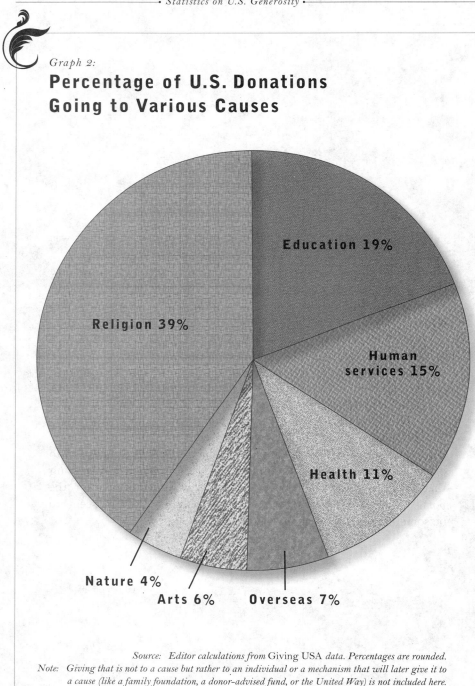

Education 19%

Human services 15%

Religion 39%

Health 11%

Nature 4%

Arts 6%

Overseas 7%

Source: Editor calculations from Giving USA *data. Percentages are rounded.*
*Note: Giving that is not to a cause but rather to an individual or a mechanism that will later give it to
a cause (like a family foundation, a donor-advised fund, or the United Way) is not included here.*

Religious causes are, and always have been, Americans' favorite charitable targets. Of course, "Religion" is a very broad category. Some of those funds are used to support houses of worship and clergy, to maintain the faith, and to proselytize future generations. Much religious charity, however, ultimately goes into sub-causes like relief for the poor, medical care, education, or aid sent to low-income countries or victims of disaster.

Keep in mind too that religious charities tend to have less access to supplemental funds than other nonprofits. Hospitals and colleges charge users fees to supplement their donated income; other nonprofits sell goods; many museums charge admission; some charities receive government grants. Churches and religious charities, however, operate mostly on their donated funds depicted in this graph.

Graph 3:
Sources of U.S. Charitable Giving

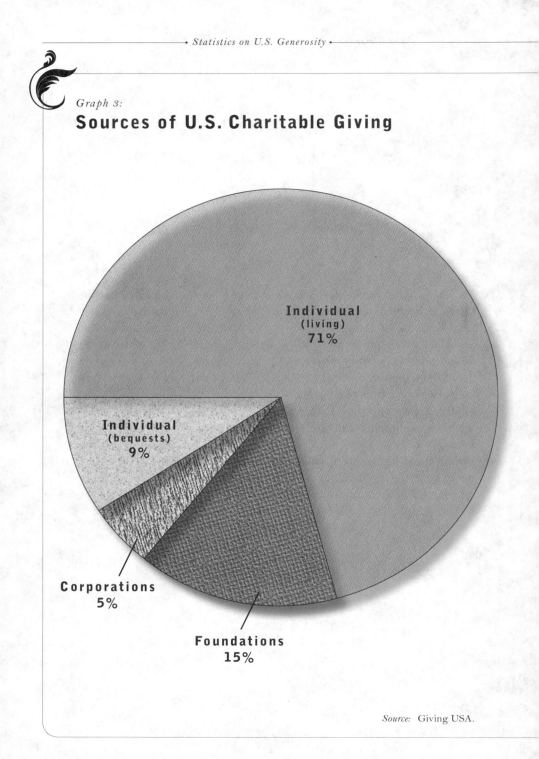

Individual
(living)
71%

Individual
(bequests)
9%

Corporations
5%

Foundations
15%

Source: Giving USA.

It's easy, amid press stories about the projects of large foundations or corporations, to forget that the vast bulk of American philanthropy is carried out by individuals. Between individual donations and bequests in wills, personal gifts come to *over four times as much*, every year, as what behemoths like the Gates, Ford, Walton, etc. foundations plus corporations give away.

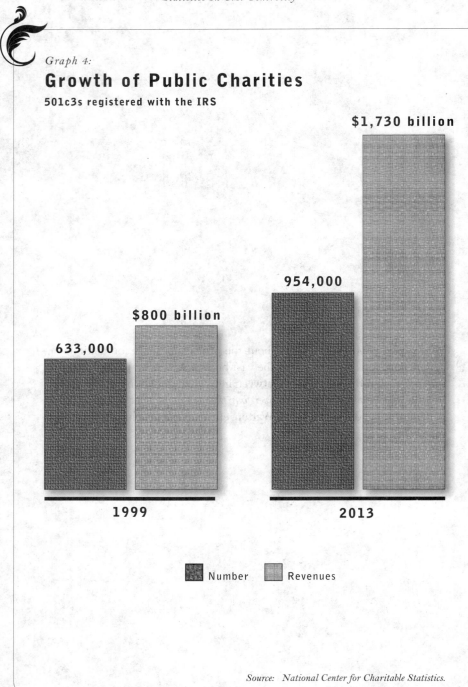

Graph 4:

Growth of Public Charities

501c3s registered with the IRS

$1,730 billion

954,000

$800 billion

633,000

1999

2013

Number   Revenues

Source: National Center for Charitable Statistics.

The number of nonprofits, and their revenues, have both grown quickly in recent years.

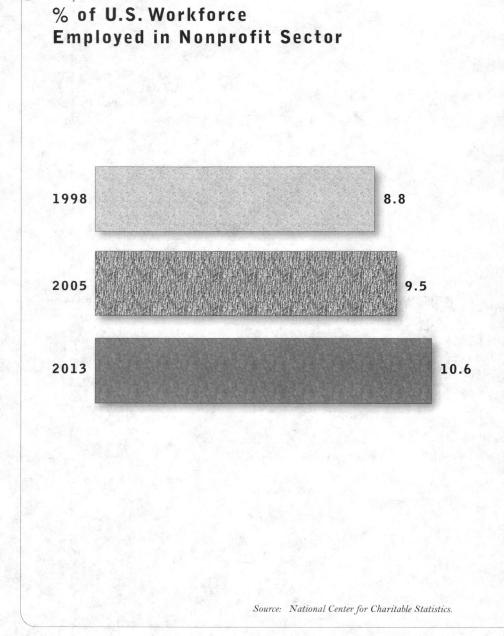

Graph 5:

% of U.S. Workforce
Employed in Nonprofit Sector

1998   8.8

2005   9.5

2013   10.6

Source: National Center for Charitable Statistics.

Nonprofits have grown faster than government and faster than the business sector over the last generation, even during boom periods.

The figures charted here actually underestimate the fraction of American manpower that goes into charitable work—because they show only paid employment, while volunteers carry out a large share of the labor poured into these groups. Various calculations of the cash value of donated labor suggest that at least an additional 50 percent of output by charities takes place invisibly because it is produced by volunteers. You'll find more statistics on American volunteering in Graphs 8 and 9.

Graph 6:

Output of Nonprofit Sector

as % of U.S. GDP

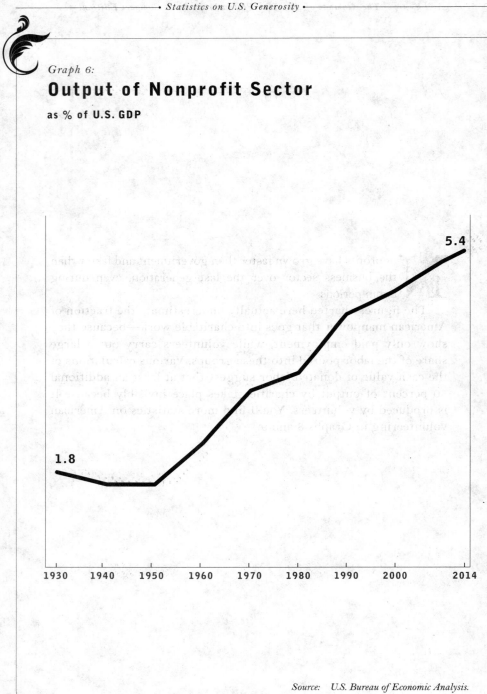

5.4

1.8

1930   1940   1950   1960   1970   1980   1990   2000   2014

Source: U.S. Bureau of Economic Analysis.

Charitable activity is becoming a bigger and bigger part of America's total economy. For perspective, consider that annual U.S. defense spending totals 4.5 percent of GDP. The nonprofit sector surpassed the vaunted "military-industrial complex" in economic scope way back in 1993.

Our charitable world is actually even bigger than this graph indicates, because its output is underestimated in several ways. The official annual statistics ignore the fact that about a third of the charitable workforce is unpaid (volunteers), and therefore invisible to the tabulators of economic activity. Also, the unusual definition of the nonprofit sector that is employed by the U.S. Bureau of Economic Analysis results in many charities that are officially registered with the IRS getting their annual output counted as part of the business sector, rather than as charitable activity.

Nonetheless, even the partial measure graphed here makes clear that philanthropic work has become a big part of our national output.

Graph 7:

Sources of Revenue of Public Charities

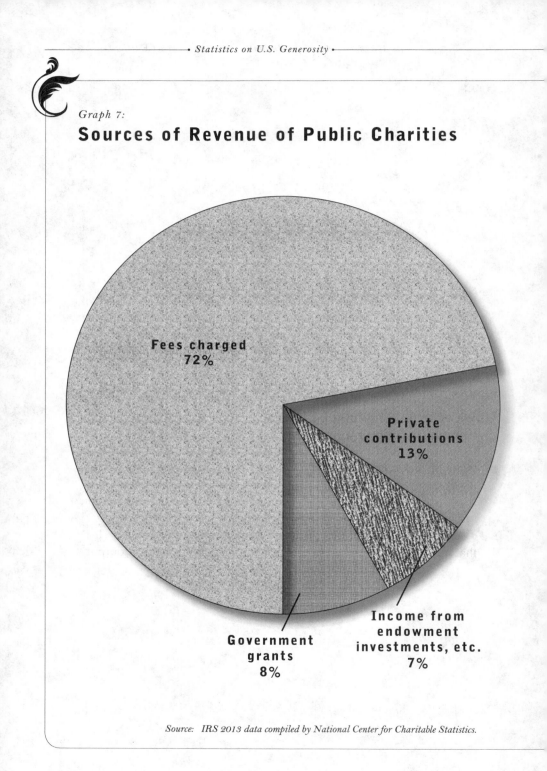

Fees charged
72%

Private
contributions
13%

Government
grants
8%

Income from
endowment
investments, etc.
7%

Source: *IRS 2013 data compiled by National Center for Charitable Statistics.*

The underappreciated fact illustrated starkly here is that many charities sell things—from used clothes to admission tickets to college educations—and rely heavily on those market revenues to keep their doors open. You can see that government grants are not a large portion of the income of U.S. public charities as a whole—annual donations plus income from invested gifts are twice as big. Of course there are also substantial government fees paid to charities as reimbursements through programs like Medicare and Medicaid. Within the "Fees charged" slice of this pie, a little more than two thirds of the money collected was private, but close to a third came from some level of government that was paying for a charitable service rendered.

Graph 8:

Volunteering in the U.S

annual number of volunteers	**63 million individuals**
% of population volunteering	**25 percent of all adults**
average time given by volunteers	**139 hours per year**
total time volunteered in the U.S.	**8.7 billion hours**

Source: U.S. Bureau of Labor Statistics, 2014 data.

This data comes from detailed time logs that statisticians ask householders to keep. In less strict definitions like phone surveys, more like 45 percent of the U.S. population say they volunteered some time to a charitable cause within the last year.

Current estimates of the dollar value of volunteered time range from $179 billion per year to more than twice that, depending on how you count.

Volunteering is closely associated with donating cash as well. One Harris study showed that Americans who volunteered gave 11 times as much money to charity in a year as those who did not volunteer.

Graph 9:

Demographics of Voluntarism

% of various groups volunteering

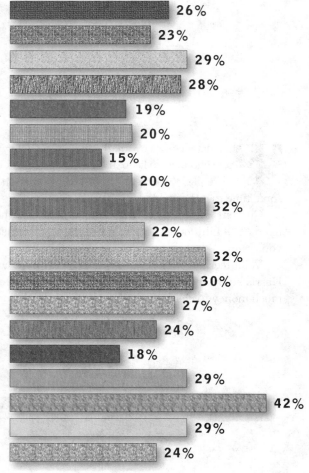

Group	%
Total U.S.	26%
Male	23%
Female	29%
White	28%
Black	19%
Asian	20%
Latino	15%
Single	20%
Married	32%
25-34	22%
35-44	32%
45-54	30%
55-64	27%
65+	24%
HS Grad	18%
Some College	29%
College Grad	42%
Employed	29%
Unemployed	24%

Source: U.S. Department of Labor, 2010 data.

All patterns courtesy of GraphicsFuel.com

Volunteering takes place at very different levels among different segments of the population. Women volunteer more than men, whites more than blacks or Latinos, married persons much more than singles. Younger and older people lag well behind 35- to 55-year-olds. The more educated are vastly likelier to give of their time. And unemployed persons don't use their extra hours to volunteer—they actually do less than those who are also holding down jobs.

Graph 10:

Proportion of Households
that Donate to Charity in a Given Year

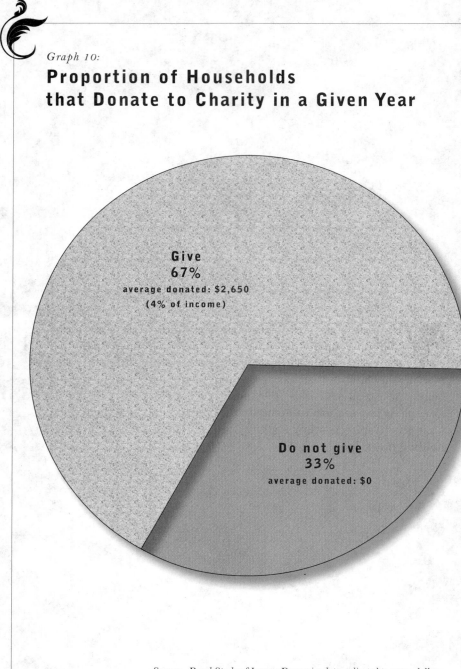

Give
67%
average donated: $2,650
(4% of income)

Do not give
33%
average donated: $0

Source: Panel Study of Income Dynamics data, adjusted to 2014 dollars.

haritability is not evenly distributed. The two thirds of households who give money actually average a hefty 4 percent of their income in gift-making. It is the other third of the population giving nothing who pull down the national average.

Graph 11:

Percentage of Households Giving to Charity By Annual Income

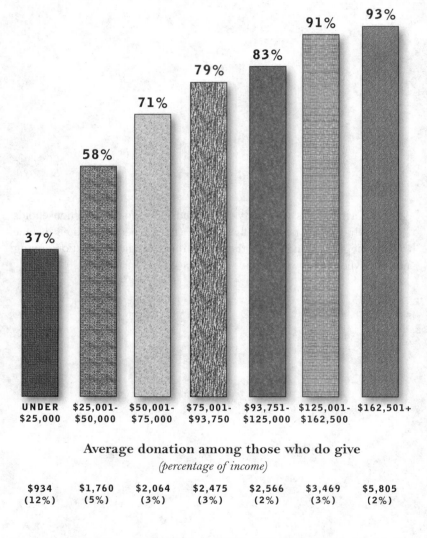

| UNDER $25,000 | $25,001-$50,000 | $50,001-$75,000 | $75,001-$93,750 | $93,751-$125,000 | $125,001-$162,500 | $162,501+ |

Average donation among those who do give
(percentage of income)

| $934 (12%) | $1,760 (5%) | $2,064 (3%) | $2,475 (3%) | $2,566 (2%) | $3,469 (3%) | $5,805 (2%) |

Source: Panel Study of Income Dynamics data, in "The Market for Charitable Giving" by John List, Journal of Economic Perspectives. *Editor's adjustment to 2014 dollars.*

An interesting pattern emerges if one studies giving by income level. As incomes rise, more and more of the people in that bracket make gifts to charity. The sizes of their gifts tend to rise as well. However: if you look at average donations as a fraction of funds available, they tend to level off at around 2-3 percent of income.

The exception to this pattern comes at the bottom of the income spectrum. Low-income households are the only ones in America where a majority do not give money to charity. Among the minority of poor who *do* give, however, a significant number are sacrificial donors—sharing double-digit portions of their incomes.

These sacrificial givers generally fall into two categories. Lots are religious, who tithe or otherwise give generously even when they have modest means. Others are elderly persons who have modest annual earnings yet are able to give because they have savings or paid-for homes and other assets that incline them to generosity.

Graph 12:

Influence of Marriage and Education
on Likelihood of Charitable Giving

all other demographic variables held constant

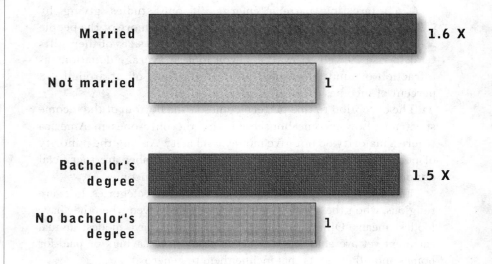

Married — 1.6 X

Not married — 1

Bachelor's degree — 1.5 X

No bachelor's degree — 1

Source: 2012 regression analysis done by Giving USA.

Just as with volunteering (Graph 9), certain factors have a strong influence on willingness to make donations. Religion (see next graph), marriage, and education are foremost among the factors that incline people to generosity. For this graph, all other variables like income, age, race, geography, and so forth were held constant. After those adjustments, it could be seen that married people give to charity at *1.6 times* the rate of counterparts who are identical in every other way except that they are unmarried. Likewise, people who have completed college are *1.5 times* as likely to give compared to an otherwise equivalent person without that education.

Graph 13:

Religion and Charitable Giving

all other demographic variables held constant

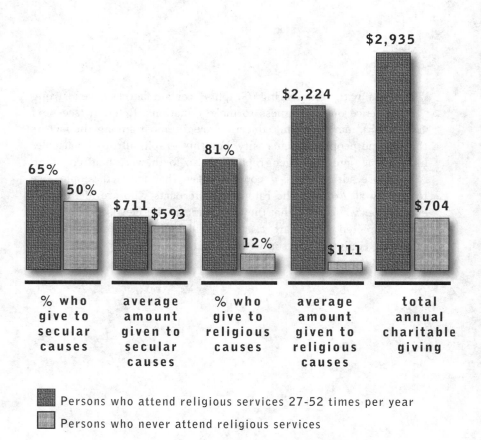

$2,935

$2,224

81%

65%

50%

$711 $593

12%

$111

$704

| % who give to secular causes | average amount given to secular causes | % who give to religious causes | average amount given to religious causes | total annual charitable giving |

■ Persons who attend religious services 27-52 times per year
■ Persons who never attend religious services

*Source: Panel Study of Income Dynamics data analyzed by
the Center on Wealth and Philanthropy. Adjusted to 2014 dollars by the editor.*

Religious faith is a central influence on giving. Religious people are much more likely than the non-religious to donate to charitable causes—including secular causes—and they give much more.

This chart holds all other demographic variables like income, race, education, etc. constant, so that when religious and non-religious counterparts are compared they are true peers in every other way. And the results show that persons who attend religious services twice a month or more give over four times as much as persons who never attend services.

We know the religious are also far more likely to volunteer. Among Americans who have volunteered within the last year, three quarters belong to a religious organization, one quarter do not.

Graph 14:

Heavy vs. Light Charitable Giving by Party Registration

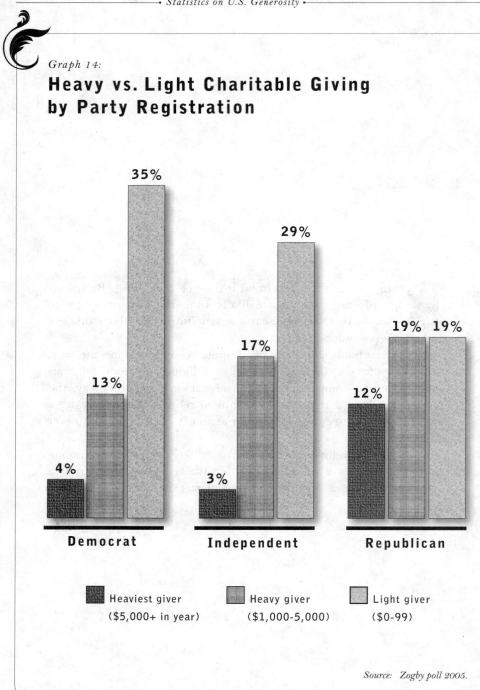

| | Heaviest giver ($5,000+ in year) | Heavy giver ($1,000-5,000) | Light giver ($0-99) |

Source: Zogby poll 2005.

Among Democrats, Independents, and Republicans alike, almost exactly half of the group averaged $100-$999 in annual charitable donations at the time of this 2005 poll. There was virtually no difference among the parties in the size of that moderate-giving group, so those results were not included in the graph to the left.

If, however, you zero in on giving that is heavier or lighter than the middle range (the bars pictured here), you find that the parties differ a lot. Democrats and Independents both had many zero-to-very-light givers to charity (less than $100 for the year), and modest numbers of heavier givers. Republicans, in comparison, had comparatively few skinflints, and numerous serious donors—31 percent sharing at least $1,000 with charity, versus 17 percent among Democrats, and 20 percent among Independents.

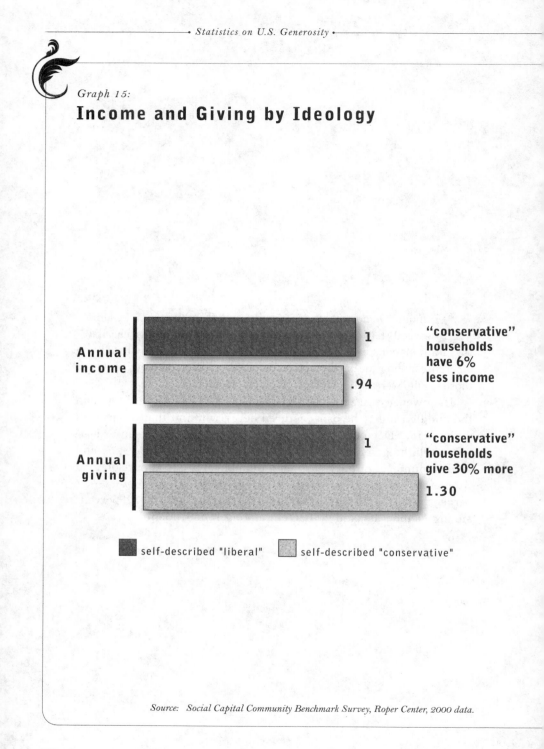

Graph 15:

Income and Giving by Ideology

Annual income

1

.94

"conservative" households have 6% less income

Annual giving

1

1.30

"conservative" households give 30% more

■ self-described "liberal" ☐ self-described "conservative"

Source: Social Capital Community Benchmark Survey, Roper Center, 2000 data.

As individual donors, conservatives are hearty givers—as made clear in this graph, the one previous, and many other data sets.

When it comes to running foundations, though, liberals tend to control the reins. Matched analyses of the major American foundations reported in the book *The New Leviathan* found 82 foundations whose staff took a clear conservative orientation in their giving, and 122 foundations whose staff operated with a clear liberal orientation. The conservative-controlled foundations had assets of $10 billion in 2010, from which they gave away $832 million annually. That same year, the liberal-controlled foundations had assets of $105 billion (more than ten times their conservative counterparts), and gave away $8.8 billion annually (11 times as much as conservative counterparts).

Many foundations end up espousing the priorities and orientations of their staff rather than the principles of the donor behind the foundation. As this has become more widely understood, some new foundations have made efforts to protect "donor intent" and be sure that funds are expended on causes compatible with the founder's views. There has also been a sharp jump of interest in "sunset" foundations—which spend all their money relatively close to the donor's lifetime, rather than existing in perpetuity, where capture by staff becomes almost inevitable. See the text accompanying Graph 18 for more details on sunsetting.

Graph 16:

Generosity of States

giving as % of adjusted gross income

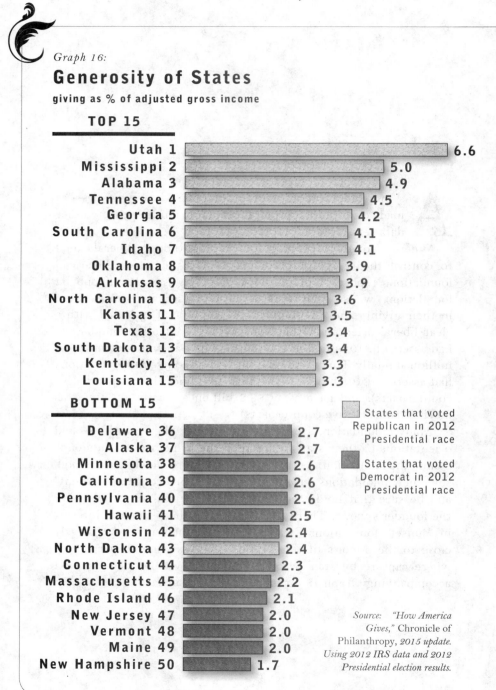

TOP 15

Utah 1	6.6
Mississippi 2	5.0
Alabama 3	4.9
Tennessee 4	4.5
Georgia 5	4.2
South Carolina 6	4.1
Idaho 7	4.1
Oklahoma 8	3.9
Arkansas 9	3.9
North Carolina 10	3.6
Kansas 11	3.5
Texas 12	3.4
South Dakota 13	3.4
Kentucky 14	3.3
Louisiana 15	3.3

BOTTOM 15

Delaware 36	2.7
Alaska 37	2.7
Minnesota 38	2.6
California 39	2.6
Pennsylvania 40	2.6
Hawaii 41	2.5
Wisconsin 42	2.4
North Dakota 43	2.4
Connecticut 44	2.3
Massachusetts 45	2.2
Rhode Island 46	2.1
New Jersey 47	2.0
Vermont 48	2.0
Maine 49	2.0
New Hampshire 50	1.7

States that voted Republican in 2012 Presidential race

States that voted Democrat in 2012 Presidential race

Source: *"How America Gives,"* Chronicle of Philanthropy, *2015 update. Using 2012 IRS data and 2012 Presidential election results.*

For the analysis graphed here, the *Chronicle of Philanthropy* analyzed official IRS data on income and giving, right down to the county level. The results showed that rural states, and specifically the Bible Belt and Mormon West, give more of themselves for charity. Other ways of measuring, carried out by different groups using alternate statistical sources, have shown essentially the same pattern. Though it comes as a surprise to some observers, it is not Americans in the high-income, urban, liberal states like Massachusetts or California who are our most generous citizens. Rather it is residents of middle-American, conservative, moderate-income, religiously active regions who step up the most.

Several observers have pointed out the political twist to this reality. When it reported its findings, the *Chronicle of Philanthropy* noted that the states that rank highest in charitable giving all voted Republican in the 2012 Presidential election, while all but a couple of the least generous states voted for the Democrat (that's what the color coding to the left reflects). Economist Arthur Brooks, author of the detailed charity analysis *Who Really Cares*, likewise states that "the electoral map and the charity map are remarkably similar." He notes "there is a persistent sterotype about charitable giving in politically progressive regions of America: while people on the political right may be hardworking and family-oriented, they tend not to be very charitable toward the less fortunate," while, "those on the political left care about vulnerable members of society, and are thus the charitable ones.... This stereotype is wrong."

Brooks points out that these differences go beyond just what households donate in money. He cites studies showing that conservatives are more likely to do things like donate blood, and to volunteer. Much of this difference he credits to the comparative religiosity of conservatives. The fact that liberals call for government to help others while conservatives feel called to help directly also seems to factor into differences in behavior.

Graph 17:

Generosity of Cities

giving as % of adjusted gross income

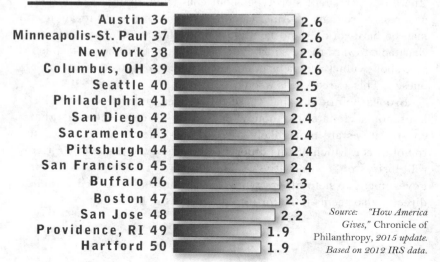

TOP 15

Salt Lake City 1	5.5
Memphis 2	5.1
Birmingham, AL 3	4.8
Atlanta 4	4.0
Nashville 5	3.9
Jacksonville, FL 6	3.8
Oklahoma City 7	3.7
Dallas-Ft. Worth 8	3.6
Charlotte 9	3.4
Virginia Beach 10	3.3
Houston 11	3.2
Indianapolis 12	3.2
Louisville 13	3.2
San Antonio 14	3.1
Orlando 15	3.1

BOTTOM 15

Austin 36	2.6
Minneapolis-St. Paul 37	2.6
New York 38	2.6
Columbus, OH 39	2.6
Seattle 40	2.5
Philadelphia 41	2.5
San Diego 42	2.4
Sacramento 43	2.4
Pittsburgh 44	2.4
San Francisco 45	2.4
Buffalo 46	2.3
Boston 47	2.3
San Jose 48	2.2
Providence, RI 49	1.9
Hartford 50	1.9

Source: "How America Gives," Chronicle of Philanthropy, 2015 update. Based on 2012 IRS data.

A pattern similar to what the previous graph showed for states is also clearly visible in this data on giving levels in America's 50 biggest cities. It is residents of our Mormon and southern Bible Belt metro areas who are our most generous citizens. Meanwhile, many of our very wealthiest urban areas—like San Francisco and Boston—rank low on generosity.

Note here the interesting divergence between Dallas and Austin. Those two cities, just 180 miles apart, share the same economic climate, exact same levels of state taxation, same basic cost of living. Where they differ rather sharply is in culture. The fact that Dallasites give almost 40 percent more to charity than Austinites underlines the powerful influence on charitable behavior exerted by factors like religious practice and political ideology.

Graph 18:

Foundation Numbers and Giving

1975-2013

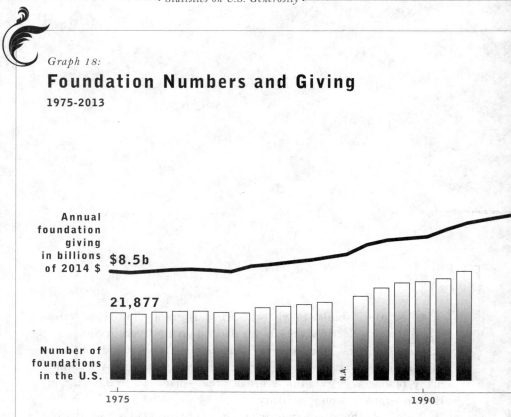

Annual foundation giving in billions of 2014 $

$8.5b

21,877

Number of foundations in the U.S.

N.A.

1975

1990

The number of private foundations, and the heft of their endowments and annual giving, have soared over the last generation.

Americans are generally happy with the growing activity of foundations in solving problems—a 2009 poll asked community leaders who have had professional contact with the charitable sector whether they thought foundations have too much, too little, or the right amount of influence on issues in their community; 51 percent answered "too little," 42 percent said "the right amount," and just 7 percent said "too much." Our own survey research in 2015 found the public inclined to give foundations and the rest of the philanthropic sector wide latitude to operate free of government regulation or interference; see Question 9 in our section "Results of an Original 2015 National Poll" in the full-length *Almanac*.

At the same time, Americans don't place foundations at the heart of our philanthropic efforts. They view small gifts from millions of

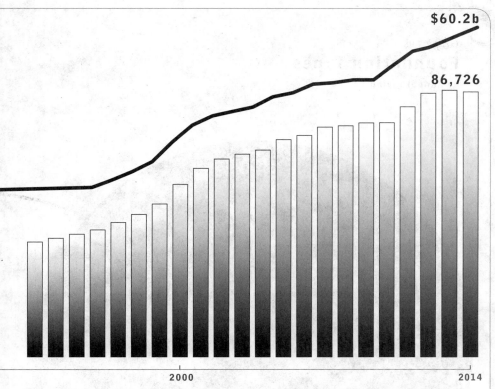

$60.2b

86,726

2000   2014

Source: Foundation Center; editor's adjustment into constant 2014 dollars.

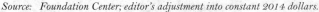

everyday donors as far more important than the big initiatives of foundations (Question 15 in our national poll). And as a factual matter they are entirely right, as Graph 3 in this section shows.

There is, however, a considerable knowledge gap when it comes to the details of how foundations operate. Only about one American out of ten, and half of community leaders, can name an extant foundation when asked by pollsters.

One interesting trend in the growth of foundations is for donors to set them up so that they spend themselves out of existence within a generation, rather than letting them exist in perpetuity. In 2010, a quarter of the assets in America's 50 largest foundations were in trusts that will sunset—compared to only 5 percent 50 years ago. Spending down allows a foundation to have a larger, quicker effect than trickling out funds indefinitely. And it reduces the likelihood of the organization drifting into purposes not approved by the donor (a problem discussed at Graph 15).

Graph 19:

Foundation Types

by annual giving

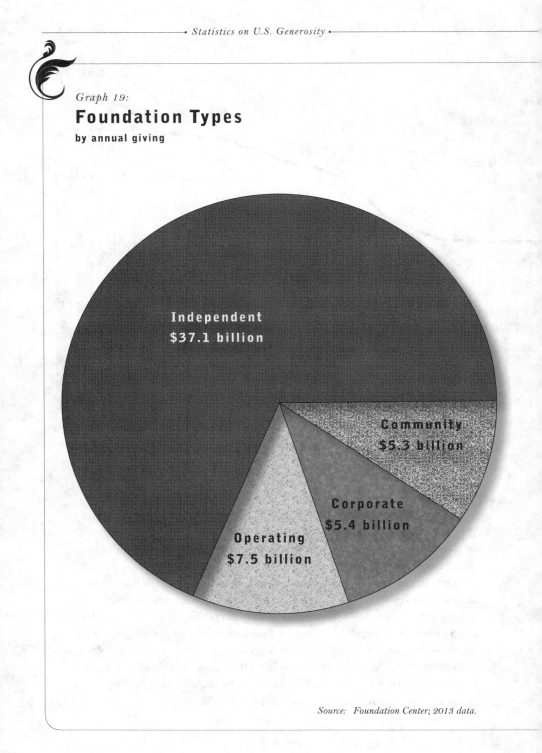

Source: Foundation Center; 2013 data.

Traditional independent foundations are by far the largest institutional givers. Community foundations pool donations from many donors within a region; there are more than 780 sprinkled across the country. Corporate foundations are a long-time presence in U.S. philanthropy. Operating foundations are a special subset that spend most of their money running their own programs, rather than disbursing funds to other charitable operators. Leading examples of some of these foundations are presented in the three graphs following.

Graph 20:

Top 50 Independent Foundations
by 2013 giving

Bill & Melinda Gates Foundation	$3,320,725,374
Ford Foundation	$560,335,883
Susan Thompson Buffett Foundation	$450,319,788
Foundation to Promote Open Society	$380,512,799
Robert Wood Johnson Foundation	$337,561,658
Walton Family Foundation	$311,719,212
David and Lucile Packard Foundation	$295,015,267
W. K. Kellogg Foundation	$294,891,874
Gordon and Betty Moore Foundation	$272,332,512
Lilly Endowment	$270,300,000
William and Flora Hewlett Foundation	$240,100,000
Andrew W. Mellon Foundation	$234,372,144
John and Catherine MacArthur Foundation	$218,542,721
Leona and Harry Helmsley Charitable Trust	$210,352,475
Bloomberg Philanthropies	$204,007,709
California Endowment	$182,809,047
Simons Foundation	$179,640,382
Robert W. Woodruff Foundation	$155,816,887
Rockefeller Foundation	$137,817,790
Carnegie Corporation of New York	$130,380,545
Kresge Foundation	$130,183,827
Duke Endowment	$127,729,045
Charles Stewart Mott Foundation	$114,442,289
Eli & Edythe Broad Foundation	$111,692,581

Source: Foundation Center.

John and James L. Knight Foundation	$107,825,135
John Templeton Foundation	$105,248,596
Howard G. Buffett Foundation	$103,284,879
Sherwood Foundation	$101,964,342
Jerome L. Greene Foundation	$100,947,352
Robertson Foundation	$99,597,042
Richard King Mellon Foundation	$99,152,041
Annie E. Casey Foundation	$98,681,016
Harry and Jeanette Weinberg Foundation	$96,929,767
Conrad N. Hilton Foundation	$92,000,000
McKnight Foundation	$86,598,229
Starr Foundation	$83,168,245
Edward C. Johnson Fund	$82,350,200
Alfred P. Sloan Foundation	$82,091,585
Laura and John Arnold Foundation	$80,519,024
William Penn Foundation	$80,099,460
JPB Foundation	$78,051,333
Doris Duke Charitable Foundation	$75,080,723
Brown Foundation	$74,487,624
Druckenmiller Foundation	$74,469,500
Michael and Susan Dell Foundation	$72,785,040
Annenberg Foundation	$70,030,812
James Irvine Foundation	$69,000,000
Houston Endowment	$64,484,305
Schusterman Family Foundation	$64,025,508
Wallace Foundation	$61,462,148

Graph 21:

Top 50 Community Foundations
by 2013 giving

Silicon Valley Community Foundation	$362,390,000
Greater Kansas City Community Foundation	$234,274,371
Foundation for the Carolinas	$180,272,727
California Community Foundation	$164,428,000
Chicago Community Trust	$150,313,429
New York Community Trust	$144,241,100
Community Foundation for Greater Atlanta	$134,633,871
Tulsa Community Foundation	$110,512,000
Boston Foundation	$105,365,000
Greater Houston Community Foundation	$98,934,435
Columbus Foundation	$95,963,350
Community Foundation for the National Capital Region	$95,397,756
San Francisco Foundation	$86,830,000
Communities Foundation of Texas	$82,493,000
Cleveland Foundation	$81,368,990
Omaha Community Foundation	$75,638,463
Greater Cincinnati Foundation	$69,133,479
Oregon Community Foundation	$66,052,201
Seattle Foundation	$65,653,979
Denver Foundation	$64,306,537
Marin Community Foundation	$62,536,631
Community Foundation of Greater Memphis	$58,341,057
Saint Paul Foundation	$54,752,338
Minneapolis Foundation	$52,591,314

Source: Foundation Center.

Community Foundation for Southeast Michigan	$52,560,486
San Diego Foundation	$50,669,000
Orange County Community Foundation	$46,816,000
Community Foundation of Middle Tennessee	$46,607,415
Pittsburgh Foundation	$42,569,107
Community First Foundation	$40,864,094
Arizona Community Foundation	$38,633,992
East Bay Community Foundation	$38,521,288
Central Indiana Community Foundation	$35,371,279
Baton Rouge Area Foundation	$35,351,731
Greater St. Louis Community Foundation	$33,338,981
Dallas Foundation	$33,204,208
Community Foundation Serving Richmond	$32,429,867
New Hampshire Charitable Foundation	$31,818,211
Community Foundation for NE Florida	$30,647,352
Greater Milwaukee Foundation	$30,050,000
Hartford Foundation for Public Giving	$29,828,016
Community Foundation of New Jersey	$28,395,393
Community Foundation of Louisville	$28,285,522
Rhode Island Foundation	$28,267,948
Delaware Community Foundation	$28,100,711
Hawaii Community Foundation	$27,361,979
Oklahoma City Community Foundation	$25,867,694
Community Foundation of Greater Des Moines	$25,228,667
Philadelphia Foundation	$24,679,393
Community Foundation for Greater New Haven	$23,670,346

Graph 22:

Top 50 Corporate Foundations

by 2013 giving

Bristol-Myers Squibb Patient Foundation	$811,433,684
Abbvie Patient Foundation	$783,366,952
Lilly Cares Foundation	$697,004,928
Merck Patient Program	$686,800,564
Genentech Access to Care Foundation	$680,278,040
Johnson & Johnson Patient Foundation	$611,680,261
GlaxoSmithKline Patient Foundation	$599,953,667
Pfizer Patient Foundation	$515,726,553
Novartis Patient Foundation	$452,745,445
Sanofi Foundation for North America	$284,044,399
Wells Fargo Foundation	$186,775,875
Walmart Foundation	$182,859,236
Boehringer Ingelheim Foundation	$179,977,010
Bank of America Charitable Foundation	$175,299,789
GE Foundation	$124,512,065
JPMorgan Chase Foundation	$115,516,001
Genzyme Charitable Foundation	$78,603,357
Citi Foundation	$78,372,150
ExxonMobil Foundation	$72,747,966
Coca-Cola Foundation	$69,658,157
Caterpillar Foundation	$55,998,836
Teva Cares Foundation	$49,164,295
PNC Foundation	$48,269,009
Johnson & Johnson Cos. Foundation	$46,445,669

Source: Foundation Center.
Note: Includes operating foundations run by pharmaceutical companies.

Intel Foundation	$45,318,315
Freddie Mac Foundation	$44,822,806
Verizon Foundation	$43,374,615
UPS Foundation	$42,895,860
MetLife Foundation	$42,488,850
Merck Company Foundation	$41,823,400
Google Foundation	$39,606,000
Goldman Sachs Foundation	$36,658,124
Bayer U.S. Patient Foundation	$34,927,912
PepsiCo Foundation	$31,730,571
Harold Simmons Foundation	$31,398,545
Bristol-Myers Squibb Foundation	$31,251,274
Blue Shield of California Foundation	$31,167,629
Newman's Own Foundation	$30,000,000
Emerson Charitable Trust	$29,059,957
General Motors Foundation	$27,627,768
General Mills Foundation	$26,898,325
Prudential Foundation	$26,859,858
Eli Lilly & Co. Foundation	$26,199,135
Valero Energy Foundation	$26,073,777
Duke Energy Foundation	$26,051,888
Nationwide Insurance Foundation	$25,558,922
Medtronic Foundation	$24,108,117
U.S. Bancorp Foundation	$23,292,965
Reckitt Benckiser Patient Foundation	$22,288,109
Ford Motor Company Fund	$21,970,680

Graph 23:

Donor-Advised Fund Growth

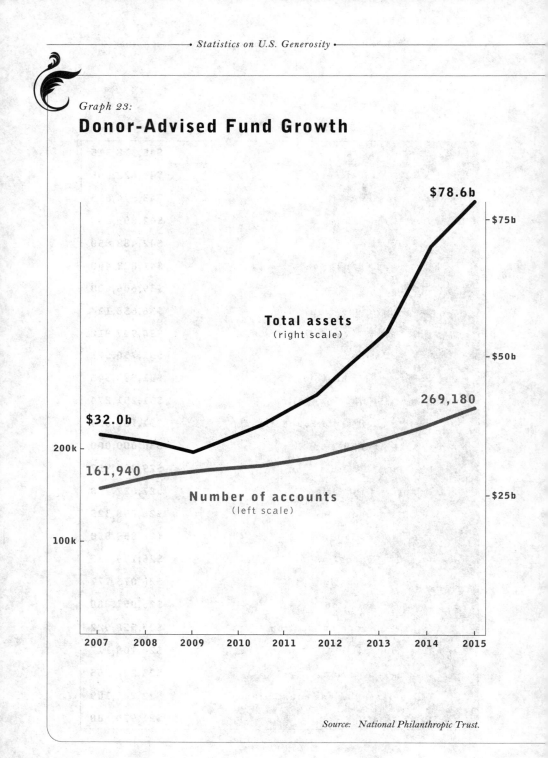

$78.6b

$75b

Total assets
(right scale)

$50b

269,180

$32.0b

200k

161,940

Number of accounts
(left scale)

$25b

100k

2007   2008   2009   2010   2011   2012   2013   2014   2015

Source: National Philanthropic Trust.

oday's very fastest-growing instrument for giving money to charitable causes is the donor-advised fund. DAFs provide givers a much simpler alternative to setting up a private foundation. Donor-advised funds now outnumber private foundations by more than two to one, and in 2015 they funneled close to $15 billion to charities favored by their contributors. DAFs are both efficient and effective: the average fund now pays out in annual charitable grants a full 21 percent of the assets contained in the fund. That's three or four times the rate at which typical foundations pay out.

Graph 24:

Top Ten Donor-Advised Funds

Today's ten largest sponsors, by assets	Type of sponsor
Fidelity Charitable Gift Fund	commercial
Schwab Charitable Fund	commercial
Vanguard Charitable Endowment Fund	commercial
National Christian Foundation	affinity
Silicon Valley Community Foundation	community
National Philanthropic Trust	affinity
Jewish Communal Fund	affinity
Greater Kansas City Community Foundation	community
New York Community Trust	community
Goldman Sachs Philanthropy Fund	commercial

Source: Chronicle of Philanthropy *2013 data; 2016 Giving Report, Fidelity Charitable.*

There are many sponsors of donor-advised funds. Most community foundations around the country offer them. So do various affinity groups like the National Christian Foundation and the many local Jewish giving federations. Today's fastest-growing sponsors of DAFs are commercial investment companies. They have made it exceptionally convenient for Americans to put away money for charity, keep it growing healthily while specific recipients are being planned, and then dispatch the donations efficiently with a few clicks of a mouse. The hundreds of thousands of individuals who have established accounts at Fidelity Charitable had granted $21 billion to charities as of 2015, with the total rising fast.

Graph 25:

Private Donations for Overseas Aid

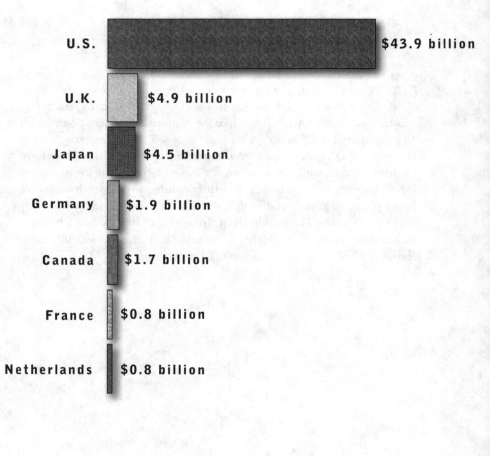

U.S.	$43.9 billion
U.K.	$4.9 billion
Japan	$4.5 billion
Germany	$1.9 billion
Canada	$1.7 billion
France	$0.8 billion
Netherlands	$0.8 billion

Source: Estimates by Center for Global Prosperity, Hudson Institute, 2014 data.

Americans are much more willing than other peoples to voluntarily donate money to help the poor and stricken in foreign lands. The figures here depict private charitable giving in various forms.

Of course there are other ways that a nation can give to less developed countries in addition to private philanthropy—official government aid, remittances to families back home by immigrants, private business investment, etc. See Graph 26 and its text for more on this subject. When you add up all of these sources of aid, the U.S. comes out far ahead of any other nation, sending $365 billion overseas annually to developing countries.

Graph 26:

U.S. Overseas Assistance

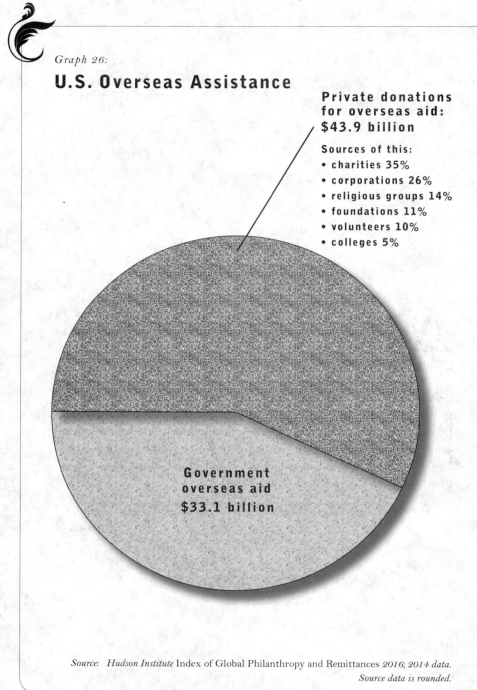

Private donations for overseas aid: $43.9 billion

Sources of this:
- charities 35%
- corporations 26%
- religious groups 14%
- foundations 11%
- volunteers 10%
- colleges 5%

Government overseas aid $33.1 billion

Source: Hudson Institute Index of Global Philanthropy and Remittances *2016; 2014 data.*

Source data is rounded.

Few people realize that private giving is now a much bigger part of how Americans aid the poor in foreign lands than official government aid. The $44 billion of annual aid depicted here comes from a variety of sources: private charities, religious groups, corporate giving, foundations, volunteers, etc.

Another very large source of economic assistance to the overseas poor, which we have chosen not to depict here but which has been painstakingly estimated in the Hudson Institute report from which this data is taken, is remittances sent back home by U.S. immigrants from poor lands. These amount to over a hundred billion dollars every year, and are more important to family welfare, health, and education in many underdeveloped countries than either private or governmental charity.

Anyone trying to understand the financial flows that aid the poor overseas must also consider one final element: private investment in developing countries. More than $179 billion of U.S. capital was committed to projects in poor nations in 2014, with for-profit aspirations. This job- and growth-creating money is probably the most important form of all of international sharing.

Graph 27:

Giving Levels by Country

individual giving only (bequests, foundation gifts, corporate donations excluded) as a % of GDP

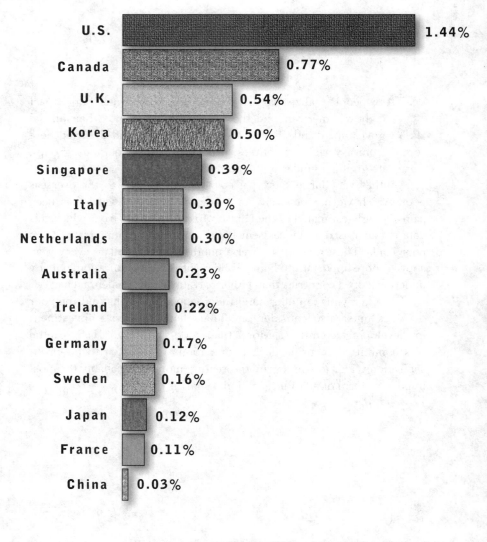

U.S.	1.44%
Canada	0.77%
U.K.	0.54%
Korea	0.50%
Singapore	0.39%
Italy	0.30%
Netherlands	0.30%
Australia	0.23%
Ireland	0.22%
Germany	0.17%
Sweden	0.16%
Japan	0.12%
France	0.11%
China	0.03%

Source: Charities Aid Foundation, data for 2011-2014.

A number of studies have been undertaken to compare the charitable giving of various countries in fair ways—adjusting for differences in standards of living, population, and so forth. All end up showing about the same relationship that is charted here: Americans are about twice as generous in our private giving as our kissing cousins the Canadians, and 3-15 *times* as charitable as the residents of other developed nations. Americans also volunteer more than almost any other wealthy people.

TIMELINE
of
AMERICAN
PHILANTHROPY
1636–2017

This timeline cumulates about a thousand significant philanthropic events that have taken place in the U.S. through the course of our history. It starts more than a century before the country's birth and runs up to 2017. Laying donor achievements next to each other in this way allows readers to see how activities in different fields add up and overlap. For added perspective, some significant moments in national affairs are sprinkled (in gray type) throughout the philanthropic milestones.

Events are listed by year and sector, and very briefly described. If you'd like to see a fuller summary of any of these accomplishments, just go to the lists of Major Philanthropic Achievements in the full-length version of *The Almanac of American Philanthropy*, look up the relevant sector and year, and you'll find additional detail. Or refer to our Hall of Fame profiles if the entry is about a great donor.

с— with assistance from Jarom McDonald

Medicine	2017	Major bonus for microbiomes
Arts	2017	Performance space in a brand-new NYC neighborhood
Prosperity	2017	Budding field of data science gets a philanthropic angel
Nature	2017	Taking fountains to dramatic new heights
Prosperity	2017	Protecting fairness in international sports
Medicine	2017	An engineer repays an old debt to charitable medical care
Education	2017	New professional schools on a rising SoCal campus
Education	2017	Meeting unmet appetites for computer science
Prosperity	2017	Funding student travel, interning, and research
Medicine	2016	A giant bet on using the immune system to fight cancer
Arts	2016	Marvelous museum is expanded by record-fast fundraising
Prosperity	2016	Opening a fossil park to the public and researchers
Overseas	2016	Israel's youngest university gets an American endowment
Arts	2016	A Smithsonian museum flourishes via private support
Prosperity	2016	Foundations and individuals join forces to help children
Education	2016	Expanding the best charter-school network in New York
Local	2016	A grateful patient creates an eye clinic to serve thousands
Medicine	2016	Creating a collaboration to boost biomedicine in NYC
Education	2016	Science education for kids, outside of school
Policy	2016	A nonprofit model for big-city newspapers
Education	2016	Rethinking school structures across a city
Religion	2016	Improving journalism on religion and the arts
Local	2016	Big bioscience boost to Indianapolis
Local	2016	Bringing dental health to a desert
Education	2016	Antonin Scalia School of Law
Education	2017	Public colleges now rely on lots of private gifts
Education	2017	More music-making at Notre Dame
Local	2017	Helping those left behind by the tech boom
Medicine	2017	Healing military brain injuries outside the V.A. bureaucracy
Religion	2017	Muslim donors fund a Catholic university
Prosperity	2017	Battling back against bad science
Arts	2017	Popular storytelling art gets a museum of its own
Medicine	2017	Bezos money for cancer research in Seattle
Medicine	2017	Mega medical gift in San Francisco is unrestricted
Religion	2016	Museum of the Bible opens in D.C.
Prosperity	2016	Pushing science discoveries into real-world improvements
Education	2016	Walton family recommits as a leader on charter schools
Medicine	2016	Two arrows aimed at difficult diseases
Medicine	2016	Supporting bio-med research with a high chance of failure
Arts	2016	A live performance hall for a once-dead place
Policy	2016	Protecting children where government didn't
Medicine	2016	Building a nationwide network for the mental health of veterans
Medicine	2016	Adding space after the Cleveland Clinic maxes out its eye care
Religion	2016	Record gift to Jewish education for college students
Prosperity	2016	Putting up resources to encourage smart science gambles
Prosperity	2016	A social-worker's gift to social work
Local	2016	One of our fastest-growing cities needed a park—and got it
Nature	2016	Separating bikers and walkers for safe recreation
Arts	2016	An art-glass specialty for Pacific Northwest museum
Education	2016	Encouraging engineering among minority students

2016	A doctor endows his medical school	Local
2015	From science fiction to reality via regenerative medicine	Medicine
2015	Homebuilder honors home state with an honors college	Local
2015	Making jailing more efficient and fair	Prosperity
2015	Roberta Buffett Elliott boosts global studies	Overseas
2015	Fostering independence for injured veterans	Policy
2015	Recycling abandoned homes	Local

History: 2015 U.S. population exceeds 321 million people

2015	Animal rehabilitation on a large scale	Nature
2015	Education held accountable by new journalism organization	Education
2015	Helping Harvard catch up in science and engineering	Prosperity
2015	Student leadership honed campuswide	Education
2015	A record for Catholic-school scholarships	Education
2014	$24 million to understand and cure allergies	Medicine
2014	Bringing Israeli spacecraft to the moon	Overseas
2014	Drug discovery as a path to economic growth	Prosperity
2014	Giving Impressionism a home in Denver	Arts
2014	Mark Zuckerberg elevates Silicon Valley philanthropy	Local
2014	Philanthropists move fast to stop Ebola's spread	Medicine
2014	Brewing up jobs for veterans	Prosperity
2014	Funding lawsuits to reform policies	Policy
2014	University of Chicago trains leaders	Policy
2014	Bloomberg backs gun control with $50 million	Policy
2014	Donors keep the lights on in Detroit	Policy

Policy	2016	Creating new tools for reviving and strengthening families
Arts	2015	Great book collection gifted to Princeton
Arts	2015	Houston Fine Arts Museum gets connected
Medicine	2015	Putting a $250M shine on NYC's hospital district
Local	2015	Tripling the size of San Antonio's community foundation
Education	2015	Doubling U. Wisconsin's endowed chairs
Medicine	2015	Cornell's biomedical engineering gap filled with $75 million gift
Overseas	2015	Gates Foundation doubles efforts to end childhood malnutrition
Policy	2015	Improving public understanding of Israel
Nature	2015	Public parks enjoy a golden age thanks to private donors
Medicine	2015	Creative approach to disease research pays off
Arts	2015	Art of Native America to Indiana
Overseas	2014	Art for Hong Kong
Arts	2014	Detroit's art heritage is saved from its debt fire
Education	2014	Engineering scholarships in Texas
Arts	2014	Half-billion gift for L.A. art museum
Nature	2014	New York's natural-history museum grants degrees
Overseas	2014	Preserving Jewish history in Tel Aviv and Venice
Education	2014	Rallying to the defense of NYC charter schools
Nature	2014	Tulsa gets the largest gift ever given for a public park
Nature	2014	A floating park on the Hudson
Prosperity	2014	Cell-science institute focused on the big picture
Policy	2014	eBay founder devotes $250 million to journalistic experiment

Category	Year	Description
Medicine		Gene-sequencing machines analyze tumors
Medicine		Johns Hopkins expands in cancer research
Arts		One more Mellon gift to the National Gallery
Medicine		Public health gets a shot in the arm
Local		Treasure trove of art for couple's hometown
Medicine		$500 million attack on cancer, times two
Overseas		Christian givers on the rise
Hall of Fame		Fisher family contributions to KIPP exceed $75M
Prosperity		Donors bring fighters to top colleges
Education		Teacher colleges rated, deficiencies revealed
Arts		Patriotic philanthropy expands Kennedy Center
Nature		Business-like conservation
Nature		Largest-ever cash gift to a national park
Arts		Notre Dame's classic architecture program
Education		The remarkable charter students of Boston
Education		Bay Area gets 25 "blended-learning" schools
Prosperity		Detecting asteroids that threaten Earth
Arts		History buff protects sacred battle sites
Education		Measuring U.S. schools against overseas counterparts
Local		A sad man makes his hometown happy
Medicine		Debt-free medical students
Local		A musical festival in the Finger Lakes
Arts		Creating a Revolutionary museum
Education		Giving students a break on textbook prices
Prosperity		Making fracking safe and efficient

2014	$35 million to help countries move toward freedom	Policy
2014	New Orleans school district goes all-charter	Education
2014	Polin Museum celebrates Jewish life	Religion
2014	Schwarzman Scholarships weave China to West	Overseas
2014	Turing Award promoted to major leagues of scientific prizes	Prosperity
2013	Boy Scout alums team up to create a haven for Scouts	Nature
2013	Johns Hopkins gets more than a billion from Bloomberg	Education
2013	New balance at the "Berkeley of the Rockies"	Policy
2013	Searle goes to the Supreme Court	Policy
2013	Urban green spaces out of thin air	Nature
2013	Aiding New York's forgotten boroughs	Local
2013	Graduate housing to encourage fresh thinking	Prosperity
2013	Met is gifted with a billion dollars	Arts
2013	Seeking biomarkers to make brain wounds visible	Medicine
2013	Regenerative medicine in San Diego	Medicine
2012	Clean water for millions of people	Overseas
2012	Gates pushes urban schools to cooperate	Local
2012	Kickstarter surpasses the NEA in arts funding	Arts
2012	Pay for performance in social reform	Prosperity
2012	Vets with technical skills linked to businesses that need them	Prosperity
2012	Number of charter schools funded by Walton reaches 1,500	Hall of Fame
2012	Building a park on a freeway	Nature
2012	Free university classes for anyone, anywhere	Education
2012	Improving the Smithsonian	Nature
2012	New deal creates a privately funded symphony hall in K.C.	Arts

Category	Year	Description
Medicine	2012	Throwing an encyclopedia at cancer
Education	2011	A major new tech hub in New York City
Local	2011	Doing disaster relief in smart ways
Local	2011	Local loans and business help linked to character
Arts	2011	Uncovering the secrets of an ancient prayer book
Overseas	2011	Bringing banking to the very poor
Policy	2011	Lessons in market economics and politics for students
Policy	2011	Rescuing states and cities from pension tsunamis
Education	2010	A big effort to fix Newark's dysfunctional schools
Education	2010	Challenging the K-12 status quo in support of students
Overseas	2010	Democracy training for developing-world leaders
Local	2010	Michigan's aeronautic high school
Overseas	2010	A technical fix to fight nuclear weaponization
Policy	2010	Climate change crusade
Policy	2010	Demonizing fracking
Overseas	2010	Radios slow warlord in suffering Africa
Nature	2009	Turning a bayou into an asset
Education	2009	Inner-city preschool experiment seeks key answers
Policy	2009	Putting budget reforms on Wisconsin's agenda
Prosperity	2009	Influential friends of community colleges give them a boost
Local	2009	Turning a whole city into a popular art gallery
Prosperity	2008	Deep support for business education
Religion	2008	Organizing Muslim giving

History: 2011 U.S. government credit rating lowered for the first time ever

Category	Year	Description
Local	2012	Wexner family strengthens Ohio State
Religion	2011	A premier collection of Biblical artifacts for the public
Arts	2011	Great art in middle America
Policy	2011	Repealing "don't ask, don't tell"
Medicine	2011	A medical empire built by philanthropy
Medicine	2011	First-ever malaria vaccine
Religion	2011	Modern Biblical art for the ages
Overseas	2011	Using collaboration to boost overseas giving
Prosperity	2011	Venture for America aims at 100,000 new jobs
Policy	2010	$27 million helps pass Obamacare
Overseas	2010	America sends out 127,000 missionaries
Education	2010	Combining school reform with legislative change
Medicine	2010	Dental care for underserved children
Overseas	2010	Taking the Giving Pledge, and philanthropy, abroad
Policy	2010	Bringing classical wisdom into modern politics
Education	2010	Creating the Common Core Standards
Education	2010	Focusing ed reform on children, not schools
Policy	2009	Transforming North Carolina into a swing state
Medicine	2009	Bridging the gap between hospital and home
Arts	2009	Private rescues for historical monuments in trouble
Overseas	2009	American gives New Zealand its largest-ever art donation
Education	2009	Linking teacher pay to student development
Education	2008	A new teacher's college based on what actually works

2008

Prosperity	Unrestricted support for scientific excellence	2008	2008	Lincoln's peaceful retreat is preserved for the public	*Arts*
Education	A citywide charter-school blitz	2008	2008	Turning Colorado's politics from blue to red	*Policy*
Religion	Investing in Catholic-school leadership	2008	2008	Tutoring millions online	*Education*

History: 2008 Credit and financial crisis sweeps globe

Policy	New journalism champions liberal causes	2008	2008	Bringing the Bible to missing languages	*Religion*
Nature	Providing a home for mustangs	2008	2008	Making the case for balancing the national books	*Policy*
Education	Opening more ivied doors to low-income students	2007	2007	Building character through sports	*Prosperity*
Religion	Giving it all to charity	2007	2007	Learning from Montana's trove of dinosaur bones	*Nature*
Overseas	Making roads less dangerous in poor countries	2007	2007	Massive investments in Midwest medicine	*Medicine*
Nature	New life for urban parks	2007	2007	Reviving high-quality history and civics instruction	*Education*
Policy	Swinging and missing on education politics	2007	2007	Shrinking childhood obesity	*Medicine*
Overseas	A popular microbank for the Rwandan people	2007	2007	A hit program boosts high-school math and science	*Education*
Nature	A tired National Mall gets a lift	2007	2007	Building an oasis in Louisiana	*Nature*
Nature	From mansion to public sanctuary	2007	2007	International campaign against tobacco use	*Overseas*
Overseas	Making property rights more secure for the poor	2007	2007	Marrying engineering with cancer research	*Medicine*
Policy	Mega-mobilization against climate change	2007	2007	Offering vets tranquility in Montana	*Local*
Medicine	Applying genomics to pediatric medicine	2006	2006	Building medical-research collaboration in NYC	*Medicine*
Prosperity	Clearing minefields for peanuts	2006	2006	Going deep underground to explore science mysteries	*Prosperity*
Policy	Jon Stryker flips Michigan politics	2006	2006	Boosting Boy Scout councils	*Local*
Policy	Organizing liberal perspectives at the state level	2006	2006	Rallying Christians to foster and adopt the hard cases	*Religion*
Medicine	Protecting millions from malaria	2006	2006	A leap forward in the quality of policy debates	*Policy*
Prosperity	Huge gift for post-9/11 veterans	2006	2006	A paragon of regional education reform	*Education*
Local	Bringing dental hygiene to the bush	2006	2006	Extending the Green Revolution to Africa	*Overseas*
Arts	Giving modern art to Los Angelenos	2006	2006	Helping poor people who are ready for change	*Prosperity*

Category	Year	Description	Year	Description	Category
Education	2006	Blastoff for blended learning	2006	New Orleans embraces school choice after Katrina	Education
Religion	2005	Colorado Christians adopt hundreds of stranded children	2006	Soros spends billions overseas	Overseas
Hall of Fame	2005	John Olin's time-limited foundation spends its last dollar	2005	A whale of an aquarium sets records in Atlanta	Nature

History: 2005 Hurricane Katrina kills 1,836, does $81 billion in damage

Category	Year	Description	Year	Description	Category
Education	2005	National intellectual infrastructure for charter schools	2005	Dole owner establishes nutrition research institute	Prosperity
Education	2005	Stepping outside old conventions in teacher training	2005	Looking out for the world's major rivers	Nature
Local	2005	A home-state initiative to promote new music	2005	Promoting a new national park in Maine	Nature
Local	2005	A school program that helps kids start businesses	2005	Restoring Yosemite Falls	Nature
Policy	2005	Democracy Alliance points donors to activist organizations	2005	Donating to a valuable science experiment—their own!	Prosperity
Education	2005	Liberal education for city kids	2005	Chopping down meth abuse by two thirds	Medicine
Arts	2005	Popularizing classical music in San Francisco	2005	Duplicating high-performing charter schools	Education
Nature	2005	Walmart conservers an acre for every acre it develops	2005	Modern-day Noah's Ark gives sanctuary to exotic species	Nature
Nature	2004	4,000 acres of public park thanks to Louisville donors	2004	Spreading change-the-world messages via "filmanthropy"	Policy
Education	2004	Sweetening the deal to attract new math teachers	2004	Medical school infusion	Medicine
Medicine	2004	Charles Feeney strengthens UC San Francisco	2004	A museum lauds technical creativity	Local
Prosperity	2003	Expanding Jewish day schools in Boston	2003	Constructing a new telescope that will far eclipse Hubble	Prosperity
Medicine	2003	Making diagnostic tests affordable in developing countries	2003	A citadel of medical research rises in Boston	Medicine
Local	2003	Using local councils to target grants	2003	Fostering classical architecture	Arts

History: 2003 Second NASA space shuttle disaster destroys Columbia

Category	Year	Description	Year	Description	Category
Medicine	2003	A big push to advance brain research	2003	Telemedicine allows physicians to reach remote patients	Local
Local	2003	Huge museum cleans out the Smithsonian's closet	2003	Streamlining progress from research to cure	Medicine
Nature	2003	Encouraging market solutions to overfishing	2003	Building private schools that poor parents clamor for	Overseas
Policy	2003	Liberal donors create a think tank with campaign muscle	2003	Business lessons in D.C.	Localy

2002

Category	Year	Achievement	Achievement	Year	Category
Religion	2002	Educating the press on religion	Charter chain uses literature to show students "the good"	2002	Education
Hall of Fame	2002	Kresge's foundation renovates Detroit riverfront	George Mitchell bolsters science	2002	Prosperity
Local	2002	Making food banks efficient	Speeding electronic health records	2002	Medicine
Arts	2002	A $100 million endorsement of poetry	An award to encourage urban public-school reform	2002	Education
Religion	2002	Christian Union carves a foothold in Ivy Leagues	An economic boost for tortured Rwanda	2002	Religion
Hall of Fame	2002	John Walton defends school choice in Cleveland	First steps in the online course movement	2002	Education
Arts	2002	$400M to Stanford in Hewlett & Packard collaboration	Training leaders for innovative schools	2001	Education
Overseas	2001	Ford educates developing-world leaders	Hometown tennis star supports Las Vegas education	2001	Local
Medicine	2001	Nearly $3 billion to nurse 9/11 wounds	Perpetual Education Fund schools needy Mormons	2001	Religion
Overseas	2001	Building microfinance into a self-sustaining industry	A New Museum for the New South	2001	Local

History: "2001 Islamists commandeer airplanes, topple Twin Towers"

Category	Year	Achievement	Achievement	Year	Category
Overseas	2001	Coca-Cola Foundation brings clean water to Africa	Emphasizing family ties to check poverty	2001	Prosperity
Local	2001	Frist Foundation rotates art through Nashville	Intel co-founder gives largest gift in college history	2001	Education
Overseas	2000	Amazon River conservation	Bold new approach to biology funded by philanthropists	2000	Medicine
Prosperity	2000	Daniels Fund polishes "diamonds in the rough"	Establishing economic incentives to save endangered lynx	2000	Nature
Local	2000	Largest gift ever for literacy	Reviving Catholic schools with a new work-study formula	2000	Religion
Education	2000	Training new-style principals to lead new-style schools	Year Up helps urban youth unlock their potential	2000	Prosperity
Overseas	2000	$66 million to build civil society after communist rule	Lifting up high-achievers among the poor	2000	Education
Overseas	2000	African universities get a big boost	An unconventional dinosaur discoverer depends on donors	2000	Nature
Arts	2000	BYUtv points the camera at wholesome entertainment	Educating donors on the "joy of generosity"	2000	Religion
Overseas	2000	Gates trains 200 scholars from 100 countries at Cambridge	Open Society pioneers the cause of gay marriage	2000	Policy
Policy	1999	DonorsTrust helps public-spirited philanthropists act	Spreading high-performing charter schools far and wide	2000	Education
Overseas	1999	Hewlett & Packard take on Chinese pollution problems	Birthright Israel funds half of U.S. Jews' pilgrimages	1999	Religion
Religion	1999	Miraculous reopening of Memphis Catholic schools	Gates Foundation revives stalled vaccination efforts	1999	Overseas

Category	Year	Description
Medicine	1999	Biomedical engineering blooms at Stanford
Arts	1999	Supercomputer brings positive animation to American culture
Arts	1999	Art bequest to San Diego
Education	1999	Careful measurement of charter-school outcomes
Nature	1999	Gorges State Park and its trove of rare plants
Education	1999	Minorities encouraged to enter scientific fields by Gates
Education	1998	BASIS creates schools as good as any in the world
Local	1998	Taking care of South Carolina
Education	1998	A Catholic college is born from Domino's Pizza fortune
Education	1998	Donors help military academies develop character
Medicine	1997	A jumpstart for Huntington's Disease research
Education	1997	Engineering education is refined at new college
Education	1997	Revolving funds for charter schools
Prosperity	1997	"Sheltered businesses" offer needy a first job
Prosperity	1997	Alleviating gang violence
Prosperity	1997	First Things First strengthens marriages and parenting
Education	1996	Helping kids build their own libraries
Local	1996	Private giving rescues New York City from decay

Category	Year	Description
Nature	1999	The High Line elevates New Yorkers
Medicine	1999	A foundation acts like a venture capitalist and scores big
Education	1999	Free tuition for music students at Yale
Medicine	1999	Huntsman Cancer Institute uses genetics to beat cancer
Nature	1999	Projecting a planetarium to new heights
Policy	1999	MoveOn.org becomes a mass donor for liberalism
Education	1998	Venture capitalists join to multiply great schools
Prosperity	1998	Andrew Grove improves vocational education
Education	1998	Private-school scholarships for disadvantaged kids
Education	1997	Bringing engineering to high schoolers in a big way
Medicine	1997	Larry Ellison funds explorations of aging
Local	1997	Volunteer health clinic fills crucial gaps in medicine
Local	1997	A fizzy way to teach kids entrepreneurship
Policy	1997	Donors show Congress the way to school choice
Education	1997	New Teacher Project finds educators in unexpected places
Local	1997	Neighborhood revival in Hartford
Prosperity	1996	Privatized space transport escapes bureaucracy
Overseas	1996	Convincing consumers to think of overseas workers

History: 1996 Welfare Reform Act passed by Congress, signed into law

Category	Year	Description
Religion	1996	A new Christian university in Russia
Prosperity	1995	Highly effective job training in Cincinnati
Local	1995	Giving gardens to Grand Rapids
Hall of Fame	1995	Washerwoman Oseola McCarty gives all to charity
Nature	1995	Cooking up nature sanctuaries in Ohio

Category	Year	Description
Local	1996	Pritzker family aids Chicago
Nature	1995	Partnering together to save an endangered fox
Arts	1995	Preserving Aaron Copland's home
Hall of Fame	1995	Gap founder Fisher takes on education reform
Policy	1995	A push against crime helps revive urban life

1995

Nature	Kentucky's largest old-growth forest is preserved	1995	1994	Gates family giving saves eight million lives	*Overseas*
Arts	Finding long-term solutions for threatened symphonies	1994	1994	Retired physician rallies volunteers to serve needy sick	*Medicine*
Local	Philanthropist chef in Seattle puts the homeless to work	1994	1994	Texans team up to push through lawsuit reform	*Policy*
Hall of Fame	Stanford finds a big friend in the Packard family	1994	1994	Top-flight new medical-research effort in the Heartland	*Medicine*
Nature	Turning old railways into recreation trails	1994	1994	Fostering complex math and science	*Prosperity*
Policy	Big donations for gay rights	1994	1994	Promoting drug legalization	*Policy*
Prosperity	Helping low-income workers break cycles of debt	1994	1994	Smoothing a path for first-generation college students	*Education*
Overseas	Banishing blindness at $25 per patient	1994	1994	Tussling over campaign finance	*Policy*
Policy	Opposing nationalized health care	1993	1993	Enhancing teaching at Catholic schools	*Religion*
Religion	Supporting traditional Lutheranism	1993	1993	Saving a storied ballet company	*Arts*

History: 1993 World Wide Web browser opens access to the Internet

Prosperity	Building popular understanding of science	1993	1993	Venture philanthropy against prostate cancer	*Medicine*
Education	How not to spend a billion dollars in education	1993	1993	Education philanthropy changes a whole town	*Local*
Overseas	Soros rescues thousands in Bosnia	1993	1993	Remaking the worst neighborhood in Atlanta	*Local*
Education	JSTOR eases research and saves college budgets	1992	1992	Disney contributions restore Florida wetlands	*Nature*
Education	Lifting a college from mediocrity to excellence	1992	1992	Math and science academy brings minority success	*Education*
Medicine	Bill Gates helps mass-produce DNA arrays	1992	1992	An unusual park combines history and nature	*Nature*
Religion	Helping secular Jews rediscover their religion	1992	1991	Campaigning against tobacco	*Policy*
Medicine	Diamond Foundation leads the charge against HIV	1991	1991	Investigating links between spirituality and health	*Medicine*
Nature	Ft. Worth Zoo finds shared human-animal interests	1991	1991	U.S.-style university bolsters democracy in E. Europe	*Overseas*
Policy	Institute for Justice litigates for liberty	1991	1991	A new order of guardians of human life	*Religion*
Education	Walton Foundation grows into major education reformer	1991	1991	A winning battle against homelessness in Chicago	*Prosperity*
Arts	$1 billion in art is donated to the Met in a single gift	1991	1991	Faux philanthropy feeds economic disaster	*Policy*
Medicine	Autism brought to public attention	1991	1991	Trying to nudge Americans away from fossil fuels	*Policy*

Category	Year	Achievement
Education	1991	Voucher program gives parents choices in schools
Medicine	1990	Taking on the top cause of preventable death

History: 1991 Soviet Union breaks up; Cold War over

Category	Year	Achievement
Arts	1990	Reviving Carnegie Hall
Education	1990	Teach For America pulls talent into schooling
Nature	1990	Letting recreation, wildlife, and lumbering coexist
Prosperity	1990	Kauffman Foundation studies entrepreneurship
Prosperity	1989	Donors pull homeless off the streets of Philly
Medicine	1989	Spotlighting bipolar disorder and schizophrenia
Nature	1989	Taking the botanical garden to new heights
Prosperity	1989	Harlem rebound built on charter schools and services
Religion	1988	Successful job training for hard cases
Nature	1988	Voluntary conservation of millions of acres
Policy	1988	Family Research Council sets up in the nation's capital
Hall of Fame	1987	John Templeton helps reconcile science and religion
Nature	1987	Using economic incentives in the wolf revival
Local	1987	Bill Daniels's bank for kids instills good financial values early
Overseas	1987	Corporations donate drugs to halt developing-world diseases
Overseas	1987	Partners In Health cares for Haitians and others abroad
Prosperity	1987	Teaching troubled kids to thrive in commerce
Overseas	1986	Bono rallies donors to fight AIDS in Africa
Local	1986	Making philanthropy more personal in Minnesota
Religion	1986	Sponsoring low-income kids at Catholic schools
Local	1986	A philanthropist invents a new kind of city

Category	Year	Achievement
Local	1991	Teaching kids the finer points of business
Medicine	1990	Fisher Houses shelter families of hospitalized military
Religion	1990	Landmark learning reconciles religion and capitalism
Religion	1990	Archive of American Jewish music created
Religion	1990	Fighting AIDS with food and fellowship
Nature	1990	Land purchases to preserve Civil War history
Education	1989	Mutual support that fixes a college-dropout problem
Nature	1989	Ted Turner brings back bison with a simple plan: eat 'em
Overseas	1989	A massive gift to battered Armenians
Overseas	1989	Focusing on property rights as a problem in poor countries
Policy	1988	Resisting race-based college admissions
Religion	1988	Training pastors for orthodox Christianity
Prosperity	1988	Donors create realistic new charity to battle NYC poverty
Policy	1987	Pew fires up climate activism
Local	1987	Encouraging experimentation to improve health
Nature	1987	Rare birds aided by a rare-bird donor
Arts	1987	Women in the arts receive a museum of their own
Arts	1987	A new generation discovers jazz at Lincoln Center
Arts	1987	Folk music heritage preserved
Policy	1986	Challenge puts a think tank in every state
Medicine	1986	Patient-centered care to make health care more humane
Medicine	1986	A push to eradicate the horrid Guinea worm
Medicine	1986	Automated DNA sequencer funded by donor angels

1986

Policy	Laying the foundation for welfare reform	1986	1986	Bradley Foundation leads school-choice revolution	*Education*
Policy	Organizing school choice	1986	1985	Rotary International leads effort to eradicate polio	*Overseas*
Prosperity	Help for immigrant families in L.A.	1985	1985	A mechanism for multiplying Mormon humanitarian aid	*Religion*
Prosperity	Training the homeless to help themselves	1985	1985	Keck Observatory boosts astrophysics	*Prosperity*
Policy	Feeding a centrist alternative at the DLC	1985	1984	Large churches join a network for mutual improvement	*Religion*
Arts	Jackson Pollock gives fortune to assist other artists	1984	1984	William Simon gives Olympic profit to a trust for athletes	*Hall of Fame*
Policy	Resisting bans on religious discourse in the public square	1984	1984	Aiding the transition from communism to open society	*Overseas*
Prosperity	Tough-love program turns many failures into workers	1984	1984	Koch brothers lay foundation for Tea Party nonprofits	*Policy*
Education	Hillsdale College drops fed. funding to guard independence	1984	1984	Packard family builds Monterey Bay Aquarium	*Nature*
Nature	Outdoor enthusiasts buy water rights to benefit fish	1983	1983	Skid Row charity helps addicts turn their lives around	*Prosperity*
Medicine	Markey Trust concentrates its giving to jolt medical research	1983	1982	Braun Labs opens up new angles in biology	*Medicine*
Medicine	Hundreds of millions invested in geriatric medicine	1982	1982	Donors save the Statue of Liberty	*Arts*
Religion	National Christian Foundation simplifies faith giving, booms	1982	1982	Land trusts take off as a voluntary method of conservation	*Nature*
Arts	A homebase for encouraging high art	1982	1982	Philanthropy takes on substance abuse	*Medicine*
Policy	Creation of the Federalist Society transforms U.S. law	1982	1982	A new network for educational excellence	*Education*
Medicine	Komen organizes progress against breast cancer	1982	1982	Emphasizing land ownership for Latin American prosperity	*Overseas*
Local	Local housing for the mentally disabled	1982	1981	Cruise-ship fortune puts wind in the sails of young artists	*Arts*
Education	Bringing phonics back to the teaching of reading	1981	1981	Sundance Film Festival is born in the Utah mountains	*Arts*
Education	Sending a class of poor children to college	1981	1981	Bringing philosophical balance to college campuses	*Policy*
Religion	Resisting church politicization	1981	1981	Peace-group philanthropy during the Cold War	*Policy*

History: 1981 AIDS virus identified

Religion	Shared medical coverage at health-care ministries	1981	1980	Milton Friedman argues for capitalism on PBS	*Policy*
Policy	Human Rights Campaign lobbies for gay rights	1980	1980	Zachary Fisher turns an aircraft carrier into a museum	*Hall of Fame*
Nature	Private conservancy takes the lead in saving Central Park	1980	1980	Bringing conservative students into campus journalism	*Policy*

1980–1976

Medicine	1980	Students learn Austrian economics
Nature	1980	Marrying economic growth and environmental protection
Medicine	1979	Nurse-Family Partnership counsels mothers, aids children
Medicine	1978	Retired cruise ship becomes hospital for the poorest
Nature	1978	A remarkable grassroots bluebird recovery
Religion	1978	Michael Novak builds an ethical argument for capitalism
Policy	1977	Cato Institute erected as libertarian think tank
Arts	1977	Bringing an Italian music festival to South Carolina
Religion	1976	Habitat builds homes to fight "poverty of spirit"
Medicine	1976	Whitaker essentially invents biomedical engineering
Nature	1976	A beachfront resort for birds

1980	Make-A-Wish helps gravely ill children live dreams	Medicine
1980	Mothers Against Drunk Driving begin their campaign	Policy
1979	MacArthur's money moves left after his death	Policy
1978	Montana donors protect Montana lands	Nature
1978	Nonprofit leads California tax revolt	Policy
1978	Antony Fisher changes Britain's diet, then politics	Policy
1977	National Journalism Center founded	Policy
1977	Microfinance invented, elevating the poorest	Overseas
1976	Tides surge supports liberal policy reform	Policy
1976	Christian study centers build mental foundation for students	Religion
1976	Major new effort ministers to prisoners	Religion

History: 1976 Apple computer company founded

Prosperity	1975	Group living success for addicts
Prosperity	1975	Volunteers, donors welcome a million Vietnamese refugees
Arts	1974	A contemporary art donation for the National Mall
Policy	1974	Linking law and economics
Overseas	1974	Clark Foundation gives tropical disease research urgency
Religion	1973	Financing mosques for a growing U.S. Muslim population
Policy	1973	Philanthropy defended by the Filer Commission
Policy	1972	Feminism gets cash infusion from Ford Foundation
Religion	1972	Templeton Prize honors "entrepreneurs of the spirit"
Policy	1972	Joe Coors brews up the Heritage Foundation
Arts	1971	Family farm transformed into one-of-a-kind arts venue
Nature	1971	Peregrine falcons are saved from the brink of extinction

1975	New champions for neurological health	Medicine
1975	First U.S. hospice established	Medicine
1974	Ronald McDonald Houses comfort worried families	Medicine
1974	J. Paul Getty opens a classical art temple	Hall of Fame
1974	Olin brings law and economics to campus	Education
1973	Chamber music blooms in Santa Fe	Arts
1973	Major upgrade of emergency medical services	Medicine
1972	Bringing fine art to Ft. Worth	Arts
1972	The most beautiful land in Texas given for public use	Nature
1971	Nautical tycoon underwrites a huge anti-cancer effort	Medicine
1971	Masterpiece Theater, brought to you by ExxonMobil	Arts

1971

Category	Description	Year		Year	Description	Category
Medicine	New attention for a neglected cause of blindness	1971		1971	Gay philanthropy begins a rapid rise	*Policy*
Policy	Using lawsuits to push the environmental agenda	1970		1970	A champion for American prairies	*Nature*
Religion	Samaritan's Purse helps the hurting without red tape	1970		1969	Saving an ancient swamp	*Nature*

History: 1969 U.S. lands a man on the moon

Category	Description	Year		Year	Description	Category
Policy	Ford Foundation backs ethnic-rights lawsuits	1969		1968	Children's Television Workshop created to open Sesame	*Education*
Arts	Many small gifts to small groups enrich NYC music	1968		1968	Pregnancy resource centers offer alternatives to abortion	*Religion*
Policy	Carnegie sets the template for college loans	1968		1968	Covenant House protects exploited teens	*Religion*
Arts	Organizing businessmen to support the arts	1968		1967	Marriage Encounter expanded to strengthen couples	*Prosperity*
Policy	Funding civil-rights lawsuits	1967		1966	Campbell's creates a quirky museum	*Arts*
Arts	Introducing Americans to Asian art	1966		1966	Reformed addict opens his house to help others recover	*Religion*
Arts	A grand patron for the arts in Houston	1966		1966	Frederic Church masterpiece—his home—is preserved	*Arts*
Policy	McGeorge Bundy steers Ford into political activism	1966		1966	Shifting the focus from school inputs to student outcomes	*Education*
Medicine	Training nurse practitioners and physician assistants	1965		1965	Making a case for arts spending	*Policy*
Policy	Giving America a report card to rate its schools	1964		1964	Warren Buffett supports abortion	*Policy*
Arts	Preserving Frank Lloyd Wright's best homes	1964		1963	A gift turns sleepy zoo into best in America	*Nature*

History: 1963 Martin Luther King delivers his "I Have a Dream" speech

Category	Description	Year		Year	Description	Category
Arts	Creating a piano Olympics	1962		1962	Donations for disarmament	*Policy*
Arts	Lincoln Center revivals	1962		1962	Danny Thomas marshals donors behind St. Jude's	*Medicine*
Overseas	Ford boosts market democracy in Latin America	1962		1962	The Green Revolution saves a billion people	*Overseas*
Arts	Advocates for New Orleans jazz	1961		1961	Hard lesson in protecting donor intent in college giving	*Education*
Prosperity	Expanding community colleges	1960		1960	Liberty Fund keeps a flame alive	*Policy*
Policy	Philanthropy puts bail on a scientific footing	1960		1959	Legal clinics become hubs for liberal political activism	*Policy*
Education	Cultural immersion for military officers	1959		1959	Stunted roots of the "War on Poverty"	*Education*

Upper timeline (above the line)

Prosperity	1958	Upending our understanding of cities
Arts	1958	Great community museums spring up across America
Policy	1957	One dogged donor backs the birth-control pill
Arts	1956	Friends fund Harper Lee to create a mockingbird
Nature	1956	Rockefellers turn Caribbean island into a national park
Prosperity	1955	Thinking up artificial intelligence
Education	1954	Bringing new rigor to the business major
Medicine	1954	Kidney victims saved by Hartford Foundation
Religion	1954	Fellowship of Christian Athletes sets out to build character
Nature	1954	U.S. Humane Society campaigns against cruelty
Medicine	1953	Howard Hughes makes super-productive medical institute

History: 1953 Structure of DNA first described by Watson and Crick

Religion	1952	Giving America a giant Bible
Prosperity	1952	Pushing bureaucracy to the side of the road saves lives
Medicine	1952	Polio is defeated by a donor-boosted vaccine
Arts	1951	Ford and Carnegie create public broadcasting
Local	1951	Scholarships aid students and their hometowns
Arts	1951	Magnificent glass museum given by corporate donor
Nature	1950	An arboretum from a grateful immigrant
Religion	1950	A highly effective Christian charity for children abroad

History: 1950 U.S. population reaches 151 million

Local	1950	Preserving immigrant heritage in North Carolina
Education	1949	Earhart educates on the power of markets

Lower timeline (below the line)

Nature	1958	Assembling a 300-acre nature sanctuary
Policy	1958	Harlem minister blazes path for the Peace Corps
Prosperity	1957	A Cold War effort to strengthen U.S. science
Religion	1956	Building evangelical infrastructure
Overseas	1956	Dedicating a life and fortune to Haiti's poor
Education	1955	Ford's huge investment in private colleges
Policy	1954	American Enterprise Institute defends business
Arts	1954	J. Paul Getty starts building his art collection
Arts	1954	Architectural philanthropy makes Columbus, Ind. a gem
Local	1954	Kentuckian leaves a fortune to strengthen his state
Arts	1953	A gifted talent scout finds artists worth supporting

Hall of Fame	1953	Conrad Hilton funds the first National Prayer Breakfast
Medicine	1952	Population controllers put money behind their worries
Education	1952	Creating "area studies" as a Cold War contribution
Policy	1952	Rockefeller III organizes population control
Nature	1951	Nature Conservancy provides attractive eco-solutions
Religion	1951	Building Christian and Jewish fellowships on campuses
Nature	1951	Private game preserves save wildlife
Policy	1950	Philanthropists make cases against communism

Religion	1950	Grassroots givers send Billy Graham into the world
Medicine	1949	Commonwealth Fund speeds cardiac-care revolution

1949

Left timeline

Arts	1949	Creating a popular festival in Aspen
Overseas	1948	American donors play crucial role in creating Israeli state
Medicine	1948	Kinsey Report is made up
Prosperity	1948	UPS founder establishes foundation for needy children
Policy	1947	Volker Fund fuels a resurgence of free-market thinking
Religion	1947	Weyerhaeuser anonymously builds evangelical groups
Policy	1946	Rockefeller keeps the U.N. in the U.S.
Policy	1946	RAND launched to institutionalize advanced research
Medicine	1945	World-leading cancer institute created by G.M. executives

History: 1945 Atomic bombs end World War II

Hall of Fame	1945	William Volker makes Mont Pelerin Society a success
Education	1944	First donations to the United Negro College Fund
Arts	1943	Taming the art of the wild West
Religion	1943	Catholic Relief Services aids Europe before government
Medicine	1941	Penicillin is uncovered, saving millions of lives

History: 1941 Attacked at Pearl Harbor, U.S. enters World War II

Religion	1941	First clubs and camps of Young Life make faith fun
Arts	1940	America enjoys Texaco's Saturday opera broadcasts
Arts	1940	Book lovers make their collections public

History: 1940 Ernest Lawrence invents cyclotron particle accelerator

Local	1940	The donor who pioneered tree replanting
Nature	1938	An oilman gives Boy Scouts a wild place to adventure

Right timeline

1949	Rockefeller II pieces together Grand Teton National Park	Nature
1948	Ballet brought to America	Arts
1948	Blasting out a memorial to Crazy Horse	Local
1947	J. Howard Pew fights for religious orthodoxy	Hall of Fame
1947	National parks get a big boost from Mellon family	Nature
1946	Making history live	Arts
1946	Bequeathing a world-leading technology library	Prosperity
1945	Lasker Prize is established to anoint medical leaders	Medicine
1945	Noble effort to preserve soil quality in Oklahoma	Local

History: 1945 Atomic bombs end World War II

1944	Heifer International helps the poor feed themselves	Overseas
1944	Rockefeller science proves DNA is the basis of heredity	Medicine
1943	Rockefeller plants first seed of Green Revolution	Overseas
1942	Tiffany, believe it or not, had to be rescued from the ashes	Arts
1941	Alfred Loomis creates model for Manhattan Project	Hall of Fame

History: 1941 Attacked at Pearl Harbor, U.S. enters World War II

1941	Philanthropy backs creation of the Pap smear test	Medicine
1940	Donor/scientist advances radar to help U.S. win WWII	Prosperity
1940	Rockefeller preserves Hudson Valley town	Arts

History: 1940 Ernest Lawrence invents cyclotron particle accelerator

1939	Jewish charities begin to raise billions	Religion
1938	A Rockefeller fund to bolster liberal Protestantism	Religion

Timeline (upper side of axis)

Arts	1938	Cloisters museum brings Middle Ages to the U.S.
Nature	1937	A Georgia-to-Maine trail created by volunteers
Religion	1937	Lilly Endowment enriches religious lives of Americans
Medicine	1937	Ending the yellow-fever scourge
Arts	1936	Creating Cooperstown and the Baseball Hall of Fame
Education	1936	Grants create modern child psychology
Policy	1936	Supporting scholarship to solve America's race dilemma
Nature	1934	A refuge for birds of prey
Arts	1933	Chicago gets a beloved museum
Arts	1933	Saving Negro spirituals from extinction
Arts	1933	Rescuing scholars from the Nazis
Arts	1932	Bringing the Bard to our national capital
Medicine	1932	Putting psychiatry on the map
Local	1931	Marquee donors to Lafayette
Arts	1931	The hall that boosted a symphony to renown
Nature	1930	Hunters save the animals they hunt
Prosperity	1930	Philanthropy allows rocketry to lift off, while others scoff
Religion	1929	A Depression-era soup kitchen that continues today
Arts	1929	From fading seaport to maritime museum

History: 1929 Stock-market crash precipitates the Great Depression

Arts	1929	Spreading great art across our Heartland
Nature	1928	Donations lead to Great Smoky Mountains park
Overseas	1928	Son of missionaries leaves money to educate Asians
Hall of Fame	1927	Herbert Hoover leads charitable response to flooding

Timeline (lower side of axis)

Medicine	1938	March of Dimes builds a culture of giving
Local	1937	A civic boost for the state of Indiana
Arts	1937	Architecture and art "of our time" from Guggenheim
Arts	1937	Andrew Mellon gives America a great art gallery
Hall of Fame	1937	Rockefeller gives away $540 million before his death
Prosperity	1936	Herbert Hoover promotes Boys & Girls Clubs
Religion	1936	Mormon welfare system combines aid and self-reliance
Medicine	1935	Inventing health insurance
Arts	1934	Centuries of art exhibited in Baltimore
Prosperity	1933	Inventing molecular biology
Religion	1933	Dorothy Day's Catholic activism
Medicine	1933	A standard nomenclature of disease
Hall of Fame	1932	By life's end, Rosenwald educates 1/4 of U.S. black kids
Prosperity	1932	Talking Books for the blind, LPs for everyone
Medicine	1931	Stemming a dangerous pandemic
Arts	1930	George Washington's birthplace becomes a monument
Nature	1930	State park bought and donated by ex-governor
Nature	1929	Woods Hole Oceanographic Institution established
Arts	1929	Museum of Modern Art as a tribute to dear Abby

Arts	1929	Rosenwald encourages black artists
Prosperity	1928	A 200-inch telescope
Religion	1928	Mass donations erect a National Cathedral
Arts	1927	Colonial Williamsburg is born

1927

Category	Year	Description
	1926	Eastman brings culture to film, Martha Graham included — *Arts*

History: 1927 Lindbergh flies from New York to Paris

Category	Year	Description
	1926	Henry Ford collects and displays treasures of Americana — *Hall of Fame*
	1925	A Rhodes mirror — *Prosperity*
	1925	George Eastman's theater builds public love of the arts — *Hall of Fame*

History: 1925 The Great Gatsby is published

Category	Year	Description
	1924	Offering the finest musical training anywhere—for free — *Arts*
	1924	Duke University laid out by its patron — *Education*
	1924	J. P. Morgan gives billion-dollar art collection to the public — *Arts*
	1923	The upstate New Yorker who produced cowboy art — *Arts*
	1922	Discovering the lifesaving secrets of insulin — *Medicine*
	1922	Celebrating black achievement — *Prosperity*
	1921	Kodak founder creates a music school — *Arts*
	1921	The family behind our first modern art museum — *Arts*
	1919	Air travel is propelled forward — *Prosperity*

History: 1920 Half a million Americans die in a flu epidemic

Category	Year	Description
	1919	Huntington Library becomes a cultural treasure in California — *Arts*
	1919	Forming private institutes to guide government — *Policy*
	1919	International leader exchanges to build understanding — *Overseas*
	1918	A Great Depression gift lifts Yale to greatness — *Education*
	1918	Carnegie popularizes pensions — *Prosperity*
	1917	Joseph Pulitzer's prize gift — *Arts*

Category	Description	Year
Medicine	Solving an urgent need for rural hospitals	
Arts	Grieving parents fund a creative colony	1926
Arts	$30 billion art collection donated by Philly fighter	1925
Hall of Fame	Julius Rosenwald encourages term limits on foundations	1925
Prosperity	The donor who sped commercial flight	1925
Religion	A Methodist infusion	1924
Local	Duke sprinkles gifts across North Carolina	1924
Education	International Education Board	1924
Religion	A shrine for liberal Protestantism	1923
Arts	Shriners Hospital treats burned children	1922
Policy	Inherited money floats the ACLU	1922
Education	Raising standards for lawyers	1921
Prosperity	Producing economic research for wise management	1920
Arts	Henry Frick donates art and mansion to fellow citizens	1919
Hall of Fame	Madam Walker leaves estate for black American causes	1919
Policy	Hoover Institution to teach lessons of war and peace	1919
Nature	Teamwork yields Acadia National Park	1919
Hall of Fame	Sears president protects employees	1918
Education	Zeroing in on troubled children	1918

Timeline (1909–1917)

Education	1917	Lincoln School experiments in education
Arts	1917	Reviving up the Harlem Renaissance
Hall of Fame	1916	Raymond Orteig speeds transatlantic flight with a prize
Nature	1916	Stephen Mather wills the National Park Service to life
Overseas	1915	Americans rally to the aid of Armenian victims
Religion	1915	Early crowdfunding at Carnegie Hall saves Jews
Overseas	1914	U.S. charities support Jews through both world wars
Prosperity	1914	The community foundation is born
Medicine	1913	Rockefeller Jr. targets venereal diseases
Overseas	1913	Rockefeller brings public health to foreign lands
Hall of Fame	1912	Julius Rosenwald coins the slogan "Give While You Live"
Arts	1912	Millennia of wisdom bound up in Loeb's Classical Library
Policy	1911	Advocates make the case for "mothers' pensions"
Religion	1911	Two physicians show an orphanage can be humane
Medicine	1910	Donor-funded study of med schools leads to major reform
Religion	1910	Catholic Charities is formed
Education	1909	Milton Hershey adopts the orphans of America as his heirs
Arts	1909	Historic Fort Ticonderoga is privately preserved

History: 1917 USSR created as first communist state
History: 1914 U.S. enters World War I
History: 1913 Armory Show in NYC introduces U.S. to modern art
History: 1908 Model T automobiles offered for sale

Religion	Quakers offer pacifist service	1917
Education	Ranch in the desert becomes a unique school for men	1917
Arts	World's largest collection of Native Americana	1916
Policy	Robert Brookings establishes the first think tank	1916
Prosperity	American cryptology is born in a private research lab	1915
Medicine	Pioneering hospital opened by Henry Ford	1915
Medicine	Preventive dental care championed by George Eastman	1914
Overseas	Rockefeller creates "cradle of modern medicine in China"	1914
Medicine	Donors and volunteers form American Cancer Society	1913
Overseas	Andrew Carnegie builds a "peace palace" in Holland	1913
Medicine	Rockefeller medical philanthropy sprouts 61 Nobel Prizes	1912
Education	MIT gets a new campus, courtesy of George Eastman	1912
Education	Nearly 5,000 rural schools spring from one man's vision	1911
Nature	Vermont's primitive beauty preserved on Camel's Hump	1911
Policy	Carnegie pours money into world peace	1910
Prosperity	Boy Scouts are set up to build character	1910
Local	First Boston marathon staged to benefit earthquake victims	1909
Medicine	Campaign begins to end hookworm in the U.S.	1909

1908

Category	Event	Year	Year	Event	Category
Hall of Fame	Henry Phipps helps inaugurate the discipline of psychiatry	1908	1908	Muir Woods turned into green sanctuary	Nature
Prosperity	Ben Franklin's trust builds a technical school in Boston	1908	1908	The Gideons stock hotels with Bibles	Religion
Arts	An artist colony is formed in New England forest	1907	1907	Quaker donor preserves "Grand Canyon of the East"	Nature
Prosperity	The Sage Foundation invents modern social work	1907	1907	Donors coalesce to educate African Americans	Education
Prosperity	Rosenwald marries business and philanthropy at Sears	1907	1906	Laying out one of America's great gardens	Nature
Medicine	A vital medical college for China	1906	1905	Methodist seed money launches Goodwill Industries	Religion

History: 1906 San Francisco destroyed by earthquake

Category	Event	Year	Year	Event	Category
Arts	Composing the Juilliard School of Music	1905	1905	Financial security for teachers	Education
Arts	Art museum rises from a Boston marsh	1903	1903	Booker T. Washington secretly funds civil-rights litigation	Policy
Education	Rockefeller & Carnegie professionalize college management	1903	1903	Scripps Institution of Oceanography is started	Nature

History: 1903 Wright brothers make first controlled airplane flight

Category	Event	Year	Year	Event	Category
Religion	Carnegie gives the gift of music via almost 8,000 organs	1902	1902	General Education Board does wonders	Education
Policy	Rockefeller sends the South to high school	1902	1901	Carnegie bolsters the university system in native Scotland	Overseas
Medicine	Death of Rockefeller's grandson leads to a great university	1901	1901	Missionaries found influential schools in the Philippines	Overseas

History: 1900 U.S. population passes 76 million

Category	Event	Year	Year	Event	Category
Religion	A cookbook helps Americanize Jewish immigrants	1900	1899	Eastman pioneers worker bonuses and profit-sharing	Prosperity
Policy	Jane Addams pushes social reform	1895	1895	Pittsburgh gets culture, courtesy of Carnegie	Arts
Nature	Creating a park to refresh working men and women	1893	1893	A bequest creates Johns Hopkins School of Medicine	Medicine
Prosperity	Immigrant-aid societies Americanize new arrivals	1892	1892	John Muir's passion fuels the Sierra Club	Policy

History: 1892 Ellis Island becomes largest entry point for immigrants

Category	Event	Year	Year	Event	Category
Religion	Massive cathedral in Manhattan begun by J. P. Morgan	1892	1892	Ned McIlhenny saves the snowy egret	Nature

Timeline — upper entries (category · year · description):

Category	Year	Description
Religion	1891	Drexel devotes fortune to Native Americans and blacks
Nature	1890	Early land preservation deal in Boston
Prosperity	1890	Hull House links poor with mentors
Education	1889	Colleges within university enrich Harvard and Yale
Local	1888	Hawaiian princess earmarks inheritance for free schools
Nature	1887	Hunters and outdoorsmen preserve animals
Education	1886	Leland Stanford creates a college that creates Silicon Valley.

History: 1886 Statue of Liberty is dedicated

Category	Year	Description
Religion	1884	Jacob Schiff powers Jewish causes
Education	1882	Pratt gives Baltimore libraries, inspiring Carnegie
Education	1881	First "School of Finance and Economy" is opened
Prosperity	1881	Trip to Switzerland yields American Red Cross
Education	1880	Teacher colleges emerge
Prosperity	1879	Between dependence and neglect

History: 1879 Edison invents light bulb

Category	Year	Description
Nature	1876	Appalachian Mountain Club provides vigorous recreation
Arts	1876	A private gallery in the city of free museums
Overseas	1874	Catholic priest raises money, gives his life, for lepers
Local	1873	A former slave gives to help build Los Angeles

History: 1872 Yellowstone National Park created

Category	Year	Description
Education	1868	Bringing literacy to former slaves
Education	1867	"Father of modern philanthropy" rebuilds the South

Timeline — lower entries (category · year · description):

Category	Year	Description
Prosperity	1892	Nathan Straus's safe-milk crusade saves thousands of kids
Education	1890	University of Chicago created by Rockefeller
Education	1890	Persistence opens and improves medical schools
Religion	1889	Nettie McCormick funds dozens of schools
Education	1888	Isaiah Williamson creates a free vocational school
Education	1887	Private giving keeps public colleges afloat
Hall of Fame	1886	J. P. Morgan subsidizes the Episcopal church

History: 1886 Statue of Liberty is dedicated

Category	Year	Description
Religion	1884	Expansion of Catholic schooling
Hall of Fame	1882	Rockefeller begins gifts to black female education
Prosperity	1881	Acculturating Jewish refugees
Arts	1881	Carnegie begins his landmark library projects
Religion	1880	Salvation Army chapters march across America
Arts	1879	Art Institute rises from the ashes of Great Chicago Fire

History: 1879 Edison invents light bulb

Category	Year	Description
Religion	1876	Invention of health food
Education	1876	Johns Hopkins University grows up on local generosity
Religion	1874	Chautauqua Institution: "most American thing in America"
Religion	1873	Temperance Movement emerges

History: 1872 Yellowstone National Park created

Category	Year	Description
Arts	1870	A great museum, thanks to J. P. Morgan and friends
Prosperity	1868	Life insurance emerges from fraternal groups

1866

A timeline of American philanthropy. Events are shown above the timeline (right-hand categories) and below the timeline (left-hand categories), arranged by year.

Below Category	Below Year	Below Event	Above Event	Above Year	Above Category
Nature	1866	Animal welfare movement finds sympathy	Private donors settle freed slaves	1865	Prosperity
Overseas	1864	China's first modern college established by missionaries	Rockefeller gives generously to Baptist colleges	1864	Religion

History: 1865 Civil War ends, preserving Union and ending slavery

Below Category	Below Year	Below Event	Above Event	Above Year	Above Category
Overseas	1863	American colleges abroad	American expatriate battles London slums	1862	Overseas
Religion	1861	Bringing 5,000 volunteers to battlefields and camps	Businessman funds a college for women	1861	Education
Prosperity	1861	Sanitary Commission protects soldiers' welfare	Southern women save Mount Vernon	1860	Arts
Education	1859	Cooper Union offers education to working classes	School for deaf children started with telegraph money	1856	Prosperity
Nature	1856	Henry Shaw pioneers the American botanical garden	Jewish community center movement gets its start	1854	Religion
Religion	1854	Judah Touro donates to devoted religion of all sorts	Connecting orphans to families	1853	Prosperity
Religion	1851	Retired sea captain imports YMCA to America	Perpetual Immigration Fund settles Mormons in West	1849	Religion

History: 1850 Third Great Awakening spurs social activism

Below Category	Below Year	Below Event	Above Event	Above Year	Above Category
Hall of Fame	1848	Girard College educates Philadelphia's poor	Pacifist fuels John Brown's insurrection	1848	Policy
Overseas	1847	Americans respond to Ireland's Great Famine	American Missionary Association resists slavery	1846	Policy
Arts	1846	Smithsonian Institution inaugurated by British bequest	Society of St. Vincent de Paul transplanted to St. Louis	1845	Religion
Education	1843	Eastern churchgoers fund Western schools	New anti-poverty work relies on personal visits	1843	Prosperity
Arts	1842	America's oldest public museum of art and culture	Fraternal lodges provide tangible benefits	1842	Prosperity
Religion	1842	Rise of religious colleges in the U.S.	Lewis Tappan adds virtue to business via credit ratings	1841	Prosperity
Policy	1841	Underwriting a legal defense that makes Africans free	Building the Underground Railroad	1837	Prosperity
Prosperity	1837	The first black college in America opens in Philadelphia	Thomas Jefferson's home is saved by a generous family	1836	Arts

History: 1835 Alexis de Tocqueville publishes influential chronicle of U.S.

Below Category	Below Year	Below Event	Above Event	Above Year	Above Category
Religion	1834	Establishing the model for medical-missionary work	Anti-Slavery Society founders start popularizing abolition	1833	Policy
Education	1833	Principled donors keep an abolitionist college alive	Philadelphia school for orphans springs from court battle	1831	Education

Prosperity	Pioneers form school for blind; Helen Keller later attends	1829	1827	Tappan brothers spur culture change via benevolent groups	*Religion*
Education	Frontier settlers band together to keep a university alive	1826	1825	Reformers separate delinquent children from adult inmates	*Prosperity*

History: 1825 Erie Canal links Midwest to New York, sparking social innovation

Hall of Fame	Judah Touro builds an early free public library	1824	1824	Stephen Rensselaer cultivates effective science education	*Education*
Overseas	American donors support Greek independence struggle	1821	1820	First Christian missionaries arrive in Hawaii	*Overseas*
Hall of Fame	Nicholas Longworth dedicates himself to "the devil's poor"	1819	1819	Offering modest-income workers a safe bank	*Prosperity*

History: 1819 Supreme Court protects private giving in Dartmouth case

Religion	American Colonization Society resettles slaves in Liberia	1816	1815	Thomas Jefferson offers his library to Congress	*Arts*
Hall of Fame	Stephen Girard bails out the United States	1813	1812	Private military contributions win the War of 1812	*Prosperity*
Religion	American missionaries minister to Native Americans	1810	1810	Five students commence major missionary effort	*Overseas*
Religion	Bible Societies take root; distribute millions of texts	1809	1809	Catholic schools created for children	*Religion*
Religion	Oldest graduate school in the U.S. is established	1807	1806	New York orphanage provides homes and futures	*Prosperity*
Hall of Fame	Studies by Benjamin Rush propel Temperance movement	1805	1805	Art academy brings European training to U.S. artists	*Arts*
Education	Rallying to create free schools	1805	1804	Early evangelicalism in Boston	*Religion*
Prosperity	Charity gives sailors a life beyond the sea	1801	1801	Charleston Jews establish Hebrew Orphan Society	*Religion*

History: 1803 Louisiana Purchase doubles the size of the U.S.A.

Religion	Rebecca Gratz founds aid societies	1801	1799	Salemites band together to build a ship for their country	*Prosperity*
Arts	Art from the sea	1799	1797	A charity by women for women	*Prosperity*
Education	George Washington makes a big gift to education	1796	1796	Stephen Girard risks his life for yellow-fever victims	*Hall of Fame*
Hall of Fame	Thomas Eddy fights cruelty in New York prisons	1796	1792	Sunday schools spread literacy and constructive behavior	*Religion*
Medicine	Second hospital in America opened in New York	1791	1786	First free walk-in clinic established by Declaration signer	*Medicine*

History: 1790 First census shows there are 3.9 million Americans

1785

Prosperity	New Yorkers fight kidnapping with education	1776
Prosperity	Patriots bankrupt themselves funding the Revolution	1773
	Education — 1785 — A frontier college is built by generous Americans	
	Hall of Fame — 1780 — Benjamin Rush pioneers movement to abolish U.S. slavery	

History: 1776 Declaration of Independence proclaims individual rights

Prosperity	A helping hand for Britons abroad	1770
Religion	Donations fund California's mission system	1768
Medicine	Philanthropy enables "father of American psychiatry"	1751
Religion	Americans warm to individual philanthropy	1740
Prosperity	Resettling the religiously persecuted	1732
	Religion — 1770 — French immigrant aids the forgotten	
	Religion — 1763 — Religious freedom enshrined by George Washington	
	Prosperity — 1743 — Nation's oldest scientific prize fuels investigators	
	Medicine — 1735 — First U.S. charity hospital endowed by dying sailor	
	Education — 1731 — Franklin and friends open the first public library in America	

History: 1731 Great Awakening sparks evangelical fervor and individualism

Prosperity	Quaker merchants offer work to Philly poor	1731
Religion	Nuns establish school, hospital, orphanage in New Orleans	1727
Education	School for slaves opened by an exiled French Protestant	1704
Prosperity	North America's first ethnic charity is founded	1657
	Prosperity — 1727 — Ben Franklin creates a network for good in Philadelphia	
	Education — 1721 — America's first endowed college chair established	
	Religion — 1681 — Quakers reform prisons, pioneer rehabilitation	
	Education — 1643 — Harvard initiates America's first fundraising campaign	

History: 1650 There are an estimated 50,400 colonists living in America

Education	First in a string of privately funded colleges opens	1636

History: 1620 Mayflower Compact pledging mutual aid is signed by 41 pilgrims

INDEX

ABOUT
The
PHILANTHROPY
ROUNDTABLE

THE PHILANTHROPY ROUNDTABLE is America's leading network of charitable donors working to strengthen our free society, uphold donor intent, and protect the freedom to give. Our members include individual philanthropists, families, corporations, and private foundations.

MISSION

The Philanthropy Roundtable's mission is to foster excellence in philanthropy, to protect philanthropic freedom, to assist donors in achieving their philanthropic intent, and to help donors advance liberty, opportunity, and personal responsibility in America and abroad.

PRINCIPLES

- Philanthropic freedom is essential to a free society
- A vibrant private sector generates the wealth that makes philanthropy possible
- Voluntary private action offers solutions to many of society's most pressing challenges
- Excellence in philanthropy is measured by results, not by good intentions
- A respect for donor intent is essential to long-term philanthropic success

SERVICES

World-class conferences

The Philanthropy Roundtable connects you with other savvy donors. Held across the nation throughout the year, our meetings assemble grantmakers and experts to develop strategies for excellent local, state, and national giving. You will hear from innovators in K-12 education, economic opportunity, higher education, national security, and other fields. Our Annual Meeting is the Roundtable's flagship event, gathering the nation's most public-spirited and influential philanthropists for debates, how-to sessions, and discussions on the best ways for private individuals to achieve powerful results through their giving. The Annual Meeting is a stimulating and enjoyable way to meet principled donors seeking the breakthroughs that can solve our nation's greatest challenges.

Specialized programs

In crucial areas important to philanthropists we've developed special programs, led by national experts in the field, that we offer free of charge to advise donors. The Roundtable's K-12 education program is our

largest and longest-running program—it has helped hundreds of donors springboard their gifts into educational excellence. We operate the best advisory in the country for philanthropists who want to support veterans, servicemembers, and their families. Economic opportunity, job training, and anti-poverty work are the focus of another of our program areas. And we have programs on character education, on family reinforcement, and on public policy change. Our specialized staff know how to get the best results, which nonprofits are most effective, and how to evaluate and refine your giving. Plus, each program has built a critical mass of donors who share your interest in that topic—to whom we can connect you for peer-to-peer learning.

A powerful voice

The Roundtable's public-policy project, the Alliance for Charitable Reform, works to advance the principles and preserve the rights of private giving. ACR educates legislators and policymakers about the central role of charitable giving in American life and the crucial importance of protecting philanthropic freedom—the ability of individuals and private organizations to determine how and where to direct their charitable assets. Active in Washington, D.C., and in the states, ACR protects charitable giving, defends the diversity of charitable causes, and battles intrusive government regulation. We believe the capacity of private initiative to address national problems must not be burdened with costly or crippling constraints.

Protection of donor interests

The Philanthropy Roundtable is the leading force in American philanthropy to protect donor intent. Generous givers want assurance that their money will be used for the specific charitable aims and purposes they believe in, not redirected to some other agenda. Unfortunately, donor intent is usually violated in increments, as foundation staff and trustees neglect or misconstrue the founder's values and drift into other purposes. Through education, practical guidance, legislative action, and individual consultation, The Philanthropy Roundtable is active in guarding donor intent. We are happy to advise you on steps you can take to ensure that your mission and goals are protected.

Must-read publications

The Almanac of American Philanthropy is our authoritative resource—a compilation of the greatest givers, greatest achievements, and greatest ideas in the field.

Philanthropy, the Roundtable's quarterly magazine, is packed with useful and beautifully written real-life stories. It offers practical examples, inspiration, detailed information, history, and clear guidance on the differences between giving that is great and giving that disappoints.

We also publish a series of guidebooks that provide detailed information on the very best ways to be effective in particular aspects of philanthropy. These guidebooks are compact, brisk, and readable. Most focus on one particular area of giving—for instance, improving teaching, charter-school expansion, support for veterans, programs that get the poor into jobs, investing in public policy, and other topics of interest to grantmakers. Real-life examples, hard numbers, first-hand experiences of other donors, recent history, and policy guidance are presented to inform and inspire savvy donors.

JOIN THE ROUNDTABLE!

When working with The Philanthropy Roundtable, members are better equipped to achieve long-lasting success with their charitable giving. Your membership in the Roundtable will make you part of a potent network that understands philanthropy and strengthens our free society. Philanthropy Roundtable members range from Forbes 400 individual givers and the largest American foundations to small family foundations and donors just beginning their charitable careers. Our members include:

- Individuals and families
- Private foundations
- Community foundations
- Venture philanthropists
- Corporate giving programs
- Large operating foundations and charities that devote more than half of their budget to external grants

Philanthropists who contribute at least $100,000 annually to charitable causes are eligible to become members of the Roundtable and register for most of our programs. Roundtable events provide you with a solicitation-free environment.

For more information on The Philanthropy Roundtable or to learn about our individual program areas, please call (202) 822-8333 or e-mail main@PhilanthropyRoundtable.org.

Also available from
The Philanthropy Roundtable

The Almanac of American Philanthropy (full-length version)
By Karl Zinsmeister

What Comes Next?
How private givers can rescue America in an era of political frustration
By Karl Zinsmeister

Uniform Champions: A Wise Giver's Guide to Excellent Assistance for Veterans
By Thomas Meyer

Learning to Be Useful: A Wise Giver's Guide to Supporting Career and
Technical Education
By David Bass

Catholic School Renaissance:
A Wise Giver's Guide to Strengthening a National Asset
By Andy Smarick and Kelly Robson

Clearing Obstacles to Work:
A Wise Giver's Guide to Fostering Self-Reliance
By David Bass

Agenda Setting: A Wise Giver's Guide to Influencing Public Policy
By John J. Miller and Karl Zinsmeister with Ashley May

Excellent Educators:
A Wise Giver's Guide to Cultivating Great Teachers and Principals
By Laura Vanderkam

From Promising to Proven:
A Wise Giver's Guide to Expanding on the Success of Charter Schools
By Karl Zinsmeister

Closing America's High-achievement Gap:
A Wise Giver's Guide to Helping Our Most Talented Students Reach Their Full Potential
By Andy Smarick

Blended Learning: A Wise Giver's Guide to Supporting Tech-assisted Teaching
By Laura Vanderkam

Serving Those Who Served:
A Wise Giver's Guide to Assisting Veterans and Military Families
By Thomas Meyer

Protecting Donor Intent:
How to Define and Safeguard Your Philanthropic Principles
By Jeffrey Cain

Transparency in Philanthropy
By John Tyler

How Public Is Private Philanthropy?
By Evelyn Brody and John Tyler

KARL ZINSMEISTER, *series editor*